CHRISTIANITY WITHOUT ANTISEMITISM

James Parkes
and the Jewish–Christian Encounter

Studies in Antisemitism

Series Editor: YEHUDA BAUER

Chairman, Vidal Sassoon International Center
for the Study of Antisemitism,
The Hebrew University of Jerusalem.

Studies in Antisemitism brings together in one series major world-wide research on this complex phenomenon—in the Western democracies and the East European regimes, in the Americas and the Islamic world—from which the student and decision-maker as well as the general public may learn. The Studies cover antisemitism, ancient and modern, from a broad range of perspectives: historical, religious, political, cultural, social, psychological and economic.

ALMOG, S.
Nationalism & Antisemitism in Modern Europe 1815–1945

ALMOG, S. (editor)
Antisemitism Through the Ages

NETTLER, R. L.
Past Trials and Present Tribulations:
A Muslim Fundamentalist's View of the Jews

REVEL-NEHER, E.
The Image of the Jew in Byzantine Art

STERN, F.
The Whitewashing of the Yellow Badge:
Antisemitism and Philosemitism in Postwar Germany

VOLOVICI, L.
Nationalist Ideology and Antisemitism:
The Case of Romanian Intellectuals in the 1930s

YADLIN, R.
An Arrogant Oppressive Spirit:
Anti-Zionism as Anti-Judaism in Egypt

CHRISTIANITY
WITHOUT ANTISEMITISM

James Parkes
and the Jewish–Christian Encounter

ROBERT ANDREW EVERETT

Published for the

Vidal Sassoon International Center for
the Study of Antisemitism (SICSA),
The Hebrew University of Jerusalem

by

PERGAMON PRESS

OXFORD · NEW YORK · SEOUL · TOKYO

U.K.	Pergamon Press Ltd., Headington Hill Hall, Oxford OX3 0BW, England
U.S.A.	Pergamon Press Inc., 660 White Plains Road, Tarrytown, New York 10591-5153, USA
KOREA	Pergamon Press Korea, KPO Box 315, Seoul 110–603, Korea
JAPAN	Pergamon Press Japan, Tsunashima Building Annex, 3-20-12 Yushima, Bunkyo-ku, Tokyo 113, Japan

Copyright © 1993 Pergamon Press Ltd.

First edition 1993

Library of Congress Cataloging-in-Publication Data
Everett, Robert Andrew.
Christianity without antisemitism : James Parkes and the Jewish-Christian encounter / by Robert Andrew Everett. -- 1st ed.
p.   cm. -- (Studies in antisemitism)
Based on the author's thesis (Ph. D.--Columbia University, 1982) originally presented under title: James Parkes, historian and theologian of Jewish-Christian relations.
Includes bibliographical references and index.
1. Parkes, James William, 1896–   . 2. Judaism--Relations--Christianity. 3. Christianity and other religions--Judaism. 4. Christianity and antisemitism.   I. Title.   II. Series.
BM535.P242E94   1993
261.2'6'092--dc20   93-9480

ISBN 0-08-041040-5

Printed in Great Britain by BPCC Wheatons Ltd, Exeter

Contents

To my mother, Jurl Ann Patton Everett,

of Blessed Memory

Her Love Knew No Bounds

TO MARIE
WHO TAUGHT ME THE MEANING OF
DIVINE GRACE AND HUMAN FORGIVENESS
AND
GAVE ME MY THREE ANGELS,
AMANDA SHOSHANNAH, JOSHUA ANDREW
AND JESSE DAVID

Foreword

IN 1934, James Parkes earned his doctorate at Oxford with a thesis later published as *The Conflict of the Church and Synagogue*. Nearly fifty years later, when Robert A. Everett defended a Columbia/Union Ph.D. dissertation on "James Parkes: Historian and Theologian of Jewish–Christian Relations," his examining committee urged its publication. The young scholar had written a careful study, researching thoroughly the life and work of his subject and becoming very well acquainted with him personally. Actively involved in discussions between Jews and Christians as well as continuing to produce articles and reviews in the field, Everett has since revised his work, which appropriately appears in book form a decade after Parkes' death, and which will materially help to keep the memory of that remarkable man and his work fresh.

Parkes often insisted that good theology cannot be based on bad history, and he made significant (and hence controversial) contributions as both historian and theologian. This ordained Anglican priest was a pioneer in carefully documenting how Christianity from its earliest centuries to the present has continuously misunderstood the nature and history of Judaism, thus tragically contributing to antisemitism in its many forms. His explorations led him to argue that there needed therefore to be among Christians some important changes in what he called the detestable habit of "theological ophthalmology"—the art of removing the motes from the eyes of others. His lifelong *Voyage of Discoveries* (the title of his autobiography) led him to such insights as that in the first five centuries of the common era came the discovery that

"Scripture could remain holy in a changing world only by interpretation, and that the interpretation must also be holy."

Parkes also provides a useful model for helping Christians to deal honestly with Judaism and Jewish history, and to shake off both historical and theological misconceptions that have caused distortions in our understanding of the Bible and of our own theological traditions. Hence he can be for us a liberator, freeing us from the burden of serious flaws in our biblical and historical interpretations—errors that have led to arrogant triumphalism and have increased the sufferings of others. In this book, Everett opens a door to the deeper understanding of James Parkes: historian, theologian, pioneer, model, and liberator.

ROBERT T. HANDY
Henry Sloane Coffin Professor
Emeritus of Church History
Union Theological Seminary, New York

Preface

THIS book is a revised version of my doctoral dissertation, which was written for Columbia University in 1982. It is an intellectual biography of James William Parkes, one of the true pioneers in the field of Jewish–Christian relations and the study of antisemitism. He remains one of the few Christian thinkers who have attempted to interpret the Jewish tradition and the Jewish experience to the Gentile world. This books deals primarily with these two aspects of Parkes' work, but in doing so, it tries to place these aspects in a context beyond the Jewish–Christian issue. Parkes was a rather competent theologian and historian, and his ideas about Jewish–Christian relations were not conceived in a vacuum. Rather, they were developed within the framework of Modernist theology, which he learned at Oxford University, and of his own historical research into the roots of antisemitism and Jewish history. I shall attempt to show how Parkes was not simply a "philosemite," itself a curious title which implies that any Christian favorable to Judaism must have ulterior motives, but rather a Modernist theologian who applied his Modernist theological critique of Christianity to the question of Jewish–Christian relations. By doing so, I hope to prove that his rather distinct "Theology of Equality" arises directly out of his Modernist leanings, and not out of some personal need to please Jews.

In addition, there is a moral dimension to Parkes' work related to his thesis that Christianity created an antisemitism unique from classical anti-Jewish rhetoric. For Parkes, "Good theology cannot be based on bad history," and he argued that much of what Christians thought about Jews and their religion was neither historically nor theologically true. Christianity's involvement in antisemitism could go unchallenged only if Christians were willing to remain antisemitic. Parkes saw the moral quandary this placed Christians in, and he attempted to provide a way for Christianity to be free of antisemitism. He wanted the Church to cease its support of a 'Theology of Victimization" of Jews which gave tacit support to the idea that it was alright to make Jews victims of oppression and intolerance. For most Christians today, the events of the Holocaust have forced them to deal with this troublesome issue, although some critics have felt that too much of this Christian rethinking of their tradition is based solely on guilt. Parkes stands out as a unique Christian thinker in this area on the grounds that he clearly saw the demonic dimensions of this Christian tradition long before the Holocaust took place. Thus, Parkes' work challenges those who think the Holocaust is the only reason for Christians to rethink their attitudes about Jews and Judaism. For Parkes, it has always been a moral issue facing the Church. The Holocaust makes it even more imperative that Christians deal with the problems.

To fully appreciate Parkes one must read his work as a whole, and not in bits and pieces. His work has a logic and consistency to it, but this is often neglected when he is read piecemeal. Read as a whole, Parkes becomes a model for Christians attempting to deal with the reality of Judaism as a living religion which retains its own validity, while still maintaining a particularistic Christian identity. In many ways, Parkes was an early proponent of Religious Pluralism, a theme which is today of concern to a growing number of Christian thinkers. To my knowledge, there has been no other such study of Parkes, and therefore, this book was worthwhile if only to expose the ideas of this unique thinker to a wider audience.

I had the distinct pleasure and honor of personally knowing Dr. Parkes, and on two occasions I visited him in England. The first time was in 1974. Returning from a period of study at Tel Aviv University, I arranged to stop over in England. Dr. Parkes and his wife, Dorothy, graciously invited me to stay with them at their home in Iwerne Minster, Dorset. There I spent a week discussing his work, enjoying his seventeenth-century cottage, sharing his fine French wines, and receiving his personal tour of Thomas

Hardy country. Since Hardy is my favorite author, this was an unexpected treat. Their hospitality knew no bounds.

In May of 1979, I spent a month doing research at Southampton University, England, where the Parkes Library is housed. Parkes gave me permission to examine all his papers, and to copy anything I needed for my study. Although he was quite ill by then and living in a nursing home in Bournemouth, I was able to visit with him on a cloudy Sunday afternoon. I discussed with him certain aspects of his work I was only then discovering. My short time with him then proved extremely valuable to the writing of this book.

I also kept up a lively correspondence with him initiated in 1971 while I was still a student at Yale Divinity School. The interest he showed in a young, struggling student exceeded anything I could have expected from someone so famous. He was truly a remarkable man, and my appreciation of his work is matched only by my admiration of his person. To my lasting regret, this study was not completed before his death. I am grateful, though, that he was able to read substantial portions of it.

I also wish to acknowledge a number of people and institutions who helped to make this book possible. To my mother and father, Jurl Ann and Robert Everett, who never wavered in their support of their perennial student of a son. To my sisters, Gail Ann and Sharon, who could always make me laugh. To my great-Grandmother, Georgia Stewart, and grandmother, Edna Patton, who taught me the true meaning of simple faith and radical love. To my grandfather, Lester Everett, who is an example of a true churchman. To the congregation of the Emanuel United Church of Christ in Irvington, New Jersey, for allowing me to be their pastor and a graduate student at the same time. To Dr. James Gilman, who stayed up with me many a late night discussing this project from the start. To the Reverend Bruce Bramlett, who shares so many of my concerns. To Dr. Robert Handy, who served as my doctoral advisor. He, more than anyone else, taught me how to do research and how to write. If one can be an academic "saint," Dr. Handy is one. To Dr. Arthur Hertzberg, who advised me on this project, and who taught me so much about Jewish history. To Dr. A. Roy and Professor Alice Eckardt, who are my intellectual "godparents." So much of what I think and what I have done stems directly from their friendship and their love. To Geoffrey Hampson of the Parkes Library, who befriended a tired and lost American student, and who has continued to be a source of information and guidance. To Wendy Buckle, formerly of the Parkes Library, who spent an entire day copying materials for me while I went walking around London. To Dr. Robert Ayers of the University of Georgia, who prepared me for a scholarly career, and instilled in me a love of Judaism and Reinhold Niebuhr. To the Faculty of Yale Divinity School, for the fine education they gave me in theology, particularly Charles Forman and Werner Rode. To the Faculty of Columbia University's Religion Department and Union Theological Seminary, for making me a better scholar. To the Graduate School of Arts and Sciences of Columbia University in New York, for their generous University Fellowship and President's Fellowship. I hope that this book justifies their investment. To the Christian Study Group on Jews and Judaism, for all their help in the field of Jewish–Christian relations. To Franklin Littell, whose friendship has been enduring and whose interest in Parkes unending. To Carl Hermann Voss, himself a pioneer in Jewish–Christian relations, and a constant source of encouragement. To Dr. Louis Feldman of Yeshiva University and my colleagues in a National Endowment for the Humanities Seminar on the Classical and Christian Roots of Antisemitism. Last, but really first, my wife, Marie, who typed the original manuscript under difficult conditions, and who has never lost faith in me. To the many not mentioned, my word of thanks for all your support and help.

July 24, 1990   ROBERT ANDREW EVERETT

Acknowledgments

THE author wishes to acknowledge the following sources for permission to use their material:

Harvard University Press, for extracts from
>H. D. A. Major, *English Modernism* (Cambridge, Mass., Harvard University Press), copyright © 1927 by the President and Fellows of Harvard College. Reprinted by permission.

University of Southampton, for extracts from
>James Parkes, *Religious Experience and the Perils of its Interpretation*, 1972.
>James Parkes, *The World of Rabbis*, 1962.
>James Parkes, *Judaism and Christianity*, 1948.
>James Parkes, *Gilon Lectures*, 1929.

SCM Press, for extracts from
>James Parkes, *Jesus, Paul and the Jews*, 1936.
>James Parkes, *The Jew and His Neighbour*, 1930.

Vallentine, Mitchell & Co. Publishers, for extracts from
>James Parkes, *The Foundations of Judaism and Christianity*.
>James Parkes, *End of an Exile*.
>James Parkes, *Prelude to Dialogue*.
>James Parkes, *Antisemitism: A Concise World History*, 1963.

The Jewish Publication Society, for extracts from
>James Parkes, *Conflict of the Church and Synagogue*, 1969.

In the following cases, the author's attempts to trace the whereabouts of the copyright holder(s) were unsuccessful; the author would be pleased for the copyright holder(s) to come forward.

1

The Life and Times of James Parkes

ON December 22, 1896, James William Parkes was born in the Manor of Rohais at Les Fauconier on the Isle of Guernsey. The Victorian era was ending, and the few years of peace before World War I were just beginning. Parkes' father, Henry, was the falconer of the manor. He was an Englishman by birth, and an engineer by training. His mother, Annie Katharine Bell Parkes, was an author. She died after a long illness when Parkes was still a young boy. Both an older brother, David, and a sister, Molly, were killed during World War I. Parkes remained on Guernsey until 1916, when he joined the British Army.

Parkes had deep family ties in the Channel Islands. A great-grandmother had lived at Trinity Manor, Jersey, and two great-great-great aunts had lived in St. Peter Port during the Napoleonic Wars. The Channel Islands have a curious identity, lying halfway between Britain and France, yet in culture belonging wholly to neither. They have served as a crossroads for the cultural influences of Britain and the Continent, yet they retain a distinct culture of their own. A good example of this is found in the clergy of Guernsey. The country clergy were, in Parkes' time, French-speaking Calvinists who accepted episcopal ordination. Throughout his life, Parkes maintained his unique identity as a Guernseyman.

Although his mother died when he was young, he singles her out as a most important influence in his life, particularly in regard to his religious outlook. The religious background of the Parkes

1

family was rather mixed: some of his relatives had been Unitarians, and his father was a convinced agnostic. He remembered his mother, however, as a deeply religious person who had a decidedly independent turn of mind. The children of the Parkes family were allowed personal freedom of religious choice, and Parkes has stated that while his brother preferred the "High Church" Anglican services, he preferred the more simple country parish churches. At one of these country churches (St. Martin's), Parkes befriended the rector's daughter, Christine Ozanne, and they remained friends all their lives. It was from his mother and Christine that Parkes received his earliest lessons in religion. Later in his life, when Parkes was to write about the nature of the Church and religion, he would show a continued appreciation for both the simplicity of the religious life he had discovered in the country parishes of Guernsey and the independence of mind he learned from his mother.

Parkes began his education at Dame School, but he soon entered the Lower School of Elizabeth College, Guernsey. Elizabeth College was an ancient institution founded by Elizabeth I to teach the Guernsey inhabitants "English and Anglican ways and to protect them from the influence of continental Protestantism." At Elizabeth College Parkes received a proper Victorian education in the classics. He was also active in the Officers' Training Corps.

Elizabeth College had a long-standing relationship with Oxford University, and Parkes sat for an Open Scholarship, in spite of the objections of his headmaster, William Campbell Penny. Parkes was encouraged by his father to sit for the examination, and with the help of his classics master, E. W. Hickie, he succeeded in passing the exam and winning a scholarship. He was to go on to Oxford as a student at Hertford College.

All of his plans, though, were interrupted by two events. First, in 1915, Parkes suffered a physical collapse. Throughout his youth, Parkes was prone to serious illness, and in his last year at school, he suffered a complete breakdown. Upon his recovery, Europe itself broke down, and World War I commenced. In 1916, he enlisted in the British Army.

As for so many of his generation, World War I was an experience that altered his life plans and shattered most of the illusions

Parkes had about the world. Although World War I continues to recede in modern memory, many of the great thinkers of the twentieth century viewed the Great War as a turning point in their lives. Parkes was very much a part of this "lost generation."

Upon entering the Army, Parkes joined the Artists' Rifles (28th London) in January 1916. Parkes' brother had been in this regiment, and according to Parkes, it was a regiment that attracted public school graduates and professional men. He was sent over to France, to Rouen and then to St. Omer. At St. Omer, he was nearly poisoned to death by bad drinking water served to him at a local café, and he was sent back to England. Upon his recovery in the summer of 1916, Parkes was sent to the Officer Cadet Battalion at Denhem, but he was then reassigned to the Staff College at Camberley. He later attended Sandhurst, the British "West Point," to complete his training. He has written in his autobiography that "in December I duly got my commission and was attached to the Queen's Royal West Surrey Regiment. I was sent down to the 3rd Queen's at Gore Court outside Sittingbourne, but almost immediately crossed over to France and arrived at the abominable 'Bull Ring' at Etaples." He shortly moved to the Ypres Salient, where he faced battle as an infantry subaltern. During this time, Parkes was exposed to mustard gas, but he did not realize the extent of the dosage of gas he had consumed until he suddenly became blind during a parade. He wound up back in England and finished the war as a second lieutenant in charge of a Brigade Gas School. He left the Army in 1917, having been poisoned by water, gassed, and having fallen prey to Dupuytren's contraction of the foot at Ypres. This last disease and the mustard gas would have recurring side-effects for the rest of his life. His career as a soldier had ended.

His war experience caused Parkes to become what he called a "half-way pacifist," although he never accepted the position completely. The war also led Parkes to view the world as being on the brink of a new age, the old age having been destroyed on the battlefields of Europe. Such ideas began to take clearer focus in 1919 when he finally entered Oxford University, where he would become active in political issues, and they would also influence his particular view of the Church and its role in the postwar world.

Oxford must have been a curious place in the years following

World War I. Most of the students were older than the usual incoming students, and after being in the trenches, their view of life was certainly different from that of most college freshmen. Parkes entered Hertford College, a small college with a little over a hundred students. The Principal was Dr. Henry Boyd, the Nestor of the University, and Lord Curzon was the Chancellor of Oxford at that time. Parkes had two tutors, E. A. Burroughs and J. D. Dennison. He took a "good second" in classical Mods, and then decided to study theology.

The decision to study theology was a thoughtful one on Parkes' part. He had not completely made up his mind about ordination in the Church of England, and he did have interests in other fields of study. He considered studying art for a time because of his talents in painting; he was a rather good watercolor artist. He also considered philosophy for a time, but he decided against it on the grounds that it was "absurd for a man to pretend to be a philosopher before he was forty." He also toyed with the idea of studying the "Greats," but in the end he decided to study theology during his last years at Oxford.

Cyril Emmet, a Church historian, was Parkes' tutor in theology, and Emmet was to have a lasting influence on Parkes.[1] Parkes chose for his special subject, "Early Christian Art and Architecture," a choice that delighted Parkes because there was no one at Oxford who could teach it. Apparently, the subject had been included on the Faculty List some years before, but no one had ever selected it as a subject. His decision annoyed the faculty, but they were obliged to allow Parkes to make such a choice since it was listed. Arrangements had to be made for Parkes to work at the British Museum with a Mr. Dalton, who was in charge of that branch of the museum, and Percy Dearmer was secured as an examiner. Parkes completed his studies in 1923, but he had to take his final examination in bed because of a bout of the measles. His examination committee—Dr. H. D. A. Major, Principal of Ripon Hall; Mr. Emmet, his tutor; Dr. Cornsell, his doctor, representing the Medicine Faculty; and another member of theology—passed him and gave him a letter which said that as far as Parkes had progressed, he had achieved a First. This letter

---

[1] Personal interview with James Parkes, May 14, 1979.

would later facilitate Parkes' admission to the doctoral program.

While a student at Oxford, Parkes engaged in many activities outside his course of studies. He befriended the chaplain of Hertford, John McLeod Campbell, and through Campbell, became interested in the Student Christian Movement. This put him in touch with many of the important Christian leaders of the time. At a SCM campaign at Oxford entitled "Religion and Life," Parkes heard and met men like William Temple, W. Maltby, and Baron Von Hugel. In 1921, Parkes traveled to Glasgow to attend the great missionary quadrennial, where Christian leaders and students from around the world had gathered. Parkes was to remain actively engaged in work with the SCM even after his graduation from Oxford.

Parkes' main activity at Oxford, however, centered around the League of Nations Union. For Parkes and his generation, the period after World War I was seen as a time for creating a new world based on new political principles. The war had shown that a new approach to world problems was needed, and the concept of the League of Nations seemed to be an admirable idea. Parkes organized, and was university secretary of, the LNU at Oxford. The University seemed an ideal setting for such activities because of its many foreign students. Parkes spent much of his last two years at Oxford working for the Union, organizing meetings and lectures, and speaking on the League at various universities and in towns and villages. Parkes found great opposition to the League among the clergy he spoke to, as well as among the gentry. The desire to preserve "the Empire" and the view that the League was unrealistic was usually the basis of the opposition. This was the first, but not the last, time that Parkes found himself at odds with a large number of Christian clergy. Parkes also wrote an article on the League for *Isis*, an Oxford University journal, in November 1921.

Parkes believed that his interest in theology and politics was quite a logical combination. He wrote in his autobiography:

> I joined the LNU because my desire for ordination was not based on any wish to escape from the contemporary world but was tied to the conviction which I shared with so many of my generation that we had to discover the moral foundations of a

way of life for the whole world which would make a repetition of the war impossible.[2]

In Parkes' time, membership in the LNU and the SCM greatly overlapped. This indicated a common concern among Christians for developing a new world order. In addition, the goals of political and social progress were commonly shared by Humanists as well as Christians, and Parkes maintained the conviction throughout his life that Christians should work with and learn from Humanists. His future criticism of Christian theology divorced from political concerns, particularly as expressed in Barthian theology, had its roots in this period of his life.

Parkes also shared a belief in "progress" with many of the liberals and "modernists" in the Anglican Church. This belief in progress as a social, political, and moral possibility was rooted in his conviction that such a hope was not the product of utopianism, but rather was based on his generation's experiences in World War I. He claimed that his generation was not "starry eyed," had seen the total breakdown of morals, politics, and society, and therefore, was determined to find an alternative to the past. As we begin to examine the development of Parkes' thought, we shall see how influential this belief in progress, established early in his life, was to be on his thinking.

Parkes worked for the LNU up to the time when he began to prepare for his theology finals in late 1921. His work involved him with international students and political affairs, and it exposed him to the reluctance of the institutional Church to think seriously about politics and the social order. He also had his first real taste of controversy at this time. A local rector of the City Church, Oxford, had attacked Parkes for supporting the idea that German students be invited to Oxford in 1922 for a conference. The rector claimed that Parkes was the product of the pernicious teachings of William Temple, Bishop of Manchester; Dr. Cairns, Professor of Dogmatics at Aberdeen University; William Inge, Dean of St. Paul's; and Dr. Selbie, Principal of Mansfield College, Oxford.

---

[2] *Voyage of Discoveries*, p. 59.

When Parkes met these men later in his life, he related this incident to them. The connection made by the local rector between Parkes' political thinking and these particular churchmen is significant because it gives one some idea as to where Parkes rested on the theological spectrum, and indeed, Parkes was quite influenced by the thinking of these men on both issues of theological doctrine and political ideas.

During his years at Oxford, Parkes seriously considered the possibility of ordination in the Church of England, and upon graduation, he offered himself as a candidate for orders in the Anglican Church. He was accepted by the Bishop of Lichfield as a candidate for ordination. This pleased Parkes very much because his family had originally come from the Warwickshire–Staffordshire border, an area under the Bishop of Lichfield's care. Parkes prepared himself to begin his career as a cleric in the quite English countryside, but other events soon interfered with his plans.

In March of 1923, Parkes was invited to join the staff of the Student Christian Movement. The invitation was quite unexpected, and it disrupted all of Parkes' plans. The SCM was at that time at the zenith of its influence and authority in Great Britain and the world. Many of the most renowned leaders of the Christian Church were involved in its activities. Parkes joined the staff in June 1923, and he was put in charge of its International Study Program. He worked closely with the Reverend Tissington Tatlow and Zoe Fairfield.

Both Tatlow and Fairfield were longtime workers in the SCM and they had a very ecumenical approach to the SCM and to theology in general. Parkes found that the SCM on the Continent was much more confessional in nature than the British branch, and relations between the two branches of SCM were often strained. In his job, Parkes was to do a great deal of traveling to Europe, meeting with various student groups. Through this activity, he became acquainted with many political radicals, including one who took part in the murder of Walter Rathenau in Germany. He also became a member of the British (Royal) Institute of International Affairs, established contacts with the National Union of Students and kept up his ties with the LNU as well. He was quite active in combating the anti-German feelings of many student groups. Through this work, Parkes became familiar with social and political climates at home and abroad, reflected in the attitudes of students.

Parkes was not to be denied a clerical career, and the Bishop of London, Winnington Ingram, accepted him as a candidate for ordination. This was not at all unusual since the bishop often ordained SCM workers. The bishop required him to sit an examination, and when Parkes asked him about the nature of the exam, he was promised that it would be an examination that would show how the candidate thought. The exam turned out to be a set of mid-Victorian questions that Parkes found impossible to answer with any seriousness. His comments about the exam are amusing, but he would end up failing.[3] He was called in by the bishop, and an understanding was finally reached. When Parkes met with the bishop's chaplain for a two-hour interview, he refused to retake the exam. Parkes was finally ordained, but only after William Temple (then the Bishop of Manchester) interceded on his behalf. Temple remained a close friend and advisor to Parkes until his death in 1944. Following ordination, Parkes served in a curacy with Archdeacon Sharpe at St. Stephen's, Hampstead.

The problems Parkes encountered during his ordination examinations reflect something of his relationship with the Church of England. He always seemed to be on the periphery of the Church throughout his career. His work in the SCM involved him too much in politics for the taste of many of his clerical peers. Later, when he addressed the issue of Christian antisemitism and Israel, he would again find himself something of a lone voice. In a conversation I had with him in 1979, Parkes recounted how he was always a bit of a maverick in the eyes of the Church, and that he often depended on Temple to protect him when things got nasty. He also stated that he thought that the nature of the Anglican Church allowed more room for mavericks of his sort than did most other churches, and he wondered how long he could have remained in some other church given the issues he came to

---

[3] *Voyage of Discoveries*, op. cit., p. 75.

address.[4] He never actually served as a full-time parish priest, but he spent much time helping churches in the parishes in which he lived. Throughout his career as a theologian and churchman, Parkes would write critically of the Church, poking fun particularly at its pomp and its myopic attitude toward change and politics. Needless to say, he more than once incurred the wrath of some bishop or other, but such incidents did little to deter him. His criticisms were always those of one who loved the Church, and we shall later see how Parkes offered many positive opinions about the Church as well as criticism. It is true, however, that his career as a churchman was a difficult one, and the problems he encountered in getting ordained were just the beginning of a very unpredictable relationship between Parkes and his fellow clergy.

Now duly ordained, Parkes began his work with the SCM in earnest. He was responsible for developing studies in international affairs, which at the time were principally devoted to the issues of war and pacifism, the League of Nations, and the colonial status of Africa and India. He traveled throughout Britain as well as Europe, and was in contact with students throughout Europe, gaining thereby a sense of the political winds of the time.

---

[4] There is in the Anglican Church an astonishing history of maverick theologians and ministers. By the time Parkes entered Oxford, the Anglican community had been in the midst of several controversies over the theology of F. D. Maurice, Charles Gore and *Lux Mundi*, the Broad Church and Modernist movements, and the Anglo-Catholic theologians. Parkes is clearly sympathetic to the more liberal Modernist school of thought. It should be noted that one of his undergraduate examiners was Dr. H. D. A. Major, a leader of the Modernist movement. None of these movements concerned themselves with the issue of Jewish–Christian relations, but in many ways, Parkes moved quite logically from some of the positions developed by the more liberal Anglican thinkers to his position on Judaism. For instance, H. J. T. Johnson writes that Hastings Rashdall, a leader of the Modernist school, had "views on the doctrine of the Blessed Trinity ... quite acceptable to liberal Jews [like] Mr. Claude Montefiore, a distinguished exponent of their philosophy" (p. 63). Recognizing the roots of Parkes' thinking in certain schools of Anglican theology is essential if one is to avoid the temptation to think that he had to create an artificial theology in order to defend his position on Judaism. Parkes also shows a noted Anglican tendency to discuss the Incarnation and the Trinity as central themes of his theology. For a quick survey of Anglican thought relevant to Parkes' development as a theologian, see the following books: Humphrey J. T. Johnson, *Anglicanism in Transition*; Roger Lloyd, *The Church of England in the Twentieth Century, Vol. II*; Arthur Michael Ramsey, *An Era of Anglican Theology*; and Alec R. Vidler, *Witness to the Light: F. D. Maurice's Message for Today*.

His first clash with the continental churches occurred when he began to work with the German Movement for Christian Students (Deutscher Christentum Studenten Verbindung—DCSV). This group held that the Gospel had nothing to do with politics, and it opposed the help being given to students by the Committee for European Student Relief (later the International Student Service, now the World Student Service). Parkes found himself constantly in conflict with the DCSV. He also found himself frustrated by the lack of any sound "theology of politics," and any ideas he had on the topic were met by skepticism and hostility. In trying to formulate his own ideas on this issue, he began to question the traditional emphasis in Christian theology on Jesus to the exclusion of God and the Holy Spirit. It is here that Parkes' particular views about the Trinity began to take shape. He wanted theology to become more widely theocentric in its emphasis, and thereby take more seriously the questions of society. He would come to argue that a proper emphasis on the First and Third persons of the Trinity would help move Christian theology in the proper direction. His colleagues at the SCM talked about this as "Jimmy's bee in his bonnet about God." This issue would concern him throughout his life, but he found little support for his position initially. At about the same time, he was growing impatient with the pacifist movement, for he was urging them to concentrate "on much more peace" not "no more war."

In 1925, Parkes traveled to Geneva, Oberagai, Venice, and Belgrade. At the World Student Christian Federation (WSCF) at Oberagai, he encountered firsthand anti-Jewish sentiments, and he quickly became aware of its special violence and quality. It was at this conference that a Central European member gave a particularly antisemitic speech which Parkes, who was chairing the session, demanded withdrawn from the proceedings. It was the first, but by no means the last, time that Parkes would encounter antisemitism among the students with whom he was working.

This conference also brought into focus the conflict between what is loosely called "Anglo-Saxon" theology and "German" theology. The "Anglo-Saxons" (British, American and Asian students) wanted to discuss Christianity's relation to social and political problems, while the "Germans" opposed such discussions and wanted only Bible studies, usually on Paul's letters. Throughout his theological writings, Parkes attacked what he called "German" theology, particularly that represented by Karl Barth. He finished his travels that year by attending the Orthodox Conference at Hapova where he was the only non-Russian in attendance. The three-hour service of the Orthodox Church he witnessed there had a profound spiritual effect on him.

Between 1922 and 1926, Parkes traveled widely, broadened his academic studies, and found himself more and more involved with the issues of politics and theology. His work with students of different countries gave him some unique insights into the problems to be faced in the future. In 1926, his contact with foreign students became even more focused when he was asked by the SCM to stay for another term and to become the warden of the Student Movement House in London, a center for foreign students. He also found time to publish two short pamphlets for the SCM—*Outline Studies on the War* (1924) and *Studies in International Relations* (1927).

In the winter of 1927, Dr. Walter Kotsching, General Secretary of the International Student Service (ISS), asked him to head up a program of cultural cooperation in Geneva. Parkes accepted, and in March of 1928 he joined the staff of ISS, going first to Prague and then to Geneva.

The ISS was a small organization located in Geneva. It had no student membership, but existed as a self-perpetuating "Assembly" registered under Swiss law. Such a self-definition saved the ISS from competing with other student groups, and allowed it to work as a coordinating body between various student groups through conferences and programs. One important conference was scheduled each year, and during Parkes' term there, from 1928 to 1935, he attended conferences at Chartres, Krams on the Danube, Oxford, Mt. Holyoke in America, and at Brno in Slovakia. It was at Chartres that Parkes presented his plans for a department of "Cultural Co-operation." Through this department, Parkes coordinated conferences on conflict, political problems, race, nationality, and other issues of the day. A main goal of these conferences was to help people learn how to "discuss" issues, but Parkes found that the idea of an "English debate" was a mystery to most of the participants. He also encountered a growing problem of nationalism, which made it increasingly difficult to group people from different countries together. In his travels, he discovered European universities to be hotbeds of nationalism and antisemitism, particularly those in Eastern Europe. This experience prevented Parkes from being surprised later by the support given to the Nazis by the university communities of Germany and other European countries.

On the whole, the time spent in Geneva was quite pleasant. He lived at No. 3 Grand Mezel, a flat in Cité, the old hill town where Calvin had lived, which he later discovered to have been the boundary between the Jewish and Christian sections of Geneva. The flat was always open to students, and there was never a lack of guests at the Parkes' flat. His church life centered around the American Church, where Everett Smith was chaplain, and he served as the acting chaplain whenever Dr. Smith was away. The rector of the Anglican Church had attacked the SCM so violently when Parkes first introduced himself that he felt it wise to worship elsewhere. He also used this time to begin to build a substantial library, and to publish a small book in 1933 entitled *International Conferences*. These were good years for Parkes, a time of growth and change.

Part of the education Parkes received while serving at the ISS involved his first introduction to Barthian theology in a formal sense. At a WSCF conference in 1928, Fritz Lieb (Karl Barth's assistant) was to lecture on four subjects: the Fall, the Incarnation, Atonement, and the Holy Spirit. Parkes recalled that three days were spent on the Fall, and only a quarter of an hour on the Holy Spirit. This was what he called his first encounter with the "full blast of the abominable heresy of Barthianism." Parkes remained critical of Barth and his followers throughout his career, and his opposition to Barth led him to be even more out of step with his colleagues as they came under the sway of Barth's influence in the 1930s.

In Parkes' view, Barth stood for everything he opposed in theology. He was particularly critical of Barth for creating a theology that seemed to reduce human responsibility in the political sphere, and produced a caricature of God beyond human recognition. Parkes believed that Barth was responsible for creating a doctrine of the universality and inescapability of human sinfulness and of our inability to do anything about the evils of the social and political world, and thus, he was making it difficult, if not impossible, for young Germans to create a theology that could deal with such problems. Parkes considered Barth responsible for undermining what little effort was being made by German churchmen to deal with postwar problems, and "thereby made the surrender to Hitler in the vital academic field so much easier to achieve."[5]

In all fairness to Barth, we should point out that Parkes' criticisms are generally leveled at what is called the "Early Barth" theology. It should also be said, however, that Parkes was not alone in his criticism of Barth; Reinhold Niebuhr's criticisms of Barth, for example, are remarkably similar to Parkes'.[6] For the most part, Parkes' criticisms stem from his contact with students and theologians influenced by Barth in the late 1920s and early 1930s. At the ISS conference Parkes was attending, he was constantly being confronted by Germans who refused to consider political and social issues as being relevant to Christianity, and they were usually quoting Barth and praising him as their mentor. It was this group of German theologians who were making it difficult for Parkes to make any headway in his agitation for a theology of politics. He has written about this in his autobiography:

> I was still looking for a real theological interpretation of the divine relation to our social and political life. I could not accept any doctrine of a purposeful creation that did not include the ultimately complete responsibility of the Creator. Anything less seemed to me just immoral. Now along came Barth proclaiming a godling who, apparently, revelled in making himself totally obscure and incomprehensible to his creation—causing unending suffering and misery thereby—

---

[5] *Voyage of Discoveries*, op. cit., p. 101.

[6] Niebuhr offers criticisms of Barth that are amazingly similar to Parkes' own. Niebuhr is critical of Barth's influence on young German pastors in Germany, and he also shared Parkes' concern over the lack of a realistic political ethic in Barth's theology. The best collection of Niebuhr's essays on Barth can be found in a book edited by D. B. Robinson: *Reinhold Niebuhr, Essays in Applied Christianity: The Church and the New World*, pp. 141–97.

and who accepted no responsibility for the result. He had been so inefficient or malicious a creator that man, his creation, could not understand his purpose or nature, however hard he tried. In fact, Barth's godling was so egotistical that he regarded it as blasphemous if he tried. It made no difference whether Barth ascribed this situation to man's fall or to man's basic nature. For the godling who gave man freewill, and did not take into account the possibility of a "fall" was so grotesquely incompetent that he had no right ever to have created man at all. Barth's perpetual insistence on the otherness of God merely enfolded him in a fog too thick to penetrate rather than in a light too brilliant for human eyes.[7]

Parkes is not so brittle in his criticism of Barth that he does not recognize Barth's role in the resistance against Hitler, but it is guarded praise, as seen in this passage:

Later, of course, when Hitler was in power and turned to attack the Lutheran Church, the disciples of Barth were the backbone of the Confessing Church; but in the years when Hitler might have been prevented from achieving power, Barth was silent, and the immense majority of Protestant leaders were silent when the dangers were already evident, and when the Jewish community of Germany was making instant appeals for Christian backing in their warning to President Hindenburg and the nation of the danger which was menacing them.[8]

These are harsh words, but from Parkes' perspective they represented accurately what he saw happen in Europe in the 1930s, especially in Germany and its churches.

In 1929, Parkes' debate with the Barthians bore its first fruits with a series of lectures delivered at a WSCF summer conference held at Gilon near Montreux in Switzerland. The lectures were entitled *Politics and the Doctrine of the Trinity*, and they provided

---

[7] *Voyage of Discoveries*, op. cit., p. 102.
[8] Ibid., pp. 101–02. See Richard Gutteridge, *Open Thy Mouth for the Dumb: The German Evangelical Church and the Jews 1879–1950*, chapter 8, for a critical view of Barth's influence on German Christians.

a surprisingly accurate outline of many of the issues which would concern Parkes throughout his life. They were read and critiqued by friends like William Temple, and revealed Parkes' struggle to develop a theology that could provide guidance to those concerned with political issues. In fact, the lectures really marked the beginning of Parkes' serious theological development, but after he delivered them, he realized just how isolated he was in his thinking. He commented on this by stating that

> the Anglo-Saxons were irritated that I spoiled sensible remarks about politics with medieval obscurantism like the Trinity, while the Barthians, of course, found it blasphemous to mention politics in the same breath as the *arcana* of theology. The real significance, however, of this attempt to sum up my thinking from Oxford onwards was that, though I conceived of the Trinity as a meaningful doctrine of the total involvement of God in the whole of his creation, yet I had not discovered any clear guidance to a theology of politics. And there the matter rested for some years.[9]

It would be nearly ten years before Parkes returned to his theological writings.

By 1930, Parkes was beginning to feel out of place with his friends at the ISS, the SCM, and the WSCF. In 1931, W. A. Visser 't Hooft became the General Secretary of the WSCF, and he was moving the organization towards the position of Barth and away from that of Parkes. English theologians and students were just beginning to come under the sway of Barth, and thus Parkes was feeling uncomfortable with his peers. By 1932, Parkes was again suffering from ill health, and for a time he considered resigning. History, however, once more intruded into Parkes' life, and he was prevented from doing so. It was at this point in his life that the Jewish question began to demand his attention. With the rise to power of Hitler in Germany, and the growing problems of Jewish, non-Aryan, and left-wing students, Parkes found himself more and more involved with the Jewish community. The magnitude of the problem was clearly perceived by Parkes, who had already experienced firsthand the anti-Jewish sentiments in Eastern

---

[9] *Voyage of Discoveries*, op. cit., p. 104.

European universities. When the ISS asked him to work on this problem, he decided to remain, and he stayed in Geneva until 1935.

During this time, he established contact with the Marks family of England, who were aiding the resettlement of refugees in England, and through them, he met Israel M. Sieff, Simon Mark's brother-in-law. Parkes' friendship with Sieff was a close one, and Sieff acted as a benefactor to Parkes at different times in his life. In addition, Parkes' work and position in Geneva made him privy to more accurate information about the events in Germany than could be obtained even in official circles. An example of this involves a story about anti-Jewish laws in Nazi Germany and a visit by Parkes to England in 1933. He recounted the story thus:

> I had stayed with Tatlow during this visit to England, and I spent the first evening telling him about the anti-Jewish measures which were actually in force in Germany, and the threats of what was to come. I had taken the precaution of bringing with me the actual texts of the German laws. Tatlow was amazed by what I showed him. He told me that he had been with the Archbishop of Canterbury (Dr. Lang) earlier in the day and that Lang had assured him that the allegations that Jews were persecuted in Germany were largely false; that he had been to see Ribbentrop—the German Ambassador—himself, and that Ribbentrop had assured him that all the stories of persecution and violence were fabrications. The Archbishop was planning to make a speech in the House of Lords on the following day repeating the assurance of Ribbentrop. Tatlow rang up the Archbishop's secretary, Alan Don, later Dean of Westminster, and arranged with me to go down to Lambeth in the morning with the texts I had brought with me. The speech was not made.[10]

As time went on, Parkes would find officials less willing than the archbishop to accept his descriptions of the plight of Jews in Nazi Europe, particularly officials in the Foreign Office.

On a personal level, Parkes was affected by the Jewish problem as well. The year 1933 was particularly difficult. Parkes refused to

---

[10] Ibid., p. 106.

attend the ISS conference in Kloster Ettal, Bavaria, because Jews were not allowed to attend. An ISS friend, Fritz Beck, correctly predicted his own murder because of his work with the ISS. Indeed, Beck's own students killed him. Even on a trip to New York to raise money, Parkes found it necessary to take precautions while meeting with the Swedish contact, Elsa Brandstrom, because of the number of Germans in the city, particularly in the Yorkville section of Manhattan. Parkes remained in touch with Brandstrom, who provided great aid to war victims, through a special code. Parkes was vaguely aware by that time that Nazi spies were in and out of his flat in Geneva, so he kept the code number under a pile of dirty dishes. He correctly assumed that this hiding place would not be discovered. During this trip, Parkes also traveled to Canada to preach at Holy Blossom Synagogue, and while there, he became friends with Maurice Eisendrath, a Reform Rabbi with whom Parkes worked closely in subsequent years.

Parkes was called back from Toronto to New York to meet with James G. McDonald, the newly named High Commissioner for Refugees. This was a position that had originated in the League of Nations, but with the League's collapse, it was now "abandoned forthwith on the steps of public charity." Parkes was sent by McDonald to meet with Felix Warburg of White Plains, New York, to discuss the problem of funding this work for refugees. Warburg and Parkes were able to make arrangements for the money, and Parkes sailed back to England with McDonald. Parkes worked with McDonald for a short while, but he resigned over the question of how the monies should be spent. Parkes felt that too much was being spent on administration, and not enough on refugees.

Parkes finally resigned from the ISS in 1934, but he remained in Geneva until 1935. The years spent there were formative years for Parkes. He had begun to develop his own theological answers to questions that were being put to him by world events, and he was becoming more deeply involved with the Jewish question. Aspects of his work that would be developed more fully in his later work have their seeds in this period. An example of this would be his opposition to missionary activities among Jews. In a letter of November 15, 1933 to W. W. Simpson, then with the Methodist

Missionary Board, he stated that "while I fully recognize the right of any Jew to join the Gentile Church, I disagree entirely with individual conversion to the present Gentile Churches being the official policy of those organizations." Simpson had asked Parkes to put him in touch with Jews for the purpose of conversion, but Parkes refused. This letter was written at a time when the missionary effort among Jews was an important activity of the Church in Britain. Parkes was quite correct when he told Simpson how he was on the "other side of the hedge" on this question of missions to the Jews. Parkes would, as a result, be in continual conflict with the mission people.

It is interesting to note that Parkes was not totally alone in his opposition to missions. In April 1934, Reverend A. Hubert Grey of London wrote to Parkes expressing his sympathy with Parkes' position, and making clear his own opposition to all missionary activities. He also agreed with Parkes that antisemitism was an evil, rooted in Christianity, that needed to be eradicated from the Church's soul. Parkes also had an exchange of letters with Rose E. Strahan of Aberdeenshire, Scotland, on this issue. Strahan was a laywoman concerned about the Jewish question, and she frequently wrote Parkes about the issue. A letter from her in October 1933 shows remarkable insight into the dangers confronting Jews in Nazi Germany, and in her opinion, such dangers constituted a danger to the Church as well. Parkes provided her with much information about the plight of Jews in Germany, and he discussed with her his own theological ideas on the matter. On the whole, however, Parkes' position was a minority one, and even friends like William Temple disagreed with him. In Temple's case, he did not believe that the relationship between Christianity and Judaism was as unique as Parkes made it out to be, and he believed that some form of mission was justified.

By the time he returned to England, Parkes had established himself as an authority on the Jewish question. He had been so involved in the matter that he turned down an opportunity to stand for the position of Chaplain of Oriel College, Oxford. In a letter of February 19, 1934, L. B. Namier, a leader of the Jewish community in England, wrote to Parkes to say that Professor Powicke, a professor of historical theology at Oxford, had suggested Parkes for the post. Parkes turned it down for fear that it would interrupt his work on the Jewish issue. A question needs to be asked, therefore, as to how Parkes, an ordained Christian minister and an ecumenical worker, came to consider this issue so important that he decided to devote his whole life to it.

This is not an idle question, but one that has great bearing on our understanding of Parkes and his work. It has been implied by critics of Parkes that he was "the Christian in the Jewish camp," and that his work suffers from being too Jewish or philosemitic in nature. A more damning implication has been that Parkes was financed by Jews like I. M. Sieff to do their bidding. Even when we proposed to do this study of Parkes' work, questions were asked about the quality of his scholarship and his proximity to the Jewish community. In my own mind, Parkes' scholarship is beyond reproach, no matter whether one agrees with his conclusions or not. More importantly, it can be shown that Parkes' interest in the Jewish question arose out of his situation in the ISS, and that initially he had very little contact with the Jewish community. I hope to show later in the study that his theological position, which was developed in the late 1920s, enabled Parkes to move logically in the direction he did regarding the relationship between Christianity and Judaism, without twisting his own theology in order to meet Jewish needs. In fact, his discovery of Judaism provided answers to questions he was asking about theology during his SCM days. But here we are jumping ahead of our study. In order to understand how Parkes became involved in the Jewish question, we need to first return to the year 1925.

We mentioned earlier the 1925 WSCF conference at Oberagai at which an Eastern European student gave an anti-Jewish speech which Parkes demanded to be withdrawn. This was his first encounter with the antisemitism then emerging in Europe, particularly in Romania, Poland, Austria, and Germany. The extent to which this antisemitism was pervading the whole of society became clearer to him as he traveled to universities in these countries. Riots were occurring between Jewish and nationalist students in many universities, causing some of them to close down completely. Parkes' initial awareness of the problem was rooted more in the disorder antisemitism was causing in the universities he was visiting for the ISS than it was in the acute and immediate danger it posed for Jewish life in the political and social arena. At this time, he was also rather oblivious to the religious dimension of antisemitism. At the Chartres Conference of July 1928, Parkes proposed that a future conference be held between Jewish students and nationalist students. He wrote that "I was generally regarded as mad for proposing such a conference, and both sides tended to inform me that I was insulting them for suggesting that they sit down with the other side. It was hopefully foreseen that the conference would end in bloodshed; but I was given permission to try the experiment."[11]

Parkes arranged for the conference to be held in January 1929 at Bierville, France, in the Chateau de Bierville, which belonged to Marc Sagnier of the Jeune République. The location was rather remote and the time of the year unusual, but Parkes hoped that this would keep the people together. Invitations were sent to the heads of Jewish and nationalist student organizations from Central and Eastern Europe, and even the president of the Deutsche Studentenschaft came, despite German objections and threats. The result was that the two sides were able to meet and hear each other out. Moreover, the non-Jewish participants were able to hear about aspects of Judaism and Jewish history that they never would have heard at home. Parkes was encouraged by both sides to continue his work on the issue, to visit their universities, and to keep the ISS active in this area. Perhaps the most important discovery made by Parkes at this time was the lack of any Christian able to speak intelligently on the Jewish issue. The ISS agreed that there was a void to be filled here, and they instructed Parkes to make a study of the Jewish problem. So Parkes began his career as a Christian scholar devoted to the Jewish question.

Parkes had some immediate decisions to make at this juncture. Should he spend his time learning Hebrew or Jewish history? Who should he meet in the Jewish community? How should he present the issue to Gentiles? The last problem would occupy Parkes throughout his life, while first two had easier solutions.

Parkes decided that he could never learn Hebrew quickly enough to use it in a scholarly fashion, particularly in regard to understanding the Talmud. For this information, he would have to use good secondary sources. He decided to concentrate on

---

[11] Ibid., p. 110.

history, and he proceeded to purchase Graetz's *History*, and read it in six months. He also made contact with Jewish leaders throughout Europe. Alexander Trich was an old friend with a good knowledge of Central and Eastern European Jewry, and he introduced Parkes to many Jewish leaders, He worked with Jewish student leaders in Poland, Hungary, and Romania, as well as with the World Union of Jewish Students, whose president, Hersch Lauterpaucht, was then a lecturer at the London School of Economics. In London, Parkes contacted Dr. Charles Singer, Professor of the History of Medicine at London University, and Rabbi Dr. Mattuck, a leader in the Liberal movement who had a good deal of sympathy with the Orthodox Jewish tradition. He also spent time with Professor Herbert Loewe of Oxford and Professor Claude Montefiore of Cambridge. Using the offices of Nathanson and Louis Laush of Paris and Berlin, and M. Slatkin of Geneva, he began to acquire a first-rate library on Judaica.

Almost from the beginning of his work, Parkes discovered that both Christians and Jews viewed his work with suspicion. Jews thought that any Christian interested in Jews had to have missionary motives underlying the interest. Many Christians resented any hint of Christian responsibility for antisemitism, and they considered any lack of interest in converting Jews as a subversion of the faith. This problem became evident to Parkes when Dr. John Mott chose Conrad Hoffman to be the first secretary of a new committee on the Christian Approach to the Jews, created by the International Missionary Council. Hoffman had worked closely with minority groups in Eastern Europe when he worked for the European Student Relief, and Mott chose him precisely because of his cordial relations with Jewish students. Parkes viewed Mott's decision as a "naked piece of religious aggression," and he found his own situation aggravated by the Hoffman appointment since Jews became more suspicious than ever of the motives of Christians working on the Jewish problem.

All this took Parkes by surprise at the time. His own work had initially involved him with the problem of antisemitism in the universities, and he had not really seen the religious dimensions of the issue. His own theological views on Jewish–Christian relations had not yet developed, and he basically held the traditional and conventional ideas he had acquired at Oxford. At the

SCM, most of the mission issues had been centered on Africa and Asia, and Parkes has said that he could not recall "missions to the Jews even being discussed." By 1930, Parkes found himself in the middle of a controversy with his Christian colleagues over this issue.

Being unable to find a suitable short study on antisemitism written in English, Parkes wrote a book on the subject entitled *The Jew and His Neighbour*. The book put him into immediate conflict with Hoffman and William Paton, secretary of the International Missionary Council. Hoffman objected to the book, which was still in press, because it blamed the Christian Church for medieval antisemitism, and because it did not support the idea that conversion to Christianity was the solution to the Jewish problem. Paton objected to Parkes' contention that the relationship between Christianity and Judaism was unique. Such a view threatened the idea of Christian universality, a favorite view of liberal Christians at that time. When Parkes tried to explain his position, he was told by Paton to "go and read his bible." This episode with Hoffman and Paton caused Parkes to write in his autobiography that he "learned very early that to evolve a new attitude to Jewish–Christian relations was to be a very lonely job."[12]

By 1931, Parkes' involvement with the Jewish issue was complete. After having traveled to America to meet with Cyrus Adler of the Jewish Theological Seminary, he returned to Europe to continue his work at conferences. Two such meetings took place at Nyon on Lake Geneva, and there he met Nahum Goldmann, later the leader of the World Jewish Congress and the World Zionist Organization, and Herman Badt, then the highest placed Jewish civil servant in any Germany ministry serving in the Prussian Home Office. At these conferences, Parkes got his first taste of Nazi racial theories through Nazi students. Dr. Wilhelm Stapel was invited by the students to lecture on the issue of Jewish "differentiated plasma" and German "undifferentiated plasma." According to Stapel, this "fact" made symbiosis impossible. In

---

[12] Ibid., p. 117.

reaction to this plasma nonsense, Parkes wrote the following verse:

My plasma lies over the ocean
My plasma is awful to see.
My plasma is all in a muddle.
Oh, who'll differentiate me?

When Goldmann and Badt left, the president of the Deutsche Studentenschaft led the singing of Parkes' *plasmalied* in their honor.

Following this conference, Parkes headed for Poland to speak on the Jewish issue to the Polish National Union for Students at the invitation of Jan Wrocznski, vice president and foreign secretary of the Union and a longtime member of the ISS. These conferences and visits to European universities were making Parkes more aware of the controversial and difficult nature of his work, and he decided that he would have to become "Herr Doktor" if he was to continue in the field. Accordingly, Parkes arranged with the ISS to begin work at Oxford on his doctorate.

The arrangement with the ISS was for Parkes to spend one term a year at Oxford, this being the minimum residence time required by the University. Parkes took his first term in 1931 at Exeter College, a college which had close historic ties with Parkes' school in Guernsey. It was through Exeter that he was offered a modest postgraduate scholarship. Oxford also accepted the letter which had been signed by his examining committee in 1922 as evidence of his ability to do a second degree despite the fact that the letter was highly irregular and probably illegal. The University accepted his book *The Jew and His Neighbour* as a first research degree requirement. Professor (later Sir Maurice) Powicke was his faculty advisor. Over the next three years, Parkes spent one term a year doing his work at Oxford.

The subject of Parkes' work at Oxford was an inquiry into the origins of antisemitism. In his book *The Jew and His Neighbour*, Parkes had begun his study with the Crusades and the massacre of Jews which took place in Europe at the time. It puzzled him that the massacres took place in cities where there had been a long Jewish presence with no real tradition of violence against them, and he decided to use his time at Oxford studying the background of the Crusades in order to discover the roots of antisemitism. He thus began his thesis project without the least idea as to what he would discover in his studies.

Having been well schooled in the classics, Parkes was already somewhat familiar with the Roman dislike of Jews and other orientals. He had never seen fit to question very seriously what he had learned about Judaism while an undergraduate. "I had understood from my good teachers at Oxford," he writes, "that all that was good in Judaism had passed to the Christian Church, and I had been content to leave it at that."[13] Of post-New Testament Judaism, he knew almost nothing. He was surprised, therefore, by what he found as his research into the origins of antisemitism proceeded.

Parkes discovered that while the antisemitism of the Hellenistic world was an example of normal human xenophobia, Christian antisemitism was the product of something entirely different:

> I was completely unprepared for the discovery that it was the Christian Church and the Christian Church alone, which turned a normal xenophobia and normal good and bad communal relations between two human societies into the unique evil of antisemitism, the most evil, and as I gradually came to realise, the most crippling sin of historic Christianity. . . . Antisemitism arises from the picture of the Jews [which] Christian theologians extracted from their reading of the Old Testament, a work whose every word they claimed to have divine authority. The Old Testament is very frank about Jewish sins and very definite in its certainty that they earned divine punishment. But it also dwelt on the love between God and Israel, and the promises of the Messianic Age. So long as both elements in the story are accepted as being about a single people, a lofty balance is retained. But Christian and theologians divided it into the story of two peoples—the virtuous Hebrews, who were pre-incarnation Christians, had all the praise and promise; and the wicked Jews had all the crimes and denunciations. This was the interpretation repeated over and over again, in every century from the third

---

[13]   Ibid., p. 121.

onwards. In the leading Church historian of the fourth century, Eusebius of Caesarea, Jews and Hebrews are biologically two distinct races.[14]

How and why antisemitism became a product of Christianity became the focus of his thesis.

In the course of his study, Parkes also discovered that the traditional Christian views of Judaism were the result of distortions of Judaism, the Jewish people, and Jewish history. For instance, Parkes found that his assumption about the Jewish responsibility for the persecution of the early Church was false. In reading through the *Lives of the Saints*, Parkes discovered that there were no references to the Jewish responsibility for the martyrdom of Pionus, Phillip, and Pontius, even though Catholic, Protestant and Jewish scholars have all agreed that Jews were responsible. He also found that Christian historical writings are deeply embedded with false accusations against Jews, and thus have helped to distort the image of Jews and Judaism in the eyes of Christians. He was also forced to make a new evaluation of post-Temple Judaism as he discovered more about Judaism and its tradition on its own terms. In this effort, he was guided by Herbert Loewe, who was in Parkes' words a "living denial of all the stock charges that Judaism is legalistic, unspiritual, formal and so on and so on." These discoveries that he made were a serious challenge to traditional Christian teachings, and he found himself being labeled "philosemitic" simply for drawing a different picture of Judaism and Jewish history.[15]

The end product of his research was a thesis which was published under the title *The Conflict of the Church and the Synagogue: A Study in the Origins of Antisemitism*. The study covered the period from the time of Jesus up through the decline of the Roman Empire, ending with the beginnings of the Dark Ages. It

---

[14] Ibid., p. 123.
[15] Edward H. Flannery, *The Anguish of the Jews*, pp. 22, 281, 53. Flannery quotes Marcel Simon in support of his position that some scholars like Parkes downplay the issues of pre-Christian antisemitism and Jewish persecution of Christians in order to support the claim that Christianity bears responsibility for the way antisemitism developed in the West. I am of the opinion that Parkes had the better argument in this debate.

contains 135,000 words including five appendices, and remains one of the most important studies on antisemitism to date. Oxford awarded him the doctorate in 1934, the same year in which Sonocino Press published the book. Having become "Herr Doktor," he returned to Geneva to finish his work with the ISS.

Before returning to Geneva, Parkes met in London with George Antonious, author of *The Arab Awakening*, to discuss the possibility of joining the Crane Foundation in New York in order to continue his work on the Jewish question. Parkes was offered £1200 a year, a home in Jerusalem to be secured by Antonious from his friend the Grand Mufti of Jerusalem, and a substantial pension. In return, Parkes would be subject to Antonious' "overriding" censorship and Parkes' pledge that he was "never to put anything on paper on the subject of the Jews except for the Crane Foundation." Parkes turned down the offer and returned to Geneva.

During his last year in Geneva, Parkes continued his writing. He published a book entitled *Jesus, Paul and the Jews*, in which he made a more detailed study of the Gospels and the Pauline letters than had been possible in his thesis. Herbert Loewe wrote the Introduction. Parkes took issue in this book with the Christian claim that the Jews had rejected Jesus, arguing instead that they have rejected the Gospel accounts of the life of Jesus and the exaggeration of Jewish failings and the distortion of their religion. He also faults Paul for giving a completely false picture of Judaism. He used the book to attack "biblical theologians," whom he believed to be perpetuating the mistaken idea that the Church does not share the Old Testament, but has an exclusive right to it and its interpretation. The book is an important aid in understanding how Parkes treats biblical material and its interpretation.

In early 1935, he was invited by the SCM to deliver a series of lectures on Judaism and Christianity at various British universities. He used this time in England to discuss with William Temple and his friends at SCM ways in which he could work in this area full time. His lectures, however, did not produce much encouragement. One lecturer at St. Ordan's, Birkenhead, protested that Parkes could not be right about Judaism, since Christians would then have to study it and there was no time in the seminary curriculum to do so. Parkes spoke in Selly Oak, Birmingham, and in York. While in York, he stayed with William Temple, who encouraged him to continue his work on Jewish–Christian relations. Temple also agreed with Parkes that the separation of Christianity and Judaism was a schism, which like all schisms, left truth divided.[16]

While in England, Parkes also approached I. M. Sieff about sponsoring his research. Parkes believed that in time Christian support would be forthcoming, but he needed immediate help. Sieff agreed to help when Parkes told him that he thought it would take at least three hundred years to complete all the work that needed to be done. He also spent time preparing for his permanent return to England. He found a house in Barley, a small village near Cambridge, hired a valet, Thomas "Len" Thomas, whom he had known when he served as warden of SCM House, and together they prepared to return to Geneva. He stopped in Guernsey to see his father, and there he received word that his flat in Geneva had been occupied by the police. Some friends even warned him not to return since they assumed that the police planned to arrest him.

The situation in Geneva developed when the Berne police received information that the Eisene Front, a Swiss Nazi group, had been instructed by the World Antisemitic Service (Der Antisemitische Weltdienst) to liquidate Parkes. Berne was the location of the famous trial over *The Protocols of the Elders of Zion* in 1934–35, which finally ruled that the book was a forgery. As a student of the Jewish question, Parkes was visited regularly by "Swiss" students to discuss the trial. He often showed these students a rare copy of the *Dialogue aux Enfers entre Montesquieu et Machiavel*—the book used as the basis for forging the *Protocols*. During this period, Parkes was also active in helping refugees from Germany, and they often spent time at Parkes' flat. What was unknown to Parkes was that his "Swiss" students were Nazi spies. Being correctly perceived as an enemy of the Nazi movement, Parkes was marked for attack.

A Nazi attempt on his life took place soon after he arrived back in Geneva. Its failure was due to the fact that the Nazi agents

---

[16] *Voyage of Discoveries*, op. cit., p. 128.

mistook his valet Thomas for Parkes, and they attacked the wrong man. Thomas sustained severe wounds, but the police acted as if the incident had never occurred, and the Nazi thugs were never caught. After nursing Thomas back to health, Parkes departed from Geneva in the spring of 1935 to return to England.

Upon returning to Barley, Parkes arranged with St. John's College, Cambridge to make use of their resources. He continued his work as he prepared a volume on the medieval period that was published in 1937 as *The Jew in the Medieval Community.* A second volume was planned, but it was never completed. The war also interrupted plans to write a two-volume work on the Church and the populace.

Parkes continued to lecture and cultivate Christian support for his work. William Temple remained a good friend and advisor to Parkes; George Bell, Bishop of Chichester and friend of Dietrich Bonhoeffer, also supported his work; as did his old friends from the SCM, Tissington Tatlow and Zoe Fairfield. But Parkes found it difficult to make much headway among ordinary Christians, and he continued to look to Sieff for support. "I was always conscious of the unfairness of a Jewish friend having to provide the necessary funds," wrote Parkes, "for fighting against the non-Jewish, in fact, Christian sin of antisemitism. But though I had quite a list of Christian supporters before the war, they could never have made a whole-time job possible."[17] The support of Sieff was unconditional, and he made no attempt to influence Parkes' ideas. Such a condition Parkes would not have tolerated, as evidenced by his refusal of the Crane Foundation offer.

In 1937, Parkes completed his book on the medieval period. In that same year, Gilbert Murray asked him to write a book on the Jewish question for the Home University Library, and as a result his book *The Jewish Problem in the Modern World* was published. In this book, Parkes wrote for the first time on the issue of Zionism. He had avoided the issue until then because he felt another Gentile writer should take up the issue. But he realized that he could no longer work on the Jewish question without addressing the problem of the Jewish homeland. This interest in Zionism would last throughout his career.

---

[17] Ibid., p. 140.

Outside of his research, Parkes was active in politics. In November 1939, Parkes went to the United States and Canada to lecture to Christian audiences on antisemitism and the refugee situation. He consulted with Canadian officials about allowing more refugees into their country. He also made a similar lecture tour of Britain. His main interest at this time, however, was the rise of British fascism under the leadership of Oswald Mosley. This interest put Parkes in touch with the Board of Deputies of British Jews.

Neville Laski (the president of the Board) and A. G. Brotman (the secretary) asked Parkes to prepare a book on the *Protocols*. The plan was to have something ready to print should the fascists provoke a controversy about it. The book was never published, but Parkes did use the material in later works. He was also involved with the Board in working to combat the fascist activity in the East End of London. On September 7, 1936, Parkes received a letter from Sidney Solomon, writing on behalf of Laski, asking for his help in enlisting Christian clergy to help in the fight against antisemitism. Mosley and his group were provoking the Jewish community in the East End, and they were attempting to poison the generally friendly relations between Christians and Jews in the area. Parkes agreed to help, and in November 1936, he produced a document entitled "Antisemitism in the East End."[18] The document outlined the problems faced by the Jewish community, and the fascist plan of attack. It was circulated among people involved in the East End situation, but the Board was not entirely in agreement with the document.

Parkes and the Board were at odds over the best approach for responding to Mosley. The Board wanted only to attack Mosley's antisemitism, but not his fascism, because they feared he might well become Prime Minister, and then the Jewish community would be in the impossible position of opposing the policy adopted by the nation. The Jewish People's Committee took the position held by most East End Jews that Mosley and everything he stood for should be attacked. Parkes agreed with the People's Committee, and the Committee's position won the day.

---

[18] James Parkes, "Antisemitism in the East End," 1936. Copy in possession of author and on file at the Parkes Library, University of Southampton, England.

Parkes also engaged in an exchange of letters with Sidney Solomon in November 1937 over the accuracy of information about German Jewry found in a pamphlet issued by the Board. The pamphlet was designed to counter German claims that Jews occupied positions of authority out of proportion to their population in Germany. Working with his Barley neighbor, Radcliffe Salaman, Parkes attempted to get the Board to issue more accurate information in a less polemical fashion. He wrote to Solomon on November 30, 1937;

> The Board has issued a pamphlet which can easily be disregarded and disproved. Dr. Salaman and I have been dealing with a memorandum sent by you at his request. It contains no more than four pages, but includes, as you yourself have admitted, several statements which have been disproved, and a large number which are disputable in that you have to defend them by elaborate casuistry.

Salaman was writing at the same time to Claude Montefiore expressing both Parkes' and his own concern over the Board's action. They both worked on producing their own report on the status of German Jews. Parkes believed that accurate information was essential if the British were to be convinced of the dangers posed to Jews by the Nazi Reich. He was afraid that actions such as that which the Board was taking would hinder efforts made on behalf of German Jews because accurate information would not be available. His own experience with the Nazis made him acutely aware of the dangers involved, but he also knew of the problems in getting the message across. He particularly feared that intemperate statements would be counter-productive, and they would be dismissed as so much propaganda.

Parkes understood the danger menacing the Western world at that time. The problem, as he saw it, was finding ways to explain the danger without making it look like unbelievable anti-German propaganda. The memory of the propaganda war of World War I made people hesitant to accept as fact the horrors taking place in Germany in the 1930s and 1940s. An example of how Parkes went about this task of making people aware is found in a series of letters sent to Parkes by a number of people in 1937. In order to make people realize the magnitude of Nazi antisemitism, Parkes sent copies of the German children's books *Bilderbuch* published by *Der Strümer*. The book was used to teach German children about Jews, and it ranks as one of the most vile pieces of antisemitism ever published. It used pictures and stories to foster hatred of Jews and reinforce stereotypes. Parkes knew that few would believe that such a book actually existed if they were not shown it. The letters sent to Parkes by the people who received copies all expressed shock and astonishment that such things were being used to teach children in Germany.[19]

Parkes also discovered himself in the middle of a controversy between Christian missionary groups and groups working with Jewish refugees. It was not long after Hitler invaded Czechoslovakia that Parkes was visited in Barley by Louis Rabinowitz. Rabinowitz had received a request from some relatives in Prague to visit an Orthodox Jewish boy whose mother had sent him to England to escape the Nazis. She had signed a document presented to her by a man who claimed the document was required by the British authorities to allow him to take responsibility for the boy. It turned out that the man was a member of an extreme Protestant missionary society, and the mother had unknowingly given her permission for the boy to be brought up as a Christian. Rabinowitz had tried to find the boy at the address given to him by the mother. He was refused admission to the place, unable to discover where the boy was, and was told that none of the boy's Jewish relatives in England would be allowed to see him. Together, Parkes and Rabinowitz traced the boy three months later to an establishment in the diocese of Rochester. The bishop of the diocese was no help since the mission group did not recognize his authority. Through some complicated procedures, the boy was finally freed, along with twenty-eight other Czech Jewish boys. Parkes wrote that "the Czech incident closed with a telegram from Rab, which must be the oddest telegram sent by a rabbi to an Anglican clergyman: 'Glad to say boy saved,' meaning that he had been rescued from Christianity and come home to Judaism."[20]

---

[19] These letters are on file at the Parkes Library, University of Southampton, England.

[20] *Voyage of Discoveries*, op. cit., pp. 149–50.

This was but one of many conflicts that Parkes had with missionary groups both during and after the war. Apparently, Parkes was often called upon to protect English Jewish children from well-meaning foster families with whom they were staying after being evacuated from cities enduring the blitz. In a letter he wrote to me on May 27, 1976, he told of another incident like the one with Rabinowitz. Certain missionary groups were using very questionable methods to induce Jewish children to join them. Parkes confronted A. Luklyn Williams, author of the noted work *Adversus Judeos* and a leader in the Church Missions to the Jews, with this information. Parkes said in the letter:

> The most important single event in the period covered is the challenge issued to the Church Mission to the Jews and other Evangelical Missions when they were trying to get Jewish children into their toils by bribery, i.e. offering food and clothing to impoverished immigrants. At the time, A. Luklyn Williams was working at the Mission and denied the accusations; he said that if it was proved, he would resign at once and have nothing more to do with them.[21]

The charges were proved to Williams' satisfaction, and he resigned. Parkes' argument with the mission people erupted from time to time into full-scale controversy with the most serious exchange coming in 1959 in a series of letters in the *Church of England Newspaper*.

Parkes' first real theological statement on the mission question appeared when he was asked to give a University sermon at Oxford in 1939. The sermon, endowed by a Principal of his former college, Hertford, was supposed to be devoted to "the application of the prophecies in the Holy Scriptures respecting the Messiah to our Lord and Saviour Jesus Christ, with an especial view to confute the arguments of Jewish commentators and to promote the conversion of Christianity of the ancient people of God." Parkes thought it ironic his being asked to deliver such a sermon since his intentions were quite opposite to the intentions of "the pious giver of the endowment." The sermon deals with a number

---

[21] Letter received from James Parkes, dated May 27, 1976.

of issues, including the tragic history of Jewish–Christian relations. Parkes concluded the sermon with this lengthy statement on missions:

> To many the answer is simply that we should try the old methods, but in a spirit of love and repentence, admitting when convenient, our past sins, but maintaining unaltered our historic conception of the relations of Christianity to Judaism. . . . I think they are wrong. . . . To me the challenge goes much deeper, and affects our whole attitude to Judaism. The men of the historic church were no less Christian, no less sincere, no less filled with missionary zeal than those who would set out today along the paths they trod to retrieve the consequences of their errors. They were not wicked men, filled with hatred and a lust for cruelty, but men who set out to do the will of God. They failed, and did incredible harm because what they set out to do was not the will of God. They believed themselves possessed of the whole truth, setting out to convert those who wholly lack it. In both beliefs they were in error. The Gentile Church to which we belong does not possess the whole truth; the synagogue of Rabbinic Judaism does not wholly lack it. Gentile Christianity and Rabbinic Judaism are two parts of the whole; the separation of the Church from the Synagogue was the first and most tragic of all the schisms in our history, it left truth divided. We have retained the person of Jesus, Judaism his religion; we have retained his teaching; Judaism the setting in which that teaching is coherent. And the same is true as we look to the developments of the two religions. While we have developed a theology far richer than anything to be found in the synagogue, they have shown the same diligence and at times extravagance, in the understanding of the life of the holy community; we have too often been pessimistic about the world, Judaism too often indifferent to the next; we have preached charity, Judaism has insisted on justice; to us the mystics alone with the infinite, to them the social reformers busy in the life of men; to us the emotional power which can raise up them that fall, to them the intellectual democracy which can strengthen such as do stand. And, if both of our

religions are facing critical times today, an analysis of the causes often reveals that it is just for the lack of that in which the other faith is strong. . . . We have failed to convert the Jews, and we shall always fail, because it is not the will of God that they should become Gentile Christians; antisemitism has failed to destroy the Jews, because it is not the will of God that essential parts of His revelation should perish. Our immediate duty to the Jews is to do all in our power to make the world safe for him to be a Jew.[22]

Given the advent of the Nazi death camps in the years that followed, Parkes' works were indeed prophetic to the Christian community. Unfortunately, history proved them destined to go unheeded. From this sermon, one can also glean the principal themes which Parkes would expand upon in his later writings on Jewish–Christian relations.

The entrance of England into World War II came as no surprise to Parkes. He had seen firsthand the evils of Nazism well before most Englishmen even knew who the Nazis were, and he had tried his best to warn his fellow countrymen about the perils which faced them. When the war came, Parkes was living in Barley, writing, studying at the library of St. John's, Cambridge, developing his thoughts on Jewish–Christian relations, and helping in local parishes. The war brought new responsibilities to Parkes. Between 1939 and 1945, one can divide Parkes' life into five different areas of work: (a) the refugee problem, (b) politics, (c) theology, (d) the Jewish question, and (e) Jewish–Christian relations.

Even before 1939, Parkes had developed close ties with organizations concerned with the refugee problem. He was often called upon for information and support in getting the British government to take the refugees more seriously. In 1942, he became a member of Eleanor Rathbone's Parliamentary Committee concerned with refugees, and he had many arguments with the Home Secretary, Herbert Morrison, over the question of rescue.[23] He

---

[22] *Voyage of Discoveries*, op. cit., pp. 154–55.
[23] See Bernard Wasserstein, *Britain and the Jews of Europe 1939–1945*, for a good survey of the history of the problem.

also helped to find places for refugees to live and work, and he often had a houseful of refugee children in his home while they awaited permanent housing. His activities in this regard often required police protection since it was feared that German agents would try to make another attempt on Parkes' life. It was through his work on the refugee question that Parkes met Dorothy Wickings. Laura Livingston, George Bell's sister-in-law, introduced them in 1941 during a lecture that Parkes was giving at Chatham House. Miss Wickings was active in the Christian Committee for Refugees, and she was the founder of the "'Thursday Group of Christian and Jews" at Bloomsbury House, where all the refugee organizations had their offices. In August of 1942, the two were married at Dorothy's home in Hildenborough.

The work with the refugees involved Parkes in politics on many levels. He shared with William Temple and other clergy an interest in the social problems of the day, and he and Temple often worked together on political issues. Parkes' own political leanings were to the left, and he was active in the Labour Party, although this was a bit unusual for an Anglican clergyman since the Anglican Church had rather close ties with the Tories. In 1942, he found himself becoming more and more active in the new radical-liberal party, "Common Wealth." This rather eclectic political movement was born of a merger between Sir Richard Acland's "Forward March," and J. B. Priestley's "1941 Committee." Parkes stated that "this group was non-, and in some cases anti-religious, and arose primarily out of the brilliant Saturday evening broadcasts of Priestley during the dark days of 1940."[24] There does not seem to have been any central purpose to Common Wealth except for its ideas about a "new democratic society." Priestley's abrupt resignation as its leader in 1942 left a vacuum, and Parkes was asked by Acland to take over as chairman. He remained temporary chairman for a number of months, and he helped the movement to organize itself. He then found himself in a power struggle with R. W. Mackay, and rather than split the movement, he quietly resigned. Parkes kept in touch with the people in the movement, but what political activity he was involved in after that tended to be in the Labour Party. Living in a

---

[24] *Voyage of Discoveries*, op. cit., p. 182.

small village dominated by Tory politics, his political life remained an interesting one.

The theological works that Parkes did during these years are essential to the tracing of his intellectual development, yet these works have remained rather obscure. One reason for this neglect is that much of the work done at this time was published under the name of "John Hadham." He chose a nom de plume in order to keep his theological work separate from the controversy attached to his work on Jewish–Christian relations. A good many people familiar with Parkes are often unaware of his work as John Hadham. This is most unfortunate because these theological writings help to provide a clear picture of how Parkes came to his understanding of the relationship between Judaism and Christianity.

The Hadham books were quite popular in England during the war. The first Hadham book appeared in 1940 as *Good God*. Not long after, *God in a World at War* appeared. In 1942, *Between God and Man* was published, and in 1944, *God and Human Progress* appeared in print. Parkes claimed that Temple told a friend that *Good God* was, in his opinion, the most important contribution to theology in the last fifty years.[25] That may be a bit of an exaggeration, but it is not surprising that Temple would like the Hadham works since they reflect a good deal of Temple's theological ideas. In many ways, these Hadham books are an extension of the 1929 lectures Parkes had given for the WSCF. Many of the themes discussed in these lectures—the Trinity, the Kingdom of God, progress and revelation, God and the ordinary, christocentric theology—are discussed once more in greater detail. If they are read carefully, these books enable one to see how Parkes developed his later theology on Judaism, since he uses many of the same ideas and themes to construct his position on Jewish–Christian relations.

Under the name of Hadham, he lectured widely on theology, and he published a number of articles, particularly in *St. Martin's Review*. On more than one occasion, he also delivered radio addresses at the request of Eric Fenn, assistant to Jimmy Welch, Director of Religious Broadcasting for the BBC. These broadcasts

---

[25] Ibid., p. 159.

got Parkes into trouble more than once. Once he did a series on intercessory prayer in which he prayed for those countries that had been deprived of their liberty by the war. The problem was that he included countries like Estonia, Latvia, and Lithuania. It was alright to pray for Poland and Czechoslovakia since the Nazis had taken them, but to mention countries taken by Russia was not permitted. England was trying to wean Russia away from her agreement with Germany, and ideas like Parkes' would not make that effort any easier.

The end of his broadcasting career came in 1943 after a series of lectures he gave called *Worship and Life*. His opening remarks were:

> I do not believe that those who have ceased to worship in churches or chapels of this country will ever return to take part in the normal services offered today. . . . They will not be brought back by the kind of tinkering with the services that is all that progressive elements in the churches have attempted so far.[26]

His remarks so offended Dr. Garbett, then Archbishop of York and Chairman of the Committee on Religious Broadcasting, that he ordered Fenn never to invite Parkes to lecture again. Parkes and Garbett had clashed earlier on the question of reform. In an article in the *Daily Telegraph* on April 1, 1942, Garbett, then Bishop of Winchester, had "dismissed with contempt, all those who complained that there was anything deeply wrong with the Church of England." Parkes found this attitude "astonishingly complacent even for a Bishop," and he responded to Garbett in a sermon delivered at Cambridge University. Garbett seemed to have won the final battle by having Parkes removed from the radio broadcasts.

The interest Parkes showed in 1929 in the issue of politics and religion continued through the war but he also continued to be disappointed in the Church's general response. The Malvern Conference called by Dr. Temple early in the war showed once again the inability of the Church of England to face its own need for reform. Parkes attempted to air his opinions on this issue in

---

[26] Ibid., p. 164–65.

the pages of *The Christian News Letter* (later the *Christian Frontier Movement*). The paper had been created by J. H. Oldham, and he often asked Parkes to write on Palestine and the Jews. He never asked for articles by Hadham. Parkes attributes this reluctance to Oldham's acceptance of Barthian theology for his own. Parkes charges that Oldham refused to allow into the *News Letter* any basic metaphysical challenges that Parkes believed to be fundamental to any renewal of religion. In February 1945, he wrote to Oldham:

> This generation is called upon to face two fundamental problems. Everything else falls into place, or takes a new character, according as we deal, or fail to deal, with these two.
>
> A. How can we discover a sense of community and common purpose which will give personality, meaning, and dignity to lives of ordinary men?
> B. What is to be the shape of our society, an issue presented—whether we like it or not, and with innumerable varieties in detail—by the choice between capitalism and socialism?
>
> For the Christian, these two questions are naturally resolved in another form: (a) How can we get men to believe in God? and (b) How can be bring the forces of Christianity into the political struggle? To be silent on these two points is to avoid the fundamental issue.[27]

The issues raised here by Parkes are basically a restatement of issues he first raised in 1929. The relationship of Christianity to politics, and questions of the community are both leitmotivs in Parkes' theology. One can get a key to his views on Judaism by keeping this in mind.

Early in the war, Parkes was asked by Chatham House to prepare material for a hypothetical peace conference. Although there was only an inkling at the time of the Nazi Final Solution, Parkes decided that two important issues to be discussed would be the problem of antisemitism and the Jewish National Home. It was in preparing these materials that he began an in-depth

---

[27] Ibid., p. 164.

investigation of Zionism. Actually, he had discussed the issue in the book he wrote for Gilbert Murray, but it was during the war years that he really grappled with the subject in greater depth.

Part of his research involved personal meetings with people who were knowledgeable about the problem. Frequent visits were made to Oxford to talk with Sir John Hope Simpson (with whom he stayed), Harold Beeley, Albert Hourani, and Professor (later Sir Hamilton) Gibbs. In addition, he also spent time with Arnold Toynbee, whom he knew through Chatham House. Parkes and Toynbee would later clash over Toynbee's interpretation of Judaism as a "fossil" and his opposition to Israel, and even at this time, Parkes said that Toynbee was interested primarily in the Hadham material. To discuss the Mandate, he met with Sir Herbert Young, Sir Ronald Storrs, and especially Leopold Amery. Amery had been in the Cabinet Office in November 1917, and was the author of a paper which combined the many viewpoints on a Jewish Homeland and clearly stated the British position. Parkes asked him a good many questions about the preparation of that text and its wording. He also met with Bert Locker and others at the Zionist headquarters in London. He lunched with Sir Arthur Wuachope, once High Commissioner for Palestine and considered by Zionists as being the most friendly of all the holders of that office.[28]

Out of this research came the book *The Emergence of the Jewish Problem*, which was published in 1946. It was not the sort of book which Chatham House had desired, and they disassociated themselves from the project. An interesting footnote to this whole venture was the refusal of the Foreign Office to accept Parkes' figures about the Final Solution. He wrote about this problem in his memoirs:

> While the section on the Nazis was being written, news was filtering in of the reality of the "final solution." In the first draft I had written that there had been 50,000 Jews murdered in cold blood. The Foreign Office crossed off a naught. More news came in. In the second draft it was half a million—

---

[28] Ibid., p. 179.

and the Foreign Office crossed off a nought. When they did the same to five million, I gave it up, and no figure is mentioned.[29]

I think this is an interesting personal anecdote with reveals just how difficult it was to get governments to take seriously the scope of the evil being perpetrated by the Germans against the Jewish people.

Parkes had a similar problem with government officials concerning his published materials on the Middle East. He wrote two short pamphlets for the Oxford Pamphlets on World Affairs Series: *Palestine* (1940), and *The Jewish Question* (1941). Concerning *The Jewish Question*, there was no problem: *Palestine*, however, caused a good deal of unhappiness in the Colonial Office. That office had demanded to see a copy of the text, and insisted that the publishers have the author make certain changes. Parkes remembered the episode:

> I was rung up one day by one of the syndics who said to me: "Tomorrow you will receive a letter from me, requesting you to make a number of changes in your manuscript. I want you to know that this letter has been dictated to me by the Colonial Office. But *we* asked you, and not the Colonial Office, to write the pamphlet, and if you do not agree to any of the changes I suggest, the pamphlet will be published exactly as you wrote it." So I refused to make any changes and the pamphlet was published exactly as I wrote it.[30]

In addition to these pamphlets, Parkes also wrote a good many short articles on the issue of the Mandate and the Jewish Homeland during this period.

On the home front, Parkes was active in the newly formed groups devoted to Jewish–Christian relations. He was instrumental in the development of the Council of Christians and Jews, an

---

[29] Ibid., p. 180.
[30] Ibid., p. 181.

organization still in existence today. Among the people who took part in forming the group were William Temple, the Roman Catholic dignitary Bishop Matthew, the Chief Rabbi of Britain, and Rabbi Dr. Mattuck. The secretary of the group was W. W. Simpson. Simpson had shifted from the pro-missionary position he had held as expressed in a letter to Parkes in 1933, and he went on to full-time service in the CCJ in England and internationally. Parkes was also busy lecturing on the issue of Jewish–Christian relations, and he wrote many articles on the topic, as well as on Christian antisemitism. In 1945, he published a book on antisemitism entitled *An Enemy of the People: Antisemitism*. The book had an American edition, and after the war, it had a German edition which was widely distributed in Germany.

With the end of the war, Parkes turned his attention almost completely to the Middle East question. In March 1946, he and his wife sailed for Palestine to have a firsthand look at the problem. Traveling by train from Port Said to Rehovah, he arrived to the welcome of Chaim Weizmann and Simon Marks. He met often with these men (as well as with Harry Sacher) in Jerusalem, and Marks offered to pay for any books Parkes found during his stay. Dr. and Mrs. Parkes were the guests of the Jewish Agency at this time, and this fact terribly upset the Anglican Bishop of Jerusalem. The Parkeses were befriended, however, by Canon Witton-Davies, the bishop's advisor on Jewish affairs, a Hebrew scholar, and a friend of Martin Buber and Joseph Klausner. Gershon Agronsky of *The Jerusalem Post* drove Parkes around the country to give him a personal look at the people and the land.

Much of the trip involved personal meetings with various leaders in the Jewish community. Meetings with Arab leaders proved more difficult to arrange. During the first week, Parkes met with Judah Magnes, Chancellor of Hebrew University, and many professors of that institution. Parkes gave a series of lectures at the University that provided the foundation for his later works on Jewish–Christian relations. The lectures were entitled: "The Foundation of the Church," "The Traditional Attitude of the Two Religions toward Each Other," "The Recognition of Judaism as a Living Religion and the Jew as a People," and "Judaism, Christianity and the Future." Parkes commented on these lectures:

These lectures marked another stage in the development of
my thinking. . . . I affirmed the equality of the two religions,
their need of each other, and the impossibility of either
absorbing the other. It was the position, so new and so
tantalising to the deeply religious Jews we met at the university, Professor Bergman and Professor Guttman, in particular, that made discussions with them, as with Buber, so
interesting.[31]

Indeed, Parkes spent a whole day with Buber at his apartment in
the Arab quarter of Deir Abu Tor discussing their ideas.

Parkes also had letters of introduction to the officials in charge
of the Mandate. While he expressed his admiration for the men,
he found them to be woefully lacking in understanding of the
Jewish question. Most of the officials were from the colonial
service, knew Arabic but not Hebrew or Yiddish, and generally
felt more comfortable with Arabs than with Jews. He wrote that:

... again and again I found myself describing inter-war
conditions in Eastern Europe in order to help them understand the whys and wherefores of the Jewish desire to
immigrate to Palestine and create a national home. From the
Jewish point of view, a few men taken from the consular
service and with experience in central and eastern Europe
would have been an immense asset.[32]

Upon returning home, Parkes decided to write a history of the
people of Palestine. He believed that such a book was absolutely
necessary, given the ignorance all the parties involved had of each
other. The book, *The History of Palestine* (later titled *Whose
Land?*), appeared in 1947. He also spent time meeting with people
back in England. He visited with Creech Jones, Colonial Secretary, to warn Jones that he believed that the British would crack
first under the strain. Not too long afterwards, things came
undone for the British. Parkes also met often with Weizmann,
Golda Mier, Ben Zvi, Abba Eban, leaders of the Histadruth, and
other Zionist leaders in England.

---

[31] Ibid., p. 192.
[32] Ibid., p. 193.

Parkes did not stay long in England upon his return. Toward the end of his Palestine trip, he had met the American Jewish leader, Stephen Wise, and Wise had invited Parkes to America to deliver the Charles William Eliot lectures at the Jewish Institute of Religion. Parkes accepted, and gave the lectures in the winter of 1946. The lectures enabled Parkes to expand on his Jerusalem talks, and they also helped him to develop further his thoughts about the equality and individuality of the two religions. He also lectured at Hebrew Union College in Cincinnati and in Chicago. The University of Chicago Press published the lectures under the title *Judaism and Christianity* in 1948.

Not long after returning to England, Israel Sieff reappeared in Parkes' life. The help Sieff had given him earlier had been discontinued during the war because of greater needs elsewhere. Now Parkes once again was given financial help by Sieff. He always seemed uncomfortable with this situation. In accepting the help earlier, he had done so with the hope that help would be forthcoming from the Christian community. That sort of help never really materialized, and so he turned again to Sieff in 1948.

> It was a difficult situation made possible only by the complete intellectual freedom which dominated our relations with IMS. But it was unnatural that the work which was largely concerned with Gentile responsibility for past and present antisemitism should have to be financed by a Jewish friend. It meant that we never asked for twopence if we could just manage with a penny-halfpenny. For we always knew we were but one of the many causes IMS supported, and the more I uncovered of the past relations of Jews and Judaism with Christians and Christianity, the more I realized the total responsibility of the Christian tradition and its manipulation for tragedies of Jewish life. . . . But the more I emphasized the Christian responsibility, the more difficult it became for us to augment our resources from Christian contributions, for the conventional attitude of Christians who are interested in Jews is to support efforts for their conversion to Christianity, and the missionary societies, the Anglican Church Mission to the Jews, and the relevant departments of the International Missionary Council, regarded me (quite rightly) as their

increasingly dangerous opponent. But I knew from the beginning that pioneering to reverse a verdict with nearly two thousand years behind it would not be easy, and Dorothy was willing to share its substantial but inevitable burden.[33]

The Sieff–Parkes connection was a long-standing one, and it has caused some commentators to question Parkes' intellectual honesty, as we mentioned earlier. A careful study of Parkes' work will reveal, however, that Sieff's influence on Parkes was limited to the financial realm. As I shall try to show, his position on Jewish–Christian relations is rooted in ideas formed early in his life, well before his contact with Sieff. The two men did have a close friendship, but to try to see it as anything else is a mistake.

For reasons that escaped Parkes, he was actually asked to present his views on the missionary question to a study conference organized at Bossey by the Committee on the Christian Approach to the Jews of the International Missionary Council. He was not surprised by the negative reaction that he received from the group, which he characterized as being wholly Barthian and biblically fundamentalist in outlook. He remembered that "condemnation was divided between myself and W. W. Simpson." The missionary people also feared the growth of the Council of Christians and Jews because they correctly suspected that such an organization held contrary views to their own. Simpson had actually been invited to Bossey to try to justify its very existence.

Parkes would continue to battle with missionary groups, and in 1955, he and Jacob Jocz, a Hebrew Christian and an active member of the Mission to the Jews Society, engaged in a debate in the *Church of England Newspaper* on the question. The debate had actually begun in 1954, when Parkes wrote a negative review of Jocz's book, *The Church and the Jewish People*, for the newspaper. In response to the question posed by the paper, "Do we need missions to the Jews?", Parkes answered, "No," H. L. Ellison, who was on the staff of the Mission Board, answered "Yes." Both men were responding in part to Jocz's book. In a letter to the paper dated March 14, 1955, Parkes outlined his objections

---

[33] Ibid., p. 208–09.

to a statement of Jocz's that the "Jews were under God's wrath." A summation of Parkes' position read:

1. Judaism and Christianity are not simply the religions for Jews and Gentiles, but they are religions that have universal application. [Notice that he is here also distancing himself from the ideas of Franz Rosenzweig.]
2. While Christianity is a missionary religion, its relationship to Judaism is unique and calls for a different approach.
3. Both Sinai and Calvary are channels for God's power.
4. Both religions are part of one revelation of God. Judaism emphasizing the community, while Christianity emphasizes the person.
5. Christians need to see this meaning of Sinai.
6. Only by doing so will we see God's purpose more clearly.[34]

Parkes' position on this issue is directly related to his theology, and he is not simply opposed to missions because he opposes antisemitism. In this view, missions to the Jews ignore the role of Sinai in God's plan for creation, and thus it constricts the Christian view of the purpose of God for the world.

Jocz was not the only person Parkes debated with over this issue. In 1959, he and George H. Stevens, editorial secretary of the Church Mission to the Jews, engaged in a long exchange of letters over Reinhold Niebuhr's opposition to missions to the Jews. Niebuhr had given an address entitled *The Relations of Christians and Jews in Western Civilization,* in which he criticizes missions to Jews by stating that "the two faiths despite differences are sufficiently alike for the Jew to find God more easily in terms of his own religious heritage than by subjecting himself to the hazards of guilt feelings involved in a conversion to a faith, which whatever its excellences, must appear to him as a symbol of an oppressive majority culture."[35] Such a challenge to the missionary work could not go unchallenged by someone like Stevens,

---

[34] Copy of letter in author's possession and on file at the Parkes Library, University of Southampton, England.
[35] Reinhold Niebuhr, *The Godly and the Ungodly: Essays on the Religious and Secular Dimensions of Modern Life,* p. 108.

and he attacked Niebuhr in a *Church of England Newspaper* articles dated April 24, 1959. Parkes was invited to respond because his name had been mentioned by Stevens as someone who held views similar to Niebuhr's. Parkes not only defended Niebuhr, but also discussed the "unsavory scandals" that had riddled the mission groups. Parkes and Stevens exchanged a series of letters and articles over the issue, and in November 1959, Parkes gave a summary of the exchange in an article in *The Jewish Chronicle* entitled, "Reinhold Niebuhr, George Stevens, and Missions to the Jews."

In a letter of May 8, 1959, Niebuhr wrote to Parkes to thank him for defending him. He told Parkes that "the opposition to my position puzzles me because it seems to me so obvious that Christians only convert marginal Jews, but it is argued that if you give up missions to the Jews you give up the right to missions. I am not impressed by this purely logical approach." Soon after, Parkes wrote Marcel Simon and stated that Niebuhr's position was pragmatic, while his was more theological; but a common bond between them did exist.[36]

While the mission controversy heated up in 1949, Parkes did not neglect his other interests. The issue of Zionism and Israel occupied much of his attention in the late 1940s and early 1950s. He wrote a book on Jerusalem in 1949, and in 1950 he published a pamphlet on Israel entitled *Israel: Intrusion or Fulfillment?*, which he sent to over 200 people for comments. In 1950, Valentine-Mitchell published Parkes' book *End of an Exile*, in which he traces the roots of Zionism in Jewish history. Recognition of his contribution to this and other issues related to Jewish–Christian relations came in 1949, when he was elected President of the Jewish Historical Society of England. He was only the second Christian ever named to the position.

On a personal level, he remained very active in his local parish by helping the Sunday services at various churches and by lecturing. He also continued to be involved in Labour Party politics. In village life, he was the chairman of the Village School Board. In 1953, Maurice Eisendrath invited him to go to Israel to

---

[36] Copy of letters on file at the Parkes Library, University of Southampton, England.

study the curious religious situation of Israel. He also was very active in the Council of Christians and Jews. Later, Eisendrath again invited him to travel, this time to America. Eisendrath wanted Parkes to spend time in the winter of 1953–54 speaking to audiences of Christian clergy under the auspices of the Union of American Hebrew Congregations on the relation of the two religions.

The tour was rather an exhausting one, and Parkes spoke in cities throughout the United States. What he found in most audiences was an almost unbelievable ignorance of Israel on the part of American Christians. This ignorance was coupled with a complete identification with the Palestinian refugees. Parkes called the experience "horrifying." He wrote of one incident that illustrated the problems he encountered. "A Quaker lady, whose views would have pleased Goebbels, explained to me that, if they did not identify their opinions completely with those of the refugees, they would not be allowed to work in the [Palestinian refugee] camps. This hideous and destructive moral cowardice was common to Catholics, Protestants, and Quakers."[37] This "hideous cowardice" Parkes speaks of still characterizes a substantial bulk of the American and world Christian community, and it is, as he wrote, "a most tragic problem, and does immense harm to the unfortunate Palestinian Arab whom it encourages to live in a world of fantasy, where none of the limitations which apply to the rest of humanity apply to them, and where they have no responsibility for any sins they have committed."[38]

The highlight of his American tour was an invitation to give the Gilkey lecture at the University of Chicago. The lecture was entitled "The Concept of a Chosen People in Judaism and Christianity." It was subsequently published as a Union of American Hebrew Congregations pamphlet. Parkes found that the tour had taken a toll on his health, and he contributes much of the strain to the fact that it was difficult work trying to change traditional ideas:

---

[37] *Voyage of Discoveries*, op. cit., p. 129.
[38] Ibid., p. 219.

It was a very heavy strain for a Christian theologian to be constantly explaining to his Christian brethren that their views of Judaism, however benevolent in intention, were theologically an intolerable offence to their Jewish neighbors, though these would be too polite or nervous to show it. In almost every discussion I had to explain that Judaism was *not* an incomplete form of Christianity, that it was *not* unchanged "Old Testament religion," that it had not ceased to be creative when BC changed to AD, and that it had to be treated as an equal in any discussion between Jews and Christians. I can say quite objectively that there was then no other Christian theologian in existence who would even have tried to perform such a task.[39]

Indeed, by the end of the tour, Parkes was on the point of a physical breakdown, and this marked the beginning of a couple of years of serious health problems. In June 1955, he suffered from a cerebral spasm, which is similar to, but not quite, a stroke. His friend Sieff helped to send him to Switzerland to recuperate, but in August 1956, he suffered a coronary thrombosis. The heart attack occurred a week after he had completed arrangements for the incorporation of the Parkes Library Limited.

The Library was formally registered in August 1956. Sieff was quite helpful in getting the project off the ground, but he was not able to provide the Library with anything approaching total financial support. There was some talk about merging it with the Wiener Library, but the project never really materialized. Some funds were then raised by dinners put together by Sieff, and the Parkes Library began to take shape. A distinguished collection of people were named as governors—Professor Alexander Altmann of Brandeis University; David Daube of Oxford; Marcel Simon of Strasbourg; Zwi Werblowski of Jerusalem; Lady Stansgate; David Kessler; Maurice Eisendrath; Canon Carlisle Witton-Davies; and Charles Singer. Today the Library is housed at the University of Southampton, England, and contains Parkes' valuable library, his letters and papers.

---

[39] Ibid., p. 220.

In spite of his ill health, Parkes continued his work. In 1959, he published a book entitled *The Foundations of Judaism and Christianity*, in which he traced the growth of rabbinic Judaism and early Christianity. He tried to show in the book that each was the natural outgrowth of its respective environment, and he argued that if the hand of God could be seen in Christianity, it could also be seen in Judaism. In many ways, the book can be seen as giving some historical background to his theological ideas. One important issue that Parkes tried to deal with in this book was the traditional Christian assumption that Judaism was a dead religion at the time of Jesus. He believed that Christians would begin to take Judaism seriously only when they realized its continued vitality and purpose in God's revelatory history. Since most Christians are ignorant of rabbinic Judaism, Parkes thought it worthwhile to write a study on the topic.

In 1960, he published his last book under the name of John Hadham. The book was called *Common Sense about Religion*. In it, he returned to his ideas about the Trinity. Reflecting on his dislike of Barthian theology, his rather Anglican appreciation of the Trinity and the Incarnation, and his deepening appreciation of Judaism, Parkes advanced his idea regarding the Trinity:

> if we substitute "channels" for "persons," and if we confine the sphere of our definition to the activity of the Diety as creator of this particular world in which we live, then an intelligible doctrine emerges which claims for *Judaism* the flow of the divine purpose into the life of the community, for *Christianity* the flow of the same purpose into the life of man as person, and for the kind of scientific *Humanism* which Charles Singer represented, the divine response to man as seeker.[40]

Parkes' ideas about a "theology of equality" between Judaism and Christianity rests on this trinitarian scheme. He also offered some thoughts about the other world religions, and he wrote appreciatively about the areas of human life which Eastern religions are better able to deal with than Western religions. He returned to a theme that first was seen in his 1929 lectures, namely, that the

---

[40] Ibid., p. 223–24.

contribution of various races and people are *irreplaceable*, and they all contribute something to God's plan for the world. Parkes believed that the world was still at an early stage of development, and he disagreed with Dietrich Bonhoeffer's idea that man had come of age in the twentieth century:

> No lesser unity than the whole of mankind would provide all the elements which would be absolutely necessary before man can claim to be "adult." At present he is best described as a rather dangerous "infant prodigy," and there is no more foolish or superficial theology than that which has proclaimed that man is now adult, and needs no God to help him.[41]

Even at the end of his career, he still found it necessary to take issue with German theologians.

In spite of his novel ideas about Judaism and Christianity, Parkes always maintained that he was an orthodox Christian. In response to questions about how he could be orthodox in such an unorthodox manner, he often referred to the fact that he tried to respond to new theological questions in a positive way rather than in a negative way. He illustrated this in a response he gave to the book *Honest to God*:

> What I hope is that the time will soon come when the contemporary theological approach will pass from the negative to the positive. Books like those by the Bishop of Woolwich assume that there was in the past a static maximum understanding of God. That maximum contains elements we cannot accept, so that we are constantly reducing the picture by having to abandon now this once treasured belief. I believe this approach to be upside down. The famous *Observer* article which launched *Honest to God* had the heading: "Our Image of God Must Go." The real heading for any generation is: OUR IMAGE OF GOD MUST GROW (*sic*). I have no desire to denounce the thirteenth century or the sixteenth for holding beliefs I cannot share. Those beliefs expressed in contemporary terms are real experiences which I can share. My job therefore is to explore the experience and to relate it to my own time in my

---

[41] Ibid., p. 227.

own terms. The result is almost always to find that the old terms were too small, not too large. And I trust that I shall go on enlarging them as long as I live.[42]

In this passage, we get an important insight into Parkes' approach to theology, and it helps one to see how he was able to move in the directions he did without feeling that it was necessary to completely abandon his own faith.

It is interesting to note that one area of theology Parkes became interested in during his later life was that of the power of Christ as healer. This interest developed because of an experience a close friend of his had during a bout with cancer. Parkes and his wife became increasingly involved with leaders of the healing movement in the Church of England, and Dorothy became a member of the international and interdenominational Order of St. Luke the Physician. Parkes' willingness to investigate this area of theology is not surprising, given his beliefs that God was active in all realms of human existence. He even wrote a number of articles on the topic for the London journal *For Health and Healing: The Magazine of the Guild of Health.*

He officially retired in 1963 to a small village in Dorset, but he continued to write on Judaism, Christianity, antisemitism and the Middle East. In 1963, he published a new study on antisemitism and, in 1964, *A History of the Jewish People.* That book was only the fourth original history of the Jews written by a Christian in the last three hundred years. In 1969, an important collection of his essays on Jewish–Christian relations were published under the title *Prelude to Dialogue,* with an introduction by Abraham J. Heschel. Throughout this time, he also wrote numerous articles and pamphlets for the Parkes Library. His life work was recognized by various honorary degrees and, in 1973, he was awarded the Nicholas and Hedy Monk Brotherhood Award by the Canadian Council of Christians and Jews.

The last years of Parkes's life were marked by increasing frailty and illness. On August 6, 1981, he died at the nursing home in Bournemouth, England, where he had lived the last four years of his life. In a laudatory obituary in *The Times* of London on August

---

[42] Ibid., p. 227.

8, it was written that "Parkes belongs to that procession of men who in dangerous ages urge upon their fellows the need to practise a degree of honest realism that alone will enable them to save mankind." Certainly a worthy epitaph for a most remarkable human being.

2

The Foundations

THE name of James Parkes has been associated almost exclusively with the issue of Jewish–Christian relations. This association has been made for good reason since Parkes is generally acknowledged as one of the foremost pioneers in the field. While Parkes certainly deserves the honor due him for the work in this area, this very honor often leads to problems in understanding his work as a whole. Parkes was thirty-five years old when he wrote his first book on the question of the relationship between Christians and Jews, and he had already established himself firmly in the ecumenical community of Europe through his work with the Student Christian Movement and the International Student Service. He used the time between his graduation from Oxford University until the publication of his first book on the Jewish question in 1929 to mature as a theological thinker, and in many ways his future work on Jewish–Christian relations had its roots in this period. He continued to write on Christian theology throughout his life, sometimes under the nom de plume of "John Hadham," but these works have been, for the most part, overlooked by people studying Parkes. This is very unfortunate because Parkes' work on Jewish–Christian relations becomes much more intelligible when one is aware of the theological foundation that underlies it. It is important, therefore, to trace the development of his theological thinking before attempting to examine his ideas about Jewish–Christian relations.

There were two major influences on Parkes' early theological development. The first was World War I. The second was the theological movement in England, particularly in the Anglican

Church, known as English Modernism. In order to begin to understand Parkes' development as a thinker, these two factors need to be taken into account.

It is something of a surprise to readers in the latter half of the twentieth century to read about the dramatic impact World War I had on European society. In spite of the fine studies like Paul Fussell's *The Great War and Modern Memory*, and Barbara Tuchman's *The Guns of August*,[1] I suspect that to most people World War I remains, at best, but a distant memory. Yet, in reading personal accounts of individuals who lived through the experience of that war, it becomes apparent that the world as it was in 1914 no longer existed when the war ended in 1918.[2] The political, social, and moral order of the human community had changed dramatically in only four years. The senseless slaughter of hundreds of thousands of soldiers on the command of generals unable to understand how the technological advances in implements of war made the ancient military codes of behavior obsolete, revealed how worthless human life had become in the eyes of those in authority. It was the first glimpse of how governments could justify the slaughter of their own civilians in the name of a "higher cause." The battlefields of Flanders and France suggested that Europe had entered an age of atrocity that would only be brought into full view during the Holocaust.

There were some people who were able to discern the signs of the time. Karl Barth's disgust at his former professors signing the declaration of support for the Kaiser's war effort caused him to rethink the nature of the Church and Christian theology. The past appeared to him to be bankrupt. To the German thinker, Eugen Rosenstock-Huessey, the Great War exposed the "spiritual lag" of academia, which could no longer provide people with

---

[1] Paul Fussell, *The Great War and Modern Memory*: Barbara Tuchman, *The Guns of August*.

[2] Barbara Tuchman writes of World War I: "The Great War of 1914–18 lies like a band of scorched earth dividing that time from ours. In wiping out so many lives which would have been operative in the years that followed, in destroying beliefs, changing ideas, and leaving incurable wounds of disillusion, it created a physical as well as a psychological gulf between two epochs." *The Proud Tower*, p. xv.

leadership, whether it be ethical, intellectual, or cultural. Rosen-stock joined with other German thinkers such as Franz Rosenz-weig, Martin Buber, Barth, Nicholas Berdyaev, and Hans Ehren-burg in forming the Patmos Circle, named after the island where St. John was said to have written his sacred texts. They chose this name because they were aware of living in an age in which speech had lost its power to break down the barriers between men and establish communication. The Patmos Circle believed that new forms of speech needed to be found.

World War I had forced such thinkers to recognize the break-down of the old standards of society and to devote the "rest of their lives, instead, to normalcy, to the new norm of this extraordinary experience."[3] The collapse of the Kaiser; the Russian Revolution; the decline of the Hapsburgs; the shattered French myth of liberty, equality and fraternity; and the social change in England all contributed to the changing landscape of world politics and culture. The genteel world of pre-1914 Europe had been brutally transformed into a world facing unknown and unexpected prob-lems with little or no guidance from the traditional sources of help.

James Parkes was a member of the "lost generation" of Europe which came of age during and after World War I. The war had exposed near-fatal gaps in the political and religious traditions in which Parkes had been raised, and he viewed the postwar period as a time in which new ways of thinking about religion and politics had to be found. Parkes believed, along with many others of his generation, that it was to be their task to develop a moral foundation that would make a "repetition of the war impossible." The situation which Parkes' generation found themselves con-fronting has been clearly expressed by Hendrik Kraemer:

> It is a well-known fact that the First World War dealt an irreparable blow to the prestige of the West in the so-called "non-Christian" world. Up until that time, in spite of inner revolt against its dominating and domineering impact on the "East," Western culture and its principles had commanded high respect and enthusiastic assent among the intelligentsia of the Eastern countries, who constituted the vanguard of the

---

[3] Eugen Rosenstock-Huessey, *Biography-Bibliography*, p. 11.

nationalist movements and the efforts for radical self-reform. These Western principles were the dynamic instruments in their efforts. The suicidal European war of 1914–18 destroyed this venerated image and caused deep disillusionment about the validity of Western culture. [It was] the inability of the West to avert a second world war and the very fact of the war, which drew the whole world into misery and destruction and saw the loss of prestige which, to the Easterner, if not the Westerner, constitutes the collapse of the West. And not only of the West as a cultural image, but also of Western Christendom.[4]

Parkes keenly felt this blow to Western civilization, and his activities in the SCM and the League of Nations Union while a student at Oxford and in the years following graduation, reflected his ongoing search for a new foundation for civilization. Clearly, his willingness to examine new ways of theological thought had roots in his experience of World War I.

As Parkes entered Oxford University in 1919, he held to the belief that the world was entering a new age. Therefore, Parkes felt that a new theology, which took seriously the issues of community as well as personal salvation, was called for by the times. Parkes also believed that the politics of the past could no longer serve the future, and he became active in groups looking for new political solutions. In his autobiography, he wrote about his reason for being active in both the SCM and the League of Nations Union at Oxford:

> I joined the League of Nations when I came up [to Oxford] because my desire for ordination was not based on any wish to escape from the contemporary world, but was tied to the conviction, which I shared with so many of my own generation, that we had to discover the moral foundations of a way of life for the whole world which would make a repetition of the war impossible. . . . There was nothing inconsistent in my finding my interest in the LNU [as well as] the SCM for

---

[4] Hendrik Kraemer, as quoted by Robert Handy in his article, "Confronting the Modern World: The Last 150 Years," in Henry Van Dusen (ed.) *Christianity on the March*, p. 54.

membership of the two bodies overlapped a great deal. . . . In those happy days, neither "liberal" nor "humanist" was a term of abuse, and humanists and committed Christians worked together over a wide area of life. Nor were we ashamed to speak of the possibility of "progress;" nor, because we did speak of it, believe in it and work for it, were we utopians or shallow or superficial. It was a generation which had seen too much of the realities of war, and which saw too clearly the immense gaps in the Christian tradition in so far as the human community was concerned, for it to be legitimate to call it "starry-eyed." Of course it failed to achieve the realisation of its hopes . . . but it was a noble failure.[5]

While this quote is a summary of events that happened early in his life, it gives a remarkably accurate description of issues that would continually reappear in his writings throughout his career. The war had shaken his confidence in the traditional ways in which politics and religion had been practiced, and Parkes saw himself as part of a new generation groping for new answers to old questions.

The war experience had made traditional theological positions subject to re-examination in Parkes' mind, and he embarked on a search for new ideas. When he arrived at Oxford, he discovered that there already existed on the English scene a theological movement which was seeking new ideas for theology. This movement was known as the Modernist movement, and it was to have the greatest influence on Parkes' early theological thinking. Evidence of its lasting influence is abundant throughout Parkes' writings, and much of the influence came, in large measure, from his professors at Oxford. His tutor, for instance, was Cyril Emmet, a noted Church historian and a leading figure in the Modernist movement. A member of Parkes' undergraduate examination committee was Dr. H. D. A. Major. Major was the principal of Ripon Hall, Oxford (a center of Modernist thinking), editor of *The Modern Churchman*, and one of the most important apologists for the movement. It was from these two men in particular that Parkes was introduced to the principles of Modernism. All in all,

---

[5] James Parkes, *Voyage of Discoveries*, p. 59.

Oxford proved a most hospitable location for someone with Parkes' concerns after the war, and in tracing the development of Parkes' thinking, one must begin with his introduction to Modernism during his Oxford years.

It is rather difficult to define Modernism. It originally began as a movement in France among liberal Roman Catholic thinkers, but it soon found a following among liberal Anglicans in England. Since it is a movement rather than a school of thought, those belonging to the movement tended to share common concerns, if not common solutions.[6] In his Noble Lectures delivered at Harvard University in 1925–26 entitled *English Modernism*, Major defined Modernism thus:

> What is Modernism? Modernism consists in the claims of the modern mind to determine what is true, right and beautiful in the light of its own experience, even though its conclusions be in contradiction to those of tradition. It is this which in practice constitutes Modernism, whether in religion, ethics, or art. The intellectual task of Modernism is the criticism of tradition in the light of research and enlarging experience, with the purpose of reformulating and reinterpreting it to serve the needs of the present age.[7]

Thus, the Modernist movement saw the development of biblical criticism, critical examination of dogma, and the idea of evolution and progress as allies in the task of re-interpreting the Christian faith for the modern world. While traditionalists were attacking these ideas as undermining the faith, the Modernists saw them as contributing to a better understanding of God and Christianity. While they were somewhat beholden to some past thinkers like F. D. Maurice, and past movements like the Broad Church movement, the Modernist movement moved in its own particular direction in reformulating Christianity. World War I only convinced those in the movement of the importance of their task. Major pointed this out clearly:

---

[6] H. D. A. Major, *English Modernism: Its Origin, Methods, and Aims*, pp. 193–94. Major supplies a list of Modernist thinkers in a footnote.

[7] Ibid., p. 8.

Christian teachers possessed of varied and mournful experience, like the Anglican army chaplains in the late war,
became convinced of the impossible and useless character of
large parts of our traditional Church theology. Mr. Studdard
Kennedy uttered the inmost convictions of many when he
said . . . "It is awful to realize that when one stands up to
preach Christ, the soldier feels that you are defending a whole
ruck of obsolete theories and antiquated muddles."[8]

Such sentiments about the effects of the war on traditional
theology were shared by Parkes in large measure.

Most Modernist thinkers shared the belief that the Church
needed to reinterpret many of its traditional teachings in the light
of modern historical research and modern science. The position of
Dean Hastings Rashdall, one of the most influencial Modernist
thinkers, reflects this attitude quite well:

It is a profound historical mistake—a pure mistake—to sup-
pose that the Church's teachings have always been the same
on all subjects. The Church would have been dead long ago if
it had been and the promise that the Holy Spirit would ever
lead the Church onto new truth would have failed. The
Church has always—and most of all in the ages in which its
influence has been most vital—been adapting its teachings to
meet the advance of knowledge in other directions.[9]

Cyril Emmet stated a similar belief in his book *Conscience,
Creeds, and Critics*:

The advanced "unorthodox" view of one generation often
becomes the accepted orthodoxy of the next. It is quite true
there is chaff mingled with the wheat. The theories of no
single school or writer are accepted in their entirety, nor are
they admitted universally. But they come in time to be
recognised as legitimate. The denial of verbal Inspiration, the
right to reinterpret the Bible "like any other book," the
questioning of the strict accuracy of some of its historical
statements, the rationalising of some of its miracles, the

---

8 Ibid., p. 100.
9 Ibid.

recognition of myth and allegory, the rejection of traditional views of Atonement, of Eternal Punishment and Hell, the attempt to restate the Incarnation in terms of modern thought—modes of thought such as these are the common-place of every theological student to-day. Even those who still fight against them would hardly urge that a clergyman who adopts them is bound to resign his orders. Yet, as we have seen, this was the cry with regard to each of these theories when it first came to prominence. They were regarded as a cloak for rank infidelity; the very foundations of Christianity and religion were being undermined.[10]

This attitude toward change, reflected in both Rashdall and Emmet, is pervasive throughout Modernist thought. They are quite fond of referring to Isaiah 43:18–19—"Remember not the former things, nor consider the things of old. Behold, I am doing a new thing; now it springs forth; do you not perceive it?"—as biblical evidence for their position. In spite of traditionalist criticism of their ideas, particularly harsh after the Modern Churchman Conference held at Girton College, Cambridge, in 1921, the Modernists insisted that their attitude toward dogma and tradition reflected the very type of critical response that had made the Church possible in the first place. Major summed up their position:

> This is the Modernist attitude toward Dogma. The Modernist is no *malleus theologoreum*. We must have a theology, but a theology which will win the modern mind: a theology, too, which in its profoundest doctrines must be proved experimentally: a theology which, if possible, shall be so simple and lucid that plain men can understand it. We must have a modern theology. The hour is overdue for its formulation.[11]

Critics of Modernism argued that the Modernist "is always so much more conscious of what he does not than what he does

---

[10] Ibid., pp. 45–46.
[11] *English Modernism*, op. cit., p. 95.

believe."[12] In part this is true, and it was bound to be true given the Modernist idea that God was always doing new things. The very idea that evolution was an essential part of human life carried with it the idea that few things could ever be dogmatically asserted. One critic, Roger Lloyd, Canon of Winchester, took exception to the seven points which Major held to be in need of Modernist reinterpretation by writing the following:

> The Modernist, then, refuses assent to the following propositions.
> 1. The conception of God the changeless despot who "from a throne in the heavens governed the earth in accordance with certain inflexible principles." In His stead the Modernist asserts "the God of emergent evolution, who is ever bringing new things to pass."
> 2. The doctrine of everlasting punishment, "grotesque, absurd, incredible."
> 3. The doctrine of the propitiatory sacrifice of Christ. Here the words in the Prayer of Consecration in the Liturgy, "who made there by his one oblation".... are called "terrible"; and objection is made to the formulae "for Jesus Christ's sake" and "through the merits of Jesus Christ" at the end of prayers.
> 4. The doctrine of original sin when interpreting original guilt; and as a consequence he refuses assent to any doctrine of baptism which goes further than a statement of baptism as necessary to assert the protection of God and to admit to the Church.
> 5. The eschatological doctrines of judgement and the second coming of Christ, but it is more the imagery under which these are traditionally asserted than the truths which these images assert which is refuted.
> 6. The belief in the infallibility of the Bible. It is not an infallible but an inspired Bible. "The statement that the Bible is the Word of God is being replaced by the statement that it contains the Word of God," and we must now accept "the assured results of criticism as to the origin, dates,

---

[12] Roger Lloyd, *The Church of England in the Twentieth Century*, vol. II, p. 33.

composition, integrity, historicity, and scientific value of various books."

7. The traditional view of divine revelation, which presented the knowledge of God as a unique system of truth miraculously communicated from heaven to earth. In its place the modernist would claim that revelation is implied in the very structure of the human mind, so that the process of thought, conscience, affection, truly understood, involve the recognition of the Infinite and Eternal. It is because we are what we are, and are becoming what we are becoming that God can and does unveil Himself to us, that is *in* us. Hence the modernist teaches that the divine method of revelation is internal—God speaking, not as Traditionalism teaches, in tones of thunder from the sky, but with a still, small voice in the human consciousness.[13]

Lloyd wrote this list to illustrate what he believed to be the weakness of the Modernist position, and he should be given credit for being fair to Major and not creating positions which the Modernists did not hold. Yet, to the Modernist, the positions listed by Major, and criticized by Lloyd, were the only positions possible for Christian theology to take if it was to have any effect in the modern world.

If there was another principle which seemed to underlie the entire Modernist enterprise besides the theme taken from Isaiah, it was the overwhelming conviction that Christianity had to take modernity into account if it was to play any part in the world after the war, and not rest on the past. Modernists like Rashdall believed that this simply required the Church to take account of the Holy Spirit's activity in the world. He concluded his last published sermon in 1921 with these words:

> Let us try to take seriously the doctrine that the Holy Spirit is teaching something—something important and something new—to the Church of our own generation; and let us—each in proportion to his leisure, his vocation, and his opportunities—try to discover what it is, and to do what we can to communicate to others whatever measure of truth God

---

[13]   Ibid., pp. 33–34.

has revealed to us and to the Church of our day. Now, as in former times, the Holy Spirit of God is saying to us: "He that hath ear, let him hear what the Spirit saith unto the churches."[14]

The Modernist movement held strongly to the belief that Christianity must make sense to the common man, and not deny what everyone knows to be true simply because Church dogma does not accept it as true. It is no longer sufficed to quote the Bible in answer to the new and vexing questions being raised, for instance, by modern science. Rather, theology would do well to see the scientific discoveries as enhancing our knowledge of God and His creation.

> Revelation did not stop with the conclusion of the New Testament. It has, in accordance with Christ's promise of the gift of Spirit, been continuously operating ever since. The Modernist believes that this revelation is made "in Christ"; that is to say it will always be found to be in harmony with those moral and spiritual ideals which He taught: it unveils their implications and applications to our expanding experience. Hence there is a special Revelation of God to each age which can be neglected only with loss and peril. . . . The Revelation contained in the Bible is not adequate of itself for this age.[15]

If one remembers the battles that raged between theology and science after Darwin published his theory of evolution, the fact that theologians of the caliber of Major and Rashdall could argue not only that theology should make peace with these discoveries, but could actually utilize them in the creation of a new theology, grows in significance. The battles the Modernists had to wage against the more traditional-minded theologians over these issues also becomes easier to understand.

Major added one more point that needs to be mentioned as well. For him, as for most Modernist theologians, the final touchstone for any theology had to be Truth, and Truth was believed to be

---

[14] *English Modernism*, op. cit., p. 121.
[15] Ibid., p. 120.

found in human reason and conscience. Major contrasted traditionalist ideas on this question with Modernist ideas:

> There is not time to deal here with many other doctrines in which the Modernist presentation differs from the traditionalist. The Modernist wished the Church to adopt them in the Modernist form for two reasons: first, they are more true in that form than in the Traditionalist form, and secondly they are able in the Modernist form to win the adhesion of the modern man: and the Modernist is convinced not only that the Church must have a true theology, but also that the individual must have a true theology too. It matters not how simple his theology is. What does matter is that it should be in accordance with the truth as he knows it. His reason and conscience, the sense of truth, and the sense of right guard the entry to the heart of the modern man; and though Christianity would fail to enter his heart, yet unless her creed can make terms with his reason and his conscience, she must remain outside.[16]

This appeal to reason and conscience in the search for truth in religious ideas is an important characteristic of Modernist thought, and it appears throughout Modernist writings.

In reading through Parkes' theological writings, it quickly becomes clear how influential Modernist thinking was upon his own thinking. If one was to read, for instance, a book of essays by Rashdall entitled *Ideas and Ideals*,[17] and then read through some of Parkes' writings, one will notice immediately the similarity of ideas and themes. Ideas similar to Rashdall's about the Atonement, progress, Logos theology, the Trinity, eternal punishment and the like, all reappear in one form or another in Parkes' writings. If one is to understand Parkes, and how his theological positions developed on many issues, including Christian–Jewish relations, one must first start with the fact that he was influenced in his thinking by the Modernist movement. Although the Modernists did not actually deal with the issue of Jewish–Christian

---

[16] Ibid., p. 121.
[17] His chapters on progress and the Atonement, for example, anticipate much of what Parkes would later argue for in his writings.

relations, their positions on biblical criticism, traditional dogma, progress and evolution, and the relation of religious belief to historical fact and modern knowledge, all helped to point Parkes in a certain theological direction. When Parkes' research into Judaism revealed to him that traditional Christian ideas about Judaism were incorrect and a new theology had to be created, his grounding in Modernist theology made it possible for him to accept the task without ever thinking that he was in any way compromising his fundamental Christian faith. In many ways, his work on Jewish–Christian relations can be seen as his application of Modernist principles to a new theological problem confronting the modern world. Recalling Major's idea about truth, Parkes was simply trying to relate his theology to his reason and his conscience when he called for a new Christian theology about Judaism.

It is essential for any student of Parkes to read his works in the light of World War I and the Modernist movement. Parkes takes to their logical conclusions certain ideas first presented in Modernist thought regarding the relationship of Christianity to other religions. While it is true that Parkes was the first to deal seriously with the Jewish–Christian problem, his approach to the problem stemmed from his early development. This is an important aspect of his thought, and I believe that it will become more obvious as we study his ideas in more detail.

Parkes produced his first serious theological statement in a series of lectures delivered at the World Student Christian Federation Conference held at Gilon, Switzerland in 1929. The overall theme of the lectures was the relationship between politics and theology, and they have a decidedly Modernist flavor to them. Underlying this theological exercise was Parkes' belief that the Trinity could provide a key to the development of a theology of politics. He had been thinking of this idea during his work with the SCM and ISS, but he had received little encouragement to pursue this line of thinking. When invited by Francis Miller, chairman of the WSCF, to give these lectures, he decided to use the opportunity to present his ideas publicly.[18] Parkes gave to these lectures the fitting title of *Politics and the Doctrine of the*

---

[18] *Voyage of Discoveries*, op. cit., p. 104.

Trinity. It is most unfortunate that they have never been published because they give a remarkable insight into the thought of
Parkes. Much of what he was to write about in later works is
anticipated in these lectures, and they help to give a student of
Parkes insight into his theological development. It is important,
therefore, that these lectures be examined in some detail.

The lectures had the following titles: "Introduction;" "The
Community and the Purpose of God;" "Politics and the Person of
Christ;" "The Person of Christ and the Holy Spirit;" and "Politics
and the Doctrine of the Trinity." These themes revolved around
his main interest at the time, and he stated that the lectures took
shape through his encounters with three groups: the League of
Nations Union, the SCM (and the ISS), and the German DCSV. In
his introductory lecture, he said that "it is in reflection on the
different ideas and the different approaches of those groups that I
myself began to think out my own attitude on the Idea of God, and
of the place of the Church, and the Christian in international
affairs."[19] It troubled Parkes that each of these groups had a
difficult time relating their ideas to both politics and religion. The
LNU people were full of idealism, often based on the life and
character of Jesus, but they had little use for the Church. The
SCM people were often committed Christians who had a difficult
time reconciling their personal religion with their concern for
economic, social, and political issues. They had little use for
institutional Christianity, and, as Parkes wrote, "they were not
simply idealists, they had a quite definite belief in God, and in His
power to influence their lives, but they found no meaning in
Christian doctrine, or in historic Christianity."[20] Parkes regretted the fact that the Church proved unable to give these people
"just the extra help" to preserve their faith and willingness to
serve God when the optimism which followed World War I began
to turn to despair. And the German DCSV, though quite different
from the other groups, also influenced his thinking. While he
disagreed with them over their severe separation of religion and

---

[19] James Parkes, "Introductory Lecture." Delivered at Gilon, Switzerland,
World Student Christian Federation Conference, 1929. Text on file at the Parkes
Library, University of Southampton, England.
[20] Ibid., pp. 1–2.

politics, he admitted that they had forced him away from a shallow optimism, and forced him to take seriously the reality of sin.

It was out of this triple background that Parkes began to formulate his own "theology of politics," and he stated that he feared appearing to the Anglo-Saxons as an "obscurantist continental" and to the continentals as a "cheerful but superficial Anglo-Saxon." In spite of these fears, Parkes proceeded to write about his ideas, and he set forth the purposes of his lectures:

> It has in the long run only one aim[:] to insist that in whatever field of life we may be busying ourselves, there is only one and the same reality, God, that wherever we turn, we find Him, and apart from Him life is a riddle without any meaning. Nothing is outside His activity. Nothing is untouched by His grace. There is no good apart from Him, no hope apart from Him, no power apart from Him. In Him we live and have our being. . . . I am not concerned in these lectures to prove the existence of God. I am assuming all of us, in very different ways perhaps, believe that the knowledge of God is the secret of life. Nor am I going to take up our time in trying to prove how serious the situation is today between nations. I am assuming that we all realize the tremendous responsibility that our citizenship lays on each one of us. What I want to do is to try to relate these two facts more closely together than is often done, and to show that these two duties, to know God, and to fulfill our responsibilities as citizens are not in conflict, that apart from God there is no true citizenship, and apart from citizenship only a mutilated knowledge of God. We must admit that as a Federation, just as our respective churches, [we] have done very little to understand the ways of God in this field of citizenship.[21]

The goal of these lectures was twofold. First, Parkes wanted to show how the community is as essential to the purpose of God as the individual. Second, he wanted to construct at least the outline of a Christian theology that concerned itself with more than individual salvation. In doing so, he hoped to be able to show that

---

[21] Ibid., p. 4.

social, political, and economic issues are as important to God as the plight of an individual soul. Parkes believed that the Church had historically left these social issues to those who were concerned with "applied Christianity," and did not believe that such issues had much to do with, "essential Christianity." He believed that such a view distorted the Church's view of God and its own mission in the world. It also helped to make it difficult, if not impossible, for the Church to address issues that were of paramount importance to people struggling to live their Christian faith in the everyday world. For Parkes, the post-World War I era demanded that this problem be rectified if the Church was to have any role in shaping the future.

The next lecture dealt with the question of the community in the purpose of God. At the start of the lecture, he argued that progress and perfection are characteristics of God's plan for the world. He stated that it is impossible for him to believe "that God in creating the world did not have an idea in His mind of what it would look like functioning according to His will," and that the "victory of the Cross is that God knows that sin has not made it finally impossible for it so to function."[22] He stressed his view that the idea of "functioning according to His will" demanded a dynamic view of creation rather than an idea of a "shabby state of completion before us."[23] The source of that dynamic is the task that man has, to know God and receive His revelation, a task which Parkes viewed as being infinite in nature. Perfection is not seen by Parkes as being a Tennysonian image of "the kindly earth shall slumber, lapped in universal," an earth which Parkes thought would be incredibly dull. Rather, perfection is the "perfect adjustment naturally and spiritually of any stage of development to what God would have it [be] at that stage."[24]

This concept of perfection involves a number of things. The first is the perfection of the individual, which involves "conversion." Parkes meant by this the "willingness of the individual to receive

---

[22] James Parkes, "The Community in the Purpose of God." Lecture delivered at Gilon, Switzerland, WSCF Conference, 1929. Text on file at the Parkes Library, University of Southampton, England.
[23] Ibid., p. 1.
[24] Ibid., p. 1.

the Righteousness of God. . . . It certainly does not mean an end of development or an impossibility of making future mistakes, but it involves an attitude of heart, in which one might put it that mistakes are not fatal."[25] Parkes did not want to suggest that individuals are therefore of first importance in God's plan for perfection, but since communities are made up of individuals, it made sense to start at this point. He stated that the "normal way in which the individual will be led into wanting to work for the Kingdom of God will doubtless be membership of a Christian Church, and a sense of individual relationship with God, a sense of a call from God."[26] He then cautioned against viewing this as a sign of superiority of those who hear God's call. He wrote about God's ability to call anyone He wants, and the need to take a holistic view of God's purpose in the world rather than a narrow view limited to the Church alone. He wrote:

> But it must not be forgotten that the initiative lies with God and not with us. We have not to construct a Kingdom of God. We have to give ourselves to God in order that He may work. Therefore, we cannot possibly say that God will not use some whose yearnings are never actually conscious of the fact that it is God they are yearning for. The Kingdom of God is no preserve of any Church or groups of Christians who have heard His voice. It is His alone, and He alone knows all the workers in it. He alone knows the whole pattern of which we see but glimpses. I want this borne in mind when I am talking of what seems to be the sense of its marks. I believe it to be of His will that we should see enough for our guidance, at every stage of our development, and at the present time it seems to me that this involves some conception of the world as a whole, since there is not a single problem before us that is not world wide in its scope, and in which failure and success will not have repercussions all over the world.[27]

Having said this, Parkes moved to the second characteristic of a world doing the will of God—what he calls fellowship. Again, he

---

[25] Ibid., p. 2.
[26] Ibid., p. 2.
[27] Ibid., p. 2.

did not limit fellowship to the Church alone, and he introduced the idea of the importance of Divine–human cooperation. He took issue with the idea that the search for God by man is essentially a lonely quest:

> An individual does not grow to perfection all by himself. At no stage of his existence is he actually absolutely alone. Not only does the fellowship of his parents shape to a large extent the course of his future life, but in everything he is inheritor of the ages, and exists in a fellowship of thought and worship far vaster than he is individually capable of realising. Moreover, it is in this fellowship that he finds God. Sometimes the loneliness of the search of the individual soul for God is overstressed. There are stages when every soul in the search will withdraw spiritually into its Arabia, and commune not with flesh and blood, but that is a stage only. The seeking of God in itself is an act of man in fellowship.[28]

Parkes carried this idea of fellowship over to a description of the Church. He argued that the genius of the Church is its ability to create a fellowship among such different types of people.

> The individual worships God in a "church"—I am not of course referring to a building—and it is through the Church that he receives grace and power to do the will of God. That design gets its meaning because lots of other corners are being done by others. It is like a carpet of many colours and intricate pattern. We are one tuft of wool, and not only meaningless, but useless by ourselves. What man is there so great that he can in himself contain the whole of God's purpose for the tiniest fraction of His creation? The fellowship is therefore of two kinds. In a fellowship man goes to God, and in a fellowship he receives God's will for himself. This at bottom is the meaning and the necessity of organized Churches, however much we see their failings.[29]

---

[28] Ibid., p. 3.
[29] Ibid., p. 3.

There is also a material aspect to fellowship which augments the spiritual side of fellowship, and it is here that Parkes introduced the idea of the interconnection of human life. This idea of interconnection is essential to the definition of life itself:

> No man is sufficient for the material and artistic sides of his own life. Books and pictures, furniture and clothes, food and warmth, all these man provides for himself in mutual service, and as God serves to have distributed his talents, so it must always be. A world in which everyone not only provided his own material needs, but wrote his own books, and painted his own pictures, made his own clothes and furniture would be a very funny place, and a very poor one. Life is based on a co-operation which allows each of us to develop our own special talents. When that is lacking as it is so often today, the result cannot be characterised as life. It is "existence."[30]

With this sort of anthropology, Parkes tried to establish the idea that individuals belong to groups, and concerns for individuals cannot be limited to a solitary soul. The interconnectedness of our life with that of others makes it mandatory that the Church take more seriously the social and communal dimensions of human life. Indeed, since God takes it seriously, it makes little sense to think Christian theology can ignore it. Parkes then went on to strengthen his argument by postulating that the contributions of nations are the third characteristic of a world doing the will of God.

Parkes distinguished between a nation and a state. "A state is a temporary and changing and quite superficial attempt to provide a political and economic executive for the nations."[31] By nations, Parkes seemed to mean something more like culture. That is, nations are those entities which produce and cultivate ideas and patterns of life from which all can draw strength and meaning. Indeed, it is through such nations/cultures that mankind's spiritual development takes shape:

---

[30] Ibid., p. 4.
[31] Ibid., p. 4.

If we are to say as I believe we can, that where we see something which has been of great value in the spiritual development of mankind, there we can see the hand of God, then I do not think we can avoid saying that nations are of the purpose of God. The world may be reduced to a sorry mess by different states, but it is only enriched by different nations. When we say Greek philosophy, or German philosophy, or French gothic, or English lyric poetry, or Italian painting, we are enriching the conception of philosophy, poetry, painting, not narrowing it. Nor can we say it is an accident that Hegel was a German, that de Vinci was Italian, Shelley an Englishman, and so on. Apart from the geographical, historical, and cultural setting of these genii, they would not have been, or would have been quite different. And the world is richer for their being intensely of their own people. It does not prevent their universal appeal. On the other hand, it seems to me equally true that no nation is able to isolate itself, or grow alone. There is nothing in the world more closely interlocked than culture, and we can borrow without impoverishing the lender, and are indebted to increase our own wealth. The confusion of national ideals with state sovereignty and exclusiveness has been nothing less than a tragedy for the nations themselves. For a nation is like an individual. It is only part of the whole. Its fullness is the whole.[32]

Parkes' position on nations extended the scope of theology beyond the individual. God is as concerned about ideas, culture, economics, and the world order as He is about the individuals who collectively constitute the nations through which God guides such things. One also gets a clearer view of why He was so concerned with the idea of the community. It is through communities, and the individuals who establish them, that God proceeds from stage to stage in the development of His idea of the world fulfilling His will and perfecting itself. Again we find Parkes stressing the interconnectedness of human life and God's plan for the world.

It is this emphasis on interconnectedness that led Parkes to his fourth characteristic of the world doing the will of God. That

---

[32] Ibid., pp. 4–5.

characteristic is his view that "the world as a whole is clearly a unit." He wrote:

> Nothing less than a world unity is adequate to the expression of the plan of God. They shall come from the East and from the West, from the North and from the South, before man can begin to see in its entirety the revelation of God to this world, or the righteousness of God revealed in it. I do not for a moment suggest that this one little world can reveal the whole of God. I say that nothing less than the whole of the world is adequate to reveal God in His relation to the world. It is equally obvious that if the world is spiritually a unit in which different parts are complementary, it is also a material unity. Nothing less than the world as a whole can express the richness of God.[33]

With these four characteristics, Parkes created the ground-work for his theology of politics. Christianity needs to be concerned with more than individual salvation because God's plan for the world goes beyond individual concerns. The community is just as essential as the individual. He emphasized the fact that he draws a sharp distinction between the community and the state, and politics as they are usually understood. While the state, and the politics related to it, plays an important role in one's life, Parkes believed that it needed to be ultimately eliminated, not redeemed. He took this position because he believed that state politics are usually in opposition to the Kingdom of God. Yet he also believed this to be the very reason Christians had to deal with the issues created by politics rather than avoiding them:

> Throughout I have claimed, not that the Church should be interested in state politics, but in the community. The whole division of the world into sovereign states, into spheres of interest, dominant and subject races, and the politics that go therewith have no place in the Kingdom of God. They are a denial of His nature and of our Sonship of Him. The whole set of ideas that accompany economic imperialism, the ideas on which armaments and alliances are based is false, and from

---

[33] Ibid., pp. 5–6.

the point of view of the Church, a meaningless beating of the
air and degradation of the Sons of God. But if we have the
courage to face these facts we must at the same time face the
fact that we for our earthly life are to struggle for the
righteousness of God in a world dominated by these ideas. We
cannot accept them, but neither can we retire from them. We
have to do battle with world imperialism in the name of world
fellowship, with the State in the name of the community, with
the neat divisions and political rivalries in the name of the
unity of the Fatherhood of God and the fellowship of the
brotherhood of man. These are but words flung in the face of
seeming realities. We must give them content.[34]

Parkes would later take a less naive position on state politics, but
these views reflect a certain point of view widespread after World
War I, particularly among those who strongly supported the
League of Nations.

Parkes' great concern about communities stemmed from his
arguments with many students and fellow workers about the role
Christianity should play in the public arena. He felt the need to
challenge their assumptions that communal and political issues
were of little concern to the Church. He claimed that if one tried to
see how God seems to work in history, and to trace the main line of
true progress, one would discover that communities have dominated historical events. The stress on individualism was, in his
view, a rather modern idea. The great discoveries in history, be
they artistic, agricultural, cultural, political, or economic have
arisen in a communal setting, and they have been the discoveries
from which humanity has never turned back. Parkes thought this
view countered both the traditional emphasis on individualism
and the problems raised by a cyclical view of history. History was
for him the constant and progressive revealing of God's plan for
the world. While it is true that the Greek city-states and the
Roman Empire, among others, have risen and fallen, their contributions as civilizations have been, in the broadest sense, both
universal and progressive. It was in this steady progress in
human history that Parkes saw the plan of God unfolding:

---

[34] Ibid., p. 6.

The mastery of man over the materials prepared for him by God, hidden for his discovery in successive ages, has steadily increased. It is not an accident that God has made the material world so rich and varied. They were set there to enrich life and that enrichment is the purpose of God; and here also beneath and beyond the temporary rise and fall of successive epochs in progress. There is movement towards an increasingly full use of the materials prepared by God to beautify and to save His creation.[35]

Parkes was making a subtle point here about God's Creation upon which he will expand later. God is as concerned, in His view, with the material world as He is with the spiritual world. Creation is still good, in spite of the Fall, and it should not be seen as evil or ungodly. It is through the material world that God works to reveal the stages of His plan. One needs to be concerned about it, and with the communities through which this plan is revealed. He never denied God's work in the nonmaterial, spiritual areas of life, but he believed it has been stressed to the improper exclusion of the material area. It is this situation he was addressing.

He anticipated the criticism that the material gains do not imply progress because they have been used for destruction, and he argued that while this has happened, it was not the necessary consequence of material progress. He offered two comments:

1. They [material riches] are given by God with absolute impartiality. The wireless sets of the righteous amateur do not work better than those of the wicked expert. The sick atheist is cured as effectively as the sick Christian.
2. They can offer as great possibilities of evil as good. That is why science can never oust religion. She possesses no moral standard. The use of them depends not upon the skill of the expert, but his spirit, his ideal, his religion.[36]

Having said this about material progress, Parkes offered his own caveat to the idea. This progress will help move man closer to

---

[35] Ibid., p. 8.
[36] Ibid., p. 8.

the Kingdom of God, but finally, it will not bring it to its fulfillment.

> I believe every step of this progress to be the work of God
> alone—God whose Fatherhood gives to all his children as
> much as they will receive. They are all steps toward His
> kingdom in a positive sense. They are more than merely
> clearing away the obstacles. But none of them will bring in
> His Kingdom. For that another program is needed—progress
> in the knowledge of God. Even here, however, it is important
> to remember that there are some of the steps briefly sugges-
> ted above [material progress] which are not just neutral. But
> they are not enough. The Key to the whole question of
> progress, the assurance that the increasing mastery of the
> working of man and nature will be rightly used, this depends
> on our answer to the question—is there an increase in the
> knowledge of God?[37]

Parkes believed that there had been such an increase, in spite of
the fact that it would be easy to be pessimistic about such an
increase of knowledge. He said that, "our knowledge of God is far
fuller even than in the Middle Ages. The answer to the question,
"Is there progress?" is often asked on the basis of happiness. I
doubt if this is a Christian basis on which to ask it, but even there I
think one could say that life was happier than a thousand years
ago."[38]

Alan Davies has argued that Parkes, in his work on Jewish–
Christian relations, is really celebrating human progress rather
than Judaism or Christianity.[39] This early lecture by Parkes
shows that Davies is only partially correct in his criticism. Parkes
does celebrate human progress, but he does so because it is an
essential ingredient of his theology. In this regard, Parkes was a
true child of Modernism.[40] God's plan for the world, in Parkes'
view, involves the steady uncovering along the way of both

---

[37] Ibid., p. 9.
[38] Ibid., p. 10.
[39] Alan Davies, *Antisemitism and the Christian Mind: The Crisis of Conscience after Auschwitz*, p. 141.
[40] *Ideas and Ideals*, op. cit. See chapter 5.

material gains and knowledge of God. Progress in human history is intimately connected to God and His relationship to creation. Human progress is not a separate phenomenon apart from God, but in fact, it is the very means by which God works His will in the world. Even setbacks like the Great War cannot halt the steady work of God to reveal His plan for the world. Parkes held to his view throughout his career, and it led to the next question that he addressed in these lectures: "If we accept the view that God is interested in the march of secular events, we must try to define what the nature of His interest is, and attempt then to see the principles on which He works."[41]

In attempting to answer his own question, Parkes postulated two characteristics of God which remain constant in his theological writings. Given what he has already said about God, it is obvious that Parkes had an idea about God being intimate and active with his creation. This becomes clear in two observations he made about the nature of God:

> Every event, whether of the individual or of the community, whatever their conscious knowledge of God may be, is of direct interest to Him as a step towards or away from His kingdom. Nothing to Him is neutral. Secondly, we need to be very careful in our use of the term "the operation of Divine Law" which suggests something impersonal and automatic. There is no "Divine Law" other than the consistency of the Divine nature. Just as "history never repeats itself," so every event is treated by Him directly, personally, originally. Divine Law does not rest on precedents. The most fascinating of the characteristics of God is His originality. We make a law, and it fulfills itself to a large extent independently of the human and individual factors. We have no evidence that God does the same. Rather we have evidence of a purpose continually renewing itself, of infinite patience, of every possibility of progress held open to the last minute, of one who knows our necessities before we ask, and who gives far more than we have the knowledge to ask for. There is conflict in the course

---

[41] "The Community in the Purpose of God," op. cit., p. 10.

of history, but there is no chance. There is defeat, but there is nothing haphazard.[42]

Parkes was careful to deny that this means that God causes everything to happen and that human freedom is negated, nor did he wish to imply that God acts in an arbitrary fashion. He did believe that the "fundamental gift of God is the power to know Him," yet what is done with that knowledge is left to mankind to decide.[43] He considered the Church's insistence on the equality of all people in the sight of God to be one of the greatest contributions the Church had made to the world, yet on the other hand, he saw that this is not the whole truth of the situation. "We believe that every individual has an equal place in the love of God," he wrote, "but men are equal neither in ability, opportunity, or responsibility."[44] Individuals with greater gifts have greater responsibilities. So too do civilizations have unequal gifts. He cited the Jews, for instance, as being a nation of greater gifts and responsibilities. But he argued that there is a "naturalness" of things which is the result of the fact that God acts in a rational fashion, and through which God works his plan for the world.

Parkes also argued that God need not be compromising in order to work out His plan. He used the example of Moses killing the Egyptian guard. He asked if God willed Moses to kill him, thus compromising God. In other words, the question is, "Does God use evil that good may come?" Parkes responded:

> What is a compromise? The interest of God covers the whole range of human activities, whether consciously religious or not. Everything which leads towards that perfection towards which He is striving is in accordance with His will, whether it were done for that reason or not. Very often it is not. It is done because it is good business or common sense. This need not surprise us, if we believe in the intelligence of God and the rational nature of His universe. We are landed in a pretty pass, if we believe that success in material things is always

---

[42] Ibid., pp. 10–11.
[43] Ibid., p. 12.
[44] Ibid., p. 12.

the result of sin. The cross was not the last word of Christ, and that a man cannot run his life well is no sign that he is therefore more virtuous than his more successful neighbour. We are apt to be sentimental about failure and suffering. They have their value, but they should not be sought for their own sake. If the purpose of God is a rational one, in the long run it is also "good business" and common sense. . . . We can say God is wonderfully compassionate toward us, and that "coincidences" do occur an astonishing number of times, that it is often on the brink that a man is saved, but there is a difference between bringing good out of evil and using evil that good may come. God is marvellously expert at the former, but there is no evidence that I can see He does the latter.[45]

In addition to this, Parkes also stated his belief in the "awful consistency of God." This consistency at times hampers God because it will tolerate no compromise. God works mercilessly to eradicate the evil which impedes His kingdom and He is tireless in the effort. Time itself is no factor, thus evils of the past continue to be attacked in the present.

On the one hand, He uses every means which leads toward His goal, and on the other, no amount of nobility will turn evil into good. In this sense, the moral consistency of God is relentless whatever it may cost, and however much the refusal to compromise may seem to retard the march towards the goal. Mercy is shown unto thousands of them that love Him, and keep His commandments, but it is also true that the unrepented sins of the fathers are visited upon the children until the evil is wiped out for good. . . . But give Him the response of the will to pay the debt, and He will see it discharged. God can wipe out evil, even more effectively than evil can wipe out good, for the one does so by creation, the other by destruction. . . . There are no statutes of limitations

---

[45] Ibid., pp. 14–15.

to the consistency of God. He does not accept that injustice may become hallowed by custom. In the end, the debt must be paid.[46]

For Parkes, the injustices for which the debt must be paid are corporate as well as personal. With this idea, he linked together his ideas about God with his effort to show the importance of the community in God's plan. To illustrate what he believed to be modern evils for which there must be corporate atonement, he cited the Jewish problem of Europe; the United States and the issue of slavery; and white empires and their exploitation of colonized races. From a theological view, Parkes argued that "there are no signs in these problems before us that God will accept compromise. It must be remembered that they are problems demanding corporate, not individual atonement."[47]

In raising the question of corporate atonement, Parkes prepared to present the strongest argument he had for the community in the purpose of God. He argued that while individuals can do much in terms of corporate atonement for social evils, they still remain related to their nation and subject to both the good and bad of their nation. One passage revealed the heart of the lecture:

> Individuals can do much, as we have seen in the improvement of relations between England and Germany since the war, which is partly the result of the work of individual English people in the different relief organizations and elsewhere, and the stands made by individual papers like the *Manchester Guardian*, but they only become effective as they affect national policy. A nation cannot benefit by the good work done by an individual unless it deliberately shares in it; but an individual can benefit by the action of his nation even though he opposed it. And he suffers also in the same way if his nation does wrong. This alone justifies us in attaching great importance to the community in the purpose of God.[48]

---

[46] Ibid., pp. 15–16.
[47] Ibid., p. 16.
[48] Ibid., p. 17.

With this passage, Parkes tied together the other parts of his lecture which set out to show the importance of the community in the purpose of God. All four characteristics mentioned earlier are woven together in this passage, and he used this passage almost to dare others to deny the importance of the community. He did so by closely linking the individual and individual achievement to the community and its actions. God's concern for an individual must also include His concern for the community because of this intimate connection. If for no other reason, therefore, the community plays an important role in the purpose of God. In addition, corporate existence also gives rise to good and evil, and given God's moral consistency in working for the good, God has a great deal of interest in what communities do concerning such issues as war, economics, race relations, and so on. It should be noted that these were all issues which Parkes dealt with in his work at the SCM and the ISS.

This lecture reflected Parkes' postwar concern about discovering a new moral foundation and a plan of action that would prevent another war. In addition, it is evident that his work at the SCM and ISS had led him to be particularly concerned about international problems in ways that move beyond the ordinary politics of nations and states. Indeed, his stress on a holistic approach to God and the world clearly reflects his own ideas about "One World," a concept prevalent among many League of Nations supporters. What troubled Parkes so much was his inability to find a suitable way to connect these concerns with theology. He dealt somewhat with theological issues in this lecture, but he saved his main theological statements for the next three lectures: "Politics and the Holy Spirit," "Politics and the Person of Christ," and "The Person of Christ and the Holy Spirit." In these lectures, he attempted to build a theological bridge to politics and to show how Christians could rethink their ideas about such themes as christology, the Incarnation, and the Trinity. The lectures marked Parkes' first serious attempt to construct his own theology.

Parkes concerned himself in these lectures with the problems that Christians have in finding any relationship between their theology and the social issues of the world. He offered this opening statement as a summary of his concerns:

It is a usual phrase for those few Christians who are interested as Christians in the affairs of the community in industry, politics, and international questions, to speak of them as "applied Christianity," as though Christianity existed as a complete whole if they were left out of account. The attitude of most other Christians is that politics are politics, economics are economics, and religion is religion. It is true to say that for the vast majority of the several hundred millions of Christians of the world, Christianity is a question of their soul, and of its prospects in the next world, and while it is concerned with this world, it is with them as individuals. If we study the Christian life and literature of the last few centuries, we find an enormous mass of profound study which on the human side turns upon this question of the individual, but of study of the meaning of our Christian religion in terms of the community, we will find very little. The interest which the churches take in the community is primarily relief not construction, it is in the form of charity, not of new ideas of society.[49]

In his first lecture, Parkes talked about God's steady work to reveal His plan for the world at various stages in history. Parkes believed that there is a constant striving by God to better not just individuals, but the community as well. Yet somewhere along the way, in his view, Christianity lost contact with the social aspect of God's purpose, and reduced itself to concern for individuals alone. The idea that matter was evil took root in Christian thinking, and in Parkes' view, this idea retarded any substantial Christian view of the community. He saw this reflected particularly in the way Christians "refer to political or economic necessity as though economics had an objective reality, independent of God, as though they were not His concern, not subject to His action, not relevant to His revelation in Christ. There is a profound dualism at work here."[50] For Parkes, the view that matter is evil negates a wide range of God's activity in the world. It was also the occasion for

---

[49] James William Parkes, "Politics and the Doctrine of the Trinity." Lecture delivered at Gilon, Switzerland, WSCF Conference, 1929. Text on file at the Parkes Library, University of Southampton, England, p. 1.

[50] Ibid., p. 2.

him to take issue with the doctrine of the Fall. This doctrine had already stirred some controversy between the German students and himself, and for Parkes, it was the source of much wrong thinking in Christian theology:

> The idea that *matter* is inherently evil is so distinctly contradicted by the very fact of a material incarnation, that except in extreme cases it is not held by people calling themselves Christian, but the doctrine of the Fall, the idea that man is inherently evil is still held with as much vigor as that with which it is denied. Some believe that the Fall is so complete that the world cannot be saved, others that progress is such an inevitable process that no study of it is necessary. These two attitudes, one pessimist, the other determinist, are widely held by Christians today. . . . Leaving aside for the moment the theological, philosophic, or scientific approach to the matter, and looking at it from a historical point, do we find that history justifies either of these views? Have we historical evidence for saying that the Fall is a complete one, in the sense in which some modern—particularly Protestant— theology interprets Paul's words "as in Adam they fell"? The interpretation seems to me profoundly untrue, both in relation to the word "Adam" and to the word "fell." The "Fall" took place long before Adam, accepting Adam as the first conscious creature, and it is not, and never was complete. To insist upon it in order to make a nicely rounded doctrine of the Redemption of Christ, is to introduce an unreal element into the Incarnation, and one which by contradicting the obvious facts as observable by the ordinary intelligent man, drives him from Christianity.[51]

The doctrine of the complete Fall of Creation was anathema to Parkes. It reduced man to a pitiful state of existence, and it effectively halted any efforts in the areas of social justice and community. In addition, it ran contrary to common sense, a touchstone for much of Parkes' theological thinking. To counter this theme, Parkes offered an allegorical argument that in the first chapter of Genesis man has two powers—the power of choice

---

[51] Ibid., pp. 2–3.

and the power to know God. Man abused the power of choice, and this is responsible for the Fall; but the power to know God was never lost, and so the Fall was not a complete one. The consequences of believing the Fall to be complete is that one "cannot escape from the dilemma that in that case, man lost all moral responsibility for his actions, and that God has no right to punish him for that."[52] In his view, the Fall was not complete, but it is one of the factors in human history and God's plan:

> The history of the world is the history of the conflict of those two facts—the abuse of choice and the knowledge of God; and though there is nothing automatic in the action of the latter, the evolutionist is right to the extent that history is the tale of the gradual victory of God. . . . If we believe in the personality of God, this leads us straight on to the idea that this victory is not accidental, that God has a plan for the world and for its evolution toward the perfection for which he conceived it, so that whereas one strand in the thread of history is the story of the thwarting of that purpose by human sin, the other strand is its gradual realisation.[53]

Redefining the nature of the Fall of Creation does not solve the problem of a Christian lack of interest in political issues because linked closely to the doctrine of the Fall is a particular view of the Incarnation. In Parkes' view, the traditional concept of the Incarnation is incomplete, and it leads to a misunderstanding of the doctrine of the Trinity. His views on these themes, which developed in his quest for a theology of politics, came to influence his later work on the nature of Judaism and Christianity.

Parkes attacked once again what he believed to be an excessive concentration on the individual by the Church. The idea that the Incarnation was for the redemption of individual souls alone is only half true. He did not deny the importance of this idea, but he argued that there must be more to it than that:

> The concentration of the Church on the individual is nowhere more conspicuous than in its conception of the person of

---

[52] Ibid., p. 4.
[53] Ibid., p. 4.

Christ and the Incarnation, and again its effects are most conspicuous in Protestant theology. A doctrine of redemption in Christ has been elaborated which has resulted in the Church completely ignoring what it calls secular history in the interest of artificial theology. In calling it artificial, I do not mean to depreciate its positive side. The doctrine of redemption in Christ remains the central doctrine of the Christian Church, and is bound so to do while the Church holds its traditional view of the meaning of the Incarnation. In so far as it means the power of Christ to change the life of the individual, it is supported by the whole experience of nineteen hundred years of Christian history; but it has been made to mean more than that. The whole of the meaning of the Incarnation has been concentrated into the act of redemption. The entire purpose of God has been hallowed into saving certain individuals in their future life. The world is transitory, a vale of sin and suffering; in Christ is escape from it, to a future beyond death. This may be an extreme form in which to express it, but it is an idea with which most of us who date back to the nineteenth century were familiarised by our churches, and which dominates a large proportion of the hymns and prayers which we still use. With such a conception of Christ, while his ethical teaching inevitably acted upon the conduct of believers, and gave rise to many great charitable movements, it was all the time in a very secondary place. The main task of the Church was to secure future bliss, not present change. It was a refuge from the world, not a challenge to it.[54]

I have quoted at length here because this passage gives a very good summary of what Parkes viewed as a major stumbling block to a theology of politics. The traditional view of the Incarnation took no account of why God even considered it important to

---

[54] James William Parkes, "Politics and the Person of Christ." Lecture delivered at Gilon, Switzerland, WSCF Conference, 1929. Text on file at the Parkes Library, University of Southampton, England, p. 1.

redeem the world in the first place.[55] This view ignores completely the role of God as creator and His plan for the world. It separates God from a large part of human history found primarily in the community. It also dwells too exclusively on the second person of the Trinity, thus perverting the unique meaning of the Trinity.

Parkes did not view the Incarnation as an event which occurred outside of history. In his words, the Incarnation has a man-ward side and a God-ward side. The man-ward side is tied up with individual redemption. The God-ward side is tied up with God's plan to move his creation toward perfection. The Incarnation enabled God to "face the burden of the world's suffering and know His power to guide it to the perfection for which he had designed it."[56] It is this side of the Incarnation that Christian theology has ignored, and it has, therefore, retarded its work in the field of politics and international affairs. Parkes called for a new approach to theology in the name of a Logos theology. In this theology, Christ is not simply the redeemer of sins, but the source of progress. He is not the sole source, but the central thread of human progress:

> The lines of all human progress converge in Christ, and from Him radiate out afresh. One doctrine of the Person of Christ

---

[55] Herbert Richardson has written about American theology in a similar fashion, and on the whole, he shows a great deal of sympathy for the Parkesian position. In comparing European theology (Reformation) with American theology he writes: "Because of this concentration on God and His Kingdom, American Christianity has tended to reduce the Reformation concentration on human sin and Jesus Christ the Redeemer to a secondary emphasis. When, as in Reformation theology, human sin and the need for redemption are made primary emphasis, the kingdom of God must be a secondary emphasis—for the very possibility of attaining that kingdom in this world must be denied. Moreover, to focus on sin and man's need for redemption forces a theology to make Jesus Christ, as Redeemer, the primary religious symbol. But in American Christianity, this Reformation emphasis on the symbol of "the cross of Jesus" is never primary. Bonhoeffer noted just this characteristic when he says that American Christianity is "still essentially religion and ethics. But because of this the person and work of Jesus Christ must, for theology, sink into the background . . . because it is not recognized as the sole ground of radical judgment (on sin) and radical forgiveness." *Toward an American Theology*, p. 109. On the whole, I found Richardson to be dealing with issues that were raised by Parkes in his theological writings. I know from a conversation with Dr. Richardson that Parkes was an influence on his theological thinking.

[56] "Politics and the Doctrine of the Trinity," op. cit., p. 5.

has got to be large enough to cover all these facts which seem to be historically true. A general doctrine of an increasing fall and decay is absolutely unrelated to them. A concentration of the individual salvation in Christ is inadequate to them. . . . Here again I think the answer to our needs is already to be found in a fresh understanding of Christian theology. The doctrine of the Logos goes back to the second century, though it seems to me that there is some confusion between the doctrine of the Logos and the Holy Spirit yet the main point is the same. . . . Whether we call the action of God in creation the Logos or the Holy Spirit makes little difference. The whole of God acts in creation. But we make a mistake if we confuse the function of one person with that of the others (in the Trinity). It is not that the activities are in any way in conflict with one another. The distinction is only necessary that we may ourselves have a clearer and more rational conception of the nature of God.[57]

Again we see Parkes stressing this theme of God's involvement with human progress on a level beyond that of individual redemption. He believed the view to be only half true that the course of history up to Christ was simply one of decline and desperation and that the Incarnation ushered in a new period in regard to the struggle of man with sin. While, on the one hand, man had fallen so low that only God could raise him, on the other hand, he had risen so high that only God could complete the process. It is this process headed toward perfection in history that is the work of the Logos, the Holy Spirit, and it involves communities. At this point, Parkes again argued that history shows that communities are where this process is most clearly seen:

When we come to study history further we find more grounds for doubting the conventional emphasis of Christianity, that is the exclusive concentration on the individual. The only corporate activity usually acknowledged is the Fall. Even the Church of England itself, according to the 39 Articles, is no more than a "congregation of faithful men." Today those Christians who reject the Fall have on the whole no corporate

---

[57] "Politics and the Person of Christ," op. cit., pp. 6–7.

activity at all acknowledged in the actual body of their Christian doctrine. But this concentration on the individual, as a unit in himself is flatly contradicted by history, as indeed it is also by psychology. As far back as we can trace history, its prime emphasis is on the community. Even if we take it as the record of great men, those great men are but the highest stone on the pyramid of their times. Moses apart from his Egypto–Hebrew setting is as incomprehensible as Shakespeare apart from Elizabethan England, and this being so can we believe in an all wise God and not believe that this grouping of men in communities is His purpose and their activities very directly His interest? The doctrine of the self-limitation of God was never supposed to apply to His wisdom. Can we, in fact, connect Him vitally with the world at all if the community as such means nothing to Him? It is either of Him or of sin, and to say that it is of sin contradicts the profoundest logic of history, and makes belief in a rational nature of the creation of God impossible. Rather the community, whether nation or Church, gives us some of the clearest spheres in which to observe Him working, and in which to trace the progress of mankind. If the progress of the communities of the world is not due to God, there is a power greater than God in the world.[58]

Later in his writings, Parkes would coin the phrase that "good theology cannot be built on bad history," and he is adamant in arguing that history is the stage upon which the Hand of God is seen. Therefore, theology has to give credence to what history has to say. His reading of history gives communities a central role in God's plan for the world, yet he found that the Christian tradition generally ignores communities. This created an incomplete theology and a distorted view of the Trinity. He insisted in his lectures that a proper understanding of the Trinity would lead to a proper understanding of communities in Christian theology. He understood the first and last person of the Trinity as having significance to communities and the second person to individuals. They work together, not separately, to give a complete theology, yet tradition

---

[58] "Politics and the Doctrine of the Trinity," op. cit., pp. 14–15.

has emphasized the second person almost to the exclusion of the other two. This is where problems occur in creating any sort of Christian theology of politics. He argued this point in one of his lectures:

> So far it might seem that we were making an artificial division in allotting as it were, the community to the first and third person of the Trinity, and leaving the individual to the second. There is some truth to this distinction, as the result of the concentration of the Church on the second person shows, but there is no need to make such distinctions, provided we do not allow the interest of the individual to be swamped in the interest of the community. It is Christ that gives significance to the individual, which he is given in no other religious or philosophical system. A Church which worships only the first and third persons would be no improvement on the present. But it is well to realise that the first preaching of Christ was about the community, "the Kingdom of God is at hand," and that the first reference to this world in the Lord's Prayer is "Thy Kingdom come." The relation of religion to the community is no more "applied Christianity" than its relation to the individual. They are two sides of the same thing, and the two together are needed to make the whole.[59]

The key point here is Parkes' desire to create a holistic theology which relates God to the whole of creation, and not just to individuals. This theme was already mentioned in the first lecture, and it carries over into these three lectures as well. The work of God includes not only individuals in search of self-perfection, but it includes all domains of human life:

> Parallel with these two movements in human history, the search for the absolute and the search for self-perfection, is the search for progress in all domains, the gradual development of the community, and its ordered life based on the sanctity of the oath, and the treaties, and the evolution of the idea of law and custom, and social responsibility, the enrichment of life by art, literature and thought, and then later by

---

[59] Ibid., p. 15.

science and commerce. All this progress I take to be the work of the Holy Spirit. Now it is evident that this division of function is for the purpose of analysis rather than devotion. Its value lies in its helping us to see life as a whole—and that allows us to give full weight to all lines that lead towards the goal, without claiming exclusive right for our own individual choice. It has also the value that it relates God in the whole of His personality to His creation, and to human life. God the creator is seen to be immanent as well as transcendent, and lest it seem a higher thing to concentrate on the absolute than on self-perfection, or on our social responsibilities, we see the way to God lies no less along the other paths since Christ and the Holy Spirit are no less God.[60]

In his quest for a holistic theology, Parkes took seriously the broad dimensions of God's activities, and he challenged the exclusive Christian position that one is saved by faith in Christ alone. He argued forcefully for a certain doctrine of universal salvation based on God's idea of perfection for His entire creation.[61] He particularly singled out the position listed in the thirteenth of the Church of England's thirty-nine Articles of Faith as being untenable if one holds to the possible activities of the first and third person of the Trinity. The thirteenth article reads:

> Work done before the Grace of Christ and the inspiration of His spirit, are not pleasant to God, for as much as they spring not from faith in Jesus Christ. . . . Yet rather, for that they were done not as God hath willed and commanded them to be done, we doubt not that they have the nature of sin.

---

[60] "Politics and the Person of Christ," op. cit. p. 8.

[61] Parkes believed that "nothing less than universal salvation is compatible with the honour of God and the responsibility of creation. . . . Perfection will be universal, just because God-in-a-human-life was *God* in a human life. . . . At any point they [human beings] may still be persisting in their refusal; but there still lies the infinity of eternity before them, and God is morally convinced that somewhere within that infinity refusal will give place to hesitation, and hesitation to acceptance. . . . Salvation is not only universal in the sense that it embraces all men; it is also complete in that it raises all men to their real perfection." John Hadham, *Good God*, pp. 66–67. Parkes holds this position throughout his work, and it is a clear indication of the influence of Modernism on his thinking.

Parkes refuted this article in no uncertain terms, and his answer helps us to see early in his writings the foundation upon which he was to build his position concerning the relationship between Christianity and Judaism without feeling that he had to compromise his own Christian faith in any way whatsoever. In commenting on the thirteenth article he writes:

> This is surely not the view which we can accept if we really believe in either the first or third persons of the Trinity. God is the Father of *all* men, and has an equal responsibility toward all, and I believe, a vision of all men made perfect. On what ground can He refuse the striving after Himself, the response of Himself within them, from those who have never known the incarnation or risen Christ. It would not be justifiable to falsify the teaching of history in order to provide a satisfactory explanation of the Holy Spirit, but it is rather true to say that Christianity, in adopting such a view as that of the article, itself falsifies, and makes rubbish of history, and that the true key to that history is to regard the whole of it as the struggle of the Holy Spirit with the sin, ignorance, and willfulness of man. It is false to say that apart from the knowledge of Christ all is sin, but it is false to say that there is no good in the world, conscious or unconscious, which is not the work of God. What other source of goodness is there in the world than God? What is the good in the individual heart but the glow and reflection of the rays of life from God Himself which is an *essential* part of its nature. Apart from it human nature is not "human nature." Apart from it indeed man is fallen, but I know of no other character in the range of history of whom it can be said that he was *absolutely* devoid of good, and so *absolutely* untouched by the influence of the Holy Spirit.[62]

In Parkes' holistic theology, God's ability to work whenever, wherever, and however He so wishes destroys any parochial interpretation of His love and revelation. Parkes was insistent that the Church be alive to the spiritual truths of other religions,

---

[62] "Politics and the Doctrine of the Trinity," op. cit., pp. 13–14.

"instead of allowing these to be discovered by her opponents."[63] Christian missions have been guilty of this attitude according to Parkes. He was also skeptical of these Christians who insist on radical conversion as the only true religious experience.

> For most of us Christianity is an affair of growth, with some it is so placid and unruffled that it appears almost to be without the cross, and we would be rash to say on a basis of our self-knowledge that this or that Christian was better than another because his religious experience seemed to correspond more closely to the convention we have set. . . . In most cases it is a gradual growth which produces the best Christians.[64]

He believed this gradual growth was part of God's plan for the community as well. All this is in line with his attack on the emphasis on individual redemption in Christian theology based on Christ alone. There is a wider area of concern in which God works, and it is not limited to the Church or to those who profess to be Christian.

He was also critical of the type of Christian ethics which limits itself to religious concerns alone. Just as God has been divorced from His creation in much of traditional theology, Parkes believed a similar divorce has taken place between God and ethics:

> It is often said that there is no such thing as a Christian ethic on the one hand, and that there are no such things as the "principles which Christ taught" on the other. These two statements come from opposite sides. The one side says that economics have their own laws, and "it is idle to say that such and such ought to be men's aim in business if in fact they are not." The other side says that Christ did not deal in ethics or principles at all. He taught men attitudes to God. Both these theories divorce God from ethics. The one suggests that there is a way in which the world can run perfectly well without Christianity or God, the other that God is not concerned with mortality. God's only desire is that all men shall worship Him.

---

[63] "Politics and the Person of Christ," op. cit., p. 2.
[64] Ibid., p. 16.

To those who do not share this view it scarcely does credit to God. He is made in effect to say, "Have communion with me, and if you also do good to your neighbour that is your own affair, not mine."[65]

Obviously, for someone like Parkes, who sees God acting in the whole of creation, limiting one's relationship to Him to a circumscribed religious setting is sheer nonsense. It detracted both from God's majesty and His concern with His creation, and it also reduced man's religious life and commitment to a series of meaningless rituals. In Parkes' view, this has been the traditional way of viewing things, and thus it has made it almost impossible to construct any sort of useful theology of politics which could inform the ordinary Christian about issues outside the realm of "personal religion."

If there was to be any change in Christian theology, Parkes believed that it needed to broaden its understanding of the Incarnation and the Trinity. That would result in Christian theology being less christocentric and more theocentric. He introduced these terms in his 1929 lectures, but they would appear repeatedly in his writings on theology and on Jewish–Christian relations. In fact, his idea about theocentric theology was to become a cornerstone for his ideas about a new Christian theology of Judaism.[66] Its appearance in these early lectures is very significant, and it casts a new light on his later works. In 1929, Parkes' contact with the Jewish question was limited to his work with Jewish student groups in Eastern Europe and his knowledge of Judaism was limited to what he had learned while at Oxford. At Oxford, Parkes had learned only that Judaism no longer served any real purpose in God's plan since the advent of Christianity. His references to Judaism in these lectures reveal common stereotypes found in Christian tradition. The Law is seen in a negative light,[67] rabbinic Judaism is characterized as legalistic,[68] Judaism

---

[65] Ibid., p. 15.

[66] For a complete statement on this issue by Parkes, see p. 208ff. in his book *Prelude to Dialogue.*

[67] Parkes, "Politics and the Person of Christ," op. cit., pp. 4, 5 and 12.

[68] Ibid., p. 8.

at the time of Jesus is seen as having been in a state of decline,[69] and Jesus is portrayed as a chief opponent of the Pharisees.[70] Parkes revised these ideas as his knowledge of Judaism increased.

I mention all this to show that Parkes' later works, which contrast christocentric and theocentric theology, are not dependent on a need to be more favorable to Judaism in order to construct his case for better Jewish–Christian relations, but rather simply the continuation of a theme found early in his work. It was his initial reinterpretation of Christianity, brought about by his desire to find a means of creating a theology of politics, which allowed him to reinterpret Christian views about Judaism, and not the influence of Judaism and his Jewish friends upon his work. His later views of Judaism are natural and logical extensions of a theology he first formulated in 1929. In his first statement about christocentric theology he writes:

> Our religion has tended to be Christocentric, and not even completely that, for we have considered only the man-ward and individual aspect of the Incarnation. It is only so that it seems possible to explain the concentration of the Church on the individual to the almost complete exclusion of the community. If we think of Christ as only the redeemer from sin of each separate individual, and as perfect of what One Man (as much modern humanitarian religion sees Him) ought to be, if we emphasise the apparent lack of interest in politics and economics in His teaching, then we can believe that Christianity is only concerned with the individual, and that apart from the knowledge of Christ by the individual the world is completely fallen; but if we relate the Incarnation directly to the purpose of God in the creation of a world which should be a unit, and not a mass of unrelated, independent individuals, however we may say it—and there may be better ways than the one I have chosen—then we are thrown back on the question: What is the purpose of God for the world, and how is it being realised? Our religion is no longer Christocentric. We are compelled to consider God the Creator whose plan is

---

[69] Ibid., p. 12.
[70] Ibid., p. 1.

either being fulfilled or thwarted and God the Holy Spirit working continually in the evolution of mankind, and that plan and that evolution become no longer an adjunct, an "applied Christianity", but something essential to the understanding of Christianity itself.[71]

Parkes concluded his lectures with a statement declaring that he was "not writing this in any sense for publication," rather he was trying to clear his own mind and get his ideas corrected and supplemented by the criticism of those few who had read the lectures, like William Temple.

Except for two short articles in *The Student Movement* in March and May of 1931, Parkes did not write again on his interpretation of Christianity as such until 1940. These later writings prove to be commentaries of sorts on his 1929 lectures, and together they provide one with a good outline of his theological thinking. In the next chapter, we shall review how he interpreted these themes in later writings.

---

[71] "Politics and the Doctrine of the Trinity," op. cit., p. 6.

3

Interpreting Christianity

IN 1931, James Parkes wrote two short articles on theology for the SCM journal *The Student Movement*: "God and my Furniture" and "Revelation and the Duster." In these two articles, he argued for a God involved in the ordinary events of life and in human history, rather than a God who is "Wholly Other." Parkes believed God was intimately involved with His creation, revealing Himself in different ways at different times. "My home and its content are my corner of the Kingdom of God," he wrote.[1] He believed God gave creation a certain loveliness, some of which is hidden, and that God enjoyed people discovering that hidden beauty. Nature and material things were viewed as part of God's revelation, particularly as people used them to create beauty. He wrote that "carving and weaving and embroidery, cut glass, and painted china, are all revelations of God's love of beauty, since they all depend on the use of materials which He has provided."[2]

A consistent theme in Parkes' theology is that the Kingdom of God is not just in the future, but that glimpses of it are available in our everyday life. He first expressed this idea in the 1929 lectures,[3] and he returned to it in 1931:

---

[1] James Parkes, "God and My Furniture," *The Student Movement*, March 1931, p. 2.

[2] Ibid., p. 3.

[3] James Parkes, "Politics and the Doctrine of the Trinity." Lecture delivered at Gilon, Switzerland, World Student Christian Conference, 1929. Text on file at the Parkes Library, Southampton, England, p. 17.

And God has given me to weave together out of all these things my home. In the office, His Kingdom is often something infinitely remote to be achieved by endless struggle and combat. We stand as watchmen looking over the desert man has made of the world and society, and are conscious only of the difficulties, and the immensity of the task. But the Kingdom of God is not just a problem. It is also something to be realised here and now; something to be enjoyed; something intensely real—in spite of all that theologians may say, something intensely simple and everyday. And in one aspect, the Kingdom consists in the beauty of creation which God made, and if the Kingdom of God is not in my home it is my fault. . . . Your home should be a perpetually new reminder of the beauty of God, and because it is made up of the expressions of that beauty, its appeal should be infinite. It should be itself creative. It should soothe, it should cheer, it should laugh with all who come into it, yourself included. It should welcome you on your return with a reminder of the fact that God is, for it is that bit of His Kingdom, which is given to you and to no one else to create, to maintain, and to render daily yet more beautiful.[4]

Parkes' insistence on the presence of God in creation was not a form of pantheism. Material creation is separate from God, but not separated from Him. It is used by God and man in a cooperative effort to help creation move closer to the perfection God intended it to have at the beginning of creation. Parkes believed that this aspect of God was often overlooked by theologians who stressed the transcendence of God to the point that God only moves in human history by miraculous intervention unrelated to everyday life. He obviously had the Barthians in mind here, and in "Revelation and the Duster," he leveled a sharp rebuke against this position.

Unless even the Barthians have underestimated the effects of the Fall, God is not primarily interested in theology. The greater part of humanity is occupied with the everyday task of living, and apparently must be so. Therefore, if God *is*, then

---

[4] "God and My Furniture," op. cit., p. 3.

in all the everyday tasks of living it should be possible to serve Him—and find Him. To the intellectual, the nature of God is often like the carrot held in front of the nose of the donkey— they can never be quite sure that they will get there in the next step. Even the Incarnation is as much a fresh puzzle as a fresh proof. But life is not made up of intellectual problems, and there is a whole side of it when intellectual proofs do not really matter, where from the pedestal of teleological possi- bility He descends to the common ground of just being God, creator, guide, inspirer of artistically, the eternal tempter, always revealing and never completely revealed, who shows a perfection only to hint at the possibility of a greater one. The true knowledge of God is a perpetual process of eating one's cake and keeping it.[5]

God's presence in the ordinary events of life does not translate for Parkes into the sanctimonious phrase "God is near." Such a statement usually carries with it the idea of fear and trembling before the Awesome Holy One. Parkes believed this kind of theological concept falls on deaf ears among ordinary people. It is just not the way most people think of or experience God. Secondly, if it was the way most people thought of God, it would be difficult to sustain any sort of relationship with Him. It would be simply overwhelming. Rather he offered this idea:

> There is usually a certain unctuous, and sentimental tone in our voice when we say, "God is very near." It has a serious side, but it is a pity we are not more often reminded of its delightful side. Of course, to live in the presence of the Absolute would not mean much to the housemaid; to live in the presence of a Personality interested in everything which is well and sincerely done, might mean more. When I look at the pair of candlesticks which want cleaning and feel too lazy to do it, it is an authentic voice of God which says: "Do you think I took the trouble to work out the particular combi- nation of positive and negative electricity which you call brass, for you to offer it to me in that condition? Go and get the

---

[5] James Parkes, "Revelation and the Duster," *The Student Movement*, May 1931, p. 8.

Brasso." And when I am obedient and get it, I am given the infinite joy of revealing another little bit of the Kingdom of God.[6]

Throughout his theological writings, Parkes delighted in describing God and His activities in such unusual terms. How many times has one read of God and housework connected in such a fashion? Revelation concerns all of God's creation, not just the specific events that have become "truths" in religious tradition. In this regard, we can see the influence of William Temple on Parkes' thinking. As we mentioned before, Temple was a close friend of Parkes, and he read and criticized almost all of Parkes' early theological works. Parkes' views on God and revelation lack the philosophical sophistication one finds in Temple's writings, but Parkes' ideas show remarkable similarity in content, if not in form, to those found in Temple's writings.

Temple argued, for instance, that revelation involved God's revelation of Himself and His plan, rather than dogmatic truths. He wrote that "what is offered to man's apprehension in any specific revelation is not truth concerning God, but the living God Himself."[7] This is similar to Parkes' ideas in the 1929 lectures and these 1931 articles. In addition, Temple argued against any sharp distinction between nature and God. All of creation is a source of God's revelation and activity, and it includes the ordinary events of life. He argued that

Unless all existence is a medium of revelation, no particular revelation is possible. . . . Either all occurrences are in some degree revelations of God, or else there is no such revelation at all; for the conditions of the possibility of any revelation require that there should be nothing which is not revelation. Only if God is revealed in the rising of a son of man from the dead.[8]

Temple also argued that he would make "no truce with any suggestion that the world for the most part goes on in its own way

---

[6] Ibid., pp. 8–9.
[7] William Temple. *Nature, Man and God*, p. 322.
[8] Ibid., p. 306.

while God intervenes now and again with an act of His own."[9]
Again we see a point of contact between Parkes' thinking and
Temple's views.

For Parkes, God acts on the stage in human history, not just
nature, but God does act in a deliberate fashion. Temple agreed
with Parkes, and he took a position quite opposite from the
Barthian position of a "wholly Other" God removed from history
and creation:

> The main field of revelation must always be in the history of
> men, rather than in the ample spaces of nature, though it is
> also true that if nature were so severed from God as to offer no
> revelation of Him at all, it would mean that there was no
> Being fitly to be called God, and therefore no revelation of
> Him either in human history or elsewhere.[10]

Both Parkes and Temple believed the end result of revelation
was faith in God, and they agreed that faith is grounded in
personal fellowship between man and God. For them both, faith is
not simply the assent to revealed doctrines of truth, but a personal
relationship between the living God and His creatures. Temple
stated:

> The life of faith is not an acceptance of doctrine any more than
> the life of the natural man is the acceptance of mathematical
> equations, or the life of the artist is the acceptance of aesthe-
> tic canons. . . . Faith is not the holding of correct doctrines,
> but personal fellowship with the living God. Correct doctrine
> will both express this, assist it and issue from it; incorrect
> doctrine will misrepresent this and hinder or prevent it.
> Doctrine is of an importance too great to be exaggerated, but
> its place is secondary, not primary. I do not believe in any
> creed, but I use creeds to express, to conserve, and to deepen
> my belief in God.[11]

---

[9] Ibid., p. 304.
[10] Ibid., p. 305.
[11] Ibid., p. 321.

Temple also felt that belief in doctrines often inhibited faith, and that such belief was not the way most people lived out their faith. As he wrote in one of his essays:

> Much of the difficulties that men find in accepting traditional Christianity is due to their belief that what is chiefly asked of them is intellectual assent to certain propositions. They may not regard these as untrue, but they refuse to affirm them until they have worked them out for themselves; they see no sufficient reason for taking them on trust. In revolt against what seems to them an exaggeration of formalism they desire a "formless faith," though they often agree, when challenged, that this would be hard to transmit from generation to generation or to propagate through the world. But if the revelation is given in events, and supremely in the historical Person of Christ, this difficulty is avoided. For an event is not vague or indefinite, even if no number of theories exhaust its significance, and men who differ profoundly in their theories of the Atonement may kneel together in penitence and gratitude at the foot of the cross.[12]

As this passage indicates, Temple was willing to acknowledge that revelation remains open to reinterpretation, and that tradition need not bind one to an inflexible position. In this regard also, Temple and Parkes were in agreement.

I have tried to illustrate some of the similarities between Parkes and Temple for a number of reasons. First, Temple's influence on Parkes in unquestionable. He was a better known figure than Parkes, and he occupies a definite place in modern theology as a progressive and liberal thinker concerned with relating Christianity to society. Second, Temple is a better theologian in the traditional sense than Parkes because he devotes more attention to the philosophical basis of his position. Yet Parkes shared a common vision with Temple, and reading Temple helps to add a dimension somewhat lacking in Parkes' work. It should be noted, however, that Parkes never made any pretense of being a philosophical theologian like Temple, and most of Parkes' writings

---

[12] Quoted in John Baillie, *The Idea of Revelation in Recent Thought*, pp. 95–6.

were directed to a more popular audience. Third, by seeing the common ground between Temple and Parkes, we realize that he was not a renegade Christian, but in fact was stating a view of the Christian faith shared by the Modernists, especially someone as important and respected as William Temple. This is not to say that there were no differences between the two men. For instance, Parkes adopted more of a Modernist position than did Temple, but referring to Temple does give a context to Parkes' thought that is easily missed and seldom acknowledged.

There is a hiatus in Parkes' theological writings between the years 1931 and 1940. The main reason for this gap was Parkes' decision to devote almost all his energy to the historical issues related to Christian antisemitism. But there were other reasons as well. By 1932, Parkes was beginning to feel a bit out of step with his colleagues at the SCM and ISS. Barth's influence was beginning to take hold in British theological circles, and Parkes felt himself being forced more and more towards the periphery. The controversy surrounding his work on the Jewish question made him hesitant about getting involved in other controversies related to theology. So, for eight years, Parkes concentrated on the historical questions affecting Christian attitudes toward Jews, a subject on which he became a leading expert. He came to discuss the theological issues concerning Jewish–Christian relations only at a later date.

The theological issues raised by Parkes in 1929 and 1931 continued to concern him, and by 1940, he had begun once again to write on a new theology that related God to all His creation. He was encouraged in this by his close friend and benefactor, Israel M. Sieff, a wealthy and influential figure in the Jewish community of England. Parkes and Sieff had met in 1932 at the urging of Simon Marks, Sieff's brother-in-law, to discuss funding Parkes' research on the Jewish question. While their initial meetings concerned the Jewish question, it was apparently Sieff who encouraged Parkes to write again on theological issues. Parkes recounted in his autobiography that in the spring of 1939, he and Sieff were discussing religion and the difficulty ordinary people had in seeing a real God in the archaic language and thought found in both Judaism and Christianity. Parkes recounted the conversation:

I then told him that I had long wanted to write a book called *Sketches of the Character of God*, in which I did not theologise or such to prove that God existed, but simply describe His activities as would those of the Prime Minister or the Archbishop of Canterbury. Writing about such people one would not begin by seeking to prove their existence, and I wanted to assume the existence of God in the same way. "But James," said IMS, "you must write it. Go and do it."[13]

It was just the sort of encouragement Parkes had been waiting for in order to set about the task.

This was not the first time that Parkes had thought about writing such a book. However, his inquiries to his friends at the Student Movement Press like Hugh Martin and Eric Fenn brought forth no encouragement. In fact, Fenn, a person Parkes greatly respected, told Parkes not to "insult the Student Movement Press by asking them to publish it." Convinced now by Sieff that the project was worthwhile, Parkes set about in the summer of 1939 to write the book. The war broke out when Parkes was two-thirds finished, and it was not until early spring 1940 that Parkes finished the manuscript. He gave it to Sieff to read and informed him that if it was to reach its proper audience it should be a Penguin special edition. Sieff was able to get it published by Penguin, even though the editor, Allen Lane, questioned its lack of evidence and proof. However, the readers at Penguin thought it was quite good, and Lane was overridden in his decision. The book appeared in the spring of 1940 under the title *Good God*. However, the author under whose name it appeared was John Hadham, and the reason for this requires some explanation.

In the course of getting the book published, Parkes decided that it would be best to write under a *nom de plume*. He did so in order to keep his theological writings from getting confused with his rather controversial books on the Jewish question. The name Hadham was picked rather arbitrarily, but the name John was picked for a particular reason. It seems that a distant relative of Parkes named John had sold some land rich in coal to someone

---

[13] James Parkes, *Voyage of Discoveries*, p. 156.

outside the family because he disliked his relatives. A vast fortune was lost to the Parkes family in the process. Since Parkes had no desire to be a coal millionaire, he was grateful to John for sparing him such a fate. Thus, the name John Hadham came to be Parkes' *nom de plume*.

This *nom de plume* is something of a problem in studying Parkes. Those familiar with his work on Jewish–Christian relations, antisemitism, and Jewish history are seldom aware of the work Parkes produced as John Hadham. A knowledge of the Hadham material contributes greatly to our understanding of Parkes' basic theological position, but unless one knows that Hadham is really Parkes, this material is of course ignored. Without the benefit of the Hadham books, one is often left wondering how Parkes arrives at some of his positions, and the link between certain ideas found in the other writings of James Parkes cannot be made.

The career of John Hadham spanned the years 1940 to 1960, but most of the work done under this name was completed between 1940 and 1944. Under the name John Hadham, Parkes published four books, numerous articles and did a series of radio broadcasts. Parkes also publicly lectured under the name Hadham, and the works of John Hadham were enormously popular in Britain during the war.

In studying these materials, one finds Parkes developing more fully the ideas first presented in the WSCF lectures of 1929. The Hadham materials dealt with themes like politics and religion, the problems of christocentric theology, the Trinity, religious language, religious truth, Divine–human co-operation, progress, perfection, holistic theology, human interdependence, and the need for a new theology in a new age. Again, one does not find Parkes dealing with these issues in the traditional philosophical-theological manner, but rather in an experiential, commonsense manner, not lacking a humorous side. A good deal of criticism is leveled at the Church and its traditions, as well as its often rigid interpretations of Scripture. The influence of Modernism is apparent throughout these writings. It could be characterized as a theology struggling to relate God to all of His creation. It is a theology that takes the future seriously without discarding all the past. It is a theology attempting to find a way to break free from parochial interpretations of God and His revelation without falling into syncretism. It is a Christian theology which argues for God's ability to act outside of the Christian experience. It is a theology which considers the human–Divine encounter in personal and corporate life more essential to God's plan for His creation than the dogmas and interpretations that arise from such encounters. Finally, it is a theology which takes the human side of the encounter as seriously as the divine side. In it all, one can discover the foundations of a theology that helped Parkes to develop a new Christian view of Judaism, and that appreciated other religious traditions as well. In his later theological writings written under both names, his theological concerns and his interest in Jewish–Christian relations become increasingly intertwined, but when one is familiar with his early Hadham writings, one gets a clearer picture of what Parkes is trying to do theologically in his later works.

In the opening pages of *Good God*, Parkes set forth a description of what could be loosely called his "theological method." Rather than creating a theology based on philosophical arguments, he wanted to produce a theology based on what can be known about God through ordinary experience and language. Such a method produced many problems for people schooled in formal theology and philosophy since the method did not fit into any of the usual categories used to classify theological thinking. Yet Parkes remained consistent throughout his theological writings in refusing to write about God in the usual theological–philosophical fashion. He aimed his writings at a more general audience, and he attempted to write in a way that would make his work available to the general public. It would be wrong to call Parkes a "popularizer," but it is correct to view him as someone who wished to be a "theologian for the public." His main theological purpose was to help people think about how God relates to them and their personal existence, rather than producing any formal arguments about God's existence. Parkes outlined his theological method very clearly in the beginning of *Good God* in this lengthy passage:

> I am not going to try and prove that God exists. As a matter of fact, it is not possible to do so because God arranged the world like that. Of course that does not mean that philosophers will

not always argue as to whether he does or not. Some will accept the probability of an "ultimate teleological conception of the universe"—which is apparently a philosophic statement of belief in God—and some will propound other solutions. This need not worry us, for God also made philosophers, and made them like that. . . . Personally, however, I am convinced that God exists, and I write on that assumption. What interests me is not whether he exists, but *assuming he exists*, what he is like, and what on earth he is up to at the present moment. I mean "what on earth" literally. Of the home life of God I know nothing, and I am equally ignorant of his relations with other planets and universes. . . . We cannot emphasize this too clearly. Theologians are foolish to claim to know about God as he really and fully is. All we know about him is related to this world of which I believe him to be the creator and sustainer. My beliefs are an interpretation of facts, the knowledge of which is open to all of us. They are the facts of geology, history, psychology, and so on. And as I *am* concerned with this world in which I happen to live, I consider it important to have as clear a picture as possible of the person who made it, and, what is more difficult to accept, did it on purpose, and has not abandoned it. . . . I shall try as far as possible to avoid abusing other people's ideas of God, although everybody knows that there are no hatreds like those engendered by the discussion of religion. And if it shocks anyone I apologize in advance. The only thing which matters is that these sketches of his character should show a real God, with a character, a personality, and a purpose of his own. I would add that they are only sketches; they do not pretend to be a complete picture or to answer every question. Moreover, I propose to describe him in perfectly ordinary language; and *in ordinary human terms*. I do the last not because I believe them to be adequate to a complete picture of God, but because, being a man, they are the only terms I understand. The only words by which a man can describe real qualities are words which allow of comparison with qualities in his own experience.[14]

---

[14] John Hadham, *Good God*, pp. 5–6.

We can see here some essential elements of Parkes' theological method. He was concerned not with formal doctrine and argument, but rather with the effect God has on a person who assumes His existence. We see him again concentrating on God's relation to creation, to the earth, rather than on theological speculation of the philosophical sort. The ordinary human dimension is again central to his thinking, and the relationship of one's experience as a human being to one's knowledge of God is of primary importance. He was also justifying his belief in the intimate connection between reason and faith when he argued:

> So far as I know, there is nothing God dislikes more than that kind of humbug which cloaks itself in false reverence. I am convinced that so far from adopting an attitude that we are not to criticise or examine his activities, He welcomes the frankest attempts to understand who He is and what He is doing. In fact it is perfectly obvious that if He were really so easily offended and of so sensitive a dignity as many religious persons assert, He would have closed down this particular planet a long time ago. For being the God of this world is no sinecure for an idealistic and egocentric autocrat. It is an occupation in which only the most complete realism is the least likely to be successful. And I am sure that He had this in mind when He started the whole process.[15]

It is clear throughout his writings that Parkes was not afraid to discuss God in rather unconventional terms, and that he sought ways which he thought made it easier for ordinary people to think about God.

Parkes was steadfast in his argument that we can only assume God's existence, not prove it. Although there was a danger that such a position could lead to agnosticism, Parkes believed that theology can borrow from science to show why a hypothesis that God exists is intellectually sound:

> To ascribe to God personality and purpose is always an act of faith. We cannot *prove* that there is a person behind the visible process of the world, or a purpose in it working out.

---

[15] Ibid., p. 6.

But it is equally impossible to prove the opposite. It is sometimes argued that it is unnecessary to assume either hypothesis, and that it is therefore, better to remain resolutely agnostic. That is, indeed, legitimate, but it is not more scientific. For just as the intellect of men works from hypothesis in the field with which the intellect can deal, so the emotional side of man, the spirit of man, is entitled to work from a hypothesis in the spiritual field. In each field men have to discover by experience whether the hypothesis is tenable or not. Only in one case the experience can be demonstrated intellectually and in the other, though conclusive to the individual concerned, it is incapable of "scientific" demonstration or contradiction. It can only be communicated in its own field, that of emotional personal experience.[16]

This idea of the "emotional, personal experience" of a person is a key idea in Parkes' theology. He did not limit it to a uniquely personal religious experience, but rather he argued for a holistic approach to man's emotional life that includes his life in corporate society as well as his individual experience. Even in talking about revelation, Parkes used emotional terms as when he states that "revelations is a natural and inevitable part of the relationship between God and man."[17] Revelation is not an isolated event in history, detached from man's everyday existence, but is indeed part of the basic fabric of life. There must be an intimate connection between man's spiritual and material existence if there is to be any real understanding of God on the part of human beings. He wrote that "spiritual movements without material foundations, spiritual exaltation without intellectual preparation, and material discoveries without spiritual vitality are all alike sterile. The idea must be made flesh. The body must have a soul. The soul must have a fitting intellectual habitation."[18] For Parkes, the way one can best understand this phenomenon is not by looking for cosmic events, but by looking at the ordinary in life. This is a theme that runs throughout Parkes' work—God is best found in the ordinary events of human life. In an article he wrote in 1941,

---

[16]   John Hadham, *God and Human Progress*, p. 80.
[17]   *Good God*, op. cit., p. 9.
[18]   *God and Human Progress*, op. cit., p. 12.

he summed up this position while talking about the essence of the Church.

> The real essence of the Church lies not in a supposed iner-
> rancy of doctrine, not in Divine authority, but in the member-
> ship of ordinary people, living ordinary lives in the palace, the
> village, the slum. For it is in the haunts of ordinary men that
> God needs men and women who combine ordinary vocations
> and ordinary interests with the extra something which arises
> from faith, which responds to calls of service and to the
> demands for sacrifice, which is never daunted by pain and
> weariness, never despairs, never grows bitter. Of course, not
> all such men are to be found in the churches, and not all the
> churches possess such characteristics. But the Body of Christ
> consists of all of them, wherever they are to be found and its
> membership can be known only to God.[19]

In part, the argument for God found in the ordinary world stemmed from Parkes' belief that revelation is the revelation of the living God to men and women in their personal lives. The idea was present in the 1929 lectures and the early articles, and it was also an important aspect of William Temple's position on revelation. Closely linked to this idea of revelation was the notion that God has a plan for the world and is working to bring it closer to its goal. Thus we return again to the four characteristics listed in the 1929 lectures as essential for a world doing the will of God—the

---

[19] John Hadham, "The God We Believe In," *St. Martin's Review*, 602–607 (April–September 1941), p. 301. Six articles were published as follows: 1. (no. 602, April 1941), pp. 129–31; 2. (no. 603, May 1941), pp. 171–73; 3. (no. 604, June 1941), pp. 211–13; 4. (no. 605, July 1941), pp. 257–59; 5. (no. 606, August 1941), pp. 299–301; 6. (no. 607, September 1941), pp. 341–43. See also John Hadham, "God and the Church," *St. Martin's Review* (August 1942), p. 166 for Parkes' ideas about God's presence in ordinary life. Six articles, with subtitles, were published as follows: 1. "The Church in Perspective" (no. 616, June 1942), pp. 142–43; 2. "The Church and the Christian Civilization" (no. 617, July 1942), pp. 156–57; 3. "The Message of the Church" (no. 619, September 1942), pp. 176–77; 5. "The Worship of the Church—I" (no. 620, October 1942), pp. 192–93; 6. "The Worship of the Church—II" (no. 621, November 1942), pp. 201–02. Second Series, two articles with subtitles, were published as follows: 1. "The Element of Adaptability: The Church in a Revolutionary Period" (no. 631, September 1943), pp. 322–23; 2. "The Element of Stability: The Church in a Revolutionary Period" (no. 632, October 1943): pp. 332–34.

progressive movement toward perfection, fellowship, corporate existence, and a holistic view of human existence. It is here that we also take up the question of God's responsibility to creation, and the issue of Divine–human cooperation in helping to move the world forward toward its intended perfection.

Although Parkes always tried to avoid discussing theology in philosophical terms, he did view the issue of freewill as being crucial to his theology. He argued that God has a plan for the world and that He is working to bring it to fulfillment. It could be asked, "why didn't God just create the world He wanted in the first place? Why go through the agony of failure and setbacks involved in the moving of the world toward its perfection?" Parkes attempted to answer this question when he wrote:

> Since the matter of the world is but the automatic conse-
> quence of the creative thought of God, a perfect "material"
> universe would have automatically come into existence as
> soon as God thought of it. This, however, would obviously
> have been an unsatisfactory activity, for such a world would
> be static and complete in a moment. And even God might find
> it a little tedious to go on continually creating such
> worlds. . . . God, therefore, decided to do something much
> more interesting, although obviously much more difficult and
> dangerous. He managed somehow, not merely to bring mat-
> ter into existence by thinking about it, but to transmit to that
> matter enough of His own vitality for the matter to be able to
> think for itself. In conventional language, he made a world
> with freewill. . . . In the beginning the scope of the freewill
> was extremely limited, as indeed was the matter out of which
> the world was to evolve. But from the first within limits of
> their power, their capacity and their need, the material
> things which he had called into being could play or refuse to
> play, the game which he was devising for them. . . . When
> God gave His thoughts their freewill, he did not at the same
> time give up thinking himself. The world is not the improvisa-
> tion of an audacious molecule of hydrogen. It is the product of
> continual and universal collaboration between thinker and
> thought, between God and His plan and the world which
> slowly grasps, absorbs and fulfills it. . . . That collaboration
> has been going on from the beginning. It is the source of

every development which has led to the fuller use of what God has prepared.[20]

God's intelligence is a divine attribute which Parkes stressed in his theology. In his view, God did not create the world haphazardly, but had a clear purpose and a direction in which He wanted it to move. In addition to this intelligence, Parkes argued for the patience of God as He works with His creation in advancing it towards its desired end. "For just as intelligence is one of the most obvious characteristics of God, so patience is another. More power could have created things all at once. Tremendous patience was needed to see an amoeba evolve over millions of years."[21] In Parkes' view, God's plan for the world is of overriding importance to God, and it sums up God's basic interest in his creation. "God is not concerned," wrote Parkes, "with any other matter except in so far as it leads mankind towards or away from the goal for which he planned it. In this sense, he is ruthless and consistent, without sentimentality and without pity. God knows no 'good old times.'"[22] God's interest in making His plan work out was an important theme in Parkes' theology, and he believed that this led directly to the idea that God is ultimately responsible for His creation and its creatures in their quest toward perfection. "God has an astonishing capacity for getting the best out of the material which, after all, He made quite deliberately and on his own responsibility."[23]

The idea of a responsible God has many ramifications for Parkes' theology. For instance, just how responsible is God for the suffering which human beings experience in their lifetime? This is a particularly pressing question to someone for whom the Holocaust is a deeply troubling event. Parkes never attempted to justify God with arguments that suffering is the result of human sin. He freely admitted that God did not make a safe world. "A most interesting aspect of the character of God is revealed by the fact that He in no way attempted," wrote Parkes, "to make a safe world. He gave a basic and rather incomplete security to life, itself at the cost of pain, but beyond that He was apparently indifferent

---

[20] *Good God*, op. cit., p. 9.
[21] Ibid., p. 74.
[22] Ibid., p. 74.
[23] "God and the Church," op. cit., p. 166.

to the dangers inherent in the products of His imagination."[24] God does not leave creation on its own, and He does take responsibility for the pains of life. "What kind of God would it be that we believed in," wrote Parkes, "if all the suffering, all the sorrow, all the tragedy of the world was to have no better compensation than the kind of individuals mankind is likely to produce in any future that we can yet see?"[25]

A cornerstone in Parkes' theology was the proposition that God takes full responsibility for guiding the world closer to its intended perfection and also for the suffering found in the world. He argued for God's responsibility throughout his writings, and it is a determining factor in any theological thinking for Parkes. As he wrote in *Good God*:

> it seems to me that all theories which, out of false reverence, attempt to minimise the entire responsibility of God for every tragedy in the world's history insult Him rather than do Him honor. No theology can escape the fact that no man ever born asked to be born or was allowed to determine the conditions of his birth. Our freewill only comes into play after the wholly arbitrary act of creating us has been performed. Moreover, it is perfectly clear that hereditary and environment exercise such influences upon each one of us that we do not start square, but with a more or less heavy handicap. Individually, we did not create the past, neither can we change it. The whole and entire responsibility for our existence at all, and for the conditions in which we are individually born, lies with God and not with us. And if He refused to accept, or in any way attempted to evade the full implications of His responsibility, He would not merely be totally unworthy of our admiration or affection, but He would be more unutterably despicable than the most contemptible criminal for whose stupid birth He was wickedly responsible. This is the fact, and any attempt to water it down is an insult both to the realism and the intelligence of God. . . . God's whole title to our unbounded admiration and affection rests on the fact that He

---

[24] *Good God*, op. cit., p. 14.
[25] "The God We Believe In," op. cit., p. 341.

has accepted His responsibility and under terms which men set and in their presence.[26]

The idea of a responsible God who cares not solely for the individuals, but society as well, followed logically from Parkes' concern about Christian theology's traditional emphasis on individuals. He argued consistently against any kind of theology which heads in the direction of "privatization." In a 1942 radio lecture delivered under the name of John Hadham, he went so far as to call the idea that "religion is a private matter" diabolical.[27] Religion is not a matter of private decision, but a way of living in the whole world as a whole person. A human being does not live in a spiritual vacuum, but in society. If a theology is to have any meaning for the whole person, it must address itself to the question of the community as well as to questions of the soul. It must be a theology which takes seriously the responsibility placed on God's shoulders to deal with the problems humans face not just in their personal life, but in their social life as well. Theology also needs to take seriously the idea of God working on the stage of history and affecting all aspects of human life.

Parkes included in his theology the argument for the idea of life after death. He believed this idea clearly indicates God's responsibility to the world and individuals. One is not to be cut off at death from the quest to perfection that God intended from the start. Nor is the world to be left in a state of incompleteness. This idea appears in *Good God* and it reappears as late as 1976 in Parkes' contribution to Simon Wiesenthal's book *The Sunflower*. In *The Sunflower*, he stated his position simply by saying that if one believes in a Creator who is

> "intelligent, responsible, and benevolent in His attitude to creation . . . and if these adjectives, however inadequate they may be, really apply to Him, then I do not see how He can face the responsibility of having endowed His creation with free-will *except* on the basis that He will bring it finally to the perfection for which He designed it. And that is impossible if the space of human life is limited to the experience we pass

---

[26] *Good God*, op. cit., p. 56.
[27] "God and the Church," op. cit., p. 201.

through between physical birth and physical death. I think it is also impossible unless the Creator possesses a moral certainty that He will redeem His whole creation."[28]

Parkes believed that, rather than negating the present as the idea of immortality had done in traditional theology, particularly since the Enlightenment destroyed the medieval superiority of the Church, the idea of immortality carried with it the seed of a theology of the world. This theology is to be built around the idea of God's taking responsibility for His creation.

If one takes Parkes' position of God's concern for all of His creation seriously, this view of his should be no surprise. He rejected out of hand the idea that the world is a "vale of tears" that one should seek to escape. Creation is a positive act of God, and it should not be denigrated by the idea that God has no interest or responsibility for it. It is so important to God that its ultimate redemption and perfection extends beyond physical existence into eternity.

> The detestable view, propagated by certain religious sects and still pervading our hymn books, that the world is a vale of tears and a kingdom of wickedness given over to the rule of the devil, is not merely folly but blasphemy. This world is, always has been, and always will be, *God's* world; and to describe it as a vale of tears after its maker has put it together with infinite prudence and enjoyment is no compliment to Him or His intelligence. . . . In the same way the idea that the interests of God are confined to individuals, and to their souls at that, is not only ridiculous, but is accountable for a good deal of modern irreligion. . . . It is curious how often religious people seem to envisage this as the whole of the intention of God without in the least considering the conceit involved in such a belief. For it has already been made evident that God expended as much thought on the world in which He set the process which should lead to man as He did on man himself. God will not be satisfied until his world reaches its perfect development.[29]

---

[28] Simon Wiesenthal, *The Sunflower*, p. 192.
[29] *Good God*, op. cit., pp. 73–4.

Parkes emphasis on God's responsibility for the world and its salvation helped to influence his views on the nature of God's character and the adjectives that could be used to describe Him. He wanted to discard the traditional attributes of God such as omnipotent, omniscient, and omnipresent in favor of such terms as benevolent, wise, and responsible. This desire was partly due to his belief that one had to speak about God as a personality, and it made sense to talk about God in personal ways easily understood by the ordinary man or woman. Another reason for his desire to talk about God in non-traditional ways stemmed from his belief that God and man were engaged in a cooperative effort in the struggle for achieving perfection in the world. If one was to cling to the traditional descriptions of God, that cooperative effort would appear to be rather one-sided. Parkes goes so far as to say that "the key today is not salvation but cooperation."[30] He believed that until our language about God and His activities reflected this shift in traditional adjectives and a proper appreciation of the Divine–human cooperative venture, the Church would not be able to offer its people any real guidance for the problems they face each day. "We are content to treat God," wrote Parkes, "as though it did not matter very much what we said about, or to Him, so long as it sounded nice or suited some other part of our argument."[31] In light of this problem, he offered this alternative.

> I am sure God would rather that we call Him "Old Mumbo" if it would become natural for one of a Board of Directors facing a difficult decision on the business issue to say, "I wonder what Old Mumbo would like us to do," whereupon all would fall into a lively debate as to how they thought God wanted them to run their business, than that we address Him as Almighty, Everlasting, the King of Kings and Lord of Lords and the rest of it, and then ask Him to do something which we know He has never done, cannot do, and in the last resort, which we do not expect Him to do, at any rate for four or five millenia. The Church is not going to play any part of value in reconstruction until it proclaims God in terms which people

---

[30] *God and Human Progress*, op. cit., p. 84.
[31] "God We Believe In," op. cit., p. 122.

understand and addresses Him in prayers which people feel to be real—and which they both want and *expect* Him to answer.[32]

Parkes reiterated the theme throughout his writings, and he believed that speaking about God in ordinary language was essential to any future theology.

In discussing this issue, Parkes revealed the Modernist influence on his thinking. He believed in the idea of progress. His was not an utopian idea that everything was changing for the better, but the belief that things were changing and theology had to take account of these changes. He certainly appreciated the traditions of the past, and he believed that it was important for people to have deep roots in the past. But he also believed that it was a serious mistake on the part of the Church to always look backwards whenever she was confronted with a new problem. He wrote that "the age which evolved our theology, our liturgies, our hymnologies, and most of our religious thinking is definitely passing. It cannot be brought back, and old formulas cannot be just passed on to a new age—the remark of Jesus very definitely applies to our present generation."[33] The new age demanded that there be an appreciation for a new understanding about God and the needs of man. Parkes offered this insight into the problem:

> The need of man today is for a God in whom they find wisdom, not one whose dominant characteristic is power. We have lost the respect for absolute power which existed in the pre-scientific world, and when we think of power we think in terms of responsibility. Constant appeals for mercy do not meet the deep-seated human need to which they once appealed. The threat of Hell and its counter-part in the appeal of an emotional outpouring of love on the Cross have lost their power because men think differently about human nature and God's responsibility for it. What would make an appeal would be the statement that the Cross involves an out-and-out acceptance of responsibility by God for all the suffering and anguish, the failure and despair in the world which

---

[32] Ibid., p. 130.
[33] Ibid., p. 341.

God made without our consent, and into which He has placed us without our having the power to determine the conditions. This would have far more meaning than the proclamation of a selective redemption of those who believe in Him. Of a God who is wisdom, men naturally ask for guidance more than mercy, and of a God who Himself accepts responsibility for His world they ask courage and endurance to play their part in His world, rather than salvation out of it.[34]

This is an important passage from Parkes' work. It summarizes his views about the need to reject a theology that stressed power and to create a theology which emphasized the wisdom and responsibility of God. Such a move would allow for the kind of cooperation between God and man that Parkes so much desired, and it clearly reflected his idea that God's plan for His creation should have a higher priority in theology than the idea of personal salvation. This idea was present in the 1929 lectures, and it is a cornerstone of his theology in general. Parkes showed here most clearly his Anglican roots, albeit of a Modernist persuasion.

Anglican theology's emphasis on the Incarnation distinguished it from continental theology, which emphasized the concept of redemption. In discussing this issue in relationship to the development of Anglican thought, Arthur Ramsey offered this observation:

> Modern Anglican theology owes many of its characteristics to the central place held within it by the Incarnation. . . . Always somewhat insular in its attitude to continental theology, Anglicanism in these years paid little heed to continental movements and writers, except when they concerned the Person of Christ, in history or dogma. . . . Furthermore, the doctrine of the Incarnate Christ as the Logos gave a constant impulse toward relating the Incarnation, wherever possible, with contemporary movements in thought or social progress.[35]

---

[34] John Hadham, "The Parson in the Pew," *The Listener*, p. 178. The introductory talk in a series of eight (by different speakers) entitled "Worship and Life," broadcast on the BBC Home Service, February 5–April 2, 1943.
[35] Arthur Michael Ramsey, *An Era of Anglican Theology*, p. 27.

Parkes fits this description of Anglican thought, but Ramsey believed that there were problems with this Anglican approach because it often led to a weakened sense of a theology of redemption:

> When the Incarnation is made the centre it easily follows that: (i) *explanation* rather than *atonement* can tend to dominate the theological scene, (ii) that *reason* can depress the place and meaning of *faith* in the approach to revealed truth, (iii) that the giving of prominence to this particular dogma can cause other categories of Biblical language and thought to recede from their rightful prominence. These weaknesses have been alleged in the long-term effects of the Anglican Incarnational theology.[36]

Parkes would not necessarily agree with Ramsey that such developments are bad, but he would certainly support the idea that Incarnational theology was more in tune with the needs of the modern world than the redemptive theology of continental theologians. Evidence of this belief was already present in his 1929 lectures, and it reappears throughout his writings.

A key to understanding this aspect of Parkes' theology lies in his attack on christocentric theology. He had already issued this challenge in 1929, and it became one of the essential features of his theology. It certainly is central in the development of his thinking concerning Jewish–Christian relations. In arguing for a theocentric theology, Parkes is really expressing his continued interest in developing a theology that would embrace the social dimensions of life. He wrote in 1941 that "it is not an artificial distinction, nor is it anti-Christian, to suggest that what men need today is not only Christ but even more God."[37] Parkes believed that the emphasis on Christ in Christian theology created a situation in which personal salvation appeared to be the only thing a Christian was concerned about, and thus it became almost impossible to create any kind of political theology for the Church. The situation after World War I demanded that Christianity

---

[36] Ibid., p. 27.
[37] "The God We Believe In," op. cit., p. 129.

rethink its theology, and in rethinking it, Parkes suggested that a theocentric theology be developed:

> We should weigh with the utmost care the meaning of every word which we address to God. But to do so we must have a very much clearer idea of who God is, what He is doing, and how He does it, than we can get out of the Bible—New Testament and Old. I am no more attacking the Bible in saying this than I am denying Christianity in saying that today we need *God* more than *Christ*. Perhaps it would be fairer to say that we need to bring our understanding of Christ; and that we need to bring our understanding of God up to the level we have reached in our understanding of the revelation God has been giving us in history, in economics, in sociology, in medicine, in psychology, up to the level of our knowledge of His revelation in the Bible.[38]

We can see once again in this passage the strong influence of Modernist thinking on Parkes. He never moved too far from this position, and as late as 1973, he was still arguing that "the world had collapsed around us because we have interpreted the relation between Creator and creation exclusively in christocentric terms."[39]

This position does carry with it a weakened theology of redemption but, unlike Ramsey, Parkes does not think this is so terrible a thing. Redemptive theology contained the idea that one had to be saved "out" of this world. For Parkes, this was no longer what man needed or what the Church should be teaching. People needed help to live in the world, not escape plans:

> The emphasis on salvation almost wholly disappeared. Men had no desire to be saved "out of" the world, but to be guided to live in it, and to learn to control it. And the idea of salvation was so bound up with the selection of the saved from a general mass who would not be saved that it was in evident conflict with new ideas of the ultimate responsibility of God for the

---

[38] Ibid., p. 130.
[39] James Parkes, "Tomorrow and all our Yesterdays," *Common Ground* vol. 27, no. 3 (autumn 1973), pp. 25–9.

whole of His creation. Just as the possession of a piano became stupid, if one were not musical, as soon as everybody could have a piano, so the idea of struggling for the purpose of being saved became meaningless when God was realised to be responsible for "saving" everyone whom He had created.[40]

Parkes realized that this position had unmistakable ramifications for other traditional Christian teachings. He saw that the shift to theocentric theology meant that one had to rethink the meaning of the life and death of Jesus. He rejected, along with Modernists like Hastings Rashdall, the idea that the forgiveness of sins is linked in any way to the death of Jesus.[41] He wrote of the responsibility of God and the role of Jesus:

> This in turn led to discoveries about the meaning of the life and death of Jesus of Nazareth. To many, of course, it reduced His significance entirely, and they found no reason to complicate their minds with arguments for his divinity. But this was not the general Christian experience. While the sentimental language about God "giving" or "sending" His only son was realised to be picture talk of a very different and primitive society, the idea of God coming into His world as the final expression and communication of His responsibility for it, was readily accepted as the crown of the idea of God as Personality. Without it the personal relation which was the heart of the conception of Divine–human collaboration in the perfection of the magnificent adventure of creation, would have been only imperfectly fulfilled.[42]

Parkes argued consistently that the importance of Jesus Christ could be understood correctly only against the backdrop of God's greater plan for creation. He rejected the exclusive language that accompanied traditional Christian theology which claimed that salvation only came through Christ. Such a position only confused ordinary people in his opinion, and it gave undue emphasis to

---

[40] John Hadham, "Faith and Institutions," p. 13. Copy on file at the Parkes Library, University of Southampton, England.
[41] Hastings Rashdall, *Ideas and Ideals*, p. 146.
[42] "Faith and Institutions," op. cit., p. 13.

personal salvation. "It is not and never had been," he wrote, "that men could approach the Godhead only through Jesus Christ."[43]

However valuable its expression in genealogical terms may have been in past history, it is doubtful whether we need today the constant emphasis on an "only son" or "God sending His only son," or approach to God "through the Son."[44]

Parkes objected to the christocentric emphasis on other grounds as well. His interest in religion and politics led him to the conclusion in 1929 that Christianity could not offer any valuable guidance in political affairs as long as it stressed personal salvation as its primary religious goal. In his view, christocentric theology was the source of the Church's failure to speak out clearly on political issues. He wrote that "it has been true throughout the Christian story that when the action which is required has passed from the personal to the impersonal—as all political acts must pass—the Churches have hesitated, faltered, and given that uncertain sound which is no summons to battle."[45] The world after World War I required more action on the political front than the Church seemed capable of offering as long as it clung stubbornly to its traditional view of Christ and salvation theology. The modern world demanded a new sort of theology which took seriously the basic relations between "an intelligent and responsible Creator and this complex creation (which He has made capable of understanding his challenge and responding to it)."[46] Parkes took this to mean that Christianity needed to look beyond its own parochial interpretations and relate itself to God's broader plan for salvation that was revealed, not only in the Christ event, but in other revelatory events as well. In order to do this, he developed a particular view of the Trinity that he called

---

[43] James Parkes, *God at Work in Science: Politics and Human Life*, p. 88.
[44] Ibid., p. 88.
[45] Ibid., p. 134.
[46] James Parkes, "Judaism and Christianity," *European Judaism* vol. 13, no. 1 (autumn 1979), p. 35. See also James Parkes, "A New Approach to the Doctrine of the Trinity," January 1951. Copy on file at the Parkes Library, Southampton, England, unpublished and James Parkes, "An Economic Trinitarianism," January 1964. Copy on file at the Parkes Library, Southampton, England.

"Economic Trinitarianism," and this view is distinctive to Parkes. Indeed, it sheds light on the development of his ideas on Jewish–Christian relations.

Parkes shared a view prevalent in Anglican theology that the Trinity provided a valuable tool for relating God to the social aspects of life. Parkes went a bit further with his own conception of the Trinity in arguing that the Trinity had a parallel in the threefold role which man has in his life. The Trinity is actually the basis of his anthropology, and here also he found support for his argument against christocentric theology. He developed his argument by describing God's activity in the world as being threefold, and then relating that to man's threefold function. From there, he argued that the Church made a serious mistake by overemphasizing the second "person" of the Trinity over the other two "persons." That is, he believed that Christianity had not fully appreciated the role of God the Creator and Holy Spirit. The Church's miserable failure in political affairs stemmed, in his view, from this lack of appreciation.

The first thing Parkes tried to do in reinterpreting the Trinity was to substitute the term "channel" for "persons" in describing the activity of God in the world.[47] He believed that the Trinity helped to explain the three modes of God's activity in the world, and he wrote that "the whole conception of God as Person will at times appear a barrier to a true understanding of the nature of the power behind the world."[48] He also believed that the traditional interpretation of the Trinity did not account for the full scope of God's power, and he again attacked christocentric thinking for being at the root of the problem:

> Today the Church in both thought and its liturgy is almost exclusively christocentric. The other members of the Trinity are thought of in terms of functions delegated to or by them, in relation to a central figure of Christ, and not in terms of separate modes of divine activity.[49]

---

[47] "Judaism and Christianity," op. cit., p. 30.
[48] *God at Work*, op. cit., p. 141.
[49] Ibid., p. 164.

This in turn has led the Church to ignore the truths involved in the other key revelations of God's power in the world. Parkes wanted to revise the current thinking about the Trinity so that "all three persons are co-eternal together and co-equal. No essential difference is made in this affirmation by speaking of modes of divine activity instead of persons."[50] One could understand this properly by referring to Sinai, Calvary, and Humanism.[51] Parkes believed that this particular trinitarian scheme helped to establish a proper relationship between the Creator and His creation, and thus made it easier to speak about the ways God operated in the world.

He related this scheme of divine activity to human experience by talking about the three basic characteristics of human life. Parkes believed that each human being experienced life as a social being, an individual, and a seeker of truth. A proper understanding of God's modes of activity in the world helped to show how God had offered help to His people in their quest to live a meaningful life. Given this idea, Parkes found himself at odds with Christian tradition:

> The dilemma in which the churches find themselves today arises from their attempt to force man's two functions as members of the community, and searcher, into the mold which the tradition and experience they have developed for man as person. They proclaim Christ as the answer to every question; they absorb the experience of the Old Testament into the status of preliminary to the New; they almost wholly leave aside the full implications of the doctrine of the triple personality of God which is the product of centuries of their own puzzled thinking.[52]

The Church's attempt to force this situation led to its inability to deal with issues that go beyond the strictly personal issues of life. As long as Christian theology remained christocentric, Parkes saw no way out of the dilemma. He did not want to deny the

---

[50] Ibid., p. 65.
[51] Ibid., p. 148–49.
[52] James Parkes, "God and His Creation," unpublished, April 1950, p. 2. Copy on file at the Parkes Library, Southampton, England.

Christian experience or the importance of Christ in the Christian life, but he did want to argue that Christian theology needed to take a more holistic approach to God's activity and begin to learn from other experiences.

> The tragedy of Christian history is its attempt to make the second revelation override the first and third. It is not a question of challenging in any way the validity of its experience of the revelation of the Incarnation and the Cross, on which it has concentrated. But Judaism has preserved the first, and we still need to learn it from the Jews; and the third we all need to consider together. While we must preserve the identity of the three modes of action, Christian as well as Jewish, experience and the present horror of scientists themselves at what they have done, warn us that the three have to be held together in a creative balance, as indissolubly one in quality and purpose as we believe to be the triune nature of God. Only then shall we begin to see the answer to the world's needs[53]

There are a number of issues in this argument about the Trinity. The influence of the Modernist belief in progress is clear. He firmly believed that "the stages of God's revelation once achieved are never lost."[54] This belief helped him to see God working to move His creation toward its intended perfection, never resting on past events or achievements alone, but always making use of what happened in the past. In this way, he was able to maintain a belief in progress without rejecting tradition in its entirety. His view of the Trinity also showed how he had come to accept the idea of evolution as a theological principal. He stated clearly that "the assertions contained in *The Origins of Species*, that creation showed a single continuous evolution from the simplest forms of life to man himself, should have been welcomed as a revelation both of the skill of the Creator and the unity of the whole creation."[55] We can see here again themes that were present in the 1929 lectures. Moreover, Parkes' trinitarian

---

[53] Ibid., p. 4.
[54] *Good God*, op. cit., p. 92.
[55] *God at Work*, op. cit., p. 117.

scheme provided a theological underpinning for the idea of human interdependence.

At this point we need to look at Parkes' theology of politics, as it were, to find the key to his trinitarian scheme.

As early as 1929, Parkes was already talking about politics, theology, and the Trinity. This was still a concern for him in 1974 when he once again coupled these concerns. In reviewing the world situation, he saw two failures that seriously threatened human survival. First, he had lived through two world wars, the Holocaust, and the unleashing of nuclear warfare. Second, he saw the advance of science and technology depleting the world's resources, while they polluted the earth, the air, and the sea. In the face of all this, he saw Christianity unable to offer any serious response to these political issues apart from ambulance work during the war. This may be a worthy endeavor, but it was hardly adequate to the problems at hand.

> It seems to me not unreasonable to set this position alongside the religious picture of the determinably christocentric Gospel, which has consistently ignored the realities of politics on one side and economics and technology on the other. There are, of course, Christians concerned with the political, economic, and scientific life, but I would maintain that there is no adequate theology to guide them. For the basic discipline involved in religion and politics are different: Christianity rests on love. Politics rests on justice and righteousness. The ultimate sanction in the use of the world's resources is truth. Put in another way, politics rests on knowing the attainable, but neither love nor a democratic vote will tell me whether my industrial activity is poisoning the river that runs beside my factory.[56]

In Chapter 1, we mentioned Parkes' affinity to Reinhold Niebuhr on a number of issues, and we can see here on understanding of the relationship between love and justice, and politics and religion that one finds in much of Niebuhr. Parkes believed that it was the traditional christocentric theology of the church that impairs its ability to deal with the political situation of the modern

---

[56] "Judaism and Christianity," op. cit., 1979, p. 35.

world. This was, in large measure, the reason he disliked the theology of Karl Barth. His concern with this issue developed early in his career, and it was not directly linked to his interest in Judaism. However, as Parkes discovered more about the genius of Judaism, he began to see how Judaism offered something that Christianity and its christocentric theology lacked:

> As I studied the post-Christian growth of Judaism I realised that what I was hearing about was a religion different from Christianity, with a different discipline of living. Unquestionably, it is this which has been responsible for the survival of the Jewish people, not, as Toynbee once asserted, just as a fossil, but as an extremely dynamic and adaptable society. . . . This challenged and indeed overthrew my previous acceptance of the culmination of the spiritual development of society as being a christocentric divine–human relationship. For I was sufficiently concerned with politics to see that it is precisely this concreteness, this sense of the attainable, which is missing in the Christian approach, but which is essential for any realistic understanding of the political situation. In the same way I realised one must face the lack of concern with truth in accepting standards and opinions. So I was launched on the path to a Trinitarian picture of the relations of the Creator to His creation. For here is the religion out of which Christianity had grown but which Christianity has clearly not superseded. Sinai is as permanent as Calvary in the divine activity within creation. The interesting question is, what is the divinely intended relation between the two equals [?].[57]

Parkes' concern with theology and politics began when he entered Oxford in 1919, and for many years, he tried to develop a theology which could adequately deal with the relationship between the two disciplines. His work on Judaism was undertaken rather separately from this specific concern. So much so that he even used a *nom de plume* in order to keep his two lines of work from being confused. Yet he finally came to the realization that

---

[57] Ibid., p. 36.

what he was learning about Judaism answered some of the very questions he was dealing with in his work on Christian theology. In a rather bold move, he decided that he needed to discover a way in which to think about God so that both Judaism and Christianity could contribute what they could to our understanding about God and His plan for the world. Here his Modernist background enabled him to think anew about traditional ideas without fearing the loss of his own Christian faith. The foundation for his ideas about Jewish–Christian relations was laid at this point.

Another issue was Parkes' interpretation of Jesus Christ. His demand for a theocentric theology meant that certain traditional ideas about Christ would have to be discarded. This had implications for his views on Jewish–Christian relations since the question of the messiahship of Jesus has been the central point of debate between Christians and Jews. In his trinitarian scheme, he already raised questions about traditional interpretations of the Christ event, and he boldly stated that one does not need to go through Jesus to reach God. What then did he think about Jesus of Nazareth and his role in God's plan for the world? Parkes interpretation of the meaning of the life of Jesus of Nazareth was closely related to his understanding of Christianity as a channel through which God revealed Himself as a Person concerned with the individual man. Without realizing this fact, it is extremely difficult to understand the role Jesus played in Parkes' theology. While he did view Jesus as being central to any interpretation of Christianity, the christology which results from his interpretation is quite weak in comparison to such theologians as Karl Barth or Wolfhart Pannenburg. In order to correctly understand Parkes on this issue, one must keep in mind the backdrop of his trinitarian interpretation of God's mode of activity in the world.

Parkes was a historian as well as a theologian, and he was always concerned with relating Jesus and his message to the historical environment in which he lived. He took seriously the fact that Jesus was born, raised, and died a Jew. Jesus was circumcised, studied at the synagogue, was bar mitzvahed, and read and preached in synagogues. The Synoptic accounts relate how Jesus was asked many times to come and preach to the people in the synagogue. Jesus' family and the people he grew up with were all Jews, part of the *am ha'aretz*, the common people of the land.[58] Knowledge of these facts are important because they help one to avoid the mistaken idea that Jesus was always in opposition to Judaism. Concern for historical facts about Jesus' life also counters those interpretations that would make the life of Jesus so cosmic in nature that it loses all its grounding in human existence and experience. Parkes consequently took particular issue with Barth when he wrote that "Jesus came on the plane of ordinary history, and in the fulness of time—our time, the time of history."[59]

Parkes was also concerned with relating the message of Jesus to its proper historical context. Much has been written about the hostility between Jesus and the Pharisees, and how Jesus offered a new religious viewpoint, entirely different from that offered by the Pharisees. Parkes did not deny that there were tensions between Jesus and some Pharisees, but he did not believe that the tension should be seen as an argument between enemies. With Jesus reported as preaching in the synagogues, we can assume that Jesus had fairly close ties with the Pharisees simply because their domain was the synagogue. Likewise, Jesus' concern for the common people and their religious life is also similar to the concerns of the Pharisees. There was a difference, however, between the two. One finds Jesus calling upon the people to view their spiritual intuition as being of central importance, while the Pharisees believed in bringing men to God by the continuous inculcation of habits which continually remind them of God's presence.[60] But the difference was more of emphasis than substance. Parkes argued "that Jesus did not think of his teaching as being a new Torah in opposition to, or destructive of, the old is shown by two passages whose authenticity is guaranteed, Matthew 5:17 and 23:2."[61] If one looks carefully at Jesus' teaching and the teachings of the Pharisees, one finds little disagreement on the basic doctrines concerning God and man, repentence and forgiveness, and other important doctrines.[62] The arguments

---

[58] James Parkes, *The Foundation of Judaism and Christianity*, p. 165.
[59] Ibid., p. 148.
[60] James Parkes, *Judaism and Christianity*, p. 64.
[61] *The Foundations of Judaism and Christianity*, op. cit., p. 158.
[62] *God at Work*, op. cit., p. 90.

between Jesus and the Pharisees are real, but Parkes believed that they had to be seen as infighting between two similar schools of thought with different emphases concerning the meaning of religious life. The Pharisees stressed the community and its religious habits, while Jesus came down more strongly on the side of the individual and his religious habits. It should also be kept in mind that the hostile picture of the Pharisees in the New Testament reflects more the tension between the early Church and the Pharisees than between Jesus and the Pharisees.[63] It is the centrality of man as person in Jesus' message which Parkes used as a key concept for his interpretation of both Christ and Christianity. As Parkes understood it, the message of Jesus offers to man as person full communion with God as person.[64]

According to Parkes' trinitarian scheme, the divine power which flowed from Sinai continues to help direct man as a social being, and it revealed God as being concerned with that aspect of man's existence. He then argued that "as a Christian, I believe that Power flows to the same extent from the life of Jesus of Nazareth."[65] That Power in this case is directed at man as person, and it revealed God as being concerned with man in that aspect of existence. The Gospels themselves are concerned with proclaiming a message about a person—Jesus of Nazareth—whom they believe to be the Messiah.[66] It is with this particular emphasis in mind that Parkes developed his interpretation of the Cross and the Incarnation.

For Parkes, the Cross and the Incarnation are interrelated because it is on the Cross that he finds the ultimate meaning of the Incarnation. He referred to the Incarnation with the phrase, God-in-human-life, that life being Jesus of Nazareth. By living within a human environment, God was able to see for Himself that man could obey His will and strive for the ultimate possibility of human perfection.[67] However, the fact that man could not easily do so also meant that God had to answer this difficult question: "Things

---

[63] Ibid., p. 90.

[64] Ibid., p. 91.

[65] James Parkes and Maurice Eisendrath, *Jewry and Jesus of Nazareth*, p. 15.

[66] *God and Human Progress*, op. cit., p. 16.

[67] *Good God*, op. cit., p. 54.

have gone wrong. Can I still put them right without violating the conditions under which I made the world?"[68] Thus God, while seeing that it is possible to live a righteous life, also felt a responsibility to provide the means of salvation for those who failed. Failure and the sense of separation from God become the essential key in God's attempt to see at what point He was unable to reach man. Thus, on the Cross, God was put to a crucial test.

The life of Jesus represented for Parkes a life of complete reliance upon God. It is because of this that the failure of the Cross represents such a great betrayal of God toward His faithful servant. Parkes boldly states that "with more justification than any human being ever born, he (Jesus) might 'curse God and die.'"[69] The failure of God to be able to redeem His faithful servant from the failure of the Cross would have meant that God's experiment in a human life had failed, and that man could get himself into a position beyond God's reach. However, Parkes interpreted the Cross as follows:

> On the Cross, God proved to Himself that He was able to accept this responsibility because He had touched by His own experience the lowest depths of human despair and failure; had realised the full meaning of human opposition; and had discovered that there was no depth to which man could fall which was beyond His reach. God had won. . . . The answer is the mysterious "Resurrection," an event which is *almost* objectively proved by the historical fact of the change in the disciples between the evening of Good Friday and Easter Sunday: but which just avoids wrecking the whole adventure by a solution which is again as simple and skillful as the manner in which he entered human life.[70]

Parkes viewed the victory of the Resurrection as providing a bridge between man and God, a "personal union."[71] In revealing Himself in this personal way, another stage in God's revelation scheme was completed. Whereas Sinai had revealed the *activity* of

---

[68] Ibid., p. 55.
[69] Ibid., p. 60.
[70] Ibid., pp. 61–63.
[71] *God at Work*, op. cit., p. 95.

an intensely personal God, Calvary revealed the *personality* of the same intensely personal God.[72] In Parkes' terms, Sinai views God as Ruler, but Christianity sees God as Person.[73]

> In this concern with man as person, nothing is taken away from the power or meaning of the working out in history of the revelation of Sinai. But, if that be true, it is equally true that something is added. . . . Now another stage was reached in the full unfolding of the extent of divine–human co-operation when, within the Sinaitic community and in "the fullness of time," God could similarly reveal the full meaning of man as person, and Jesus of Nazareth stepped on to the stage of history. This did not replace Sinai, nor could, on the other hand, Sinai simply absorb it and continue unchanged. It did not contradict Sinai, but in the life and teaching of Jesus the revelation and the new revelation stand together in creative tension.[74]

The new dimension of God which was introduced by Calvary involved the idea of Atonement, that is, divine acceptance of responsibility for the sins and suffering of man. As Parkes understood it, this introduced an aspect of God which was not of concern to the Jewish tradition. The idea that God is merciful and forgiving is not foreign to Judaism, despite the commonplace and incorrect belief that the God of the Old Testament is vengeful, while the God of the New Testament is loving. Rather, the point of difference is the Christian idea that it cost God something to be merciful and forgiving. Such a concept meant the introduction of a theological system that Judaism never possessed or cared to cultivate. The Cross represents God-in-a-human-life who must suffer in order to find the means of redemption for fallen man. This raises the problematic concept of Jesus Christ being both human and divine, a concept traditionally dealt with in the idea of the Trinity.

Parkes believed that it was essential that Christians emphasize neither one nor the other, but rather accept the paradox involved.

---

[72] Ibid., p. 100.
[73] Ibid., p. 94.
[74] *The Foundations of Judaism and Christianity*, op. cit., p. 130.

Without giving up the concept of God the Father and Creator, the Christian must also see God as a Person who lived in the world as an individual.[75] Through this experience and paradox, one sees new dimensions of God's love and mercy and their relationship to human life. It is through this paradoxical view of Jesus' life that man can see both his possibilities to live according to God's will, and at the same time, see God's love and mercy directed toward him if and when he should fail. Man is thus able to strive toward what he should be without fear of failure since the victory over the failure of the Cross shows that he is never beyond the reach of God. It is, for Parkes, God's experiment as a God-in-human-life that has made this possible.

In light of all this, Parkes accepted the Christian claim that Jesus was the Messiah, but with a qualification. Parkes' interest in Jewish history and tradition made him aware of the differences between Jewish messianic expectations and the life of Jesus. As far as he was concerned, Christians were mistaken to expect Jews to accept Jesus as the Messiah or to argue that he fulfilled Jewish expectations of the Messiah.

> Jesus was not the Messiah as envisioned by the prophets. . . . There is one basic difference from the reality of the Incarnation. No prophet envisaged a Messiah who would be rejected by his own people, or would depend for recognition on the personal surrender of each of his followers.[76]

He also adopted the thesis that Jesus had little, if any, messianic consciousness. Parkes took seriously the finding of biblical critics, and he viewed the claims that Jesus makes of being the Messiah as being later insertions on the part of the Gospel authors: "I do not, for example, take as words actually spoken by Jesus those, especially in St. John's Gospel, in which Jesus declares openly he is the Messiah and Son of God. These words are the authors' interpretations."[77] Parkes understood why the early Church felt the need to fit Jesus into the messianic expectations of the Hebrew

---

[75] *Good God*, op. cit., p. 44.
[76] *The Foundations of Judaism and Christianity*, op. cit., p. 145.
[77] John Hadham, *Common Sense About Religion*, p. 88. See also *Jewry and Jesus of Nazareth*, p. 20.

scriptures, given the debate that was going on between the Church and the Synagogue over the question of Jesus' messianic title. In his view, however, an honest examination of Jewish expectations, even apocalyptic expectations, revealed a great difference between Christian claims and Jewish claims. One clear difference between the two concerned the political overtones of the Jewish expectations. These overtones are missing in Christian claims, and they are frequently criticized by Christian writers. Thus it is, as Parkes said, difficult to fit the career of Jesus into the traditional forms "of messianic expectations."[78]

Parkes' attempt to see more clearly how Jesus does or does not fit into the messianic prophesies was not an attempt on his part to dismantle the Church's claims for Jesus. Rather, it was an attempt to more clearly understand what it is about Jesus that makes it possible for Christians to make any such claims at all. It was here that he turned to St. Paul for an understanding of the claim that Jesus was the Messiah. "Almost all the permanent value of Paul lies in the four words, 'new life in Christ'," wrote Parkes[79] Here again we can see the stress on the *personal* aspect of Christianity about which Parkes is so keen. Paul's mystical interpretation of Christ is an accurate one as far as Parkes is concerned. "To Paul," he wrote, "the Christ Jesus reconciling God and man was part of the very structure of creation. It is not something imposed from without at a moment in history, it was part of the very web of history,"[80] It is the emphasis of Atonement—reconciliation—which represents a point of agreement between Paul and Parkes. For Parkes, "the Atonement does not bring Christ into the centre of New Testament theology. That is always God, and distinguished from whatever title is ascribed to Christ. But it is by Atonement that we have access to the Father."[81]

Parkes was also very concerned with the question of the damnation of those who do not believe Jesus to be the Messiah. On this issue he took a completely Modernist position, and he rejected out

---

[78] The Foundations of Judaism and Christianity, op. cit., p. 149.
[79] *Jewry and Jesus of Nazareth*, op. cit., p. 17.
[80] *The Foundations of Judaism and Christianity*, op. cit., p. 220.
[81] Ibid., p. 220.

of hand the idea of Eternal punishment in Hell for those who have not been "saved." He found this particular tradition of the Christian Church to be most offensive. He also found it to be a stumbling block for Jewish–Christian relations, and it was the source for many of his battles with missionary groups. Parkes found it very strange for the Church to preach about Jesus as a man of love and compassion, and then teach that anyone not believing in Jesus as the Messiah would burn in Hell. He found it particularly disappointing that so much of the New Testament confirmed this distasteful belief. He wrote that "one had to admit that the New Testament, while it demands of man that he should love his enemies, contains few examples of the manifestations of that love toward either Pharisees or Judaizers, the enemies *par excellence* of the first century Christians."[82] Parkes was concerned that Christians used the "Good News" of the Gospel of Jesus Christ, not to start life anew, but to condemn those who do not believe as they do. The fact that Christians have been unable to come to terms with the universal truths of Christianity without understanding that this does not mean that only one interpretation is possible was a serious failure of the Church and her teachings in the mind of Parkes.[83] He argued consistently for a more dynamic view of God's revelation in history, and he steadfastly refused to limit the knowledge of God to one revelatory event alone. This reflected his Modernist sympathies, and it was a crucial factor in his attempt to write a new theology of Jewish–Christian relations. The condemnation of people who do not believe in Jesus ignores both the message of Jesus and the power of God to save all men. Parkes believed that theology must always struggle against ideas about faith and salvation that are narrow, static, and self-righteous.

In Parkes' theology, Jesus is always a reconciler of men, not a divider. The horrendous doctrines that make some people sheep and others goats condemned to Hell, had no place in the theological thinking of James Parkes. Jesus may well have been the most influential man in history as far as Parkes was concerned, but he

---

[82] James Parkes, *Prelude to Dialogue*, p. 194.
[83] Ibid., p. 176.

was not the end of history. In summing up his views, Parkes wrote:

> This terrible doctrine caused Christian theologians to lay a unique emphasis on the punishments of Hell. It was the authority for every form of intolerance, and the Inquisition justified itself by the belief that the tortures which it imposed in this life might save its victims from worse and more lengthy tortures in the world to come. In modern times a whole theology has been developed, binding the figure of Jesus himself in the bondage of apocalyptic eschatology, whereas any survey of his significance in Christian history makes it evident that he is a "seminal" figure and in no sense an "eschatal" one. He initiated much, he terminated nothing.[84]

The idea that Jesus was a seminal figure rather than an eschatal figure also reflected his Modernist sympathies. Such an idea left open the possibility of new interpretations of the life and death of Jesus Christ, of further revelations of God to the world. This position does not deny the significance of the life of Jesus, but it does place it within the wider context of God's overall plan for the perfection of creation. If we turn now from Jesus to Parkes' ideas about the nature of the Church, we can see a similar application of Modernist ideas.

In his autobiography, Parkes wrote that as a boy he always preferred the simple "low Church" country parish service to the "high Church" city parish service. His mature thoughts on the nature of the Church reflected a continued appreciation for simplicity, and a view of the Church that caused some critics of John Hadham to ask, "why do you always leave out the Church, or denounce it, or make fun of it?"[85] This kind of criticism was frequently leveled at Parkes because his view of the Church included no false sentimentality, and he was often very critical of the Church's stances on many issues. This criticism arose from a

---

[84] James Parkes, *Religious Experience and the Perils of Its Interpretation*, (the Ninth Montefiore Lecture (Southampton: the University of Southampton, 1972), p. 11.
[85] "The God We Believe In," op. cit., p. 299.

deep-seated love of the Church and his hope that the Church would begin to face up to the challenges of the modern age. The Modernist approach that Parkes took toward theology was carried over to his writings on the Church, and his thoughts on the nature of the church can be read as a Modernist challenge to traditional ecclesiology.

For Parkes, the Church was a distinctly human institution with a divine mission, and one was not to confuse the two. He believed that the Church was a product of organic growth, rooted in the three civilizations of Greece, Rome and most particularly, Israel. He argued that the "Church is creative when its blood is flowing through the body of a civilisation."[86] In light of this intimate connection between the Church and civilization, Parkes believed that one could only understand the real nature of the Church by appeal to historical facts and not to theological fancy. He wrote in *St. Martin's Review*:

> One thing is certain, that no claim can be made on behalf of the Church which has to take refuge in mystical evasion of ascertainable facts. And certain facts *are* ascertainable. Jesus left a body of Jewish disciples, to whom he gave [the] command to spread his teaching. They were loyal members within the body of Judaism. The Church as a separate institution does not ever emerge in apostolic times—only a body of Jews (and their Gentile converts) who were distinguished from other Jews (and Gentile converts) by their belief that the Messiah had come and was to be identified with Jesus of Nazareth, and who lived, quarrelled, and fought out their controversies within the broad bosom of the Synagogue.[87]

Parkes believed that a proper view of the Church's organic, historical roots prevented one from using language that attributed to the Church qualities it did not possess. He was particularly critical of ideas that made the Church the sole receptor of Truth, "the Bride of Christ," infallible, and above all, immune from human criticism. This he stated clearly and often:

---

[86] "God and the Church,"op. cit., p. 5.
[87] "The God We Believe In," op. cit., p. 299.

Moreover, since the beginning of our independent career, the Church has constantly been wrong in matters of faith, of morals, and of practice. The history of the Church carries no proof of inerrancy, and the use of such phrases as the Bride of Christ or Body of Christ to convey the idea of the possession of absolute truth and superhuman authority by any existing ecclesiastical organisation is the language not of mysticism but of emotional sentimentalism. It is unlikely that the world will ever be impressed by such phrases again.[88]

Parkes realized that his approach to the nature of the Church would prove problematic to many within the Church. There seemed inherent in his position an attack on the very foundation of the Church and a serious challenge to its authority. Yet he insisted that the Church was and remains a human institution, and, therefore, subject to all the ambiguities of the human condition. He defended his view:

Historically all the institutions of the Churches are human; all their formulations are liable to error and, at best, are transitory; their members are no better than they should be; as vested interests they rightly move men to every emotion save those of admiration or respect; their capacity for hypocrisy is unique; their self deception appears limitless. Do they matter? Should we be better without them? The answer lies between the emotionalism of the Christian apologist, and the equally emotional extremism of the rationalist or Marxian denouncer.[89]

Parkes' criticisms of the Church were those of one who deeply loved the Church, but who was concerned about its future. His voice was that of a prophet from within who sought to awaken the Church from its complacency, and there was no desire on his part to destroy it. He appreciated the Church's task to teach the world about God, but he believed its efforts fell short of the mark. In urging the Church back to a proper course, Parkes' Modernist sympathies are most evident:

---

[88] Ibid., p. 300.
[89] Ibid., p. 300.

> The message of the Church is a message about God—who He
> is, what He is doing, and what offers men and wants from
> them. It must always revolve about the two basic realities—
> the unchanging God and the changing contemporary scene.
> Eternity and the present movement are the two ultimate
> realities of the world. It is the task of the Church to make each
> real in its intimate relation to the other.[90]

Parkes believed that the Church could meet its challenge only by
a constant renewal of its message in the light of new knowledge
and discoveries. In this regard, he saw a distinct similarity
between the Church and the State, both of whom he believed had
a responsibility to win souls *into* the world, not out of it. Here
again he was arguing against the idea that the Church could be
"other-worldly," even in regard to its most important mission:

> All the distinctions between a divine Church and a human
> State are inherently false. But they have different, if recipro-
> cal tasks. The task of the Church is indeed [the] winning of
> souls, but the winning of them *into*, not out of the world. The
> interests of the Church and State are in this matter identical,
> but again they express them differently. The division is not
> between this world and the next, between the needs of the
> soul and the body. It is the difference in methods of tackling
> the same problems, and that problem is the creation of a
> civilisation in which the human beings God has created
> advance, if only a little, along the path to perfection which
> God has designed for them. . . . The source of all power is God;
> every step taken by the State is as much His concern as every
> action of the Church.[91]

We can see in this statement of Parkes a repetition of a number
of themes first presented in the 1929 lectures. He again attacked
the notion of "other-worldly" theology, and he made a case for the
Church to be concerned with social and communal issues. He saw
the Church as giving guidance to men and women in the world
they lived in every day. True, the Church had to be concerned

---

[90] "God and the Church,"op. cit., p. 9.
[91] Ibid., p. 6.

about God and divine things, but, faithful to his Modernist roots, he did not think that this contradicted the idea of the Church relating its message to everyday issues. To do this, however, the Church had to always renew its message. In this sense, he believed the State did a better job, and he urged the Church to take a lesson from the State. The very question of renewal also raised questions about the amount of truth the Church could claim for itself.

> But the Church and State need constantly to renew their programme and their message. The State realised this more frequently than the Church. For the fact that the message of the Church is concerned with the eternal verities of the nature of God and men led the Church into believing that her interpretation of these verities is itself unchanging. She ignores the fact that every fresh discovery, every fresh theory about human life and society, every political or philosophical dictum is, from her point of view, a statement, even if a totally wrong statement, about the nature and the activities of God, and needs most careful consideration in relation to her existing pronouncements on the particular subject concerned. That is the main trouble with the Churches today. Several centuries which God has filled fuller of revelation of Himself than almost any other period of human history, have been almost entirely ignored by her, and now when she is dimly aware that something is wrong, she can only meet it by a passionate urge to "go back." But the world will not go back.[92]

Parkes had no illusions about the difficulty in implementing in the Church the mechanism for constant renewal. He knew full well that humankind was basically conservative, and they were most conservative in matters of religion. He reflected the influence of his teacher, Cyril Emmet, when he wrote:

> The necessity for the constant renewal of the message of the Church poses a most difficult problem of method, a problem which the Church bodies have not even faced, let alone

---

[92] Ibid., p. 9.

solved. It is one of the most urgent problems before this generation, for private liberties of prophesying is no effective substitute for a public and responsible constant review and renewal of life. We have totally forgotten the speed with which the heresy of yesterday became the orthodoxy of today in the creative centuries of Christian theology.[93]

Parkes believed that the Church's failure to respond to new ideas and needs ran the risk of violent reform. Like a good Modernist, he believed that

God's revelation and human experience will not stand still; and the evils of a doctrine become ossified, and of a reform become violent, are so evident, and are writ so large on the pages of the Christian tradition, that it is worth any effort to find ways in which the values of its millenial tradition can be combined in a living reality with the changing needs and demands of an ever opening vista."[94]

Parkes had his own ideas about what pitfalls the Church should avoid and what objections it should pursue. He listed three problems the Church should avoid:

1. Satisfying itself with freedom of discussion in irresponsible self-aeration, as did the philosophic schools of Greece.
2. Attempting to run the civil society itself, attaching legal sanctions to all the moral duties it proclaims, and giving an exaggerated religious authority to apparently necessary political maneuvers as do pure theocracies such as that of Calvin.
3. Detaching itself from public life and the movements of intellectual and civic development surrounding it, as did the Lutheran Church.[95]

He knew that it would be no easy task "to find a course between the pitfalls, but such must be the aim of a Church which desires to present a truly living Gospel"[96] He did have some ideas of his own

---

[93] Ibid., p. 10.
[94] Ibid., pp. 12–13.
[95] Ibid., p. 11.
[96] Ibid., p. 11.

for meeting this problem, and he offered the following list of objectives for the Church:

1. The first necessity is a network of men who are so situated (both geographically and economically) that they can reach the whole population and offer them regular religious leadership and instruction. A church which is not a teaching church is useless (N.B. *uplift* is not a synonym for teaching).

2. The second necessity is a system of authority by which some control can be exercised over the teaching given. Uniformity is not necessary either in form or content, but while "wider still and wider may thy bounds be set" might well be the motto of the Church of England (to take an outstanding example of authoritarian toleration) it is necessary to have some clear idea of the body of doctrine and practice within which variety is not only tolerated but to be encouraged.

3. The third necessity is the constant renewal of the body of doctrine and that is the task to which the Churches will have to give very serious attention before they can hope to be fit to create a new civilisation.[97]

In considering Parkes' suggestions, one can clearly see the Modernist influence on his thinking; he believed that constant criticism was essential for good health in the Church. His idea of an evolution of the Church, based on the constant renewal of ideas and the belief that God is always doing new things, stemmed directly from Modernist teachings. In addition to the Modernist influence, however, one must keep in mind that Parkes always remained a good Anglican. A. Roy Eckardt has called Parkes "the Anglican of Anglicans," and Parkes was not shy about accepting such a title. He did believe that "it is out of the Anglican experience rather than that of any other Church that a new creative spirit is likely to emerge."[98] His belief in the Anglican system was not simply a parochial protest, but based on his

---

[97] Ibid., p. 12.
[98] Ibid., p. 13.

conviction that the "Anglican position with its irrational compromises and its formal austerities is at any rate preferable to the uniformity and claims to infallibility of Rome."[99] He thought that it would be a good idea for the Anglican Church to

> create a permanent Community of perhaps a dozen men whose task it would be to review continually the doctrine and worship of the Church in the light of the thought, the knowledge and the experience of their day. While the core of this work would be undertaken by a Community in which men might pass the remainder of their lives, these men would not form an Order closed from the world. Both by their own movements, and by drawing in men and women from the different aspects of the life of the Church and Nation, they would keep themselves and the whole Church continually alive to the changing world.[100]

I doubt if Parkes believed such an Order would ever come into existence, but it is an intriguing idea and in line with his overall scheme for constant renewal in the Church.

Parkes had a rather strange clerical career in the Church of England. Although ordained, he never served as a parish priest in a full-time capacity, but he did spend a good deal of time helping out in local parish churches in need of an interim minister. As limited as his experience in the parish was, Parkes' academic work on the nature of the Church reflected an appreciation of the ordinary congregation and its role in God's plan. This appreciation he related back to the nature of the original Church revealed in the choice of the disciples:

> No Church is the body or bride of Christ. But it can be said that the Churches are the continuation of the Incarnation— of the Incarnation of the penetrating, resolute, patient, perfect spirit of the Twelve, the twelve stupid, quarreling, timid—and so far as one was concerned, traitorous— disciples. It is one of the masterpieces of the life of Christ that he chose twelve disciples so like ourselves in all their faults

---

[99] Ibid., p. 13.
[100] Ibid., p. 13.

and foibles that none of us dare say that there is not enough good material dormant in us for God to use us for His purposes.[101]

Parkes had great faith in ability of ordinary parishioners to respond to God's call, but he had much less faith in those who governed the Church to provide these people with the proper means and guidance to respond.

Parkes had some concrete solutions for helping the Church be more responsive to God's call. Upon review, his suggestions are a surprising mixture of Modernist ideas and traditional values. He firmly believed that a Church which worshipped properly would be a Church able to meet the challenges of a new age. Parkes believed that the Church could structure its worship in such a way that it would affect the lives of people in the congregation provided that the Church remembered that its two main objectives were "to reveal a clear picture to the world—and ourselves—of the God we believe in; and, secondly, to help ourselves—and the world—into right relations with God."[102] One thing that a Church should do is experiment in worship. He took the position

> that where a congregation, that is the priest and the Church council, desire liberty to experiment with their services, the Bishop should, if he considers them to be a fit congregation, give them license to do [so], on condition that he receives a copy of any service they use. If this suggestion be condemned as illegal, then I suggest that one or two bishops might have the courage to do it in spite of that; and if this causes apoplexy to become endemic in the homes of ecclesiastical lawyers, whose duty it is to keep bishops in the paths of legality for their (bishops) pockets' sakes, that the lawyers be allowed to do their worst. And if there be a congregation that sincerely desires to experiment, and honestly proposes to accept the hard work which experiment involves, but cannot get permission to do so, then I suggest that it make a solemn

---

[101] "The God We Believe In," op. cit., p. 301.
[102] Ibid., p. 211.

announcement that it proposes to accept its own responsibility before God for its determination, and allows whoever likes to take what action they care or wish to take against them. I have not the slightest prejudice against rebellion, and rebellion on this issue is long overdue.[103]

Parkes had great confidence in the "common folk" of the Church to produce results when needed. Much of this confidence was rooted in his own ideas about God being interested and involved in the ordinary events of life rather than in the theological convolutions of theologians and bishops. There was also a feeling on his part that such experiments as he called for would make worship more relevant and meaningful, and in the process, change the basic nature of one's relationship to God. Aside from the elements of drama and education, two important aspects of worship, Parkes also stressed the underlying function of propaganda in a worship service:

It is here that the question of constant repetition becomes important. Everybody would probably admit the value of familiar symbols like the National Anthem or the familiar forms like the ceremonies of Parliament. But it is not the symbols themselves which gives anything reality. The monarchy is real because we tell friendly stories about the members of the royal family, as well as because on occasion they are surrounded with all the pomp and ceremonies of millennial tradition. The difficulty is that we never tell funny stories about God or even laugh in Church. And in consequence our relations with Him are formal where they should be familiar, and coldly remote when they should be awe-inspiring or overwhelming.[104]

Here again, we can see how Parkes applied his thinking about God and the nature of theology to his views on the nature of the Church.

---

[103] Ibid., p. 211.
[104] Ibid., p. 212.

His belief that simplicity and the ordinary are the keys to a proper worship of God is best illustrated in his opinion of the Eucharist. Parkes believed that this was the center of Christian worship, and that a proper understanding of the Eucharist gives one a proper understanding of the nature of the Church. For Parkes, the very elements of the Eucharist, bread and wine, gave an insight into the nature of the Church. The ordinariness of Church life was, for him, the secret of its genius. It is God's ability to bring forth from the ordinary the extraordinary that makes the Church a vehicle for God's grace. The sign of this aspect of the Church's nature can be found in the fact that Jesus chose the most essential and ordinary of human foods, bread and wine, as the symbols of God's love and redemption. By keeping this ordinariness and simplicity before her, the Church is able to meet the demands and expectations of God. That is why the Eucharist is the center of the worship of the Church:

> There can be no other centre of Christian worship. The imperishable beauty of this central service lies in its utter simplicity, and it is a tragedy that so many irrelevant controversies have clustered around it. And yet it is wrong to call them irrelevant, for their very existence is testimony to men's realisation that here is the centre of their faith, and to their determination to reach the deepest possible understanding of every aspect of its meaning. We do not fight so bitterly about such things which do not matter. But in the long run, transubstantiation and consubstantiation, or the treatment of the elements throughout as bread and wine, can make no difference, for the simplest doctrine is so sublime that men's minds cannot reach it.[105]

It was Parkes' view that from this "simplest doctrine" one can draw the whole message of the Church. In summing up that message, he wrote:

> At the end of his days, when His Body was going to pass from men's sight, when His Blood was going to be shed in a last and

---

[105] "God and the Church," op. cit., p. 15.

supreme act of adventure and self-giving, God-in-a-human-life took the simplest and most universal elements of man's nourishment, bread and wine; and said to His followers, take these, break and share them among you in remembrance of me; they are my body and blood, given to you after this body is withdrawn from you, so that through you I may go on living in the world. I will possess your body; the blood you will shed for me is mine; as I once came into the world in Jesus of Nazareth, so I will ever come into the world in you my followers; as I died for the world, so will you die with me for the world. The whole service is *outward* from the recipient to the world, just because the service is meaningless unless it is *inward*—that is that those who receive are offering themselves, "their souls and bodies, to be a reasonable, holy and living sacrifice" in union with God Himself. Paul completed the words "this is my body which is given for you" when he said to one of his churches "ye are the body of Christ and members one of another." For we are the bread and wine offered by the priest, that in them God may again, in and through our lives, be incarnate and so continue His eternal task of the redeeming and perfecting of His Creation.[106]

When read carefully, this passage reveals that unusual mixture of Modernist ideas and traditional values that have characterized Parkes' position on the Church.

Finally, we need to mention what Parkes believed to be the goal of worship. He was very concerned that the Church was failing to reach the common man, and he thought the aimless tampering with services by bishops and the like was making this situation worse rather than better. Parkes believed that if the Church was going to attract men to its services, it must offer them three things of fundamental importance.

(a) Answers to questions which they are asking.
(b) A picture of a satisfying life in which they can participate.

---

[106] Ibid., p. 16.

(c) A sense of anchorage and spiritual security.[107]

In Parkes' view, any worship service of the Church should try to make every effort to address these three fundamental needs of human beings. His willingness to experiment and do new things in worship stemmed in large measure from his feeling that the Church was not meeting these needs and so was unable to attract people to its services.

We have examined Parkes' ideas about the nature of the Church in some detail because they represent a practical application of his theological principles. Throughout these writings, Parkes is a Modernist attempting to show how traditional values can be dealt with in a creative fashion. He adopted a rather consistent view of the "evolution" of religious thought and the growth of the Church to support his claims, and in this regard he clearly reflected his Modernist roots. In many ways, his position is that the Church, like Jesus, is a seminal institution still on its way to becoming what it should be. In summary, this passage helps to clarify his overall position:

> God Himself is unchanging, but it is not the most godlike of human qualities to apply the same truism to all religious forms and formulas. But until it has ceased to create any feeling of discomfort among the congregations that theological expressions and liturgical practices may be different this Sunday from last, any change would merely stabilize the Church in the ideas of the 1940s instead of the 440s or the 1540s; and I doubt whether that would even be an improvement. . . . For it is true on all sides that, in their thinking, churchmen and theologians have not accepted even the beginnings of belief in evolution. For surely it means that when things are wrong, we may turn to the *past* to find out *why* they are wrong, but that we normally expect to find means of putting them right by research and experiment on the basis of our *present* knowledge. When a doctor is dissatisfied with the current treatment of a disease, it would never occur to him to consult Galen and Culpepper. He does some research on it, making use of every modern device. But, the

---

[107] Ibid., pp. 22–4.

churchman *instinctively* turns to the past. He becomes an
Augustinian, a neo-Thomist, a neo-Lutheran, or a Fundamentalist or what-not. His argument is that all truth is
already hidden in these great ones, but it has not been fully
exploited; something in them has been missed, so let us find it
out and that will cure our present troubles. To a limited
extent this is always true, and even doctors are capable of
being interested in the history of science. One can, indeed,
admit that it is truer in religion than in any field of human
activity, for the relation of the individual soul to God is an
unchanging one. But the past can only reveal and remind; it
cannot replace the responsibility of any generation for its own
faith. . . . In a word, this frank and fundamental Modernism
needs both humility as well as courage, and the help of
tradition as well as the help of modern knowledge. For it will
do little except make itself unpopular if it refuses to recognize
the greatness and—for its time—the rightness of the past, as
well as the enormous value of ordinary men, of roots, and the
longer the roots the better.[108]

If one has a proper understanding of Parkes' ideas about the
Church, in addition to an awareness of his overall theological
position, one will be better able to understand how he constructed
his position concerning Jewish–Christian relations. But before we
move on that issue we need to look briefly at his opinion about the
interpretation and authority of Scripture, and his ideas about the
future needs of Christian theology.

One of the distinguishing features of Modernist thought in
Britain was its acceptance of the critical method in interpreting
Scripture. Earlier English biblical critics, like Charles Gore and
others in the *Lux Mundi* group, had applied critical tools to the
Old Testament, but they hesitated to do the same to the New
Testament. Modernism had no such sensitivies, and both testa-
ments were subject to critical examination in Modernist thought.
Modernist thinkers took exception to the idea that the Bible was
the infallible "Word of God," and while they viewed it as central to
the Christian faith, they were careful in the kind of authority they

---

[108] "The God We Believe In," op. cit., pp. 342–43.

delegated to it. H. D. A. Major offered a definition of the Modernist outlook:

> Assertions of Biblical infallibility and finality, after a hard struggle, are being abandoned by educated English Christians, and belief in an infallible Bible is being replaced by belief in an inspired Bible. The statement that the Bible is the Word of God is being replaced by the statement that it contains the Word of God, not the only one, but the clearest and most authoritative for practical purposes. Modernists recognize that the Bible relates the history of the religious and moral evolution of Israel which culminated in the Gospel of Jesus and the foundation of the Christian Church. The Bible is necessary to the historical understanding of the origin and development of our own religion; it not only furnishes its student with magnificent narratives of prophetic preaching, devotional aspiration, noble and heroic examples of loyalty to truth and righteousness: it provides him in addition with a key to the higher interpretation of the Universe—its moral and spiritual interpretation; that key unlocks the door through which we see God as the source, director, and consummator of the whole creative process, and when once we have seen God in the Bible we can then see Him operating in nature, in human history, and in the human soul. The Bible teaches how we may enter into communion with Him and both learn His will and do it. . . . The Modernists urges the Traditionalist to accept the assured results of criticism as to the origins, dates, composition, integrity, historicity, and scientific value of the various books. The test of the moral and spiritual value of the Bible is the test of experience.[109]

Major's description of the Modernist view of the Bible is important because it was one of the issues which caused the greatest controversy between them and the traditionalists. Regarding Parkes, it gives some guidance as to the approach he took on biblical issues since he took a decidedly Modernist approach to the question of biblical authority and interpretation.

---

[109] *English Modernism*, pp. 117–18.

Like a good Modernist, Parkes was critical of any attempt to understand the Bible without regard to historical and literary criticism. Attempts to make the Bible infallible and beyond critical examination reduced the Bible and its message to a mockery in his eyes. Given his view of a God constantly active and revealing new things about Himself, a static view of biblical authority would produce a restrictive view of God and severely limit our understanding of Him. He wrote in 1940 that "the gospels were never meant to be the final truth; and they are certainly not all true. The incredibly subtle thing which God has done is to make His own figure so tower above that which his disciples have written of Him, that the figure itself continually corrects their mistakes."[110] This view of Scripture is in line with the basic thesis of Parkes' theology, although it is difficult to say whether his view of Scripture informs his theology or his theology informs his view of Scripture. It can be said, however, that he was as cautious in the amount of authority he wished to give Scripture as he was concerning the authority of the Church:

> Man is always anxious to establish authority, and endows every religious doctrine which he accepts with an objective authority which God has most carefully and scrupulously refused it. The "divine" authority of either Church or the Bible is an entirely human idea, and completely contrary to everything which God has shown Himself."[111]

Parkes' Modernist background made him very sympathetic to the idea that the Bible had to be read critically. He rejected out of hand any form of Biblical fundamentalism, though he believed that the Bible offered a good guide for those seeking to understand God and His work. But it was only a guide and not the final word. His own sympathies with the Modernist notion of "religious evolution" made this position inevitable. In *Good God*, he wrote:

> The idea that the "early Church" and the books of the New Testament embody the whole truth, from which we have subsequently declined, reduces the whole brave adventure of

---

[110] *Good God*, op. cit., p. 50.
[111] Ibid., p. 36.

God-in-a-human-life to the level of a rather pointless melo-
drama. For to introduce a point into history, after which
everything looks back instead of forward, makes nonsense of
all that God has done in His creation over millions of years. If
we don't know a good deal more about Jesus now than did the
first disciples, then we ought to be ashamed of ourselves. And
subsequent generations will know a lot more than we do.[112]

This attitude toward Scripture is in line with the rest of Parkes'
theological position. He shared the Modernist view that human
reason was a tool of theological investigation and not its enemy.
His appreciation of Humanism and the scientific method of
searching for truth colored his view of Scripture, and he was
unafraid of exposing Scripture to the historical and literary
scrutiny of Biblical critics. In his view, "modern biblical and
religious scholarship has begun to take its place beside the rest,
and the whole of human knowledge and experience has become
capable of being illuminated by the same light—the light of the
objective search for truth."[113]

One problem that Parkes had with traditional interpretations
of the Bible was the emphasis placed on its being the "Word of
God" rather than a record of "the activity of God." In order to
understand this view, we need to refer to a statement of William
Temple that Parkes was fond of quoting: "Revelation is an *event*:
its *interpretation* is our responsibility." From Parkes' viewpoint,
the Bible had been too often read without any interpretation. It
locked God, as it were, within the covers of a book, thus closing off
any idea of God's continuing activity. This was contrary to his idea
of an active God. He saw the Bible as an important tool in helping
one interpret God's activity, but he believed that it was not our
only source of knowledge about God's activity. He saw biblical
criticism opening up new avenues for understanding God's
activity rather than undermining biblical authority. The idea
that the Bible is "the Word of God" left men with the problem of
accounting for the fact that the Bible could be used as an authority
to burn witches, defend slavery, enforce capital punishment for

---

[112] Ibid., p. 49.
[113] *God and Human Progress*, op. cit., p. 59.

innumerable offences, support apartheid, believe in a burning Hell, to harbor a distorted picture of Judaism, and create an image of Jesus that made him unworthy of our admiration.[114] Parkes preferred another attitude toward biblical texts which held that "the Bible describes the *activity of God*, as interpreted by men who with their whole hearts believed in Him." But, Parkes urged us to bear in mind, the men who wrote it were men of widely different understanding, and of widely different times and environments, and their writings covered more than a thousand years of history.[115]

Implicit in such an attitude was the belief that each generation has the right and responsibility to interpret the text as befits its time and knowledge.

> One may believe that the Bible was written by men who agreed in believing that the central factor in history is the activity of God. But they were men of widely different sensitivity and outlook. It is urgently necessary to say that this belief is as profound, and as penetrating as the other. For believers in biblical infallibility constantly imply that this other belief belittles the Bible, is devised to blur the distinction between truth and falsehood, seeks to get rid of the challenge of religion, is privately known by its proponents to be untrue, and so on. All that is false. Critics may possess such views and such desires. But these are not the necessary consequences of refusing to accept the Bible literally as the Word of God.[116]

As an alternative to this position, Parkes offered the following:

> The fascinating thing about the Bible is the common conviction of its writers that material power and intellectual activity are not the central dynamic of history, but that the real dynamic is the activity of God in His creation. Every writer interpreted the Divine activity in accordance with the knowledge of his time; and there lies on us the responsibility

---

[114] *Prelude to Dialogue*, op. cit., pp. 202–03.
[115] Ibid., p. 202.
[116] Ibid., p. 203.

to interpret it with the knowledge available in our own time. It will be for tomorrow to interpret it afresh in accordance with the knowledge of tomorrow. To me such an attitude to the Bible presents a far more compelling and attractive picture of the activity of God than those seven words "the Bible is the Word of God" could ever do.[117]

This view of the Bible, its authority, and its place in Christian theology is an aspect of Parkes' theology that grew in importance when he began to create his version of a Christian theology of Judaism. It is important that we see here how his view was an outgrowth of his Modernist background, and how it fits into his overall theological scheme.

As we have seen, Parkes believed that the era after World War I required a rethinking of traditional values and disciplines. He saw the contemporary world going through revolutionary changes while religion clung desperately to the past. In his opinion, this would not do because the New Age demanded a New Theology. In examining Parkes' theological writings, we have tried to see just how Parkes would go about creating a new theology. As late as 1972, however, he still found himself at odds with much of the theology being produced, and in the Montefiore Lecture given at the University of Southampton in 1972, he produced one of his last important statements on the topic of a New Theology for a New Age.

This lecture began with an echo from the past, with the first sentences of the texts sounding very much like some of his earliest statements of 1929:

> For Western Man, the whole sense of living within a secure and stable world has vanished; and in the collapse of the traditional supports of society the failure of religion has certainly been a very important factor; and therein lies the reason for my title [*Religious Experience and the Perils of Its Interpretation*]. For I believe that the failure is due, not to the fact that religion itself rested on a human hallucination, but to failures in its interpretation. And my choice of a university

---

[117] Ibid., p. 204.

audience for the subject rests on my conviction that universities could play an irreplacable role in the building of the spiritual as well as the scientific foundation of a new age.[118]

Parkes believed that this problem was complicated by modern man's insistence on being able to control his existence without the help of God. There seemed to be a striking contradiction between man's view of himself and his actual situation. Parkes compared the present period to the period of the Dark Ages that followed the fall of classical civilization. He saw the enemy today, not as barbarian invaders, but as the white-collar criminal, the terrorist, and the guerilla, who each are able to exploit the complexity of our society for their own needs and desires. Parkes did see some hope in all this mess, and he wrote:

> Facing our increasing danger, I find it a great help to recognize that mankind is still very young. As an infant prodigy he has reached the moon; but his political activities would be perfectly comprehensible to Alcibiades or Nebuchadnezzer. We have as yet no conception of what an adult humanity would be like or what would be the range of man's adult capacities. . . . I do not believe that an adult humanity is automatically secularised or atheistic. But I am quite sure that not one of the religious institutions of the world, eastern or western, is in its present form capable of guiding us through the dangers and difficulties which lie ahead, though I believe equally that all have amassed experience in the past which is essential for the future.[119]

In his lecture, Parkes concentrated on the three ethical monotheisms of the West: Judaism, Christianity, and Islam. Parkes developed an interest and appreciation for Eastern and African religions in his later years, and he believed that they had much to offer the West. His sense of the importance of history, however, led him to concentrate in this lecture, and his work in general, on the Western religions. He offered the following view:

---

[118] *Religious Experience and the Perils of Its Interpretation*, p. 4.
[119] Ibid., p. 5.

They attribute a central significance to the actual events of history as the sphere of the divine activity; and they see themselves as agents of a divine plan for the fulfillment of history. Consequently the interpretation which they have put upon their religious experience has, to an identifiable extent, determined historical events. The present world, the product of centuries of [W]estern predominance, is largely the product of the way in which the three monotheisms have interpreted their responsibility to their vision of the divine mandate in history.[120]

How these three religious traditions interpreted their vision was of great interest to Parkes. He believed that the human dimension of religious interpretation was something a tradition acknowledged about other traditions, but seldom about itself. The interpretation of the experience of the Divine in human life also raised questions about cultural limitations, the role of human reason, the historical context, and so on.

I want to identify the human element quite precisely. I accept that religious experience is contact with a reality which is eternal and unchanging. But he to whom this contact is vouchsafed can accept of it only such part as his cultural inheritance and environment enable him to understand. That in turn is, very likely, more than he can communicate to his contemporaries, [and] the communication is necessarily reinterpreted in the still more partial and imperfect categories suitable to a whole community and its institutions. The limitations of human understanding are thus of fundamental importance, simply because it is that understanding which guides the personal, social, and political possibilities of those communities which accept as divine revelation the interpretation of the religious experience of their founders and leaders.[121]

For a Modernist thinker like Parkes, it was very important to establish the human dimension of religious interpretation in

---

[120] Ibid., p. 5.
[121] Ibid., p. 5.

order to support the call for a rethinking of traditional religious values and traditions. The Modernists were always being challenged by the charge that they were tearing down what was sacred in the past. Their critics viewed them as a threat to the very foundations of the faith. Parkes believed that the new age into which he believed the world had entered after World War I required a serious re-examination of religious interpretations, but he also realized the problems involved in achieving such a goal. In his view, "there are at least four fields in which past religious interpretations block the paths to that fundamental re-examination which is needed in a period as revolutionary as the contemporary world."[122] He listed the four fields as follows:

A. First, there are interpretations which, from the beginning, were wrong. The eschatological prison built around the life of Jesus of Nazareth is an obvious example. The magnification of the Creator at the expense of denigrating the creation, as evidenced by al-Ashari (a tenth-century Muslim theologian) is another. (Parkes would include Karl Barth as a source of such thinking in contemporary Christian theology.)

B. Secondly, there is the tendency to give permanent divine authority to an interpretation because, at the time it was formulated, it was obviously right. The result is that the interpretation remains unchangeable when the conditions of its formulations have changed or vanished. This is particularly apt to happen when a religious community is forced on to the defensive, and so clings to the past. Rabbinic Judaism has been especially exposed to this danger, but the same can be seen in Christian sects exposed to similar stagnation and restriction.

C. Thirdly, there is a general situation that religion is by its nature conservative, and the world surrounding it is equally by its nature perpetually changing. New interpretations creative at the time they were evolved, quickly become restrictive. A good many examples could be found in the battles of the Reformation. Calling on

---

[122] Ibid., p. 11.

Scripture to challenge abuses in the medieval church, the Reformers unwittingly created new problems leading to new abuses.

D. Fourth, an interpretation is apt to concentrate on an aspect of life instead of being concerned with the whole of it. The outstanding example of this is undoubtedly Christianity, and the fact is directly relevant to our present situation. The proclamation of "salvation in the name of Jesus Christ" met with so widespread a response when it was first preached, and that response has been so often repeated in every century and corner of the globe, that the Christian tradition has far too much ignored the fact that humanity is not only committed to finding salvation in this world's environment, but needs also to govern the world, and to explore and use the world's resources, two fields which involve as many profound moral problems as man's personal destiny.[123]

If we read this list in conjunction with the development of Parkes' theological thinking, we can see that it is a litany of his most pressing concerns.

Parkes also added other concerns to this list. The problem of Scriptural authority, for instance, was one that ran through Christianity, Judaism, and Islam. There is also the question of credal conformity. Parkes saw the problem here as being three-fold. Total conformity made a religion inflexible. Yet the usual alternatives were either that "all religions were equally good" or the rejection of any idea of transcendence whatsoever. Even the reform movements seemed to be on the wrong track. He wrote that "at present reform movements in all three religions tend to look backwards rather than forwards for their inspiration."[124] All this was complicated by the fact that none of the three religions ever seemed able to develop a sense of mutual relationship with each other. Added to that was the problem all three religions had with the emergence of Humanism, a movement Parkes thought very highly of. We can see here that Parkes was raising issues late

---

[123]   Ibid., p. 12.
[124]   Ibid., p. 13.

in his life almost identical to issues he raised when he first began to write. The Modernist agenda was still central to his thinking, but its success in the Church seems to have been quite limited.

Parkes held the belief that past religious experiences, experiences that were the source of a tradition, needed to be reinterpreted in a creative manner. He did not foresee the development of any new religion, but he did think that this reinterpretation needed to take account of two important factors. In his view, any new interpretation needed to communicate the contact between the eternal reality and human life in language that is accessible and understandable to contemporary man. He believed that there were two fundamental points in which our needs have progressed beyond those of the men who created our past religious values. The first required us to think about God in terms of responsibility rather than power. The second concerned the doctrine of man. Parkes believed that any reinterpretation of the doctrine of man "must be based on the fact that humanity is inextricably a unity. Anthropology, sociology, and psychology alike reveal that 'we are all members one of another.' There are no limits to our mutual dependence or to our mutual influence."[125] Parkes foresaw problems for this reinterpretation because "the responsibility of the Creator, and the unity of mankind are ideas which are so novel to the theological thinking and liturgical expression of most churches that they are in no position to take the initiative in meeting a crisis as urgent as that which now impends on the whole world."[126] He looked to the universities for help since they had discovered "that past interpretations are rightly subject to continual reassessment without having to reject the past."[127] One way in which this support could be secured for theology would be by the integration of theologians and theological faculties more closely into the academic community.

Parkes' closing statement in the Montefiore lecture is worth quoting at length because it is a splendid recapitulation of his hopes and concerns.

---

[125] Ibid., p. 14.
[126] Ibid., p. 15.
[127] Ibid., p. 15.

I do not believe that what lies beyond our present confusion is a New Age of faith. Many generations will pass before we achieve a world-wide unity of outlook. What lies before this generation is something unprecedented. It is a loyal co-operation between many types of mind and outlook, many different philosophies of life, united in common recognition of the seriousness of our situation. For the first time in human history the whole of human life has been thrown into the melting pot. Our obscene politics, our waste and pollution, our dehumanisation of the person, alike proclaim our past failure. . . . I am encouraged to demand a human co-operation which over-rides traditional differences and antagonisms, because I am convinced that today we can only interpret our religious experience in terms of a responsible and intelligent Creator who is equally committed to the whole of creation. He cannot limit his responsibility to those who accept him, any more than those who desire to understand and co-operate with him can limit their activity to like-minded colleagues. There needs to be a new understanding of co-operation across historic barriers. Yet, though the area in which we accept "both and" must be widened, there is still an inescapable area in which we have to choose "either or." Such an interpretation is obviously as perilous as those of previous ages, but there is no safe way forward. . . . We are inevitably moving into a world where every aspect of life demands new exploration, but also invites new co-operations. Both for those who interpret life in theistic terms and for those who do not, it will be a co-operation in which all human qualities of intellect, of insight, and of imagination, will be stretched to the full, as much as qualities usually associated with religion—love, compassion, sacrifice. But it is in such co-operation that we shall begin to discover the range and capacities of adult man.[128]

This is an appropriate place to end our survey of Parkes' theological development. We have dwelt at some length on this material because so much of it is unfamiliar to so many. In

---

[128] Ibid., pp. 17–18.

addition, an understanding of Parkes' theological views of Christianity is invaluable in helping one to understand his ideas about Jewish–Christian relations. As we have said, Parkes was a Modernist theologian who used many of his Modernist ideas and principles to develop his views on Jewish–Christian relations. We shall now turn to this aspect of his work, but we must always keep in mind the basic theological position that we have just traced. By so doing, we shall gain a better understanding of the unity of his work.

4

The Rediscovery of Judaism

CHRISTIANS have traditionally thought of Judaism as a religion that is arid, legalistic, and no longer viable. It is viewed as the religion that prepared the way for Christianity, but with the coming of Christ, lost its ability to meet the spiritual needs of humanity. Jewish Scriptures have an historical importance for the Christian, but the correct interpretation of the texts is believed to be found only in the Christian tradition. There is a high regard for the prophets of ancient Israel, but Judaism after the prophets is regarded as being in a state of moral and spiritual decline. Christian tradition has held Israel accountable for the prophets' deaths and Jesus' death. Rabbinic Judaism is unknown to most Christians, and their knowledge of Judaism tends to come almost completely from the New Testament. Out of this situation arises a picture of Judiasm that is distorted and inaccurate, but one which informs most Christians, be they trained theologians or laypersons. There have been a few Christian thinkers, however, who have tried to counter this image of Judaism with a more historically accurate and theologically sympathetic interpretation. James Parkes was such a thinker, but even Parkes began with a traditional view of Judaism. It was only through his personal contacts with Jews and his involvement with the Jewish question that he came to realize that what he had learned about Judaism through the Church and at Oxford was not true.

Parkes' reputation as an expert on Jewish issues is such that it is difficult to imagine him ever accepting the traditional stereotypes of Judaism. Yet there was nothing in his background to prepare him for the role he was to play in the effort to revise Christian ideas about Judaism. It was not until 1928 that he

161

became involved at all in issues related to Jewish affairs, but then it was initially with issues dealing with the politics of antisemitism. His activity in this field created something of a chain reaction in his thinking, and an evolution in his thought began to take place. Parkes relates this development:

> I knew nothing special about Jews, and my knowledge of Judaism came from the normal equipment of an Oxford trained theologian. I had been taught that post-Christian Judaism was an arid and meaningless legalism, and I had seen no reason to waste time studying it. In consequence, when I started in Geneva I knew nothing of the post-Biblical history of the Jews or of Judaism. But I soon discovered that I could not begin to understand university antisemitism without knowing something of Jewish history. . . . I soon discovered that to know Jewish history was not enough; for Jewish history was meaningless except as an expression of Judaism; and by then I could call on the friendship of orthodox and liberal, traditionalist and reformer, for guidance. For I realized that one history and destiny expressed itself in the widest variety of opinions. . . . Intellectual honesty early compelled me to abandon the belief that post-Christian Judaism was a collection of niggardly and unspiritual legalisms; for it was obvious that such a "religion" could not have sustained Jewry through the centuries of massacres, persecution, denigration and contumely with which I had become ashamedly familiar, and for which the responsibility lies squarely on the Christian Church.[1]

Parkes' evolution continued until he reached the point where he not only saw the value of Judaism and the Jewish experience, but he argued for it being an equal to Christianity.

There was some initial hesitation on his part to change his thinking in any dramatic way. At first, he felt that Judaism had more good than normally ascribed to it, but that it was still not as good as Christianity.[2] He finally rejected this position as being too

---

[1] "Christendom and the Synagogue," *Frontier*, vol. 2, no. 4 (winter 1959), pp. 271–72.
[2] Ibid., p. 272.

artificial. Personal contacts with Jews like Claude Montefiore and
Herbert Loewe convinced him that individual Jews could possess
a spiritual life. Missionary tracts tried to present the argument
that such men were exceptions to the rule, and that ordinary Jews
were indeed arid, rigid, legalistic, and intolerant. Parkes' growing
knowledge of all that the Jew had suffered at the hands of
Christianity and Islam made him appreciative not of the rigidity,
but of the fact that Judaism had been able to foster any sort of
spirituality at all under such adverse conditions.[3] These personal
experiences were soon coupled with his growing historical awareness that the traditional Christian view of Judaism as a religion in
a state of moral and spiritual decline at the time of Jesus had no
basis in fact at all. His attempt to retain his traditional viewpoint
as much as possible fell victim to this discovery.

How can we characterize this new insight by Parkes? In 1960,
he wrote in the foreword of one of his most important books, *The
Foundations of Judaism and Christianity*, this summary of his
evolution:

> It is unfortunate that Christian scholars of the Old Testa-
> ment have chosen to call all or part of the period of Jewish
> history which begins with the return from exile by the title of
> "*Spat-Judenthum*," "*Bas-Judaisme*," or "*Late-Judaism*."
> They inevitably imply thereby that Judaism was about to
> pass away, whereas in fact it had just come into existence;
> and that its passing was preceded by a decline in stature,
> whereas the key-note of the period is the attempt to weave
> the teaching of the prophets into the life of the people. It
> would be just as accurate to describe the Elizabethan Age as
> "Bas-Moyen-age" or the early north-Italian renascence as
> "spat-Lombardisch." Bad history cannot be the foundation
> for good theology. This attitude to the period arises from their
> natural desires to show that Christianity is firmly rooted in
> the Old Testament, and in God's covenant with the Children
> of Israel. And it has been traditionally regarded as a necess-
> ary corollary to this belief to present the Church as the *only*
> legitimate successor to the grandeur of the prophets and the

---

[3] Ibid., p. 273.

responsibilities of the covenant. Since, in this view, all that was of permanent value in Jewish history was soon to pass to the credit of the Christian Church, this period following the return is automatically, if unconsciously, looked at through spectacles which focus the sight only on evidence for the decline and the passing of the spiritual authority of Judaism.[4]

This passage reflects the position where Parkes wound up in his thinking about the traditional ideas on Judaism, but it also reflects where he began to change.

As Parkes' traditional outlook began to be challenged, certain ideas of that tradition came under attack. He wrote that "the final blow came when I had a fresh look at the half-millennium after the return from exile, which I had learnt to think of as one of decline, of the narrowness of Ezra, the dwindling of the Remnant, the deadening influence of the priestly code, and the suspension of prophecy until the times of the Messiah.[5] What Parkes discovered in his research of the period that started with the Babylonian captivity and the second century of the Common Era, contradicted the traditional Christian interpretation of Judaism. Far from being a period of moral and spiritual decline, Parkes discovered a period full of new and exciting innovation that proved invaluable to Judaism following the fall of the Temple in AD 70. He offered the following observations as an alternative to the traditional Christian position:

> Let us look at a few hall-marks of that allegedly arid five hundred years. It saw the development of synagogue worship—copied today in church and mosque—a worship which was congregational, regular, without priesthood or sacrifice, and combined prayer, praise and instruction. It evolved the idea of Holy Scripture, and included history as a sphere of revelation. It discovered that Scripture could remain holy in a changing world only by interpretation, and that the interpretation must also be holy. It found that religion was not an affair of priest and cult, but of the moral living of ordinary men. It was, therefore, something to be

---

[4] James Parkes, *The Foundations of Judaism and Christianity*, pp. ix–x.
[5] "Christendom and the Synagogue," op. cit., p. 272.

taught, and teachers of Torah spread through the scattered people. It was also something to die for, and the period witnessed the first ordinary men and women who gave their lives for their personal faith—the martyrs of the Maccabean War.[6]

The views that Parkes put forward here are not particularly novel to anyone familiar with Jewish tradition and its development. The fact does remain, however, that most Christians would not recognize this description of Judaism right before and immediately after the time of Jesus. There had been a few other Christian writers who took a view similar to Parkes, and he often expressed his debt to their work. He was particularly influenced by the words of the American scholar George Foot Moore, and the English scholar R. Travers Herford. Moore and Herford have not been without influence, but there has been a strange reluctance on the part of Christians to base their interpretation of Judaism on Jewish texts and sources. Traditionally, most Christian interpretations of Judaism have stemmed directly from Christian sources, particularly the New Testament materials and the Patristic writings. Much of the material on Judaism in these writings is polemical, and a distorted view of Judaism is conveyed through them. This continues to be a problem today. Recently, Paul Van Buren has pointed out that "the mass of so-called scholars since Moore's time who have not yet grasped Moore's simple point that if you want to learn about early Judaism, the material is fully available in the Jewish writings of the time.[7] Parkes read Moore, and he often referred to him as a source for explaining Jewish ideas about the meaning of the Law/Torah, sin, repentence, God, etc.

In his attempt to construct a new Christian understanding of Judaism, Parkes took issue with those who would see the work done by Ezra in the years following the Babylonian Exile as being parochial and narrow. Negative comments about Ezra usually stem from his attack upon intermarriage, but Parkes took a much

---

[6] Ibid., p. 273.
[7] Paul Van Buren, *The Problem of a Christian Theology of the People of Israel*. Unpublished paper distributed to members of the NCCJ's Israel Study Group, November 14, 1981.

more positive view of Ezra's work. The Exile was, in Parkes' view, the point of which the "religion of Israel" began to change into Judaism. The Message of Sinai was that God was the only God, and He was the God of all creation. This was coupled with the message that God was a moral God who would reward righteousness and punish iniquity.[8] The Babylonian Exile was a period of transition with three new developments.

1. The past history and law of the nation were collected and edited to provide an authoritative base for action and teaching.
2. The weekly day of rest was turned into a weekly day of religious worship and instruction independent of the sacrificial ritual of the Temple and so created the synagogue.
3. The dynamic of religious leadership turned from proclamation and denunciation to instruction and encouragement.[9]

Rather than being the beginning of the decline of Judaism, as Christian tradition so often called it, the time between the return from Babylon to the Fall of the Temple was really a period in which Judaism developed spiritual and pragmatic tools that helped it survive the onslaught from the pagan and budding Christian world.

Parkes gave a great deal of credit to Ezra for transforming the religion of Israel into Judaism. The Exile had demonstrated how vulnerable the Israelites were to losing their tradition if it remained centered primarily in the Temple at Jerusalem. An Exile like the one in Babylon made such a tradition nearly impossible to maintain. By creating a system of worship based on local synagogues, collecting important texts and canonizing them, and stressing the importance of educating the people as a whole, Ezra laid the foundations for the survival of Judaism. Parkes wrote of Ezra:

> It is difficult to realise what an extraordinary and unparalleled innovation was this determination of Ezra. The religion

---

[8] James Parkes, *The World of the Rabbis*, p. 6.
[9] Ibid., p. 7.

of Israel had been betrayed as often as it had been upheld by both king and people. But to neither would it have appeared as something to be regularly *taught*. It was primarily a matter of priesthood and cultus; it imposed on ordinary people a conformity to tradition, a certain moral code, a sense of belonging, which was instilled into them from time to time by a local or wandering priest or prophet. But it was not systematised or universal. It was the [E]xile which had provided a time for reflection and self-examination; and it was Ezra who turned the results of this reflection and self-examination into unprecedented religious forms. It is not surprising that the rabbis declared that, if Torah had not been revealed to Moses, Ezra would have been worthy to receive it.[10]

The impact of the reforms instituted by Ezra was profound. Not only did they allow Judaism to survive in dangerous times, they also provided the basis for the two monotheisms that developed out of Judaism—Christianity and Islam. Parkes wrote that

> it was amazing that this period of five hundred years pro-
> duced these three novelties which still, two thousand five
> hundred years later, form the basis of the religious life of the
> Jewish, the Christian, and the Moslem world. We still have
> weekly worship containing the same elements of prayer,
> praise and teaching; we still strive after the ideal of teaching
> our whole population their religious and social duties; all
> three faiths still venerate in various special ways the collec-
> tion of books sacred to their religion.[11]

Parkes believed that if anyone doubted the achievement of Ezra, that person would do well to look at the pages of the New Testament for proof. He thought that here one could find evidence as to how the reforms of Ezra had taken root within the Jewish community. What annoyed him so much was the refusal of Christians to take the evidence seriously:

---

[10] Ibid., p. 8.
[11] James Parkes, *Jews in the Christian Tradition*, p. 10.

The New Testament on almost every page bears witness to the work of all anonymous teachers of Torah. There are synagogues all through the villages of Galilee visited by Jesus of Nazareth and his disciples; there was a religious language which ordinary people understood; they listened, because they were accustomed to listen to religious teaching. Jesus, though a Galilean *am ha'aretz*, could read and was familiar with his Bible. Peter, though also a Galilean *am ha'aretz*, could say that he had never eaten anything which was not *kosher*. Both could assume that their audiences would recognize a quotation from Scriptures. Moreover Paul shows that the same ability to read, the same knowledge of the Scriptures, and the same worship of the synagogue, existed all through the Diaspora in the Greco–Roman world. It would be fascinating to know how these diaspora Jews were taught, to be able to trace the links which bound them to Jerusalem, and to know what was the organization which supplied their teachers and ensured their orthodoxy. In fact, we are coming, with the Dead Sea Scrolls as well as the early Church fathers, to know more about heretical Jewish movements than we do about the mainstream of Jewish development.[12]

Parkes believed that Christians needed to take seriously the fact that Jesus lived at a time when Judaism was reaching a spiritual crest, not wallowing in moral decline.[13] He believed that this point had been overlooked because of the nature of prophecy in Judaism at that time. Christians held the prophets in such high esteem that they saw the period after the prophets to be one of decay. What was not acknowledged was the role played by Ezra and his reforms in transforming the teaching of the prophets into a way of life that could be followed by the people. Without these reforms, there was a good chance that the prophets would have been entirely forgotten. In considering this problem, he wrote about the decline of prophecy, and the views of Jews and Christians concerning this period.

---

[12] *The World of the Rabbis*, op. cit., p. 10. See also *The Foundations of Judaism and Christianity*, p. xii.
[13] "Christendom and the Synagogue," op. cit., p. 273.

The Jews have reasons for regarding this period as one of growth. But some Christian scholars treat it as one of decline because there was an almost complete cessation of prophecy. The great figures of the kingdom and the exile, men like Elijah, Isaiah and Jeremiah, had no successors of quite their splendour. As time went on, even lesser prophets became fewer and fewer, until it came to be believed by Jews that prophecy had ceased until the coming of the Messiah. Nothing so majestic took their place. Since, therefore, the prophets have always seemed to Christians to be the centre of the Old Testament, Christians have held that the religious temperature had cooled. This opinion was confirmed by the increase in purely ritual and ceremonial regulations and the growth of the power of the priesthood. Judaism comes to be called by a term which automatically conveys disapproval— "legalistic."[14]

From Parkes' point of view, much of the Christian misunderstanding of the nature of Judaism stems directly from a misunderstanding of the work Ezra tried to do. This was coupled with a refusual to see just how effectively these reforms were put into place so that by the time of Jesus idolatry was no longer a major problem, Scriptures were familiar to even the simplest of people, and synagogues were playing an important role in their spiritual life.

Parkes' re-evaluation of the period between the Exile and Jesus had an important implication for his view of Judaism as a whole. The dead, arid religion he had been taught about at Oxford was nowhere to be found historically. What he discovered, instead, was a vital and active religion engaged in a healthy debate with itself over the proper course it should take to ensure its survival in an uncertain world. In weighing the historical evidence he discovered, Parkes concluded that the picture of Judaism that most Christians obtained from New Testament literature was a distortion, from which sprang all sorts of negative implications. In his book *Jesus, Paul and the Jews*, published in 1936, he stated the problem quite clearly:

---

[14]   *Jews in the Christian Tradition*, op. cit., p. 10.

The question has been posed in its bluntest terms for the sake of clarity. The question which arises from it is this: that the Gospels as a complete source for a study of the Pharisees are quite inadequate it is not possible to deny; that the picture of the "Law" describes no known form of Judaism is equally certain: but is the error to be ascribed to Jesus and Paul, or is it to be found in the evangelists on the one hand and our misunderstanding on the other? The question is one of capital importance in the sphere of Jewish–Christian relationships. If it be true that the picture of Judaism, which (with the Gospels and Epistles for basis) has been consistently given since the second century, is in reality unjust to the Jews, then the reparation which the Christian Church owes to Judaism is one so terrible that it is not possible to evaluate it. For from this conception springs the whole growth of anti-Semitism and the age-long tragedy of the Jewish people.[15]

Parkes was repeating here what he had already said in his earlier work *The Conflict of the Church and Synagogue*.[16] It is an essential part of his position on the problem of antisemitism and Jewish–Christian relations. Nothing could be done to free the Church from complicity in the evil of antisemitism as long as it insisted that its biblical picture of Judaism is a correct one because an honest study of Judaism shows that it is not a correct view.

It is quite interesting to see just how far Parkes had developed in his thinking about the nature of Judaism. In the 1929 lectures discussed in Chapter 2, some of Parkes' remarks revealed his own acceptance of the traditional Christian view of the "law" and its function in Judaism. He too stressed the role of the prophets. But as he began his study of the Jewish question for the WSCF and came into personal contact with Jews, he discovered a new image of Jewish tradition. His ability to adapt to this changing view can be traced to the fact that his background in Modernism made it possible for him to take a critical view of Scripture and Christian tradition without feeling the need to give up Christianity

---

[15] Parkes, *Jesus, Paul and the Jews*, with a foreword by Herbert M. J. Loewe, p. 12.
[16] *The Conflict of the Church and Synagogue*, p. 158.

altogether. The Modernist desire to base theology on some appeal to Truth also influenced his thinking on the need for Christians to take into account the actual nature of Judaism and not cling to a traditional, but incorrect, view. He believed that there had to be a serious effort on the part of the Church to correct her teachings regarding Judaism. It would require taking seriously materials outside the Christian community, and here he relied a great deal on the work of Moore and Herford and some liberal Jewish writers like Claude Montefiore and Israel Abrahams who were also trying to offer a fresh perspective of Judaism to the Christian community. Parkes was unrelenting in his position. He wrote in 1936:

> In recent years, and in certain Churches, there has certainly been an effort to present a fairer and therefore more attractive picture of Judaism than is traditional in Christianity, but the effort has not gone far enough or deep enough. It is not sufficient to insist on the greatness of the prophets or on the moral value of the Pentateuch. It is not enough to present excuses or express contrition for the persecution of the Jews in the centuries of Christian history. A still more difficult task is to present a new and fairer picture of the opponents of Jesus and Paul themselves. And there is yet a further stage to be reached before the Christian can claim a clear conscience on this matter: the recognition that a living and vital Judaism has survived the separation between Judaism and Christianity, survived in the purpose of God, not as the medieval scholar would claim as a permanent warning to the sin of killing the Messiah, but because of the possession of an autonomous and essential witness to the nature of the relationships of God to His Creation.[17]

If Christian theology was to have any value, it would have to take into account a new understanding of Judaism and its role in God's overall plan for Creation. He believed that the Church would never correctly understand its role if it continued to believe and foster an incorrect and dishonest view of Judaism. He was

---

[17] *Jesus, Paul and the Jews*, op. cit., pp. 14–15.

fully aware of the problems this posed for the Christian community, but the belittling of Judaism and its post-Christian developments by Christian writers could no longer be tolerated in the face of the facts he had uncovered:

> Being personally a Christian, my task is to deal with my own failures; how the Jew may approach his lies between him and God—a fact almost universally forgotten by the theological writers who are never so confident as when pointing out the errors of other sects. Theological ophthalmology—or the removing the motes from the eyes of others—is the hall-mark of the Christian writing on Judaism from Justin Martyr to Karl Barth, and from the beginning to end it is as universally detestable as it is usually inaccurate. One can say with perfect security that the average Christian scholar is not only much more familiar with the less disagreeable sides of Rabbinic Judaism than with the similar sides of historic Christian theology, but he is much more familiar with them than are 99 per cent of the Rabbinic Jews themselves. If we ever desire that the Jews may make an objective study of the best in Christianity, we might surely begin by teaching our own folk the best in Judaism.[18]

Parkes saw that any reinterpretation of Judaism in the Christian community would require a new appraisal of the Pharisees. This would not be an easy task because the image of the Pharisees one received from the New Testament was almost completely negative. There has also developed a tradition of referring to anything legalistic and spiritually bankrupt as being "Pharisaic." One finds the term in *Webster's New World Dictionary* defined as "emphasizing or observing the letter but not the spirit of religious law; self-righteous; sanctimonious; pretending to be highly moral or virtuous without actually being so; hypocritical." This sort of image has pervaded Christian teachings about the so-called enemies of Jesus, and it has been used to give credence to the idea

---

[18] Ibid., p. 19.

that Judaism is inferior to Christianity. In the course of his study of Judaism, Parkes discovered an entirely different picture of the Pharisees.

The Pharisees arose as an organized sect in Judaism around the time of the Maccabean period, and they were considered by Parkes to be the "sole authentic heirs of the line of development which opens with the Babylonian Exile and the return, and which is still giving the world the worship of the synagogue, church, and mosque, the conception (at any rate in the Western world) of the Holy Scriptures, whether Old and New Testament and the Quran, as well as making a substantial contribution to both education and law."[19] The Pharisees were the ones who argued that the "oral tradition" interpreting the Law was as important as the written Law. Their main opponents in this debate were the Sadducees. The Pharisees differed from the Essenes in that they were concerned with the whole "people of Israel" and not an exclusive sect. The Pharisees were the "teachers of Torah," their domain was the local synagogue, and their constituency was the *am ha'aretz*, the common people. The Pharisaic method of constant interpretation of the Law, the emphasis on education, and the desire to create a Jewish way of life that could be followed by even the simplest of people enabled the Pharisees to survive the events of AD 70 and become the dominant force in Judaism. Rabbinic Judaism is the product of this movement.

During the time of Jesus, the Pharisees were locked in battle with the Sadducees for power in the Jewish world. The Sadducees had close ties with the Temple and the Roman authorities, but the Pharisees were stronger outside Jerusalem in areas where the synagogues held sway. What we know about the early life of Jesus would seem to indicate that his main source of knowledge about the Jewish tradition came from the synagogue and the "teachers of Torah," the Pharisees. Although the *locus classicus* for the attitude of Jesus to Judaism is usually found in the denunciations of the Pharisees found in all the Gospels, Parkes is correct when

---

[19] *The Foundations of Judaism and Christianity*, op. cit., p. 133.

he points out that "the picture of the Pharisees presented in the Gospels is so one-sided that in some cases Jesus is represented as accusing the Pharisees of customs and actions which were as strongly condemned by them as by Himself."[20] He took issue with the traditional Christian notion that Jesus taught something totally original. He argued instead that one could only understand what Jesus taught by referring to his contact with the Judaism of his day. Modern scholarship had begun to reveal the essentially Jewish nature of the teachings of Jesus, and Parkes felt it was essential for Christians to become more aware of this aspect of Jesus' life. Parkes offered this assessment of the relation of Jesus to Judaism.

> He was born a Jew, and passed the early part of His life, and probably the early years of His manhood also, in a Galilean village. In spite of the fact that there were many non-Jewish elements in Galilee, it is not possible to ascribe a non-Jewish basis to His teachings. He was certainly not a Hellenist. Nor would He have been deprived of adequate Jewish instruction by His remoteness from Jerusalem. Through the activity of the Pharisees there were synagogues in most Jewish villages, and in them serious religious teaching was given. For the Jewish synagogue was not a "church" but a "school" (in Yiddish a synagogue today is still a "school") and a community centre. The important point for us to note is that all the systematic and regular teaching which Jesus would receive as a boy and as an adolescent, came from the Pharisees.[21]

For Parkes, this contact with Pharisaism in the life of Jesus was very significant because it gave one a clue as to where the roots of Jesus' teachings were to be found. The fundamental teachings of the Pharisees were defined by Parkes as follows:

---

[20] *Jesus, Paul and the Jews*, op. cit., p. 11.

[21] Ibid., p. 57. There has been a considerable amount of literature written recently on the Pharisees. John Pawlikowski lists a number of these works in an article he wrote that appeared in a recent publication. See *Antisemitism and the Foundations of Christianity*, edited by Alan T. Davies, p. 166. This book was dedicated to James Parkes, and he wrote the introduction to it.

God willed Israel to live by the Torah. He revealed His Torah to Moses. But because the words of God are the words of an Infinite Being, there is contained in them not merely the surface meaning but infinite wisdom, and for this reason they never grow old. For fresh interpretations can continually be found therein, and by this means they are permanently adequate to the needs of changing times, and changing responsibilities.[22]

Parkes believed that the Pharisaic influence on Jesus' teachings was clear. He considered the debate between Jesus and certain Pharisees in the Gospels understandable since there were great debates going on among the different schools of Pharisaic thought all the time. At the time of Jesus, there were the two great schools of Pharisaic thought: the school of Shammai was known to be more strict in its interpretation; the school of Hillel was known as the more "liberal" school. Jesus' attitude toward the Law seems to reflect the influence of Hillel. The great debates in the Gospels between Jesus and Pharisees were not unlike similar debates found in other Pharisaic texts. Jesus did seem to stress the quest for the highest ideal of ethics, and such idealism often comes into conflict with those more concerned about conserving and passing on a tradition. But any debate between Jesus and Pharisees needed to be seen, in Parkes' opinion, as a debate between people who shared a similar set of principles but had differing interpretations:

> Jesus, like the Pharisees, accepted Torah as the Divine Revelation of the nature of God, of the right relations between God and man, and of the right relations between man and man. Like the Pharisees, and opposed to the Sadducees, He believed that the written word needed continual interpretation in order that its underlying spiritual value might be kept clear. But His method was that of a popular preacher, and not a "scribe." He was not a full member of the Pharisaic

---

[22] Ibid., p. 58.

party, though like them he used the synagogue and its opportunities.[23]

Parkes did believe that Jesus was very mindful of the danger of externalism and the problems that could arise if concentration on Halachic details caused the average Jew to become separated from the way of Torah. But these concerns were also recognized by the different schools of Pharisaism.

In examining the different schools of thought in Judaism at the time of Jesus, Parkes found in the Pharisees the basis upon which Jesus could have offered his interpretation of the Law. "The Pharisees," wrote Parkes, "recognised that certain duties overrode the commandments to perform other duties with which they conflicted. Jesus asked for an extensive development of this idea, in order that fundamental moral duties should never be obscured."[24] This discovery of Parkes was in sharp contrast to traditional Christian views of the Pharisees, but as a good Modernist and historical scholar, this was not a deterrent to Parkes. It was perfectly acceptable to challenge traditional ideas when the facts contradicted them.

One can also detect another Modernist theme in Parkes' thinking. Earlier we mentioned Parkes' disagreement with Karl Barth's assertion that Jesus appeared on the historical scene as a cosmic intrusion. Parkes believed Jesus had come in the fullness of history, and it was to history that one had to turn to make sense of the Incarnation. In attempting to take the Incarnation seriously, one had to determine the historical condition of Judaism at the time of Jesus in order to understand how and why Jesus said the things he said. The more he discovered about the Pharisees, the more he could see the roots of Jesus' thinking. Jesus' teachings were Pharisaical in nature, and appreciation of the nature of Pharisaism helps one to gain a better understanding of Jesus. This does not deny Jesus' originality, but he was able to cultivate his originality because the Pharisaical method encouraged just that sort of thinking. Parkes' Modernist sympathies, then,

---

[23] Ibid., p. 58. For information on the differences between Hillel and Shammai, see Nahum N. Glatzer, *Hillel the Elder*; R. Travers Herford, *The Pharisees*; George Foot Moore, *Judaism*, 3 volumes.

[24] Ibid., p. 85.

allowed him to interpret Scripture and the life of Jesus in ways that may have been unavailable to someone trained in a different school of Christian thought.

We have dwelt on this question of the relationship of Jesus to the Pharisees because Parkes saw how essential it was to get Christians to appreciate the Pharisees if they were to appreciate anything about Judaism as it developed after the time of Jesus. A total denunciation of Pharisaism would lead logically to a denunciation of anything they helped to develop later in history. Judaism as we know it today is an outgrowth of the efforts of the Pharisees to preserve the Jewish tradition after the fall of the Temple in AD 70. Parkes knew that Rabbinic Judaism was a mystery to even most educated Christians, and it was generally dismissed as the religion of the Pharisees. The image of Judaism as a dead, arid, legalistic religion in Christian tradition has its roots in the picture of the Pharisees presented in the Gospels. Unless one could get Christians to see beyond the negative picture of the Gospels and get them to see that Jesus himself was well within the circles of the Pharisaic movement, there could be little hope of changing traditional Christian images of Judaism.

Any appreciation of Judaism needs to begin with the achievement of the Pharisees after the fall of the Temple in the year AD 70. Traditional Christian teachings had generally regarded this period as one of decline for Judaism. This is reflected in the rather widespread ignorance of Rabbinic Judaism among Christians. The fall of the Temple was regarded as a sign of God's displeasure over the Jews' alleged murder of Jesus Christ. The Jews were said to have been scattered over the face of the earth to wander eternally as punishment for their sins. Anything that occurred within the Jewish community was of no significance since their role in God's plan for the world had now been taken over by the Church. There appeared very little reason for Christians to concern themselves with the Jews except to keep them from leading good, simple folk away from the truth of Christianity. Anything that needed to be known about Judaism could be found in the pages of what came to be known in the Christian world as the "Old Testament."

Parkes took exception to this traditional scheme. The traditional position was not borne out by the facts, and it required the

Christian to accept judgments about Judaism that are totally unfounded. While the Hebrew Scriptures do supply a great deal of information about Judaism, they are not sufficient to give Christians an accurate picture of the Jews:

> Some claim that, as we have the Old Testament as Holy Scripture, we have all that Judaism has. But the issue is not the bare possession, but what each religion does with it; and the treatment of each is wholly different. Judaism, like Christianity, is a religion which is rooted in its sacred scriptures, but we do not find the maturity of the Church in the New Testament, and we do not find rabbinic Judaism in the Old. . . . If we cannot understand Judaism unless we are familiar with its development in post-biblical times, we have at the same time to look at it in its creative period, before it had been marked and even deformed by the millennial persecution of Church and Mosque. . . . It is not fair to judge Judaism by the present rigidity of orthodoxy or the uncertainty of reform: both are the product of a hard, long, and tragic history.[25]

Parkes made a total break with traditional Christian teachings by demanding that the period after the fall of the Temple be seen as the creative period in Jewish history rather than a period of defeat.

The events that led up to the Roman destruction of the Temple divided the Jewish community into roughly three parties. There were those who sought the independence of the Jews from Roman domination. This movement was crushed in a series of wars with Rome. There were those who staked Jewish survival on the fortunes of the Temple in Jerusalem. They were crushed when the Romans took over Jerusalem and destroyed the Temple. The Sadducees ceased to be a major force within Judaism at that time. Finally there were those who clung to the Torah as the source of Jewish existence. These people were led by the Pharisees, and they survived the period of Roman destruction because of their amazing resourcefulness and imagination. What we know as Judaism today is an outgrowth of this movement.

---

[25] "Christendom and the Synagogue," op. cit., p. 274.

In Parkes' judgment, Christian history has neglected to take this aspect of Jewish history seriously. In writing about this period of Jewish history, Parkes had high praise for the accomplishments of the leader of the Tannaitic (Torah and tradition) group, Rabbi Johann Ben Zakki, and the members of the academy created at Jabneh. Parkes referred to this group of teachers by the traditional term "Vineyard," and he argued that they were responsible for creating the means by which Judaism was able to survive the destruction of the Temple and endure as a community of faith.

> The period from which we learn most is that which lies between the destruction of State and Temple and the completion of the Talmud, a period of about four hundred years. The rabbis took over a defeated nation with its political and spiritual centres shattered; they had not only to "rescue the perishing" but also to provide a basis for communal life valid from China to the Pillars of Hercules, which would be self-perpetuating and independent of any central authority. The miracle of the system they created must be measured by the fact that Jews not only survived into modern times, but that those nineteenth and twentieth century Jews whose immediate background was the ghetto and the apparently dead world of Talmudic exegesis, provided in a dozen countries a surprising number of political, social and scientific leaders, instinct with the understanding of the contemporary world and its spiritual and social problems.[26]

Parkes credited the rabbis with an astonishing ability to preserve tradition while dealing creatively with new problems for which the past tradition offered little or no help. Into their hands fell the task of preserving not only the religious tradition of the people, but the people themselves. He attributed much of this genius to the nature of rabbinic Judaism as it developed. He listed four characteristics which he thought were outstanding:

    (a) the nature of the rabbinic academy,
    (b) the rabbinic doctrine of interpretation,

---

[26] Ibid., p. 274.

(c) the rabbinic doctrine of communal authority,
(d) the acceptance of the actual situation as the basis on which their thought evolved.[27]

The nature of the academy was significant to him because it was so unlike the Christian tradition. The academy was made up of people from all occupations of the community and from all economic classes. There was no professional clergy, and there was also no particular clerical authority. The strength of this organization laid, in Parkes' view, in the fact that the affairs of the people were discussed and determined by the "experience of the community as a whole."[28] This aspect of the rabbinic transition was very significant to him.

The rabbinic doctrine of interpretation of the Torah and the oral tradition had its roots in the debate between the Pharisees and the Sadducees. The Sadducees had refused to agree to the idea that new interpretations of the Torah were justified, while the Pharisees took the opposite point of view. The Pharisees agreed that it may not be easy to see how their interpretations followed from the words of Torah, but they never hesitated to defend the position that they had a right and a duty to interpret. In their minds, the Torah contained the words of God, but so did the oral interpretations. This position enabled the rabbis to operate under a principle which stated: "we do not lay on the people burdens which are beyond their power to support."[29] Parkes believed that this principle gave the rabbis an amazing amount of freedom to modify, adapt and even abolish commandments that were no longer feasible under the new and difficult situations Jews were finding themselves in after the fall of the Temple.

The doctrine of communal authority was essential in enabling Jews to survive without a centralized source of authority. Each Jewish community was responsible for defining their own loyalty to Judaism and the people of Israel. Rabbis could be called upon for leadership, and they were often given a considerable degree of authority. But their authority stemmed from the community's

---

[27] Ibid., p. 275.
[28] Ibid., p. 275. This concern of Parkes about the relationship between religion and the community has already been discussed in previous chapters.
[29] *The World of the Rabbis*, op. cit., p. 4.

willingness to grant it to them. An outgrowth of this doctrine was the evolution of the *responsa* by which a community could seek the advice of any rabbi on the problem facing it. This doctrine helped communities adjust to specific problems forced on them by the local environment in which they lived, while they still were able to remain within the wider community of Jews around the world. Parkes called this a "fascinating and bewildering decentralization," and he believed that such a system should have, to all appearances, been a source of hundreds of Jewish orthodoxies. He was quick to point out, however, that Judaism had remained remarkable free from the sorts of schisms that have plagued Christianity, and only one major schism appeared in Judaism between the first Christian century and the eighteenth.[30]

The fourth characteristic which impressed Parkes was Judaism's acceptance of actual situations. He often stated that "as Christianity is the religion of the unattainable, Judaism is the religion of the attainable."[31] If Judaism was to survive as a religion that dealt with the needs of the community, it had to keep in focus the actual needs and situations in which it found itself. It would have done no good to saddle the community with a lot of lofty ideals that bore no relationship to the actual situation the people were in. Parkes believed that this emphasis in Judaism on the attainable as the rule of the community enabled the Jews to survive under circumstances that could have very easily destroyed them.

In the previous chapters, we discussed Parkes' interest in relating Christianity to politics, economics, and other social problems. He never seemed to be able to find a satisfactory means of doing this. He did discover something in Judaism that appealed to him very much concerning this problem. The "dead religion" he had been taught about at Oxford proved to be a valuable guide in helping him to see how religion can be related to the broader questions of the community. The task that faced the rabbis was one of finding a way to provide the basis for the whole of normal Jewish life in a world where Jewish communities were scattered everywhere. He praised their work.

---

[30] "Christendom and the Synagogue," op. cit., p. 276.
[31] Ibid., p. 276.

The rabbis provided a total way of life, personal, domestic, social, and economic. They were realists about the dependent position of the communities, and their dependence on non-Jewish rulers. They were extremely realistic and precise about the temptations to apostasy to which Jews would be subjected in the most varying conditions; and in their discussions of what should be done or not done "for the sake of the name of God" they struck an exquisite balance between the necessity of preserving Jews, and that of preserving Judaism. Torah was something to *live* by, so that there was much that could be sacrificed to save life. It is astonishing to record this of a religion and a people with an unsurpassed role of martyrs, many thousands of whom could have saved their lives by accepting the religion of their persecutors.[32]

Parkes believed that the nature of rabbinic Judaism was such that it could be considered the religion that addressed the human being as social creature. In Judaism, Parkes found an interest in communal affairs that he had not found in Christianity. The very nature of Judaism compelled it to be concerned with the "people of Israel," and its development reflected that concern. There was not the sharp distinction made by Christianity between the "secular" and the "sacred" in the Jewish tradition, and this alone would have made Judaism important to Parkes.

The communal nature of Judaism was stressed by Parkes in all of his writings, and it formed the basis for his ideas about Jewish–Christian relations. The genius of the rabbis was to take seriously the concept of the peoplehood of Israel first and then deal with individual problems within that context. Survival was the key to rabbinic thinking, and Parkes believed that the rabbis lived up to the task they confronted after AD 70. Out of the efforts of the rabbis sprang institutions that enabled the Jews to survive in diverse and difficult situations.

The Sabbath, the Synagogue, and the school between them emphasized the communal element in Judaism and the communal responsibility for the lives of members of the community. No man could perform his *mitwoth* for another, but no

---

[32] *The World of the Rabbis*, op. cit., p. 4.

man could perform a synagogal service by himself. In the widely scattered Diaspora these institutions maintained the unity of Judaism and provided an element of uniformity within its multiplicity of circumstances.[33]

Parkes believed that most Christians did not understand this aspect of the development of Judaism, and therefore they did not see what he took to be the logical implications of Judaism's communal nature.

The discoveries that Parkes made about the nature of Judaism offered him an answer to the questions he had asked earlier about the relationship of religion to politics and society. The theology of Barth had stressed the otherness of God. In rabbinic Judaism, Parkes found a concept of God wrapped in the events of everyday life. He thought that the "proper field of theology was the nature and purpose of the Creator for this particular world," and he was looking for a way to talk about a God who would "desire a man to evolve who would be capable of full co-operation with him, of understanding his purpose, and of guiding his whole life in all its aspects by that understanding."[34] Parkes found in his study of the development of Judaism the positive impulsion for his theological thinking to counter the negative impulsion of Barth. He found Judaism comparatively free of the theological baggage that often preoccupied Christianity; there was a minimum of systematic metaphysics, little interest in salvation, and no coherent doctrine of personal survival after death. Moreover, he discovered that, contrary to traditional Christian beliefs, the Jewish religion was not an incomplete form of Christianity, but rather an entirely different kind of religion.

> Consequently my first important discovery was that Judaism was not an incomplete form of Christianity nor just a different religion, but *a different kind of religion stemming from the same divine origin and revelation.* The essence of the difference is expressed in the two completely different senses in which Jews and Christians speak of themselves as a

---

[33] *The Foundations of Judaism and Christianity*, op. cit., p. 308.
[34] James Parkes, *The Interplay of Judaism and Jewish History*, p. 6.

"chosen people." For the Jew it is the whole natural community which has been chosen for a special responsibility. For
the Christian it is a new community chosen out of the natural
communities of the world.[35]

For Parkes, this discovery unlocked many new ideas, and it is
upon this belief that Judaism and Christianity are two different
kinds of religions that he tried to construct a new Christian
approach to Judaism.

Obviously, Parkes' view of Judaism is quite different from
traditional Christian teachings. The very thing that Parkes said
Judaism, to its good fortune, lacked are often used by Christian
commentators as a measure of the usefulness of a religion. The
problems Judaism would pose for a Christian who thinks that the
main concern of a religion is the spiritual salvation of its members
is obvious. Traditionally there has been little of the speculation
concerning life after death in Judaism as opposed to Christianity.
Parkes believed that Christian missions to Jews were misguided
not only because they were not part of God's plan for creation, but
also because they approached the Jews in a way totally foreign to
them. Rabbinic literature concerned itself with the survival of the
people in the world now, and it trusted in God for the ultimate
salvation of Israel. But it was always Israel that was to be saved.
One can also find in Judaism a very strong tradition that sees a
place for "the righteous among the nations" in the world to
come.[36] Parkes believed that a study of rabbinic literature would
reveal this fact immediately. The rabbis made no attempt to
produce any works comparable to Christian theologians or Greek
philosophers.

It was the whole people down to its most stupid and recalci-
trant members that the rabbis were concerned with and

---

[35] Ibid., p. 7.

[36] Arthur Hertzberg writes about this tradition. "In the time of Bar Kokhba's
rebellion in the second century, against the tyranny of Rome, the question as to
whether non-Jews have a share in the life to come was seriously discussed, and
even at that time the accepted decision was that of Rabbi Joshua that the
righteous ones among the nations have a share in the life to come." See
"Conversion: A Jewish Approach" in *Jewish Heritage Reader*, edited by Morris
Adler, p. 199.

neither theologians nor philosophers thought in terms of more than a selected community from within a nation; and it was the whole every-day life that they were concerned with, not with that portion of life which might be subsumed under the heading of religion.[37]

Parkes believed that Christians had misunderstood the meaning and the nature of the Law in Judaism because they kept trying to fit Judaism into a Christian mold. By teaching the people that survival rested on their adherence to "the way of Torah," the rabbis had provided a means by which Judaism could grow and adjust to changing times without losing its rootedness. What Christian writers usually called "the Law," Parkes called "Torah." "For nothing has contributed more to the misunderstanding between the two religions," he wrote, "than the fact that the Septuagint translated the word "Torah" by the narrower word *nomos* and the English still further reduced the meaning by rendering *nomos* as *law*. For *law* is narrower than *nomos*, and *nomos* is narrower than "Torah.""[38] He referred to both Moore and Herford as scholars who rejected the traditional Christian negative interpretation of the Law. He quoted Herford, who said of Torah: "It does not, and never did mean Law. It means, and always has meant, Teaching."[39]

According to Judaism, the Law is not a burden to be regretted, but rather it is "a burden of Joy." By obeying the Law, one does the will of God. To perform one of these commandments is a *mizwoth*, a good deed. The Law is not a symbol of sin, as the Christians have said it is, but a sign of God's plan and man's cooperation. In Parkes' interpretation,

the rabbis firmly believed that the main purpose of God in giving the Torah to Israel, whether in written Scripture or the oral law, was to give to men a complete set of *halakoth*, that is, if we may call it, a blueprint of a human society so acting in the whole of its life as to do honour to its Creator and

---

[37] *The Foundations of Judaism and Christianity*, op. cit., p. 284.
[38] Ibid., p. xv.
[39] Ibid., as quoted.

to enjoy to the fullest possible extent the good gifts, material, spiritual, and intellectual which he had given them.[40]

Through the observance of the Law, the way of Torah, the rabbis provided the people a way in which to incorporate the essence of Judaism into the most common events of everyday life. Parkes saw Judaism as a religion that taught the Law and encouraged its performance. It became the means by which a Jew could develop his/her identity, and identify other Jews as well. The Torah conveyed the Law, the Halacha, and Jews responded by performing. Performance and responsibility were stressed in Judaism and the upshot of this was the lessening of any need to talk about salvation. One did not desire to be saved from the world in Judaism; rather, one was taught the proper way in which to live in the world. In Parkes' mind, this was the strength of Judaism and also the very place where Christian misunderstanding about Judaism begins.

What Parkes discovered about Judaism as he began his study of it in the early 1930s developed into a profound appreciation of the Jewish tradition. He discarded traditional teachings about Judaism, and he argued for a new Christian approach to Judaism and its role in human history and God's plan for creation. What he found in Judaism filled many of the gaps he had discovered in Christianity when he began to examine the issue of the relation of religion to politics and society. Judaism appeared to be tailor-made for such concerns. He stated quite bluntly that "the distinction between religion and political or social life is a separation which Judaism and its predecessor, the religion of Israel, has consistently refused to accept."[41] If we keep in mind the concern that Parkes had over the separation he felt Christianity made between politics and religion, it becomes easier to see why he felt so strongly about the need for Christians to appreciate what Judaism could teach. For Parkes, Judaism was a religion that enabled its adherents to think about politics, economics, ethics, the community, the common life, education and a host of other

---

[40] Ibid., p. 284.
[41] James Parkes, "God and the Jews," *The Twentieth Century*, vol. 170, (autumn 1961), p. 52.

social and communal problems within the framework of a religious tradition. Given his concerns stated in the 1929 lectures and throughout his other theological writings, he found that the continuous interplay of religion and people throughout Jewish history compared quite favorably to the Augustinian view of the Two Cities or Luther's two-kingdom doctrine. Karl Barth seemed to continue this traditional view of the relationship of Christianity to politics, and I believe it is safe to assume that Parkes much preferred the Jewish approach to the question.

Parkes believed that he need not abandon his own Christian faith because of his discovery, but he did believe that it was essential for Christians to rediscover Judaism and its message. The message of Sinai was essential for Christian self-understanding. That message had been ignored by Christians and he is quite frank in stating that Christian hatred of Jews was the source of this problem. He addressed this problem quite clearly when he wrote:

> I am a very orthodox and traditional Christian in my acceptance of the rightness of those who founded the Christian Church on their experience of Jesus of Nazareth. But their explanation that this experience involved the rejection of Judaism and the substitution of the Christian Church as the new, and only, Israel of God was, I am convinced, wrong. And *their response* to that explanation once they had the power under Constantine to enforce it, was the greatest single disaster in the whole of Christian history. For not only did it begin a process which has a continuous presence from the first repressive measures in Roman Law to the Holocaust and to Russian and Arab antisemitism today; it deprived the whole Christian experience of any understanding and acceptance of the revelation of Sinai.[42]

What Parkes learned about Judaism compelled him to reject the traditional teachings of the Church about Judaism in the name of intellectual honesty. In addition, Parkes believed that as a Christian he could understand the revelation of Calvary properly only if he also properly understood the revelation at Sinai. To do any less

---

[42] James Parkes, *Tradition and the Challenge of the Times*, p. 8.

would leave a Christian with an incomplete understanding of Christianity's role in God's plan for creation. This is a reversal of traditional Christian claims, but one which Parkes argued for throughout his writings on Jewish–Christian relations.

Parkes was able to revise his thinking about Judaism because of his Modernist roots and his historical training. Traditional Christian teachings did not have an aura of infallibility for him, and when he began to make a study of Judaism proper, he discovered how inaccurate traditional ideas about Judaism had been in Christian tradition. The Modernist position stressed truth as a criteria for any theological statement. When Parkes discovered that Judaism was not a dead, arid, legalistic religion but a vibrant and living tradition of the Jewish people, he could only respond with a plea for a new Christian position.

Parkes reached this position through studies which he began at the request of the WCSF in 1929. He unexpectedly discovered in Judaism the kind of approach to religion and politics he had been seeking in Christianity since the early twenties, and expressed clearly in the 1929 lectures. This rediscovery of Judaism marked the beginning of Parkes' quest for a new Jewish–Christian understanding. Coupled with this was his work on the problem of Christian antisemitism, also begun in the late 1920s and early 1930s. The roots of Parkes theology of Jewish–Christian relations also can be traced back to this period. When one reads Parkes in this context, his positions become clearer, and they can be seen as a logical development of his early theological and historical thinking. That is why it is so important to be aware of how Parkes came to discover Judaism anew and revised his thinking in the light of his discoveries.

5

Antisemitism and a New Theology

In 1929, the International Student Services asked Parkes to devote his time and energy to the "Jewish Question." Antisemitic riots were taking place in many European universities, and the Nazi party and other anti-Jewish organizations were growing in political strength in Germany, Austria and Poland. During his work at ISS, Parkes had already encountered antisemitic sentiments on university campuses, and he arranged for a conference to take place in France on that very issue. He accepted the assignment to do research and writing on the question, and the results of his labor was the publication of his book *The Jew and His Neighbour* in June 1930. From that time until his death in 1981, Parkes devoted the major part of his life to the study of antisemitism and the problem of Jewish–Christian relations.

Parkes was, indeed, a pioneer in this field, and his was often a lonely, prophetic voice. As he wrote in his autobiography, "I learned very early that to evolve a new attitude to Jewish–Christian relations was to be a lonely job." Today a growing number of Christians have engaged in the task of rethinking Christianity's traditional position on Judaism and the Jewish people, and most point to the Holocaust and the establishment of the State of Israel as important factors in their thinking. The pioneering aspects of Parkes' work can be shown by the fact that he was writing about the Christian roots of antisemitism and the roots of the Jewish state long before either the Holocaust occurred or the State of Israel was founded. This is a noteworthy aspect of his work. In the modern dialogue, there has been some concern

189

that Christian rethinking of its traditional claims concerning Jews was merely a "Christian guilt trip" over what happened in the Holocaust, and that Christian support for the State of Israel was based on this guilt rather than carefully thought-out arguments. Parkes' work is a forceful counter to this argument, for even his early works raised questions about the roots of antisemitism in Christian thought based on theological integrity and moral concerns. If the Holocaust has motivated contemporary Christians to re-examine their tradition, Parkes' work demonstrates that this was a problem prior to the Holocaust and that the issue would still be before the Church even if the Holocaust had never occurred. Christian concern about antisemitism in the teaching of the Church is not a product of the Holocaust; rather the more troubling question arises about whether the Holocaust was in some measure the result of Christian antisemitism. Parkes believed that this charge against the Church could be made, and he attempted to create a new theology which would enable Christianity to affirm Judaism as a valid religious tradition with equal status to Christianity in God's overall plan for creation and the redemption of creation. The groundwork for his new theological thinking was laid prior to the Holocaust, but the Holocaust added an even greater moral dimension to the problem. I think it is safe to say that Parkes was almost alone in the Christian world in seeing the full demonic dimensions of Christian antisemitism prior to the Nazi era, and certainly one of the first to think about the theological implications of any attempt to rid Christianity of its antisemitic tradition. In this time after the Holocaust, James Parkes stands out as an important model for the Christian community as it struggles with antisemitism and the creation of a new theology.

In this post-Holocaust period, a growing number of Protestant and Roman Catholic scholars have begun to scrutinize the Christian tradition in a search for the roots of antisemitism in Christian teachings. Difficult problems arise for Christians who realize that the Church must rethink some basic theological positions if there is to be any success in removing antisemitism from the Christian mind. Astute observers have seen that the Church cannot simply condemn antisemitism as an evil without also correcting those traditional teachings that have contributed to antisemitic ideas.

It is easy to condemn something as evil as antisemitism, but it is much more difficult to admit complicity in the problem and begin the process of eliminating antisemitic teachings from one's own tradition. Failure to do so, however, would place the Church in the morally untenable situation of condemning something that it helps to perpetuate by its own teachings. It could be charged that failure to correct its antisemitic teachings provides, in essence, a post-Holocaust justification for the murderers who systematically set out to kill nearly six million human beings—men, women and children—simply because they were Jews. Even if the Church does go about its proper task of correcting its antisemitic teachings, it must still face up to the charge that it helped to contribute to the fate of the Jews during the Holocaust. In the words of A. Roy Eckardt: "Could there be a more damning judgement upon the Church of our century than this one—that not until after the day of Auschwitz did Christians see fit to fabricate a correction of the record."[1]

To many Jews and Christians, Auschwitz, the symbol of the Holocaust, is an historical event that radically affects our religious traditions and the ways in which we think about the past and the future. Franklin Littell has called it an "Alpine Event" in human history resented by many modern Christian teachers because it requires a theological reappraisal and demands an admission of guilt.[2] The Canadian theologian Alan Davies has written that, "For Christians, Auschwitz, geographically and symbolically located in the heart of Christian Europe, suggests the moral disorder of the 'Christian' civilization that permitted the Nazi philosophy to grow in its midst."[3] Eckardt has suggested that the dating of years should now be marked as B.A. (Before Auschwitz) and A.A. (After Auschwitz).[4] In the face of the events of the Holocaust, the Christian is confronted with the task of

---

[1] A. Roy Eckardt, "Can there be a Jewish–Christian Relationship?", *The Journal of Bible and Religion*, vol. 33, no. 2 (April 1965), p. 124.

[2] Franklin Littell, *The Crucifixion of the Jews: The Failure of Christians to Understand the Jewish Experience*, p. 2.

[3] Alan Davies, *Antisemitism and the Christian Mind: The Crisis of Conscience after Auschwitz*, p. 37.

[4] A. Roy Eckardt, "Is the Holocaust Unique?", *Worldview*, vol. 17. no. 9 (September 1974), p. 32.

examining the role of the Church in developing the conditions that allowed the Death Camps of Nazi Europe to be built. Understanding the historical and theological development of the anti-Jewish tradition in Christianity is essential to that task, and the need to reinterpret the tradition is a necessary corollary to it. The pioneering work of James Parkes provides a guide for Christians seeking to repudiate the antisemitism of the past and to acquire a new and better understanding of the relationship between Judaism and Christianity. It is of considerable significance that this would have been the case even if the Holocaust had never occurred. The fact that Christianity must deal with its antisemitic past today in light of the Holocaust makes Parkes an important thinker to be reckoned with, and someone who deserves more attention than he has previously been given. As both an historian and theologian, James Parkes is a major figure in post-Holocaust Christian thought.

In his first book on antisemitism, Parkes traced the problem of Jewish–Gentile relations from modern times to the massacre of Jews in Europe during the first Crusade in 1096. *The Jew and His Neighbour* did not stress religious antisemitism, and Parkes was fairly optimistic about overcoming the "Jewish Problem" with a healthy dose of patience, goodwill, intelligence and human action.[5] The book reveals just how naive Parkes was concerning the depth of the problem, and it also shows that he shared some of the prejudices of his time. Malcolm Diamond points out that Parkes made reference to the idea that some Jews may well have participated in the writing of the notorious *Protocols of the Elders of Zion,* and that he was somewhat guilty of making character references to Jews without any supporting evidence.[6] Diamond also demonstrates that as late as 1945 Parkes made some indictments against Jews who deviated from the norm of English behavior in his book *An Enemy of the People.*[7] These observations

---

[5] James Parkes, *The Jew and His Neighbour: A Study of the Causes of Anti-Semitism*, p. 11.
[6] Malcolm Diamond, "Honesty in the Christian–Jewish Interchange," *Journal of the Bible and Religion*, vol. 33, No. 2 (1965), p. 117. Diamond cites p. 184 of *The Jew and His Neighbour*, op. cit.
[7] Ibid., p. 118.

of Diamond's are helpful in showing that Parkes' ideas about Jews and antisemitism went through various stages of evolution. As Diamond showed, Parkes changed his position a number of times, and the questionable statements of earlier works were eliminated in books written at a later time. Parkes, in fact, did a considerable amount of work in debunking the myth of the "Protocols," and his knowledge of the topic was one reason the Swiss Nazis made an attempt on his life during the famous Berne Trial of 1934–35.

It is evident that Parkes's thinking in 1930 was still in its infancy from the fact that he traced antisemitism only back to 1096. But one question continued to concern him: "I had begun the story of *The Jew and His Neighbour* with the massacres of the first Crusade. But the question was always in my mind: why did these massacres take place in cities where there was already a long Jewish residence, and with no tradition of violence? So I determined to take as my thesis a study of the period behind the crusades, and the beginnings of antisemitism."[8]

Parkes was able to pursue this topic because his work on the "Jewish Question" for the ISS had made him an "expert" of sorts on the topic. Both he and the ISS decided that he should work for a doctoral degree at Oxford on the subject of antisemitism. He began his work at Oxford with no preconceived notions about what he would find. In his autobiography, he recalled how he began his research:

> My subject was an enquiry into the origins of antisemitism. I could not more closely define it, as I was in considerable doubt as to what I should find. I had been a classical scholar and was familiar with the dislike of Jews and other orientals among the Romans of good Latin stock. I knew Cicero's pretence that it was dangerous to offend Jews of Rome—though I did not know whether it was a typical Cicerionian flight of rhetoric or a genuine fear. But I knew very little either of patristic attitudes or of later Roman legislation. Of post–New Testament Judaism I knew nothing at all. I had understood from

---

[8] James Parkes, *Voyage of Discoveries*, p. 120.

my teachers at Oxford that all that was good in the Old Testament had passed to the Christian Church, and I had been content to leave it at that.[9]

As Parkes continued his research, he discovered many troubling facts that led him to the conclusion that the roots of antisemitism were to be found in the teachings of the Christian Church. His findings were published in 1934 as *The Conflict of the Church and Synagogue: A Study in the Origins of Antisemitism.*

The result of his study led Parkes to argue that "classical" antisemitism in Greek and Roman culture differed from Christian antisemitism. There is clearly a question in Parkes' mind as to whether or not the anti-Jewish sentiments of Greek and Roman writers should even be called antisemitism. His reasoning for questioning this is based on a distinction he makes between the idea of "anti-Jewish" and "antisemitic." This was not merely a semantic problem, but an important factor in his reasoning as to why Christian antisemitism is not merely a problem introduced into Christianity by Gentile converts, but rather a unique problem introduced by Christianity itself.

According to Parkes, antisemitism is an "abnormal hostility." Hostility directed at Jews is antisemitic when it is abnormal in the sense that there is no adequate explanation for the form or the severity of its manifestation in the actual contemporary conduct of the Jews against whom it is directed.[10] This abnormal hostility is not to be confused with "anti-Jewishness" or "anti-Judaism."[11]

> Antisemitism is a quite definable social scourge and its definition is not difficult. As long as Jews are disliked for the conduct which can in fact be attributed to them—even if it is exaggerated or maliciously interpreted—so long is the feeling anti-Jewish, and comparable to other dislikes which pervade our imperfect society. But when Jews are hated for conduct of which they have not been guilty, for crimes which in fact they

---

[9] Ibid., p. 120.
[10] "Antisemitism from Caesar to Luther," *Query* (1938), pp. 12–13.
[11] *An Enemy of the People: Antisemitism*, p. 65.

have never committed, then we are in the presence of antisemitism.[12]

He sustained this argument throughout his writings, and he
wrote in 1963:

> For what differentiates antisemitism from other group preju-
> dices, whether suffered by Jews or any other people, is that
> group prejudice is normally related to something contempor-
> ary, something which actually happened, even if it be
> wrongly or distortedly interpreted; whereas antisemitism
> has almost no relationship to the actual world, and rests on a
> figment of the imagination perpetually bolstered up by other
> figments.[13]

This contrast between "anti-Jewish" and "antisemitic" forms the
backdrop for the way in which Parkes compares and contrasts the
relationship of the Jews to the Greco-Roman world to their
relationship with Christianity and Christendom.

In *The Conflict of the Church and Synagogue,* Parkes begins by
raising a question about a reference to "classical antisemitism"
found in scholarly works on the history of the period, particularly
those by German scholars. Parkes had a rather traditional education with emphasis on Greek and Latin that gave him ready
access to classical texts. He came to the conclusion that much that
had been written about the Jews in the ancient world and the
issue of Gentile hostility was too narrow in perspective. He
thought the German scholars in particular argued for a deep-
seated hatred of Jews among non-Jews

> in a desire to prove that antisemitism was something which
> inevitably accompanied the Jew wherever he went, and
> which was due to his own racial and unalterable character-
> istics. Insofar as all these studies wish to generalize on the
> position of the Jews in the ancient world from an examination
> of the hostility to which they were undoubtedly subject in
> certain places and at certain times, they exhibit the weakness

---

[12] James Parkes, "Jews, Christians and God," p. 4. See also *Antisemitism: A
Concise World History*, pp. 64–65.
[13] *Antisemitism: A Concise World History,* op. cit., p. 62.

of not taking into account the implications of contemporary Jewish missionary activity and its known sources. They also omit the peculiar character of the Alexandrian situation, and the inevitable difficulties of the adjustment of a monotheistic people in a polytheistic world.[14]

In Parkes' view, the Jews of the ancient world were not the target of unrelieved hatred, but were in many ways merely one group among many, with some peculiar habits. They seem to have aroused little interest up to the time of Alexander, and the scanty references to them in all of classical literature seems to show that they were pretty much an accepted or ignored part of ancient society. Jews could be found throughout the Roman Empire, and they were engaged in numerous occupations, so economics seldom played a role in generating anti-Jewish feelings, with the exception perhaps of Alexandria. Parkes takes seriously Strabo's statement that the Jews "have already settled in every city, and it is not easy to find a spot on earth which this tribe has not occupied and where it has not asserted itself," as evidence of a Jewish presence throughout the ancient world.[15]

Parkes did think that the Jews posed a curious problem for the ancient world, whose polytheistic leaning brought with it a certain degree of religious toleration. For Judaism was a religion that did not allow for such tolerance since it was a strictly monotheistic religion. Of all the Gods of the ancient world, only the Jewish God appeared so haughty and aloof. This put the Jews in the ambiguous position of expecting toleration, but not giving much in return. It also created some problems for ancient rulers, for the Jews had to be exempted from certain civic duties that conflicted with their religious law. Parkes explained the dilemma of these rulers:

> To give toleration to Yahweh was to suppress in favor of the Jews the punishment to which the omission of these acts exposed them. The laws had to be suspended in their favor. Special privileges had to be granted them—for an exception in favor of a minority is a privilege. But to refuse this

---

[14]   James Parkes, *The Conflict of the Church and Synagogue*, p. 2.
[15]   Ibid., pp. 7, 13.

toleration was to run counter to the ancient principle of tolerance, and was to render the practice of Judaism impossible. This was the dilemma: persecution or privilege.[16]

The fact is, however, that Jews were able to gain these privileges and to maintain them even when revolts were taking place in Judea.

Parkes sees this as important for understanding the place of the Jew in the ancient world. In spite of their demands for special treatment, they were basically allowed to exist untouched. Roman authorities granted them the special status of *peregrini* in 161 BC which allowed them to be judged by their own laws. In 110 BC, they secured the same privileges for Jews in all kingdoms and states allied with Rome, independent of the citizenship that some Jews had already obtained. Julius Caesar affirmed these privileges by granting them permission to "live according to their own laws." According to Parkes, "this formed the *magna carta* of the Jews in the Roman Empire, being frequently reaffirmed in general terms by subsequent emperors."[17] It is not until the time of the Christian emperors that this status of the Jews was upset.[18]

Parkes knew that such privileges had a tendency to bring a sometimes unwanted prominence to the Jewish people, but he cautions that this can easily be exaggerated and misinterpreted. Even with their privileges, Jews were no more visible than others.

> In the main, they were indistinguishable from the other inhabitants of the Mediterranean cities. They were not the only "orientals," and they were of the same race and appearance as the Syrians and the Phoenicians who had been dwelling in Greece, Italy and Spain for centuries. They lived in groups, for the convenience of the Synagogue worship and of common life, but so did the other foreign groups in all the great cities of the empire. . . . The immense majority were in relatively humble walks of society, since a large proportion of them began their life in the diaspora as slaves.[19]

---

[16] Ibid., p. 9. Parkes quotes a long passage from J. Juster, *Les Juif dans l'empire Romain*, vol. I, p. 213, in support of his argument.
[17] Ibid., p. 8.
[18] Ibid., p. 11.
[19] Ibid., p. 12.

On the other hand, there is no doubt that anti-Jewish opinion did arise from time to time and for various reasons. The Jewish religion could not help attracting attention, and in the eyes of most Greek and Roman philosophers, it was hardly appealing. While the stress on a rigid moral code in Judaism met with approval, the rituals of Judaism appeared ridiculous, and the Jewish refusal to accept other Gods seemed excessively intolerant. Judaism appeared to many Greek writers as a curious mix of philosophy and superstition. "Whereas the Greek intellectual stood in sharp opposition to the simple-minded Greek who worshipped the gods, the Jewish philosopher, in other words, teachers in the Synagogue, believed intensely in the Jewish religion."[20] Intellectually then, Judaism suffered by comparison to Greek philosophy, and it became an object of derision in certain intellectual circles.[21]

On the popular level, the privileges extended to Jews at times gave life to anger among the other citizens of the empire. Partly, it was a typical reaction of a majority resenting any privilege given to a minority. At other times, it was due to the fact that Jews were relieved of some economic burdens that went along with participation in the civic cult. Questions about Jewish loyalty to the emperor arose, and this point was often aggravated by Jewish support for an independent Jewish state and their sending money to the Temple in Jerusalem.[22]

Jewish intolerance and exclusivism, so unattractive to Greek philosophers, and the special favors granted Jews by the Romans clearly gave non-Jews reasons to suspect and dislike them. Charges were sometimes made that Jews were misanthropes (a charge later leveled at Christians), antisocial, gloomy and insular. Their resistance to compromise on their religious beliefs caused them many problems. This adherence to their own standards and

---

[20] Ibid., p. 14.

[21] For a thorough survey of the Jews in acient literature, see M. Stern, *Greek and Latin Authors on Jews and Judaism* (Jerusalem, 1974 and 1980). See also the articles by Louis Feldman and Shaye Cohen in *History and Hate: The Dimensions of Anti-Semitism* (Philadelphia: Jewish Publication Society, 1986).

[22] James Parkes, "Christian Influence on the Status of Jews in Europe," in *Historica Judaica*, vol. 1, no. 1 (November 1938), p. 31. Also see *Conflict*, pp. 21–22.

beliefs in the pluralistic society of an ancient city made them vulnerable to the charge of being antisocial and clannish. It is a mistake to regard such manifestations of anti-Jewish feelings as antisemitism, according to Parkes, since these feelings parallel similar xenophobias. The only ancient hostility that could be called antisemitic in the sense that it evolved a completely untrue and abusive account of the Jews and their origins may be found in Egypt, and especially in Alexandria.[23] But, here again, Parkes sees the anti-Jewish activities in Alexandria as having an explanation rooted in reality.[24]

Alexandria was an exception to many rules in the ancient world. A large city that Parkes thought was rather artificially created by Alexander the Great, Alexandria was home to a number of different groups, all seeking power and security. It tended to be turbulent, and at times, the turbulence turned to anarchy and violence. The Jews found themselves viewed as outsiders, economically successful, and holders of various privileges but not citizenship.

Its Egyptian location added another problem unique to the Jews. The Jewish holiday of Passover portrayed the Egyptians in a very unfavorable manner, and this aggravated the situation. That "ill feeling expressed itself in a counter-story of the Exodus addressed by the Egyptians to the Jews."[25] Many of the charges made against Jews stemmed from the writing of anti-Jewish Egyptians like Manetho, Damocritus, and Apion. Charges were made that Jews were lepers, worshipped the head of an ass, committed cannibalism and hated all humanity. The picture painted of the Jew was such that no charge appeared too extreme.

> With these stories in the air, it is easy to see how the negative exclusiveness of the Jews was attributed to malevolence, and how this malevolence could be translated into active hostility, as when Lysimachus (also of Alexandria) alleged that they were commanded to overthrow and destroy all altars and

---

[23] James Parkes, *A History of the Jewish People*, p. 32.
[24] Louis Feldman, op. cit., argues that popular hostility toward Jews was more deep seated that Parkes seems to think and was more easily defined as antisemitism.
[25] "Jews, Christians and God," op. cit., p. 14.

temples—a charge which was true enough in the old independent days of Palestine itself, but which happened outside of
Palestine on rare occasions and under special provocation.[26]

The anti-Jewish riots reported by Philo and Josephus indicate
that there were serious problems for Jews, but here again, Parkes
sees the Alexandrian situation as somewhat unique in the ancient
world, believing that as a manifestation of conflict between competing social and ethnic groups it was understandable, but not
justifiable.

> The presence of a group, powerful both numerically and
> commercially, but not taking part in the common life of the
> city [Alexandria], was bound to be a source of jealousy and
> friction. It perpetually marks out the Jews as having inter-
> ests other than those of the rest of the inhabitants, and at the
> same time, it would give the Jews themselves a permanent
> feeling of malaise which would not tend to promote peaceful
> relations. We know that the Jews attempted to obtain both
> citizenship and a share of the public life of the city.[27]

The Jews also antagonized the local Egyptians by forming an
alliance with the Romans, whom the Egyptians hated even more
than the previous rulers, the Ptolemies. The troubles that arose in
Alexandria during the time of Caligula was well described by
Claudius, in Parkes' view, as "a war between Jews and the rest of
the population."

Can we then see this as the first incident which steps beyond
anti-Jewishness into antisemitism? Parkes thought not. Rather,
he finds Alexandria to be untypical of the ancient world, and
basically an example of social conflict in no way unique or abnormal. It seems, however, that Parkes may be making some very
fine distinctions here. The absurd charges made against Jews and
their religious practices seems to go beyond simple social conflict.
Yet, for Parkes, that which we would call antisemitism is not yet
visible in the ancient world.

---

[26] *The Conflict of the Church and Synagogue*, op. cit., p. 17.
[27] Ibid., p. 18.

Parkes also argued that the legal status of the Jews in the Roman Empire counters the belief in a universal deep-seated hatred of Jews. The many privileges they gained from Caesar were continually reaffirmed, and they became a *"religio licita."* There is some question as to whether this is a legal phrase, but it does help to explain the Jewish status in the empire. According to Parkes, "in Roman law, the Jews formed a 'collegium' rather than a 'religio' and as such it had a right to retain their own observances."[28] The one constant objection against the Jews among the Romans was that they were "utterly exclusive," but that was nothing new. What is clear is that Jews were able to survive, and even thrive, in the Roman Empire. Even in times when revolts against Rome were going on in Judea, the status of Jews elsewhere in the Empire did not change. Their expulsion from Rome in 139 BC does not seem to have been very long term since they appear quite well re-established when Pompey took Jerusalem in 63 BC. Jews continued to live on basically friendly terms with the Romans, and during Herod's period, Jews enjoyed a relative amount of security under Roman protection.

The situation between Jews and Romans began to change during the first half of the first century AD, particularly in Judaea. While the Jewish upper class tended to cultivated Hellenistic ways, ordinary Jews and groups like the Pharisees and Zealots hated the Romans and their rule over the former Jewish state. The desire for freedom from the yoke of Roman rule was coupled with "the flood of Messiahs who sprang up in the first half of the first century."[29] The hope-for Messiah would free Palestine of the Roman threat to the Jewish way of life and restore Israel to her proper place in history. Incidents between the Jews and the Romans increased tensions, some of which are recorded in the New Testament. Ultimately, war broke out in AD 65 and AD 135, with disastrous results for Jewish political aspirations. "Under such circumstances," wrote Parkes, "it is amazing that outside Palestine the Romans showed the moderation to leave Jewish

---

[28] Ibid., p. 8. See also the article by Solomon Grayzel, "The Jews and Roman Law," *The Jewish Quarterly Review*, vol. 59 (1968–69), footnote on p. 95, where he challenges Parkes' idea about "collegium."
[29] Ibid., p. 22.

privileges untouched, especially as the troubles in Palestine were spasmodically accompanied by serious troubles in various other eastern provinces of the empire."[30]

There were occasions when Roman anger spilled over and certain privileges were taken away, as when Hadrian forbad circumcision, but the Jewish rights gained under Caesar largely prevailed in the empire up until the fall of Rome. One place you can begin to see a difference is in the writings of the Roman authors that treat of the Jewish wars. Parkes believed that this can be seen by comparing the writing of Horace and Ovid on the Jews with that of Juvenal and Martial, the latter being clearly more hostile in nature. The writings of Seneca and Tacitus also reflect this change.[31]

The fact that Jews were able to retain their privileges even in times of war with Rome is a central point in Parkes' argument against the idea that antisemitism was deeply ingrained in classical culture. In addition, he argues that the success of Jewish missionary activity in the Diaspora also counters any assumption that Jews were universally hated and despised.[32]

---

[30] Ibid., p. 23.

[31] See M. Stern, op. cit.

[32] John Gager, *The Origins of Antisemitism: Attitudes toward Judaism in Pagan and Christian Antiquity* for a recent discussion of these issues. Gager is in basic agreement with Parkes, although he tends to use the works of Marcel Simon and Jules Isaac to support his work position more than Parkes' work. Nonetheless, it is significant, in my mind, that this new interest in the roots of Christian antisemitism as distinct from pagan antisemitism does not go much beyond what Parkes said, although Gager is clearly a first-rate classical scholar who was able to fill in many of the gaps in Parkes' thought. From Gager's few references to Parkes, it is not clear to me how much of Parkes he read. He tends to depend on Alan Davies' assessment of Parkes, which I think is somewhat limited. Rosemary Ruether in her book *Faith and Fratricide: The Theological Roots of Antisemitism* also tends to agree with Parkes about pagan antisemitism, but she too seems limited in her knowledge of Parkes and often cites John Seaver's book as a primary source for her ideas. Seaver's book, however, is rather a blatant copy of Parkes' *The Conflict of the Church and Synagogue*. Ruether's book did, however, bring to the center of theological discussion many of the issues Parkes raised nearly fifty years earlier and in many ways corroborates Parkes' ideas about Christian antisemitism, although I think Parkes would disagree to some extent with her ideas of Christology being the left hand of antisemitism. I base this on the idea that Parkes believed that Christology read in a theocentric manner could be free of antisemitism.

Parkes links Jewish missionary activity closely with the messianic movements that began to sweep the Jewish world in the first century AD. Such messianic excitement drew attention to the Jewish religion and accentuated among the Jews their activity as missionaries, but it also became a menace to Jewish security.[33] The combination of the two posed a challenge to Rome on both political and religious grounds, and in Parkes' view, ultimately destroyed the peace between Rome and Jerusalem.

Parkes took the position that Judaism actively sought converts in the ancient world and that Judaism remained opened to Gentiles who wished to imitate Jews without being converted—the God-fearers."

> The synagogue did attract widespread interest and a variety of degrees of adherence among Gentile neighbours of the Hellenistic Jews, and these Jews were prepared to welcome such interest and adherence. Paul might have had new things to say about the status of the Gentiles who accepted his message; but he did not have to argue that Gentiles had a right to hear it—they were there already listening to him in the synagogue or in whatever other places Jews forgathered.[34]

Jewish missionary activity seems to challenge the assumption of classical and contemporary writers that ancient Judaism was aloof, indifferent and exclusive. According to Parkes, "The exclusive connection between the God of Israel, the children of Israel and the Land of Israel was broken by two developments."[35] The first was the universalist view of the prophets and their vision. The second was the Diaspora of Jews into foreign lands. Both developments encouraged a missionary attitude among Jews which proved to be very successful in drawing in Gentile converts.[36]

It is not clear just how many Gentiles converted to Judaism because the hard evidence is scant. It does seem clear, however,

---

[33] Ibid., p. 23.
[34] James Parkes, *The Foundations of Judaism and Christianity*, pp. 108–9. Parkes used B. J. Bamberger's book *Proselytism in the Talmudic Period* as his reference on this subject.
[35] Ibid., p. 109.
[36] Ibid. See also *A History of the Jewish People*, op. cit., p. 33.

that Jewish indifference or hatred toward non-Jews seems not to have been a factor in Diaspora life, at least in the sense that non-Jews wished to be like Jews. The Jewish ethical code, a strict moral life and a strong family structure, had a great appeal to many non-Jews. The antiquity of Judaism and its monotheism also played well in certain Gentile circles. That there were converts is without question:

> We hear directly and indirectly of a number of converts to Judaism during the period before the destruction of the Temple. Sometimes the references are casual, as in the inclusion among the first deacons of the Jerusalem Church of "Nicolaus, a proselyte of Antioch" and sometimes we possess a substantial narrative. By far the most famous converts were the royal family of Adiabene who early in the first century of the Christian era became Jews. Adiabene was a small Mesopotamian kingdom, but it is doubtful if many of the population followed the example of the royal house. Or the implication may be indirect: the works of Philo imply a considerable number of Gentile hearers, for his discussion of Greek philosophy would have been of limited interest to a purely Jewish audience.[37]

Parkes also viewed the negative references to Gentile converts to Judaism in Tacitus and Juvenal as further evidence of Jewish missions.[38]

There were Roman restrictions of Jewish missions, however, based largely on the legal status of Jews. Gentile attraction to Judaism caused little problem to the authorities, but actual conversion did cause a problem. Converts could not legally claim to be Jews because public law only allowed that a Jew was one who was born a Jew. Such a person could alone claim the legal exemptions and privileges allowed to Jews; converts could not do so. Parkes argues that "Technically, proselytising among the non-[J]ews was an indictable offence, but it was only in moments of stress, such as accompanied the second Jewish war that the

---

[37] Ibid., p. 110.
[38] James Parkes, "Rome, Pagan and Christian," in *Judaism and Christianity*, vol. II, H. Loewe, ed., p. 117. See also *Conflict*, p. 24.

Roman authorities attempted to enforce the law. Otherwise, they turned a blind eye to conversion to Judaism, knowing by experience that the convert was a better rather than a worse citizen after his conversion."[39] How they know this fact Parkes does not say, and it seems, at best, an hypothetical idea. But the question of legal status may well have prevented more Gentiles from converting to Judaism, and since "the worship and teaching of the synagogue were always open to those who were not members of the community . . . formal conversion might well appear to them unnecessary."[40]

The Romans were always suspicious of Eastern religious missionary movements, not just the Jews, but Jews, being spread throughout the empire, posed a special problem. Jews were "dangerous" because they did not honor the "gods" of the state and thus were perceived as "atheists." Converts to Judaism increased the number of "atheists" who could legitimately escape certain obligations to the state by becoming Jewish. Judaism walked a thin line between legitimacy and seditiousness by virtue of the privileges granted to them, and it would seem that seeking converts would have jeopardized that legal status because of the legal restrictions concerning who was a Jew. Yet, Parkes maintained, Judaism pursued an active missionary course, and he believes that evidence of this is found in the way in which Gentiles ultimately found their way into the Church:

> The foundation of the Gentile Church was laid almost exclusively among the proselytes or people already interested in Judaism. The transition by which these groups passed from partial membership of Judaism to full membership of the Christian Church was an eay one. Had the synagogues of the Diaspora insisted primarily on the ritual and not the moral and ethical implications of Judaism, on observance of the letter rather than on the spirit of the Law, it is doubtful if this transition would have ever taken place except in a few individual cases. What Christianity offered them was not something completely different, but the same thing with, in

[39] Christian Influence on the Status of the Jews in Europe, op. cit., p. 31.
[40] *The Conflict of the Church and Synagogue*, op. cit., p. 111.

addition, the power of Jesus Christ in the place of the disadvantages and other ritual prescriptions.[41]

The Greco-Roman world, in Parkes' view, did not have an unrelieved hatred for Jews. It is a mixed picture in which Jews are seen in both a positive and negative light. Jewish–Gentile relations were not unique, but rather followed a sociologically "normal" pattern of interaction between groups that view each other with suspicion and hostility because of religious and social differences, but that also make adjustments to live together and even influence each other. Where hostility arises, Parkes sees identifiable causes and it is limited to these causes. There were clearly hostilities between Jews and other groups in the Roman Empire, and there were many problems for Jews to deal with, but this does not account, in Parkes' mind, for the development of antisemitism that begins to appear by the late first century. Parkes sees an irony in what develops for that which changed the normal pattern of Jewish–Gentile relations was the action of the Christian Church. For Parkes, the irony is that the triumph of Christianity should have reduced the problem. He sums up the issue in light of the Jewish wars:

> The struggle left blood on both sides, but essentially the advent of Christianity to power removed all the causes of the conflict. For the reasons which inspired the Jews inspired also the Christians, and the victory of the Christian attitude to "atheism" and to the missionary activity should have brought political peace to the Jews. Instead the advent of Christianity perpetuated their tragedy. The reasons for this have nothing to do with the old enmities. They are found only in the conflict of Christianity with its parent religion.[42]

Parkes is consistent in his belief that Christianity and Christian theologians were to blame for the unique evil of antisemitism. He wrote of his doctoral research that, "the central and overpowering, indeed horrifying conclusion, which that research brought me, was the total responsibility of the Christian Church for

---

[41] Ibid., p. 25.
[42] Ibid., p. 26.

turning a normal xenophobia into the unique disease of antisemitism."[43] It was the theologically based hatred that would be disseminated by patristic theology and Church councils that set Christian views of Jews apart from classical attitudes, or even Moslem attitudes toward Jews. While Jewish–Moslem relations were hardly as idyllic as is sometimes imagined, the Jews never suffered "the sustained theological denigration and the conscious falsification of their history which they had to endure wherever they lived in a Christian environment."[44]

Parkes' arguments rests on his belief that one can find an anti-Jewish polemic within the Gospels themselves, and this polemic became more and more vitriolic in the hands of an increasingly Gentile Church and its theologians. In a number of works, Parkes traces what he sees as the growing hostility toward Jews in the Gospels. The Gospel picture of Jesus portrays him as being in conflict with various Jewish groups, but it is a contradictory picture. In the synoptic Gospels, Jesus' enemies vary, and Parkes tries to illustrate how different stories in Mark, which do not reflect a particularly hostile tone, become increasingly hostile toward Jews when Luke and Matthew add certain passages.[45] "There is," he writes, "an unmistakable increase in hostility in

---

[43] James Parkes, *Prelude to Dialogue*, p. 190.

[44] Ibid., p. 190. In Gager's survey of this problem, he argues that Marcel Simon and Jules Isaac follow Parkes in their basic premises concerning the uniqueness of Christian antisemitism. Like Parkes, both these thinkers argue that the theological component introduced something that differed from classical thought. They would also agree with Parkes about the roots of the problem being found within the New Testament itself. There is a debate about the difference between antisemitism and anti-Jewish rhetoric, but Gager thinks both Simon and Isaac side with Parkes in thinking that the line between these two ideas is not easily distinguished and that systematic hostility towards Jews began with Christian teachings. Rosemary Ruether, A. Roy and Alice Eckardt and Franklin Littell are among contemporary Christian thinkers who argue along the same lines. Perhaps the most interesting figure in recent times is Gregory Baum, who began by defending the New Testament against these charges, but came over to a more Parkesian position upon reading Ruether's *Faith and Fratricide*. It strikes me as curious that many of these contemporary thinkers do not always acknowledge Parkes as being one of the first thinkers to argue for this position. Gager seems quite unaware of what Parkes had to say about classical views even though he and Parkes are in fundamental agreement. What many scholars today find to be a recent discovery, Parkes was arguing nearly fifty years ago.

[45] *The Conflict of the Church and Synagogue*, op. cit., pp. 38–43, where Parkes traces certain passages through the different Gospels.

the tone of the three synoptists if they are read in the historical order of their appearance."[46] The Gospel of John presents a new set of problems. In this Gospel, the distinction between Jewish groups collapses, and "the Jews" now become Jesus' unrelenting opponent.[47] The picture of Judaism which emerges from the Gospels is of a religion that is dead, arid and legalistic. Jesus' Jewish roots are not denied, but he is seen as moving away from Judaism and offering something new in its place, even though he seems to affirm most of Judaism in his teachings. Parkes believed that this increased hostility in the Gospels is a reflection of the growing tensions between the Church and the Synagogue in the first century, even before a permanent break between them took place. This tension Parkes finds at least understandable, if read as a debate between Jews about the meaning of Judaism and messianic hopes. The real problem arose when passages were read without the benefit of historical background, and when they became the sole source of information about Judaism and the Jewish people for the Christian community.

One charge that stems from the Gospels would become a taproot for Christian antisemitism. That is the charge that the Jews killed Jesus: the deicide charge. All the Gospels make this charge in one form or another, particularly in the following passages: Matt. 27:11–26; Mark 14:1, 11, 43ff, 55, 64, and 15:11–15; Luke 23:1–25 and John 19:1–16. Outside of the Gospels, one

---

[46] Ibid., p. 42.

[47] Ibid., pp. 82ff. See also *Jesus, Paul and the Jews*, op. cit., for Parkes' most complete treatment of biblical texts. Concerning John see pp. 53–55. John's Gospel is particularly problematic concerning Jews because of the language and the charges leveled at Jews. Some recent works are useful on this account: John Townsend, "The Gospel of John and the Jews: The Story of a Religious Divorce," in *Antisemitism and the Foundations of Christianity*, Alan Davies, ed. David Granskou, "Anti-Judaism and the Passion Accounts in the Fourth Gospel," in *Anti-Judaism in Early Christianity: Paul and the Gospels*, vol. I, Peter Richardson with David Granskou, ed. This volume contains a number of important essays on the Gospels and anti-Jewish thought. The second volume deals with patristic issues. Norman Beck, *Mature Christianity: The Recognition and Repudiation of the Anti-Jewish Polemic of the New Testament* is an exhaustive survey of New Testament literature and anti-Jewish thought. Many of these writers see John as more complicated than Parkes did on the question of its anti-Jewish bias, but few disagree that it has been used within the tradition to give biblical authority to anti-Jewish ideas.

finds this charge made in Acts 2:22–24, 32, 36 and once in the writings of Paul in First Thessalonians 2:14–16. Historians of antisemitism often isolate this charge as a major contributor to the perpetuation of Christian antisemitism. Parkes was aware of the power of this charge and the evils it had created. He wrote in 1930 that it was this charge that the Crusaders had used to justify their slaughter of Jews throughout Europe in 1096. He wrote that, "the immediate cause of the first popular attack upon the Jews was the appeal of the Crusaders: 'Will you offer your lives for the recovery of the Holy Places, and leave in peace those who are actually responsible for the death of the Saviour.'"[48]

Parkes was tentative in 1934 about his own position concerning the deicide charge. He thought that if the Romans had been entirely responsible for Jesus' death, the Gospel writers would not have mentioned Jewish participation at all since the early Church was trying to attract Jews. Yet he also saw that if there was no Roman responsibility, they would not have been mentioned at all since the Church was trying to curry favor with the Romans.[49] But Parkes was clear about the fact that if some Jewish authorities were in any way involved, it was neither historically true nor morally feasible to blame all Jews. He pointed out that the Pharisees are not mentioned in the accounts of the trial, and they are even seen as warning Jesus about the dangers he faced in Jerusalem. If one is to charge the Sadducees, whose authority was centered in Jerusalem, with culpability, one has also to remember that they opposed not just Jesus, but the Pharisees as well. In addition, they benefited the most from Roman goodwill, and they would have been most anxious to keep the Romans happy and silence any sort of Jewish messianic stirring that could upset the Roman rulers.

Parkes came to realize in the course of his studies that there were questions concerning the trial's legality according to Jewish law, and that it was perhaps wrong to blame the Jews for crucifying Jesus when crucifixion was a Roman form of execution reserved for political enemies of the state. On this matter, Parkes came to be influenced by Paul Winter's book *On the Trail of Jesus*.

---

[48] *The Jew and His Neighbour*, op. cit., p. 70.
[49] *The Conflict of the Church and Synagogue*, op. cit., pp. 45–46.

Parkes wrote a review of Winter's book in which he agrees with Winter's contention that primary responsibility must be placed on the Roman authorities. "It was only when the Church was trying to ingratiate itself with the Roman authorities—which was just at the period when the traditions were crystallising into our present Gospels—that Pilate tended to be exonerated and the Jews to be blamed."[50]

The deicide charge carried with it the idea that the Jews were to be punished eternally for their crime against God. It was used to explain the fall of Jerusalem in AD 70, and the Jewish Diaspora was linked to the belief that Jews were driven from their homeland as punishment for killing Jesus. The legend of the Wandering Jew has its roots in this myth. For Parkes, these were not academic questions, but ideas that gave life to a hatred of the Jewish people in the minds of Christians, and justified the idea that Jews were a reprobate people deserving of any punishment that befell them. This idea would gain Augustine's approval, and it appears over and again in Christian writings. Dietrich Bonhoeffer would write in 1934 a statement that draws directly on this tradition: "The Church of Christ has never lost sight of the thought that the 'chosen people' who nailed the Redeemer of the world to the Cross must bear the curse of its action through the long history of suffering.[51] Historically, one can trace how Holy Week was often a dangerous time for Jews living in Christian communities. During this period, Jews were often attacked physically by Christians stirred up by sermons about the "Christ-killers." Parkes had firsthand knowledge of this from his work in Europe, and he wrote in 1936:

---

[50] Parkes' review of Paul Winter, *On the Trail of Jesus*. Unpublished review on file at Southampton University, The Parkes Library, p. 3.

[51] Dietrich Bonhoeffer. *No Rusty Swords* (London: Collins, 1970), p. 222. Bonhoeffer scholars like J. Patrick Kelly object to using this passage out of context of Bonhoeffer's other writings on the Jews. I think, however, that this quote from someone otherwise so sensitive to antisemitism shows just how engrained this idea had become in the Christian mind. Until very recent times, Parkes was one of the few Christians to raise questions about the deicide charge and see the full implications of it on Christian attitudes toward Jews. In the last twenty-five years, most Churches have repudiated this charge, but its hold on the Christian mind is seen in how it continues to be used by Christian antisemites to support their position. It is often used to bemoan the fact that Jews now control Jerusalem.

Is it possible that, in spite of the fact that in full consciousness of the situation Jesus a few hours later asked from the Cross: "Father forgive them for they know not what they do," God has actually cursed the entire Jewish people throughout history? This is no academic question. I have met a responsible leader of the German Christian Student Movement who pointed out publicly that *even if converted* the Jews could not escape Hell, because the curse they invoked on themselves was eternal, but that knowing the mercifulness of God we might just hope that for their conversion they would receive only a *mitis damnatio*—a mitigation of the pains. Moreover in a book by a Presbyterian of Jewish origin which appeared a year or two ago I found the astonishing phrase that "Our Lord prayed the Father not to lay charge of His death against his people, but I am not sure that this prayer included the priestlings, for it was they who compassed His death." With tremendous magnanimity in the supreme moment of His life, Jesus – then implored God to forgive those who were not guilty!!! So long as anything which concerns Judeo-Christian relations is capable of creating such aberrations among Christian thinkers, it is not academic to demand a reconsideration of the original situation.[52]

In Parkes' view, the deicide charge was the taproot of Christian antisemitism. It was an idea that moved beyond mere xenophobia to a metaphysical statement about Jews and their ontological condition. From this charge sprang what I have called a "Christian theology of victimization" that implicated the Church in

---

[52] *Jesus, Paul and the Jews*, op. cit., pp. 22–23. Parkes' call for a reconsideration of the original situation is very similar to that of the Catholic theologian, David Tracy, who has called for the Church to apply an "hermeneutic of suspicion" to its texts to eliminate any vestige of antisemitism. Tracy says that such an hermeneutic may discover that "later historical events can even challenge not the founding religious event but the authoritative response to that event." Quoted in Arthur Cohen, "The Holocaust and Christian Theology," in *Judaism and Christianity under National Socialism* (Jerusalem: The Historical Society of Israel, 1988), fn. 6, p. 436. In many ways, much of Parkes' writings were an attempt to apply just such an hermeneutic of suspicion to the whole Christian tradition's view of Jews and Judaism, and to create a new interpretation of the founding events.

encouraging hatred of Jews based on a theological premise.[53]
Here I think Parkes' early definition of what constitutes antisemitism meets its test, and the roots of antisemitism in Christian teachings can be discovered in the deicide charge.

Although the deicide charge had a devastating effect on Jewish–Christian relations over the centuries, Parkes argued that initially it wasn't the deicide charge that lead to the ultimate separation of the Church and Synagogue, but rather their quarrel over the meaning of the Jewish Law. Parkes took the position that Jesus never intended to supersede Judaism with a new religion or to denigrate the Jewish tradition. Jesus the Jew was not the problem, but rather that which the Church came to teach about Jesus concerning the Law. Parkes traced this problem directly to the teachings of Paul, and he saw Paul's ideas about the Law as a continual source of misinformation and misunderstanding that has made it difficult for Christians to affirm anything positive about Judaism. Parkes seemed to think, however, that Paul himself is not so much the problem as it is his Gentile interpreters who read Paul outside a Jewish context and with no clear distinction as to whom Paul was addressing in his letters.

The question of Paul's writings and their relationship to the development of Christian antisemitism has received renewed attention in the last few years in the writings of Krister Stendahl, E. P. Sanders, Lloyd Gaston and John Gager.[54] A good deal of

---

[53] Robert Everett, "A Reply to Hyam Maccoby," in *The Origins of the Holocaust: Christian Antisemitism* (New York: The Institute for Holocaust Studies of the City University of New York/Columbia University Press, 1986).

[54] Krister Stendahl, *Paul among Jews and Gentiles* (Philadelphia: Fortress Press, 1976); John Gager, op. cit. E. P. Sanders, *Paul and Palestinian Judaism* and *Paul, the Law and the Jewish People*; Lloyd Gaston, *Paul and the Torah*. The writings of W. D. Davies need also to be mentioned. Davies was a contemporary of Parkes and influenced Parkes to a degree. What is interesting about all these recent authors is that they support much of what Parkes said much earlier, but they are all able to bring a much greater understanding of biblical studies to their works. Still, it is worth noting that Parkes was questioning the traditional interpretation of Paul and his views about Judaism well before it became commonplace to do so. Of all the writers, Gaston seems closest to Parkes in the way he presents Paul's ideas. Sanders is less optimistic about the use of Paul in Jewish–Christian dialogue, but he does seem to give some support to Parkes' notion of two covenants working within God's redemptive plan. For a critical review of this "revisionist" school of Pauline thought, including Parkes, see R. David Kaylor, *Paul's Covenant Community: Jews and Gentiles in Romans*.

attention is now being given to the audience to which Paul was writing, and the point is made that much of what Paul said about the Law in a negative vein was addressed not to Jews but to Judaizers, that is, Gentiles who thought they had to abide by the Jewish Law when they became Christian. The problem stems in large part from Paul's own contradictory views about the Law. He seems to refer to the Law in several ways, and one needs to be aware of this when reading Paul, lest one think he has a systematic and consistent point of view. For Parkes, this is where the difficulties arise for Christians. In Romans 7, the Law refers to external regulations of conduct. In other passages, it seems to refer to Torah—Judaism as practiced by Jews. But, in Galatians, he seems to be concerned primarily with ritual and ceremonial laws of Judaism as they affect Gentile converts. Yet the traditional Christian reading of Paul led to the view that Judaism had indeed been superseded by Christianity, and that the Law was of no value, and little or no attention was paid to whom Paul was addressing concerning the Law.

Parkes argued that Paul never attacked the religion of his ancestors or the importance of the Law. He urged readers to ignore the "midrash" on Paul by Christian commentators, and simply read the letters themselves to adduce the meaning of the letters to those addressed rather than the theological superstructure that had been built over them. On the whole, Parkes believed that Paul's ideas about the Law referred not to Judaism *per se*, but to ideas about how Gentiles could be welcomed into the Church without having to adopt the ritual aspects of Judaism. The Law question was concerned with entrance requirements; it was not an evaluation of Judaism and its adherence to the Law.[55]

The argument that the Law could not bring salvation is not reason to think that Paul thought the Law was of no value to Jews. Parkes argued that there was nothing in Judaism that said that it did. Thus Paul is hardly saying anything particularly anti-Jewish in this regard. Also, the dichotomy between Faith and Works found in Galatians was a false one in Parkes' mind, and not

---

[55] "The Church and the Jewish People in Light of Biblical Teachings," p. 7. Unpublished manuscript. See also *The Foundations of Judaism and Christianity*, op. cit., and *Jesus, Paul and the Jews*.

Paul's own position. This is a difficult problem because it has come to symbolize for many Christians the main difference between Christianity and Judaism. The reformers, reading Paul, would pick this up as a central theme, and radical reformers were often condemned as "Judaizers" because of their emphasis on performance and works.[56]

Yet Paul does make claims about Jesus Christ that seem to present a problem when one is trying to argue that he does not see Christianity superseding Judaism. Parkes thinks the idea that Paul needed to break the narrow shell of Judaism in order to make Christianity a universal world religion is the wrong way to view his works. In Parkes' view, no Pharisee would have disagreed with Paul that Judaism would become a universal religion with the coming of the messianic age. "There was no 'halakah' on the point, and there were many—all equally orthodox—interpretations of how that universalising would take place."[57] Parkes argues that the Council of Jerusalem took the most liberal interpretation of the question.

Parkes sees Paul as dealing with three factors that determine his work: (1) uncertainty about the proper relationship between Judaism and the Church; (2) his distress over the non-acceptance of their messianic proclamation by the majority of the Jewish people; (3) perplexity as to why the Messiah delayed of his return. These three points form the background of Paul's letters and his speeches in Acts, and they also result in his rather complex and contradictory ideas about these problems.

> In the factual situation which Paul had to meet there were two Israels. There was the Jewish people who, in the mass, remained faithful to the Mosaic Torah, and there was a new body, composed of Jews and Gentiles, who were coming to regard themselves messianically as a new and true "Israel of God." Paul did not accept this duality. He did not accept a rejection of the "old" Israel and the substitution of a new one. Like the rabbis, he did not accept automatic membership of

---

[56] *The Foundation of Judaism and Christianity*, op. cit., p. 199.
[57] "The Church and Jewish People in Light of Biblical Teachings," op. cit., p. 7.

the Kingdom as a consequence of physical birth—there were Jews who by their own sin shut themselves out of the life to come—but he looked forward to the time when "all Israel" will be saved." That "Israel" would be one with the Gentile believers without distinction in the messianic kingdom. This was a position amply supported by reference to the prophets and there was no reason for Paul to feel "un-Jewish" in putting it forward. There is also no evidence that he even wavered in his conviction that this is how history would develop.[58]

Yet what are we to make of Paul's insistence that belief in Christ brings salvation? Paul's letter to the Romans includes the famous passage found in chapters 9–11 of that epistle, where he tries to give his views on the relationship of Christianity to Judaism. It is often seen by modern Christians as a sanction for dialogue with Jews. Paul clearly argues there for one view of salvation history in which both Jews and Gentiles would be saved. In fact, the Jewish rejection of the Christian message is seen as a means by which there can be an interim time in which the Gentiles can catch up with the Jews. At the coming of the Kingdom of God, both would be gathered up. Yet questions remain as to what role Judaism plays in God's salvation plan. Surely, a Jew would not accept Paul's diagnosis of their condition, yet Paul is careful to fully include Jews in God's plan. Romans 9, particularly stresses this point, and the theme of a remnant comes straight out of Isaiah. This passage has a curious history in that it was often used to defend Jews from Christian mobs during the Middle Ages, and probably prevented their complete extinction in Christian society. As Parkes points out, "for it was argued that if they were completely extinguished there would be none to provide the converted remnant which was to be the final crown of the Church."[59] Yet can Romans 9–11 gives us any positive views about Judaism?

Parkes seems to be of two minds on this. In the *Conflict*, he seems to argue that Paul does take a supersessionist line against

---

[58] *The Foundations of Judaism and Christianity*, op. cit., p. 199.
[59] *The Conflict of the Church and Synagogue*, op. cit., p. 55.

Judaism, but in his later works, particularly *Foundations*, he seems to argue that Paul did not see Judaism's value as a religion being transferred to Christianity. I think it could be argued that as Parkes' thought matured, he came to see Paul's ideas as even more complex than he originally thought, and he began to stress the audience to whom Paul was addressing as opposed to fitting Paul into traditional readings of his works.

It is worth noting how Parkes viewed this problem of the Law and the audience to whom Paul was writing. Parkes saw it as a triangular argument summarized as follows:

> *Paul argued:* the Messiah has come; my task is to preach Him to the Gentiles. Those who accept Him enter the New Israel by baptism, the new ceremonial which replaces circumcision for the Gentiles. With the New Israel distinctions between Jews and Gentiles have ceased to exist; and although the Ceremonial Law is still valid for Jews; it is impossible for Gentiles.

> *The Judaisers argued:* the Messiah has come, but entry into His Kingdom is by the old terms of loyalty in full to the covenant given to Moses. Christ fulfills that covenant; He does not supersede it in any detail. Gentiles must be admitted to the Messianic Kingdom, but for admission they must become Jews.

> *The Jewish opponents of Paul argued:* the Messiah has not come, therefore action taken upon the assumption that He has is false. In the present circumstances there is no authority for the admission of Gentiles to the Synagogue on new and more liberal conditions than formerly.[60]

This triangular argument remained an "in-house" problem until the Church finally decided that all Christians were to abandon the Law. The question was no longer whether the Law was still binding on Gentiles who accepted the Messiah, but whether it was ever binding on anyone in the way in which the Jews understood it. Now the Law was contrasted to the Gospel as a different and erroneous way of life. In such a condition it is not unnatural that

---

[60] James Parkes, *The Jew in the Medieval Community: A Study of His Political and Economic Situation*. (1976 edition), pp. 8–9.

the fury, which in the days of Paul had been local, became a general hatred of the sect, and an uncompromising rejection of fellowship with them.[61]

Parkes faults Paul as being a source of Christian antisemitism on the grounds that his words about the Law were easily used by later authors to buttress their opposition to Judaism. In his view, Gentile Christianity's one-sided development, which came to regard salvation as the be-all and end-all of religion, came to see Paul's condemnation of the Law for not giving what it never set out to give a "termination and replacement of the revelation of Sinai." Yet he wants to defend Paul from this attitude because Paul had not foreseen the ultimate separation of the Church and Synagogue. Paul's ideas would prove a seedbed for anti-Jewish thought over the centuries.

It is important in our study of Parkes to realize that he did not accept Paul's judgment of the Law or Judaism. He knew that his position would not be easily accepted because he was disagreeing with long-held beliefs and interpretations. He freely admitted that he had accepted the traditional Pauline view he had learned at Oxford until his research forced him to reassess his position. He was always guided by the belief that "good theology cannot be built on bad history," and he came to the conclusion that Christians had distorted and misinterpreted Judaism and its true nature because of the New Testament ideas. Parkes' conclusions about Paul's role in these problems are important in understanding his own ideas on the questions.

> That Paul in his attack upon the Law was doing it less than justice can be said without detracting from the greatness of the Apostle. The Christian will probably say in reply: "Did not Paul himself know all about it? Was he not born and bred a Jew? Was he not a 'Pharisee of Pharisees'? Had he not been 'zealous beyond those of his own age in the Jews' religion'? Was he not 'as touching the law, blameless'? Who could be a better and more reliable witness upon the question of what the Jews' religion is really about?" Yes. Did not Paul abandon the Jews' religion? Did he not write about it long years after

---

[61] Ibid., (1976 edition), pp. 8–9.

he had been converted to a different religion? And is it not common knowledge that a convert seldom takes the same view of the religion he has left as those who remain in it? The fact remains, however, that the Christian Church adopted without enquiry the Pauline estimate of the Jewish religion. The ultimate redemption of Israel on which Paul pinned his deepest faith was rarely referred to by Patristic writers. The inadequacy of the Law and the forfeiture of the promises, was the continual accusation against the Jews. By the time the Book of Revelation was written at the very end of the century, it was already possible to speak of the redeemed of the Church in terms of the twelve tribes of Israel without appearing strange.[62]

As Paul's views gained more authority in the Christian community, his views on Jews and Judaism became central to Christian thinkers. How easy it was to turn much of Paul on its head is illustrated by the way in which Marcion would come to see himself as the true disciple of Paul, and urge that the Church cut itself completely off from Judaism. Paul never would have dreamed of such a thing, but his teachings lead in that direction, however unintentionally.

Concerning other books of the New Testament, Parkes considered the first Epistle to Peter and the Epistle to the Hebrews as being problematic concerning their views of the Law and the question of the viability of Judaism. The Epistle to James seems to be an exception of sorts, given its rather positive attitude toward the relationship of faith and works. Parkes sees it as an exceptional book from the Apostolic Age:

> Its calm and quiet tone, and its exclusive preoccupation with the building up of practical saintliness, impress the reader at once. The absence of Christological arguments has led some scholars to see in it a Jewish epistle adapted for Christian purposes. While this view is not generally accepted, it is a commentary on the self-contradiction of conventional views of Judaism that this, in many ways the most attractive of Apostolic writing, should be attributed by anyone to Jewish

---

[62] *The Conflict of the Church and Synagogue*, op. cit., p. 57.

authorship without it being realised that such an attribution condemned the view that Judaism was dead and arid. It is impossible to tell what the attitude of the author to the Law. . . . All we can safely deduce from it is that the question of the Law was not so universally a burning issue as we might be tempted to think from the works of Paul.[63]

As we mentioned before, Parkes saw the Gospel of John as being particularly bitter in its attitude toward Judaism and the Jewish people, even while it makes some surprising statements that seem at first glance to be rather positive toward Judaism. One central problem with the Book of John is that it is so popular with the ordinary Christian that it has an enormous influence on Christian thinking. Parkes argued that John writes with the presupposition that a separation between the Jewish and Christian communities had already taken place, and the growing hostility is clearly reflected in the text. John assumes the separation and believes that further arguments with the Jews are pointless. Jews are now assumed to be the enemies of Christianity, and Christianity is presented as a universal faith whose Jewish roots are downplayed.

> A careful reading of the book shows an amazing contrast in spiritual tone between the discourses addressed to the disciples and those addressed to "the Jews," and while the former constitute some of the most exquisite treasures of Christian literature, the latter are unreal, unattractive and at times almost repulsive. We can attribute the one, even if indirectly to a personal memory. But the other is a reflection of the bitterness of the end of the first century.[64]

As the New Testament writings became canonized and gained authority in the Church, certain ideas about the Jewish people and Judaism began to emerge. It also happened that historical events occurred that gave to Christians evidence of what they believed to be God's displeasure with the Jews. The fall of the Temple in AD 70, and the failure of Jewish uprisings against the

---

[63] Ibid., p. 59.
[64] Ibid., p. 60.

Romans struck serious blows to the Jewish community and forced it into a defensive position. The opposition offered by the rabbis to Christianity was expressed in the formulation of the *Minim* by Samuel the Small, also known as the 18 Benedictions.[65] A nineteenth benediction cut off the Jewish-Christians from the synagogue, and it offered a condemnation of the Nazarenes. What contact there had been between Jews who believed in Jesus and those who did not believe was greatly reduced, and the atmosphere became increasingly hostile.

The claims made by the Church about Jesus being the Messiah were rooted in the messianic prophecies of the Hebrew Scripture. As the separation between the two communities became more pronounced, a battle ensued over the proper interpretation of the scriptures. The fall of Jerusalem was seen by the Christians as a sign that Jews no longer had favor with God. Parkes points to three Christian documents from the second century as evidence of this new attack on Judaism. Parkes specifically mentions Justin Martyr's *Dialogue with Trypho* and Ignatius' *To the Philadelphians* and *The Epistle to Barnabas*. Justin clearly states his opposition to the Jewish–Christians who still seek to follow Jewish Law and states that he would have nothing to do with any one of them who attempted to propagate their views among Gentile Christians. Thus Judaism's adherence to the Law became a basis for separation from them and from those Jews who sought to also be Christians. "Such an attitude to Judaism," stated Parkes, "is the disastrous consequence of setting the extravagance of Paul before the measured and sober attitude of Jesus himself, a consequence from which the Church is still suffering.[66] For Parkes, this is a clear example of how the increasingly Gentile nature of the Church was introducing a radical separation between the two communities that neither Jesus nor Paul had envisioned.

Parkes maintained that by the second century the Church had become a Gentile Church, and the question now raised about

---

[65] Ibid., p. 78. See also David Flusser, "The Jewish–Christian Schism," Part II in *Immanuel*, summer 1983, pp. 32–34, where he argues that the *Birkath ha-Minim* mention of the Christians (*Nozrim*, i.e. Nazoreans) was a later interpolation.

[66] *The Foundations of Judaism and Christianity*, op. cit., p. 222.

Judaism dealt with the promises and "fulfillment" of prophecy rather than the Law. Parkes argued that the Gentile Church falsified Jewish history in order to support their claims about Jesus. This attitude led to the belief that only the Church knew how to interpret scripture, that it had possessed the truth before the Jews had rejected it, and that the Church existed already at the beginning of revealed history.[67] The Hebrew scriptures were turned into a "vast quarry with no other function than to prove, by any exegesis however far-fetched, arguments . . . to prove the reality of the Messianic claims about Jesus."[68]

The inner logic of the Christian position led to another assumption that also denigrated Judaism. The Christian claim that Jesus was the Messiah of Israel, based on their interpretation of Scripture, meant that the Church was the "true Israel." This is an important part of Parkes' thesis that the Church developed an antisemitic tradition from its own teachings:

> The Messianic question once settled, there were inevitable deductions to be made by the Christian writers. If Jesus was the Messiah promised to Israel, then they were the true Israel. It is here that we see how inevitable was the defamation of the actual history of the Jews, for if the Gentiles were the true Israel, then the Jews had all the time been sailing under false colors. That they were the true Israel they proved by innumerable passages from the prophets, in which God speaks of His rejection of His own people, and His acceptance of the Gentiles. Little by little, the Church was read back into the whole of Old Testament history, and Christian history was shown to be older than Jewish history in that it dated from the creation, and not from Sinai, or even Abraham. Continual references to Christ were found in the Old Testament, and it was "the Christ of God" who appeared to Abraham, gave divine instructions to Isaac, and held converse with Moses and the later prophets.[69]

---

[67] *The Conflict of the Church and Synagogue*, op. cit., p. 87.
[68] Ibid., p. 99.
[69] Ibid., p. 100.

From this general outline of ideas, the Church came to create an image of Judaism as a dead, arid, legalistic religion lacking in spirit and grace, and the Jewish people came to be characterized as evil monsters, liars, and children of the devil. Parkes argued that antisemitism owed its origins to the way in which the Church formulated and maintained the following claims for itself: (1) The Torah was a temporary revelation that has been replaced by the Incarnation. (2) As a result of their rejection of the claims of Jesus to be the Messiah, Jews have ceased to be the "true Israel." (3) All the promises of the Old Testament have been transferred from the Jews to the Christian Church.[70] Add to these the deicide charge and one begins to see how the early Church Fathers drew out certain implications about Jews and their religion that developed into the antisemitic tradition of the Christian Church.

In his survey of the fourth-century Church Fathers, Parkes found the Jews portrayed in this literature as corporately and individually a detestable and reprobate people. A clear demarcation was made between the "promises" and the "denunciations" found in the Old Testament. The promises were applied to Christians, while the denunciations were applied to the Jews. As Parkes pointed out, "If you take all the promises and allot them to the Christian right from the time of Abraham, and then take all the denunciations and allot them to the Jews, and present the result as a divinely drawn picture of Jewish character, you cannot be surprised if ordinary people come to believe that Jews are a hateful people."[71] This sort of dichotomy took an even more bizarre twist in the hands of the fourth-century historian Eusebius, who made a very sharp distinction between "Hebrews" and "Jews." The Hebrews were the heroes of the Bible, while the Jews were those under God's condemnation. Thus people like Abraham and Moses were claimed by Eusebius to be Christians or "proto-Christians." Not only did such an idea allow the Church to claim the Jewish scriptures as their own without involving them in a defense of their break with Judaism, it also provided them with an argument for Christian antiquity. This was very important in the

---

[70] James Parkes, "The Jews as Presented in Roman Catholic Education," p. 3.
[71] Ibid., p. 3.

ancient world for establishing the merits of a religion, and Christians were often hard pressed to find justification for creating what appeared to many to be a new religion or merely an offshoot of Judaism whose validity was questionable. In addition, this sort of dichotomy made Jews look even more contemptible.[72]

A constant attack ensued against Judaism and the Jewish people in sermons, letters, and prayers. Perhaps the most famous of these types of sermons are those of John Chrysostom of Antioch, whose eight sermons against the Jews delivered in AD 387 displayed, according to Parkes, "a bitterness and lack of sensitivity unusual even in that place and century."[73] The case of Chrysostom is interesting since he felt compelled to deliver these sermons because so many of his flock in Antioch had close ties with the Jewish community, and apparently were attracted to the synagogue. Evidence here that Judaism had not ceased to be an attractive alternative to Christianity as late as the fourth century puts to rest the belief that Christianity entirely dominated the day in religious matters. This is a point often missed by Christians who have a rather static view of the religious world after the appearance of the Church. Chrysostom was quite concerned for the "faith" of his flock and the ways in which Judaism was "endangering" it. He launched an attack upon the synagogue. He charged the Jews with murdering their own children for the devil, repeated the deicide charge, claimed the synagogue to be a house of idolatry and the Devil, and charged that it was blasphemous for Christians to enter into one.[74] He continued by stating that God hated the Jews, that they worshipped the Devil, and urged Christians to hate them. "I hate the Jews," he preached, "for they have the Law and they insult it." Parkes commented: "It is evident that Chrysostom's Jew was a theological necessity rather than a living person. If he looked different from the actual Jews living in Antioch it was part of the malice of the Jews, one of the snares of the devil, set to catch the unwary

---

[72] *The Conflict of the Church and Synagogue*, op. cit., p. 162.
[73] Ibid., p. 163.
[74] Ibid., p. 164.

Christians."[75] While one could argue that Chrysostom was addressing a real problem in terms of keeping his people at home, and therefore his concern was not necessarily antisemitic, the fantastic charges that he makes about the Jews and their religion seems to fall under Parkes' definition of antisemitism as opposed to mere anti-Jewish xenophobia. The problems in Antioch appear to prove that everyday relations with Jews were not as problematic for ordinary Christians as the theologians wanted them to be.

Chrysostom the Golden Mouth, as he was called, was but one Church Father who attacked the Jews for one reason or another, but his sermons were certainly among the most vitriolic. Patristic writers like Augustine, Jerome, Ambrose, Cyril and Basil also had little good to say about the Jews. Parkes makes this charge against them:

> The Jew as he is encountered in the pages of fourth century writers is not a human being at all. He is a "monster," a theological abstraction of superhuman cunning and malice, and more than superhuman blindness. He is rarely charged with human crimes, and little evidence against him is drawn from contemporary behavior, or his action in contemporary events.[76]

Parkes blamed this distorted picture of the Jews on the way in which Scripture was interpreted by the Fathers. The insistence by Christian writers of this period on separating the promises and the curses and applying all the former to the Church and the latter to the Jews led to insidious results.

> The Father obtained the perspective of a distorting mirror and drew faithfully what they saw. The monstrosity of Israel was evident to them. There was not one single virtuous action in their history. She had been a perpetual disappointment to God, in spite of all the wonderful things He had done for her.

---

[75] Ibid., p. 166. See chapter 5 of *The Conflict of the Church and Synagogue*, op. cit., for Parkes' rather substantial survey of this material. See also Robert Wilken, *John Chrysostum and the Jews* for an excellent discussion of Christian–Jewish relations in the fourth century and the place of Chrysostom in the development of anti-Jewish thinking in the Church.

[76] Ibid., p. 158.

For it was impossible to separate these from the main strain in the history of the people. The Church might claim all the virtuous actions of the Old Testament for a kind of pre-existent Church, but she could not deny that the people had been led out of Egypt, guided by day and night across the desert, and into the Promised Land. But their record was one of nothing but disobedience, and their ultimate rejection was almost inevitable from the very beginning. The one mystery which the Fathers never attempted to solve was why, if they were really like that, God had either chosen them, or having done so, had expected them, after a career of unchanging and unrepentant malice and vice, to accept His final revelation in Christ.[77]

There was also a certain ambivalence in much of what the Fathers had to say, as if they were never quite sure what to do with Judaism or the Jews. Jerome, for example, spoke of the Jews in light of his eschatology, but he gives three different opinions of what will happen to them. At times he argues for a complete rejection by God of the Jews. Other times he believes only a remnant will be saved. Then again, he takes a more Pauline view in saying that all of Israel will be gathered up, but only after the Gentiles have been saved. But in each case there is no positive role for Jews to play. They are merely pawns in the Christian eschatological scheme of things.

The anti-Jewish and anti-Judaism writings of the Fathers has come to be known as *Adversus Judaeos*. The appeal of this tradition was always back to Scripture, both Testaments. Parkes' argument that the New Testament laid the foundation of Christian antisemitism is given some support by its constant use by the Church Fathers to "proof text" their arguments against the Jews. A. Roy Eckardt has added his voice to this proposition by writing: "Those who seek to declare the New Testament innocent of antisemitism are hard put to explain how New Testament Christianity could have become a foundation reference for Christian antisemitism throughout the ages. Every instance of Christian

---

[77] Ibid., p. 159.

antisemitism in post-biblical history is directly or indirectly trace-able to the events or reputed events in the New Testament."[78] By the fourth century, this anti-Jewish tradition had taken a firm hold in the Christian Church. Its most sacred literature gave it support (whether intentional or not), and commentaries of the literature enlarged upon the charges against the Jews. While this was taking place in the theological realm, events in the political life of the Roman Empire began to affect Jewish–Christian re-lations.

Up until the fourth century, Christianity had been engaged in a struggle to gain recognition from Rome as a legitimate religion. Judaism had been awarded that status centuries before, and it had enjoyed a measure of toleration from the Romans. Unlike Christianity, Judaism's antiquity was recognized and appreciated by most people. With Constantine's recognition of Christianity, the whole situation changed. Christianity now won favor in the eyes of the empire, and it used its newly won strength to among other things legislate against the Jews. It was also now able to call Church councils, and while no council ever dealt solely with Judaism, they each contributed something to the crippling of Jewish rights in the empire. The very first law passed by Rome under Christian influence in October of AD 315 read:

> We desire the Jews and their elders and patriarchs to be informed that if after the passage of this law anyone who flees from their gloomy sect to the worship of God is pursued by them with stones or any other molestations, as we know is at present happening, the offender shall immediately be con-signed to the flames, with all those who have taken part in the offense. But if any person shall join himself to their evil sect, and give himself to their assemblies ("brothels"), he shall suffer the same punishment.[79]

The Roman tradition of protecting Judaism proved too strong to be dislodged immediately, but the rights of Jews were slowly

---

[78] A. Roy Eckardt, *Your People, My People*, p. 12.
[79] James Parkes, *Judaism and Christianity*, p. 119. See also Apendix of *The Conflict of the Church and Synagogue*, op. cit., for a list of laws concerning Jews, pp. 379–404.

whittled away over the centuries. Jewish rights became hostage to the whims of secular rulers and princes. The laws that deprived Jews of their rights were often written in abusive and contemptuous language. It became perfectly legitimate to humiliate Jews and their religion. The picture drawn by Christian theologians went a long way in justifying this sort of attitude. This would prove to be an important element in the creation of the Christian attitude up through modern times.

> Here also a tradition was created for medieval development, and medieval Popes adopted the same contradictory policy that everything was legitimate which humiliated the Jews and kept them in a state of subjection, even when they were requesting their flock neither actually to murder them nor to do them violence. This belief in the necessity of humiliation did not, however, stop short at abusive language. It became a cardinal point of Christian policy that Jews were to be excluded from all dignitaries, and from the possession of any office which gave them jurisdiction over Christians, and this policy which was first initiated by Honorius at the beginning of the fifth century remained in force until the emancipation of the Jews in the nineteenth century, even though secular authorities frequently offended the Church by employing Jews in departments of state service where their capacities were of special value.[80]

The restrictions of civil rights were followed closely by restrictions on religious rights. Whatever appeared offensive to Christians was subject to restriction. Justinian attempted to regulate synagogue services, and he introduced questions about the Talmud for the first time. Ambrose threatened the emperor with excommunication if he rebuilt a synagogue that had been burned down by a mob of Christians. A Visigothic king, Erwing, followed plans similar to Ambrose. The Middle Ages concentrated primarily on the censorship of Jewish books, and Talmuds were frequently burned.[81] The Talmud was a mysterious book to most Christians, and it was often subject to attack. The one really hostile Jewish

---

[80] James Parkes, "Christian Influence on the Status of Jews in Europe," p. 33.
[81] Ibid., p. 33–34.

book was *Sepher Toldoth Jeshu*, a rather scurrilous biography of Jesus. But, on the whole, Jewish literature devoted little attention to Christianity. Efforts to suppress Jewish books were generally motivated by fear of the unknown and hatred for anything Jewish. By the ninth century, the Roman laws which had given protection to Jews had been steadily undercut. The Jews found themselves without the rights of citizenship. They had become "strangers within a society which was beginning to think of itself as 'Christendom.' "[82]

The only period of time in which Jews found favor was during the Carolingian period. Charlemagne and Louis the Pious both found the Jews to be helpful in government, commerce, and intellectual circles. Their favorable view of the Jews, however, incurred the wrath of the Archbishop of Lyons, Agobard. Agobard feared the influence that Jews would have over the rulers, and he could not tolerate Jews in positions of authority over Christians.[83] The image of the Jew as an inferior, a member of a deicidal race, was compromised by the attitude of the Carolingian princes. Agobard wrote some very bitter denunciations against the Jews at this time, but his fears about Jewish control proved shortlived. Jews entered the Middle Ages without legal rights, and they were in many lands merely the property of princes and kings.

The Jews found themselves under a system that required them to seek the "protection" of princes from ecclesiastical humiliation. Here was a difference between Roman and medieval times. "In Roman days the Jews enjoyed all the liberty which the action of the Church had not withdrawn from them; in the Middle Ages they enjoyed no right except such as the princes directly conferred on them."[84] Although this system often protected Jews from harsh treatment at the hands of the Church, it came with a price. For while Jews could not be expelled easily from a country without the consent of the princes who owned them, the princes in turn exacted a price out of the Jews for their protection. That price generally took the form of a prince using his Jews to act as

---

[82] Ibid., p. 34.
[83] Ibid., p. 35. See also James Parkes, *The Jew in the Medieval Community: A Study of His Political and Economic Situation*, pp. 19–33, 53–57.
[84] Ibid., p. 36. See also *The Jew in the Medieval Community*, op. cit., pp. 24–25

collectors of money through usury from untaxed classes of the population. This would have a profound effect on the basic relations between the Jew and his Gentile neighbor, and it gave rise to the myth of the Jewish moneylender.

> The use of the Jews as usurers for the advantage of the royal treasury involved the concession to them of very definite and extensive privileges, and these privileges not only allowed the Jews to acquire a position of wealth and influence, but also—and this was the tragedy—only allow them to acquire this position by the exploitation of the other subjects of the prince. It was only an abstract conception of the consequences of deicide which had previously resented the admission of the Jews to equality with Christians, even if a more real fear of religious influence had led to legislation against intimacy between Jews and the Christian commonfolk. In the struggle against the Jews in the twelfth century onwards a much deeper motive came into play—the need for protecting the poorer and weaker classes of society from merciless extortion, backed by all the protection of the royal courts. If it be legitimate to reproach the Church with her belief and propagation of the ideas of ritual murders, of the profanation of the hosts, and the poisoning of wells—and it is legitimate to level this reproach against her—in her struggle against usury she was genuinely on the side of angels. . . . That struggle was directed even more against Christian usury than Jewish, and the traditional conception of usury as a Jewish monopoly is a myth. But while this is true, it also remains true that a large number of Jews were usurers, and that, though medieval testimony is amusingly unanimous in preferring them to their Christian competitors, they were an abominable scourge in any medieval society.[85]

The situation that the Jews were placed in by being the "protected" agents of the princes ultimately proved disastrous. By the fifteenth century, conditions led to the financial ruin of the Jewish community. Once their economic value to the princes

---

[85] Ibid., p. 37. See also *The Jew in the Medieval Community*, op. cit., chapters VIII and IX.

departed, the princes no longer had any reason to protect them against the Church or a populace that had grown to resent them. While some Jews maintained a favored status, most of European Jewry was cast into misery. The legacy of Jewish usury, however, lingered long afterwards.

> But the public had not forgotten the extortion of the Jewish usurer, and the Church still considered the Jews as deicides, capable of ritual murders and every form of anti-Christian malice. It is these legends which still remain alive today in many parts of Europe, and make antisemitism a complex of historical as well as modern causes.[86]

The new economic factor in antisemitism only helped to reinforce the traditional theological antisemitism that had been created in the Church over a thousand-year period.

In 1096, the traditional humiliation of the Jews at the hands of the Church broke out in another form of terror. The call for a Crusade to free the Holy Land from the infidel produced a tremendous religious enthusiasm, and with it the first widespread hostilities against the Jews began. Before this time, Jewish life was tolerated by the Christian antisemitic tradition, for a quirk in Christian theology maintained that Jews would convert at the second coming of Christ. Consequently, Romans 9–11 was often cited by popes in their attempts to protect Jews under attack.[87] The Crusaders were, however, more faithful to the inner logic of the anti-Jewish tradition of the Church when they slaughtered Jews in France and Germany in 1096, while they made their way to the Holy Land.

> The immediate cause of the first popular attack upon the Jews was the appeal of the crusaders. "Will you offer your lives for the recovery of the holy places, and leave in peace those who are actually responsible for the death of the Saviour?" Crusaders plundered impartially any whom they met, whether Christian or Jew, and others in their zeal for

---

[86] Ibid., p. 38.
[87] See Solomon Grayzel, *The Church and the Jews in the XIIIth Century*, p. 12. Edward Synan, *The Popes and the Jews in the Middle Ages* (New York: Macmillan, 1965–67, pp. 19, 33ff.

the Christian religion baptised the Jews instead of massacring them, but as time went on their hatred was more and more concentrated exclusively upon the Jews and upon death rather than conversion.[88]

The point that Parkes raised about Christians able to justify the murder of Jews because of a theological doctrine like deicide reveals the truly demonic dimensions of the antisemitic tradition of Christianity.

The Jew in the Middle Ages found himself under constant attacks from the Christian community. Laws passed which prohibited social intercourse between Jews and Christians, Talmuds were destroyed, Jewish ghettos were established, special badges were prescribed for Jews, and restrictions were placed on synagogue construction and Jewish worship. In addition, theological antisemitism was disseminated among the populace by means of passion plays, art, literature, and sermons.[89] The Jew was always pictured as the monstrous abstraction found in the writings of the New Testament and the Church Fathers. The Jews were seen as agents of the Devil, guilty of deicide, sworn enemies of Christian society and the Christian people. Limited to the practice of usury as a means for making a living, the Jew was seen as sapping the life from Christendom. New charges were brought against the Jewish community that were directly related to the traditional charges of deicide and reprobation. These charges included the crime of ritual murder and desecration of the Host, the Jewish conspiracy myth, the legend of the Wandering Jew and the Jew as poisoner of the wells and the cause of the Black Plague.

The charge that Jews were agents of the Devil was supported in a peculiar way. Jewish doctors tended to be superior to other doctors, and since they were said not to believe in the true God of Christianity, their power was seen to have come from Satan in an attempt to lure Christian folk away from their faith. All these charges helped to create in the minds of the Christian population

---

[88] *The Jew and His Neighbour*, op. cit., p. 70.
[89] Leon Poliakov, *The History of Anti-Semitism*, vol. I, pp. 123ff.

of Europe an image of the Jewish people noteworthy for its evil connotations, and for the total distortion of the actual Jewish condition. Joshua Trachenburg has written:

> The most vivid impression to be gained from a reading of medieval allusions to the Jews is of hatred so vast and abysmal, so intense, that it leaves one gasping for comprehension. The unending piling up of vile epithets, and accusations and curses, the consistent representation of the Jew as the epitome of everything evil and abominable, for whom in particular, the unbounded scorn and contumely of the Christian world were reserved must convince the most casual student that we are dealing here with a fantacism altogether subjective and non-rational.[90]

In commenting on Trachenburg's observation, Parkes wrote that "it is quite impossible to accept the idea that feelings which must merit such a description could arise from dislike of the usurer! The Jew as devil, the Jew whose badge was a scorpion, the symbol of falsity, owes its origin to religion, not to economics."[91]

It is important to remember that the supremacy of the Church in Europe during the Middle Ages led to the anti-Jewish bias of the Church being woven into the very fabric of European civilization. The art of the age reflected the "monstrous" image of the Jew that Parkes blamed the Church Fathers for creating. The art of a civilization is often an index to its hopes and fears, a mirror of its subconscious memories and the myths by which it lives and sustains itself. The art of the Middle Ages illustrates just how deeply ingrained the hatred and distortion of the Jew had become in Christian society. During the medieval period, the Church was the patron of the arts, and given its hostility toward the Jews, "it is not surprising at all that art, its protégé, should have proved anything but sympathetic to it. . . . And, indeed, we find art playing a very important role in disseminating distorted conceptions and false notions of the Jews, often depicting them in

---

[90] Quoted in *Judaism and Christianity*, op. cit., p. 126.
[91] Ibid., p. 126.

unnatural colors and derogatory poses, sometimes even as fright-
ful monsters without any redeeming qualities."[92] The artist,
wrote Joseph Reider, was "able to fan the bias and hatred of the
populace . . . by contributing his or her share in formulating and
promulgating the well-known myth of his Satanic majesty, the
medieval Jew."[93] The famous twin female statues depicting the
triumphant Church opposed to the defeated and blind synagogue,
figures which still adorn many European churches and town halls,
helped to reinforce the negative image of the Jew. One can also
find the Jew depicted in numerous pictures and reliefs by the
figure of a sow, a cruel, ironic statement on the kosher laws, and
this image was used by theologians, like Martin Luther, in
sermons and tracts as an allusion to Jews.

Perhaps the most pervasive and most damaging image created
by the medieval artist was that of the external appearance of the
stereotype Jew. This figure quickly became the basic image of the
Jew in the popular imagination, and anyone familiar with Nazi
caricatures of Jews will find this image to be a frightfully contemporary one. Reider describes this image:

> As to the Jew himself he hardly fared much better at the
> hands of the biased artist. From the beginning of European
> art in the early Christian centuries, a ridiculous type was
> created to represent the Jew, generally a gnarled and decre-
> pit being with sharply pointed and well-accentuated features,
> weak-kneed and woe-begone, with a pointed, dishevelled
> beard, clad in a loose gaberdine, with some sort of round cap.
> In the later Middle Ages, beginning with the twelfth century,
> the conical or funnel shaped hat and the yellow badge were
> added. This satirical figure, modelled after the controversial
> literature of those days, was intended to arouse aversion and
> disgust in the people beholding it, especially when juxtaposed
> with the lusty and robust Christian type. . . . To make sure of
> its wide distribution and universal propagation it was not

---

[92] Joseph Reider, "Jews in Medieval Art," in Koppel Pinson, ed. *Essays in Antisemitism*, p. 93.
[93] Ibid.

only sculptured inside and outside of churches and cathedrals, but also graphically illuminated in Bibles, prayer books, and hymnals used at home. For curiously enough, this type was applied to Old Testament characters and Biblical patriarchs, prophets, kings and poets were often pictured in the dejected posture and unsavory garb of medieval Jews. . . . This is a particularly Northern European (Germany) motif.[94]

As the Middle Ages progressed, contacts between Jews and Christians became more tenuous, and these artistic representations were taken by the populace as actually depicting the real Jew.

By the end of the Middle Ages, the Church had succeeded in making antisemitism an accepted part of European life. Socially, legally, artistically, and theologically the Church had created an image of the Jew that was inferior in every way to the self-image of the Christian Gentile. The Jew was always an outsider, an alien to Christian society. All the fantastic charges against the Jew— child killer, God killer, well poisoner, spreaders of Black Plague, agents of the Devil—all seemed plausible to the mass of common people because of the basic ontological and spiritual difference between Jews and all other human beings; a difference that the Church continued to preach as the truth about the Jews. The common man was taught that it was an authority as great as Holy Scripture that said that the Jews were a deicidal race, children of the Devil, and doomed to eternal suffering. The French historian, Jules Isaac, has called this "the teaching of contempt." Generation after generation of European Christians were taught this teaching of contempt, and antisemitism became an essential part of the European consciousness. And, while the roots of antisemitism are to be found in Christian teachings, the negative image of the Jew was able to survive on its own even when some of the Church's power was lost. The Jews were the only group of people who failed to accommodate themselves to the "Christianization" of Europe, and therefore the Jewish community always remained under suspicion in a civilization created and ruled by Christian ideals and symbols. This, in itself, would be sufficient to make the

---

[94] Ibid., p. 99.

Jews a likely target of distrust and fear, but coupled with the theological doctrines that justified such a distrust and fear, the results were often disastrous for the Jews. Conversion, expulsion, and finally extermination characterized the Jewish experience in Christendom.[95]

When one talks about the medieval Church, one is speaking primarily of the Roman Catholic Church. It should be pointed out, however, that one important position of the Church remained unchanged by the Reformation. Protestant ideas about Jews in no way reformed past ideas. Parkes accurately observed that "the breakdown in the medieval unity of Christendom had no immediate effects on the relations with Jews. The Reformers and the New Church Fathers shared the opinions of the old in such matters and works were printed by Catholics and Protestants alike, following the old line."[96] The teaching of contempt, therefore, became part of both the Protestant and the Catholic tradition. Martin Luther, for example, wrote some of the most scandalous antisemitic literature ever published. He urged Christians to burn Talmuds and synagogues and expel Jews from Christian lands.[97] Luther would be quoted by Nazi war criminals as part of their defense.[98] John Calvin's Geneva forbade Jews from residing within its city limits. One could say that the Roman Catholic's anti-Jewish position was rooted primarily in the writings of the Church Fathers, while the Protestants looked to the writings of the Reformers themselves. Both traditions were supplemented by the antisemitic tradition found in the New Testament itself.

With such a heritage behind him, the common man in Europe had little cause to doubt the authority and legitimacy of antisemitism. Thus there were few attempts at purging anti-Jewish feelings from Christian society. Christian Europe was able to justify antisemitism as being part of God's will that one should hate the Jews for their crimes against Jesus Christ and humanity.

---

[95] A. Roy Eckardt, *Elder and Younger Brothers: The Encounter of Jews and Christians*, p. 12.

[96] *Judaism and Christianity*, op. cit., p. 136. See also Aarne Siirala, "Reflection from a Lutheran Position," in Eva Fleischner, ed., *Auschwitz: Beginning of a New Era?*; and Friedrich Heer, *God's First Love*.

[97] Siirala, op. cit., pp. 135ff and Heer, op. cit., pp. 128–34.

[98] A. Roy Eckhardt, *Elder and Younger Brothers*, op. cit., p. 13.

All the distortions, caricatures, and charges against the Jews could be justified on these grounds. The suffering of Jews was merely proof that God was continuing to punish them.

> It is likewise impossible to overemphasize the importance of the fact that the ability of the common man to believe anything which is told him about the Jews derives ultimately from a millennium of Christian preaching throughout a period when there was no social or economic fact or moral or ethical standard of belief which distinguished him from his Jewish neighbours. It is wrong to identify the medieval situation either with Egyptian or Greco-Roman anti-Jewish feelings, for the essential difference is that the latter hostilities were based on views of actual Jewish conduct or were part of the normal frictions of group life; while the former were unrelated to any facts in the Jewish situation and derived solely from an imaginary portrait of "the Jews" drawn by the theologians.[99]

This distortion of Jewish life, this teaching of contempt, was passed down by the Church from generation to generation through its liturgy, prayers, and educational materials. Modern studies have shown how Christian educational materials persist even today in portraying the Jew in a negative light, thus fostering suspicion and hatred of the Jew in the minds of young Christians.[100] Of course, this creates a reservoir of hatred and suspicion that can and has been exploited by antisemites over the years. Commenting on the role of Christian education in the development of antisemitic attitudes among the masses of Christians, Parkes wrote:

> In dealing with the religious element of antisemitism, the normal teaching of the Christian religion cannot be omitted. Though it would be unfair to say that the ordinary "Sunday School" or the religious teaching elsewhere was intentionally antisemitic, yet it remains true that in the immense majority

---

[99] *Judaism and Christianity*, op. cit., p. 125.
[100] Examples of some modern studies are Clair Huchet Bishop, *How Catholics Look at Jews: Inquiries into Italian and French Teaching Material*; and Bernard Olson, *Faith and Prejudice*.

of cases the Jews are simply presented as the people who killed Christ and who opposed and persecuted Paul and the early Apostles. The Gospel caricature of the Pharisees is all they are taught about the Jewish religion. The result is inevitably to create a dislike of the modern Jew in the mind of the child, since it is only with these events that he connects the word "Jew."[101]

Parkes also believed that the Church would have to make a serious self-examination of its liturgy to see whether or not the liturgy was helping to perpetuate an anti-Jewish bias in the minds of the people. He felt this was particularly true concerning the use of Scripture in the liturgy.[102]

This distorted conception of the Jewish people and their history begins early in the Christian mind, and quite logically, those who learn only this about Jews have a very difficult time separating myth from reality. The mythological caricature of the Jew usually overwhelms the Jew of reality in the minds of Christians. From Parkes' point of view, that has been the history of Christian attitudes toward Jews in Christendom.

By the time the modern period of European history began in the eighteenth century, the Jews had occupied the role of the outsider, the alien, in Christian society for nearly fifteen hundred years. The Jewish experience in medieval Europe was one of suffering, persecution, forced conversion, expulsion from almost every European country, and at times, martyrdom and death. The experience imprinted itself upon the Jewish soul, and historical memories of that time continued to inform the Jewish community in the modern period. The sense of history and the power that historical memories can exert over a people should not be underestimated. In times of change, chaos, and crisis, past experiences and images are often called upon for guidance. But just as the past came to influence Jewish life in the modern period, so too did the past continue to influence Gentile–Christian life. Historians who view modern antisemitism as being only political, economic, or

---

[101] *The Jew and His Neighbours*, op. cit., p. 120.
[102] James Parkes, Introduction to the 1976 edition of *The Jew in the Medieval Community* (unrevised), op. cit., pp. 4–5.

racial in character fail to account for the persistence and the pervasiveness of anti-Jewish symbols and charges in European society. The long history of Christian animosity and persecution of Jews resulted in a situation in which Jews could be blamed for any sort of problem, whether or not they were in any way involved. Parkes argued that there had been created a sort of "instinctive antisemitism" among the masses. He encountered this frequently in his travels in Eastern Europe, and in 1930, he wrote the following:

> Dislike of the Jew is now quite instinctive and unreflected to the majority of Europeans, whether they be economically affected by them or not. They do not look for any particular reason why they should have them. They may even recognize candidly that they have no special reason; but that only confirms them more rigidly in the idea that either it is an "instinct" or that there is a deep supernatural cause for it—or that the whole fault lies with the other fellow. . . . The roots (of instinctive antisemitism) will be of two kinds. There will be the original causes of the popular outbursts which marked the 11th century, the beginning of the long persecution of the Jews in Europe. In addition there will be the question as to how far these will be causes of popular indignation and time's accretions to them have a real foundation in the relation of Jewish and Christian society today. The fact that conditions have entirely changed since the 11th century no more minimizes the importance of this inquiry than the fact that the original inhibitions which have caused the complex may have disappeared long before the psychologist begins to handle the case. Moreover, old accusations are still brought up in moments of tenseness, and even if forgotten, they are the fundamental cause of the instinctive dislike of the Jew.[103]

This "instinctive" antisemitism, rooted in the Christian teachings of the past, was incorporated into the fabric of European culture well before the modern age arrived with the Enlightenment. Although Parkes was well aware of the many new factors that contributed to antisemitism, he believed that one could only

---

[103] *The Jew and His Neighbour*, op. cit., p. 50.

understand modern antisemitism if it is seen as having Christian antisemitism at its foundation. Even the anti-Christian anti-semites, like the German racists, made concessions to this fact when they attempted to prove that Jesus was an Aryan, and when they attempted to construct a German–Christian thelogy.[104] Parkes would agree with Uriel Tal who wrote of nineteenth-century Germany, "what still attracted the masses was the classical, traditional Christian anti-Judaism, however adapted it might have been to the new economic situations."[105] Parkes did not disregard the new forms of antisemitism that appeared during and after the Enlightenment, but he believed that what made the masses so susceptible to anti-Jewish propaganda was the under-lying continuation of Christian antisemitism. The Enlighten-ment, the French Revolution, the Revolutions of 1848, the eman-cipation of the Jews, and the anti-religious sentiments of many modern antisemites all contributed something new to the prob-lem.[106] But how much of an impact did these events and new thinkers have on the common man and his perception of the Jews? The bulk of the European population still continued to be practis-ing Christians and to cling to at least a nominal Christian identity. For Parkes, it seemed far more likely that the Church's persistence in teaching its anti-Jewish tradition from the pulpit and in the church schools, kept the masses of Europe conscious and suspicious of the Jews even in the modern period.

While this position is a matter of debate among historians, Parkes is not alone in his position. The noted French historian, Leon Poliakov, has also written about the lingering influence of Christian antisemitism in the modern period:

> How many sceptics or doubters, how many champions of irreligion or of purified religion found, like Voltaire, that they were good Christians and good Catholics when they came face to face with Jews. It can be noted in this context that very many heritages of survivals of this type of emotional pre-disposition "imbibed at mother's breast" still exist. The

---

[104] Uriel Tal, *Christians and Jews in Germany*, pp. 278–79.
[105] Uriel Tal, *Religious and Anti-Religious Roots of Modern Antisemitism*, p. 12.
[106] See James Parkes, *The Emergence of the Jewish Problem*, pp. 91–233.

means whereby they are transmitted are still not entirely understood. In Catholic France prejudices of this kind still linger against Protestants, those other victims of erstwhile persecution and hereditary enemies of yore; the Jews' identity in this sense was much more pronounced, and their efforts to modify or even obliterate it only aggravated Christian prejudice more. Moreover, while the ancient teaching of contempt, in its orthodox form or in its various heretical disguises (like Wagnerian mythology), went on, the old religious passions continued to have their effect, converging with those of the new crusades by atheists. A large number of nineteenth-century ideologists thus played their tribute to a tradition which Charles Maurras described as the "antisemitic genius of the West."[107]

Parkes gave a lengthy account of the influence of Christian antisemitism on the development of modern antisemitism in his book *Judaism and Christianity*:

> In general, it must be said of modern antisemitism that its strength lies in the political and economic rather than in the religious field. Yet neither Protestant nor Catholic, nor Eastern Orthodox Churches, can dissociate themselves from considerable responsibility both for the rekindling of the flames of Jew-hatred and for aiding in the dissemination of the poison of antisemitism. At the very beginning of modern political antisemitism in the 1880s, the Lutheran Court Chaplain, Adolf Stöcker, was leading the German antisemitic movement from Berlin, while a young Roman Catholic priest, August Rohling, was distributing anti-Jewish propaganda from his press and pulpit in the Rhineland. Rohling later was given a professorship at the, then Austrian, University of Prague, where he specialised in the encouragement of every libel of the Talmud and in the repetition of accusations of ritual murder. In the last decade of the nineteenth-century the circles of political Roman Catholicism in France were heavily compromised in the *Affaire Dreyfus*. Meanwhile in the territory of the Orthodox Churches matters were no

---

[107] Leon Poliakoy, *The History of Antisemitism*, vol. III, pp. 464–65.

better. In the Balkan countries the blood accusations thrived, not without assistance from the Orthodox clergy. In Russia, the Orthodox Church was equally gravely guilty, in addition to conniving at the forced baptism of military recruits and at the general anti-Jewish policy of the Tsarist bureaucracy. Some of the Protestant theological colleges in Germany were hotbeds of National-Socialism even before Hitler came to power. Of the Roman Catholics it is enough to mention Father Coughlin in the United States and of the Orthodox Professor Cuza at the University of Jassy in Romania, neither of whom was disowned by his church until it was clear that the harm he was doing to its reputation was greater than the success with which he fomented antisemitism. . . . Immense though the output of modern antisemitism has been, there is really nothing really new in the works of such men as Canon Rohling. He had merely dug ignorantly in the vast quarry of Eisenmenger and his followers have done the same. There is, in fact, only one surprising element in modern antisemitism, and that is not a new one. It is the success with which in central and eastern Europe it has proved possible to resurrect among both Roman Catholics and Eastern Orthodox Christians the legend of ritual murder. There are almost more examples of the accusation in the years between 1880 and 1945 than in the whole Middle Ages, and the legend was revived because it was still of great value to nineteenth-century political antisemitism to be able to rely on an unbroken tradition of religious hostility, which could be exploited for political ends.[108]

To talk of modern antisemitism as a post-Christian phenomenon is to talk about antisemitism as if it was uprooted from its basic source and survived. This was not the case. The political and economic antisemites could never have gained their support from the populace unless there had been this long history of Christian antisemitism still operating in Europe that conditioned the people

---

[108] *Judaism and Christianity*, op. cit., p. 137.

to believe anything they heard about the "evil" Jews. It is doubtful that the racial antisemites could have achieved their ends had it not been for their success in making racism and Christianity appear compatible in dealing with the Jewish question. As A. Roy Eckardt points out: "To refer to modern antisemitism as a post-Christian creation of pseudo-culture and mass manipulation is to utter a half-truth. Obviously, antisemitism directly violates Christian moral standards. But to identify modern antisemitism with something 'post-Christian' is to shut one's eyes to the intimate and centuries long association of Christianity and Antisemitism."[109] The Christian roots of antisemitism provided a justification to the masses for being antisemitic. As such, it was very easy for even anti-Christian antisemites to exploit this condition in Western civilization for their own purposes. The modern period is less secular and anti-religious than is generally assumed. The Church may not appear to be all that powerful, but the residue of nearly two thousand years of Christian civilization is still a powerful influence on Western society. To most non-Jews living in the West, Christianity is still their source of religious identification and consciousness. One has only to look at a calendar to see the holidays that are celebrated by the community at large for an example of this influence. As such, we should not ignore the anti-Jewish tradition of the Church that Parkes helped to bring to light through his writings.

It was this tradition that helped to lay the foundation for the Nazi Holocaust. This is, of course, a very controversial point, but Parkes is clearly among those who sees a direct connection between what the Church had taught about Jews and the events

---

[109] A. Roy Eckardt, *Elder and Younger Brother*, p. 15. The issue of racism and Christian antisemitism is often dismissed on the grounds that Christian ethics opposes racism in all forms. Yet Christian attitudes toward Jews have never been completely free of racist overtones. One can find it in the Spanish Inquisition, where Jews remained Jews in the eyes of the Church even after conversion on the grounds that it didn't change their blood. In an important, but little-known article, Alan Davies has shown how the myth of an Aryan Christ has not been lacking in Christian antisemitism. See Davies, "The Aryan Christ: A Motif in Christian Antisemitism," *Journal of Ecumenical Studies*, vol. XII, no. 4, (Fall 1975), pp. 569–81.

of the Holocaust. In his clearest statement on this matter, Parkes wrote:

> That which changed the normal pattern of Jewish–Gentile relations was the action of the Christian Church. The statement is tragic, but the evidence is inescapable. What is still more tragic is that there is no break in the line which leads from the beginning of the denigration of Judaism in the formative period of Christian history, from the exclusion of Jews from civic equality in the period of the Church's first triumph in the fourth century, through the horrors of the Middle Ages, to the Death Camps of Hitler in our own day. Other causes indeed came in during the passage through the centuries; the motives and climate of the Nazi period owed nothing to Christian teaching; individual Christians risked and forfeited their lives in rescuing victims. But so far as the Churches are concerned the line is still unbroken by any adequate recognition of the sin, by any corporate act of amendment or repentance.[110]

Parkes' view here is at odds with many other interpreters of modern antisemitism. Jacob Katz, for example, thinks that while there is some linkage between Christianity and modern antisemitism, it is not a particularly strong one.[111] Hannah Arendt takes a decidedly opposite point of view to Parkes, distinguishing racial antisemitism from religious antisemitism.[112] Parkes is not unaware of the racial component of modern antisemitism, but he does not think this, in itself, negates the influence of religious antisemitism in modern culture; ancient prejudices still survived, and they made Jews vulnerable to anti-Jewish passions. Moreover, he sees much of modern antisemitism as being a variation on older themes. So, while he acknowledges some new forms of antisemitism, he stresses the importance of recognizing the ongoing influence of traditional Christian antisemitism. In this regard, Parkes is opposed to the idea that Christian antisemitism was in

---

[110] *Antisemitism: A Concise World History*, op. cit., p. 60.
[111] Jacob Katz, *From Prejudice to Destruction: Anti-Semitism, 1700–1933*.
[112] Hannah Arendt, *The Origins of Totalitarianism*, Part One: "Antisemitism."

no way responsible for the Holocaust. The straight line he talks about may be somewhat more circuitous, but there is a link to be made.[113]

It is noteworthy that Parkes seems to have been one of the earliest thinkers to discuss the Church's relationship with Fascism/Nazism. In 1944, he wrote in *God and Human Progress* a critique of the Christian Church's failure to encourage and promote religious tolerance. He found it odd that the State had to be the place where ideas about religious toleration had to develop. He also noted the relationship between German Fascism and the political teachings of Luther, particularly the development of the Two Kingdoms theory in Lutheran theology. Remembering that he wrote this in 1944, it deserves our attention.

> German Fascism has roots deep both in German and contemporary economic history. To deduce its German form merely from the frustration of defeat in 1919, or the supposedly diabolical character of the Treaty of Versailles, is superficial. Other nations have been defeated in history, and defeat has resulted in a spiritual rebirth; and the Treaty of Versailles was stupid rather than malevolent. Its real roots go back, not indeed to the Teutonic barbarians of Roman times, but to the disastrous religion of Luther. Lutheranism left a vacuum on the political side where the medieval Church had left merely an incompetence. The absence of any constructive political idea in Lutheranism meant that Germany remained a patchwork of ineffective principalities while [other nations] were acquiring vigorous national characteristics. The exaggerated philosophies defying the State of which Germany in the nineteenth century was the home, arose as psychological compensations for this weakness; and the mass of political theory was proportionate to the lack of actual political power.[114]

---

[113] I am indebted to the Reverend Peter Gilbert of Toronto, Canada, himself a Parkes scholar, for highlighting this aspect of Parkes for me. Reverend Gilbert is currently writing a doctoral thesis on Parkes' interpretation of antisemitism.
[114] James Parkes, *God and Human Progress*, p. 55.

Parkes then goes on to discuss the relationship between Luther and Hitler in a remarkably perceptive fashion. In linking the two, Parkes remarked:

> As Luther had appealed to the Germans of the sixteenth century by a religious emphasis on their vague pessimism, individualism, and emotionalism, so Hitler in the twentieth won still greater support by appealing to this political frustration, and giving them something to obey, with the promise of supreme glory in proportion to their obedience—the supreme glory of a German State triumphant over all its rivals and opponents.[115]

Here, I think, Parkes shows a keen insight into the issue of the relationship between Christianity and the Holocaust by illustrating not just the antisemitic connection, but also the problem Christians faced when trying to form a political alternative to the fascist message.

Parkes does not limit this critique of Christianity to Germany. He also wrote knowingly about the comfortable relationship many Church bodies had with fascist regimes throughout Europe. He argued that the Churches on the Continent occupied a "disgraceful rather than an honourable position" in dealing with this problem. In a withering blast at the Churches, he wrote:

> Although there have been individuals on the side of the angels, there is not one of the great sections of Christendom which has not corporately given proof of being far more closely allied with the forces of darkness than with the forces of light. It is not necessary to go further back than the end of the last war to justify this terrible assertion. The record of the Vatican is not encouraging. It did nothing to oppose Fascism in Italy, it hastened to conclude a Concordat with National Socialism in 1933, and even today [1944] its utterances are platitudinous and ambiguous, except in relation to Russia, where it sees nothing but atheism. In Spain the conduct of the Roman Catholic Church has been deplorable. In Poland and

---

[115] Ibid.

elsewhere large sections of the same Church has been identified with Fascist and antisemitic movements without provoking action from the Vatican or the national hierarchies. The Orthodox Church in Romania has allowed itself to be identified with both racial antisemitism and Fascism. German Protestants gave a wide measure of support to National Socialism, right up to the moment when it began to persecute the Churches themselves.[116]

Parkes' indictment of the pro-fascist elements of the Churches is made even more emphatic by what he saw as a total lack of corporate activity on the other side of the issue. For Parkes, the problem is not solved by church members claiming that the "Church is not concerned with politics." Even if that were true, the Church should still be concerned about the moral outrages being perpetuated by the Nazis against the Jews and liberal members of society. Parkes also notes that even those pastors and laypersons who resisted Hitler and Fascism often came from "reactionary" elements in the Church, and they received little or no help from their institutional families.

The issues that Parkes addressed here in 1944 have become topics of great concern in contemporary Christian circles that are grappling with the meaning of the Holocaust for both Judaism and Christianity.[117] While Parkes is best known for his work on antisemitism, he really needs to be remembered as one of the first Christian thinkers to recognize the whole matrix of problems that Fascism/Nazism raised for the Church. It needs to be further noted that he was also very active in England fighting Oswald Mosley and his Fascist party. For those dealing with these problems, Parkes is quite a unique and important historical figure.

Parkes waged an ongoing struggle with antisemitism on both the political and religious front. He discussed in his book *Antisemitism* measures that could be taken by the state to protect its citizens from discrimination and hate-mongering. He felt that

---

[116] Ibid., pp. 69–70.

[117] See, for example, the numerous articles in *Remembering for the Future*, Yehuda Bauer, ed. (Oxford: Pergamon Press, 1989) related to the themes raised here. See also *Judaism and Christianity under the Impact of National Socialism*, Otto Dov Kulka and Paul Mendes-Flohr, eds.

democratic states were particularly vulnerable to hate groups because of the clash between personal freedoms and the group freedoms. Safeguarding the rights of minority groups is a difficult task, but one which the state must deal with in democratic states. Parkes believed that legislating measures that prohibit certain activities was necessary. He listed four such possible measures:

1. The prohibition of Racial Discrimination in hotels, places of public resort and employment;
2. The extension, to the protection of a group, of the laws against libel and defamation already in force for the protection of an individual;
3. The exclusion, from the traditional liberty of speech, of opinions and policies designed to destroy that liberty;
4. The prohibition of marching or wearing uniforms for political purposes.[118]

Parkes dismisses those who say that such values cannot be legislated. He believed that wise legislation can indeed educate people, and the problems that such legislation is trying to deal with require more than benign neglect. He points out, for example, that there are already measures on the books that protect people from libel and defamation. To believe that hate groups will just go away ignores the realities of the problem and the dangers faced by minority groups. The "sterilisation of prejudice" was, for Parkes, of utmost importance for a civilized society. What he truly feared was a democratic state allowing some of its basic principles to be its undoing. The attempt to deny to any group in society the same rights that others claimed, and used as their right to deny others the same rights, must be challenged.

On the religious front, Parkes felt that the Church needed to confront its own antisemitic past and make amends. While he praised the Church for its struggle against racism and other prejudices, he found its efforts to eradicate antisemitism less noteworthy:

> In most issues of group prejudice the record of the Churches is increasingly admirable. To find a prejudice against colour is

---

[118] *Antisemitism: A Concise World History*, op. cit., p. 168.

extremely rate. But, in dealing with the very tap root of group prejudice, antisemitism, they have not yet faced the fact that, whether any manifestation of it may be primarily political or economic in character, the responsibility is theirs that generation after generation of children first hear of the Jewish people in their scripture lessons, learn that "the Jews" killed Jesus, make no distinction between Jews of that day and Jews of this, and so grow up disposed to credit the outpourings of a Hitler or his successors.[119]

The Church, therefore, is a central player in the battle against antisemitism because of its direct or indirect influence on the way Christians think about Jews. Thus, while many modern thinkers seem to make the Church a marginal contributor to modern antisemitism, Parkes takes the position that the Church remains a principal source of antisemitic teachings, and that it is incumbent upon the Christian community to eliminate the anti-Jewish teachings of its own tradition. As we have seen, this involves not merely a historical acknowledgment of the problem, but a rethinking of some basic theological ideas of Christianity. It is here that Parkes makes some unique contributions to the quest for producing a Christian theology free of antisemitism.

Parkes saw that a new theology would have to be developed by the Church if it was to ever free itself of its antisemitic tradition. While a growing number of Christians today share this belief in varying degrees, Parkes can safely be pointed to as one of the first Christians to see the theological implications involved in the battle against antisemitism. He wrote in 1934, for instance, this rather remarkable statement, given what was soon to transpire in Europe:

> The Christian public as a whole, the great and overwhelming majority of the hundreds and millions of nominal Christians still believe that "the Jews" killed Jesus, that they are a people rejected by their God, that all the beauty of their Bible

---

[119] Ibid., p. 178.

belongs to the Christian Church and not to those by whom it was written; and if on this ground, so carefully prepared, modern antisemites have reared a structure of racial and economic propaganda, the final responsibility still rests with those who prepared the soil, created the deformation of a whole people, and so made these ineptitudes incredible.[120]

We must again emphasize how Parkes was thinking about this problem prior to the Holocaust. He is an important thinker for Christians concerned about antisemitism if for no other reason than to show that theological antisemitism was a problem before the Nazi Holocaust. Parkes believed that the Church could divest itself of responsibility for this problem only by a deliberate, sustained and official revision of its teachings about Jews and Judaism.

The dialogue between Christians and Jews is a unique one among world religions because they share so much, including large bodies of Scripture, yet the history of animosity between the two traditions has few rivals. All inter-religious dialogue projects have certain common problems in Parkes' view: "All of us are apt to have inherited the idea that if my religion be true yours must be false, and some of us are not prepared just to leap on the band wagon of the alternative that all religions are equally true, and it doesn't matter which one accepts. Religious unity poses new and difficult problems which we have not worked out yet."[121]

Parkes is usually associated solely with Jewish–Christian issues, but as we have seen in the chapter on Christian theology, Parkes brings to the Jewish–Christian issue a much broader theological concern related to the question, "How does a Christian account for the religious experience of other people?" Parkes is an early advocate of religious pluralism, and with the growing interest in this problem, Parkes is someone worth going back to look at again. Not just for what he says about Judaism and

---

[120] *The Conflict of the Church and Synagogue*, op cit., p. 376.
[121] *Prelude to Dialogue*, op. cit., p. 63.

Christianity, but for his whole approach to the problem of how one maintains a particularistic Christian identity while appreciating the religious traditions of other peoples. In this regard, I would suggest that Parkes has much in common with Ernst Troeltsch.[122]

Interfaith dialogue works, according to Parkes, only when both sides can recognize and accept the integrity of the experience of the other. The problem in the Jewish–Christian dialogue has been Christianity's insistence that Judaism had nothing to offer.

> The conception of Judaism as the preliminary to Christianity has remained the basic—one might say the "official"— attitude in all the Churches down to the present time. Apart from rabid antisemitism, one would not expect the abuse of Judaism in the modern approach which one finds too often in the earlier centuries. But the theology is the same. With the coming of Christianity, Judaism becomes *functus officio* in the divine economy.[123]

That being the case, there has not really been any serious dialogue between Christians and Jews. Jews have basically been given an either/or presentation of Christianity with no acknowledgment or even hint that Judaism might have some value in and of itself.

---

[122] See Ernst Troeltsch's, *Christian Thought, Its History and Application,* particularly his essay, "Christianity Among World Religions." An excellent introduction to Troeltsch's theological ideas can be found in Sarah Coakley, *Christ without Absolutes: A Study of the Christology of Ernst Troeltsch.* I was struck in reading through Coakley by a great many ideas of Troeltsch that reminded me of Parkes. Parkes himself does not mention Troeltsch, but when I defended my original doctoral thesis, Dr. Wayne Proudfoot of the Columbia University Religion Department specifically asked me about Troeltsch and Parkes. I think there is a fruitful line of inquiry here. A good summary of Troeltsch's ideas can be found in Claude Welch, *Protestant Thought in the Nineteenth Century*, Volume Two (New Haven, Conn.: Yale University Press, 1985), pp. 266–303. As we shall see, Parkes and Troeltsch do share a common concern about creating a "theocentric" as opposed to a "christocentric" theology for Christianity.

[123] *Prelude to Dialogue*, op. cit., p. 63.

The work which Parkes did on the history of antisemitism and Jewish history forced him to reject the traditional teachings about Jews that supported the *functus officio* theme in Christian theology. His favorite motto, "Good theology cannot be based on bad history," is at the heart of his theological revision. It does not necessarily follow that good history will automatically produce good theology, but Parkes believed that any new Christian theology about Judaism would have to account for the historical evidence that militated against its anti-Jewish tradition. He also foresaw the argument that one should not tamper with Christian tradition "just to please the Jews." Parkes felt that changes had to be made in Christian theology for its own sake, for its own integrity, and not simply to ingratiate oneself with others. The moral necessity of creating a new Christian understanding of the Church's relationship with Judaism is clearly outlined in this passage:

> What of those Christians who cannot sincerely maintain such a position? Can they any longer escape their responsibility for doing something about a tradition, however ancient or revered, which has produced such results? Of what value is the freedom given to scholarship to search and declare what it believes to be true, if scholars assume no moral responsibility for the result of the research? And here the charge, which lies on all Christian congregations involved, must be held to lie with especial responsibility on the shoulders of Christian scholarship. It has so far refused the responsibility, but history will not thereby hold it innocent.[124]

Parkes took this moral challenge seriously, and he attempted to provide the foundations for a new theological perspective on Jewish–Christian relations. He proposed a change in four basic elements of the Church's traditional view of Judaism. In many ways, they flow directly from his Modernist interpretation of

---

[124] *Judaism and Christianity*, op. cit., p. 167.

Christianity, which we have already discussed. The four changes that Parkes thought essential are:

1. The Church needs to accept that the New Testament is incorrect in much of what it teaches about Jews and their religion, and the Church needs to pay more attention to the historical facts about Judaism and Jewish history.
2. The Church needs to qualify its claims of incorporating all religious truth, and acknowledge the validity of other religious traditions.
3. Christian theology should make a shift from christocentric theology to theocentric theology.
4. Christianity needs to relate to Judaism on the basis of a "Theology of Equality."

Parkes' approach to biblical materials is entirely cast in the Modernist framework of his thought. He is opposed to any fundamentalist interpretation of Scripture. Thus he is more open to using extra-biblical materials in constructing his new theology than many Christians would be. In his view, however, there are two reasons why the Bible cannot be our sole source of information in creating a new theology. First, the biblical pictures of both Judaism and Christianity are limited. While they cover many years of development, they cannot be expected to tell us anything about the two religious traditions after the first century. Even then not all the materials needed to understand the first century are found in the Bible. There is little about the evolution of the synagogue or the history of biblical interpretation, yet both are essential to understand Judaism. From the Christian side, we find almost nothing about the development of the Church after the events in Acts, nor do we find anything about how and why the two communities, Christian and Jewish, ultimately separated. As we discussed earlier, Parkes is of the mind that what Paul had to say about Christianity's relationship to Judaism did not include any idea of their separation, and much that appears negative toward Judaism is really directed at Judaizers and not Jews.

In addition, how one approaches the texts can influence what one thinks. Here he is concerned with the role of modern biblical scholarship and its influence on Church teachings, as opposed to a fundamentalist interpretation of the Bible and the use of "proof texts" to create an anti-Jewish bias. He makes one very interesting point about "liberal" interpreters of the Bible and their use of Scripture when forming their ideas about the relationship of the Church to Judaism. Parkes points out that "many, who do not hold the 'fundamentalist' view of the Scriptures . . . do not realise that they make constant use of arguments justifiable only on the fundamentalist hypothesis."[125] What Parkes has to say here is very important, and it is still very relevant today. It has often struck me that Christians who on all other issues may take a decidedly liberal stance, often become quite "fundamentalist" when asked to rethink traditional Christian views of Judaism. It is worth quoting Parkes here at length.

> [Non-fundamentalists] in their description of the religion of the Old Testament fit their facts to support an already formed hypothesis as to its relation to that of the New. They stress a covenant relationship with Abraham and ignore it in relation to Sinai; they speak of the Law as a single incident and emphasise only the giving of it by God, ignoring the fact that it is in Sinai that the covenant relationship reaches its climax. They speak of the prophets as though they followed the Law and, indeed, replaced it by something nobler; and they describe the prophetic contribution in terms drawn from their Christian theology. From the prophets they then make a sudden jump to the Incarnation, presenting in their whole picture an entirely unhistorical sequence which completely misrepresents the religious developments of Judaism, and, in particular, obscures the essential fact that it was Pharisaism and not the prophets which prepared the way for the Incarnation and created the setting of the teaching of Jesus of Nazareth. All this is legitimate, only on the fundamentalist thesis; for the text of the Old Testament does place the prophets after the Law, and it says nothing of the beginnings

---

[125] "The Church and the Jewish People in the Light of Biblical Teaching," paper read at the Ecumenical Institute's Conference on "The Church and the Jewish People," in November 1948 at Chateau de Bossey, France. It is regrettable that this excellent article was never published. Parkes makes some very important comments on the Bible and Jewish–Christian relations. It is on file at the Parkes Library in Southampton University.

or the teachings of Pharisaism. For others it is necessary to seek to understand the actual sequence of events, the actual content and objective of Judaism, and above all, when we come to the conflicts recorded in the Gospels and Epistles, to relate the information they contain to our knowledge from non-Biblical sources of the situation with which they deal.[126]

This passage tells us a great deal about the way Parkes approached the biblical materials and why he felt it so important that that Christian thinking about Judaisn not be limited to biblical texts alone. We also see here the theme constant in Parkes' thought that history must inform our theology, and where history proves previous theological ideas wrong, changes must be made.[127]

Here also Parkes' Modernist impulse is very much at work. He insisted that the New Testament picture of Jews and Judaism be properly corrected in light of the historical facts about the Pharisees, the development of Jewish Law, Rabbinic Judaism and its teachings and so on. This does not mean that one should conclude that there was no tension between Jesus and the Jewish leaders of the day, but it does mean that the image of Judaism should not be based on the one-sided portrayal of it found in the New Testament. Parkes was critical of the idea that the New Testament supplied the Christian with all he needed to know. He wrote that "if, in fact, the apostolic age had been far purer and better than all subsequent Christian epochs, it would be a poor commentary on the intelligence of God."[128] Concerning the teachings of Paul, he wrote that "it is no good asking me how I reconcile my views with those found in the Epistle to the Romans. I don't, and I long ago discovered the question irrelevant. In St. Paul's days, neither developed rabbinic Judaism nor Nicene Christianity existed. But it is with these we have to reckon with today."[129] While Scripture

---

[126]   Ibid., pp. 1–2.
[127]   A. Roy Eckardt's book, *For Righteousness' Sake* offers an excellent study about how and why history must affect the way in which one formulates theological ideas.
[128]   *God and Human Progress*, op. cit., p. 15.
[129]   *Prelude to Dialogue*, op. cit., p. 188.

is central to the Church, when it comes to developing its understanding of the relationship of Christianity to Judaism, it cannot provide the sole basis for creating a relevant theology. Here Parkes is not showing only his Modernist roots, but his Anglican roots as well.

Parkes' willingness to subject Scripture to this type of critical analysis was crucial to his position. As we have seen, he believed that the roots of Christian antisemitism could be traced back to the New Testament, and that therefore something had to be done to help people interpret it anew. This position would prove unacceptable to fundamentalists, but he was astute enough to know why even more liberal interpreters would also find it problematic. Yet he saw no other way of dealing with Christian antisemitism. The anti-Jewish passages in the New Testament remain a key problem in the Jewish–Christian dialogue. Parkes believed that a Christian need not cling to a literal interpretation of the text on the grounds that "we can teach that the living Christ is, has been and always will be, the corrective of what at any time, and in any way, men have said or written about him."[130] Concerning biblical criticism, he wrote that "such an attitude to the Bible presents a far more compelling and attractive picture of the activity of God that those seven words 'the Bible is the Word of God' could ever do."[131] This critical approach to Scripture was clearly the way Christians must go if they were to eradicate antisemitism from their tradition.

A second point that Parkes considered important also had Modernist roots. Throughout his writings, Parkes took issue with the idea that Christianity possessed all possible religious truth, and every other religion was somehow an incomplete form of the Christian faith. This idea lies at the heart of the Christian anti-Jewish tradition. He wrote that "the claims of the [C]hurch to the truth is one thing; the claim they so frequently make to complete or absolute truth at this youthful stage of the world's existence is on a par with all other claims to omniscience associated with

---

[130] *Judaism and the Jewish People in their World Setting at the End of 1973*, p. 12.
[131] *Prelude to Dialogue*, op. cit., p. 204.

extreme youth."[132] Parkes does not deny that the Church has access to truths about God. He believes Christianity has much to say about God and to offer the world. But he does not believe that Christianity alone knows God, while all other religions are false or incomplete. The Church needs to see its truth as being a *corner of* God's truth, not a *corner on* God's truth.

This is an aspect of Parkes' thinking that is not very well known to those familiar with his work on Jewish–Christian relations, yet it is essential for one to be aware of it in order to understand the basic principles on which he constructs his new theology of Jewish–Christian relations. Parkes is really working within a much broader theological context when he argues that Judaism and Christianity are equals. His ideas arise from a basic theological outlook that accepts the idea that God did not limit Divine revelation to Christianity alone. Parkes believed that a new attitude was beginning to develop within Christianity concerning other religions that offered the possibility of approaching other world religions on an equal footing:

> In the past scholarship had little influence on the ordinary attitude to other religions. The traditional Christian belief was that they were temptations of the devil, and there were practices which explained this belief. Today we are invited to accept an impossible alternative. We are told that other religions are not of the devil, but that they are *man-made*, and as such unacceptable to God. Continental Protestants are particularly liable to adopt this belief and can twist some biblical verse to their support. This is where common sense and continental theology speak different languages, and it would not be common sense for the former to compromise. For there is either a common root in God for all sincere religious striving of his children, or he may be a good enough God for continental theologians, but that is the limit of his kingdom, his power and his glory. . . . If we are to claim that history shows one central line of divine revelation—that which came from Judea—then, confronted as we are today with the potential unity of the whole world, we need to clear our minds

---

[132] *Good God*, op. cit., p. 36.

on two points. We must abandon entirely the idea that eternal damnation awaits those who, in this life, did or did not accept Christian salvation. . . . But we must also have a convincing picture of the relations of that central line of revelation with religions outside it.[133]

Parkes argued that when Christians talk with Jews they needed to stop setting up the discussion around the question "We believe in Jesus as Messiah and they do not." That question does not exhaust the whole content of the Christian faith, nor is the belief that the Messiah has not yet come the whole content of Judaism. Rather Parkes offered three postulates around which dialogue could take place.

1. Neither side yet possesses the final totality of truth so that each is prepared to recognize that there exist truths which it has still to learn.
2. Each side recognizes that the other side possesses essential aspects of truth, in its own right (i.e. Jews would have to recognize that Christianity is more than a perverted form of Judaism, the Christians would need to abandon their belief that they "took over" the whole of what was of value in the Old Testament and so possess everything which the Jews had and more).
3. Both sides recognize that, where there is not complete conformity, there is sufficient similarity in the conception of one God, of the purposes of creation, and the nature of man as the son of God, for each to accept that the doctrine of the other contains elements of truth.[134]

It is clear that such postulates are not the ones most Christians use in dealing with other religions, much less Judaism, but Parkes

---

[133] *Common Sense about Religion*, pp. 64–66. This concern with religious pluralism has become a hotly debated issue in Christian circles today. See Paul Knitter, *No Other Name: A Critical Survey of Christian Attitudes Toward the World Religions* for an excellent introduction to the problem. Although Knitter mentions Parkes only in conjunction with the Jewish–Christian dialogue, it is important to note that Parkes was raising similar questions about Christianity's relationship to world religions nearly forty years ago.

[134] "Notes on 'Ex Aequo' discussion between Jews and Christians," unpublished manuscript, 1944, p. 1.

was of the mind that true dialogue takes place only when both partners can acknowledge the possibility of truth in the others, position without giving up their own claims to truth. But any claims to truth must be tempered by the fact that human beings cannot ever possess absolute truth, particularly concerning God.

Parkes thought that there was not any essential difference between Judaism and Christianity concerning the nature of God. He argued that the Nicene doctrine of God in no way compromises divine unity, and that its christological claims in no way infringe on that unity. He admitted, though, that neither his Jewish nor Christians friends agreed with him on this point. But he maintained that Judaism and Christianity shared a common view about the manner in which the Infinite expressed itself in history. He argued for the position that just as the Christian doctrine of the Second Person of the Trinity asserts that the Infinite can be expressed in the finite, the Jewish doctrine of Torah expresses a similar idea. He bases his belief on the idea that had not Alexandrian Jewish thinkers been cut off in their attempt to interpret Judaism for Greek thought, they would have arrived at a concept similar to that of the Christian doctrine of the Trinity.

> We both believe [he wrote] that the Infinite was expressed through the finite; we both believe that the eternal God intervened in history and that man's salvation (we may differ somewhat in the content we give to this word) is intimately related to and dependent on this intervention. The Jew says that the crown of that revelation was Torah in its continually creative interpretation. The Christian says that it is in Jesus and in the living Christ.[135]

For Parkes, the significant point is that both communities have experienced the Infinite within the finite, and while their point of reference is different as well as its accompanying interpretation, their basic experience is similar enough to provide grounds for a discussion as equals. He also states that it is precisely their similarities that cause them to have such heated quarrels with each other. While each has a strong case to make on their own

---

[135] Ibid., p. 2.

behalf, they can also discover, if they are willing to meet each other as equals, that each has what the other one lacks.

Although it would be easy to dwell on the negative aspects of Christian antisemitism, Parkes made an honest effort to move beyond guilt and shame for the Christian past and forge ahead with new ideas on how the two faiths could relate to each other. In a letter he wrote to me in 1972, he outlined what he believed should be the underlying motivation for the quest for a theology without antisemitism. "What is worth doing," he said, "is the understanding of the positive problem of deepening, broadening, and developing the intellectual and spiritual understanding of the basic Jewish–Christian relationship in the purpose of God; and then encouraging of the dialogue which should emerge from such an understanding."[136] His efforts to produce a theology based on such premises lead to what I call his "theology of equality," aspects of which we have already discussed.

Parkes' "theology of equality" rests on the premise that "Sinai and Calvary exist in creative tension by which neither can absorb the other."[137] It would require Christians to rethink how their experience of God fits into the history of revelation.

> There could be three ways in which this new understanding of the Divine–human relationships could be related to that already possessed in Judaism. They could be thought of as in opposition to each other; they could be absorbed into each other so that the clear edges of each were smoothed over to give an appearance of unity; or they could be held in creative tension. The first was adopted by the Christian Church, largely through the influence of Paul; the third has not been tried. The second was adopted by "Judeo-Christians."[138]

For Parkes, the time had come to work to make the third possibility a living option for Christians.

This theology of equality could work only if Christian theology became less exclusively christocentric and more widely theocentric. This was not an idea that Parkes arrived at through his work

---

[136] Letter in Author's possession.
[137] *The Foundations of Judaism and Christianity*, op. cit., p. 204.
[138] Ibid., p. 227.

with Judaism, but rather it was already present in his thinking as early as the 1929 lectures. By theocentric theology, Parkes meant that Christian theology would define itself in the light of God's many revelations in history, including Sinai, rather than by christocentric theology that defined Christianity and everything else on the revelation of Jesus Christ alone. Parkes knew full well that he was setting himself in opposition to almost all traditional Christian thinking in this regard. Christocentric theology has determined most of Christian theology over the centuries. It has only been in recent time that one finds Christian thinkers even considering the possibilities of a theocentric Christian theology. One can see this new development in the writings of Christian theologians like A. Roy Eckardt, Paul Van Buren, and John Hick. But in general, such ideas have not been part of mainstream Christian thought. Christocentric theologians like Barth and Pannenburg have been more prominent. Parkes wrote, "It was natural that in the first flush of excitement the early church thought the acceptance of Christ was all that mattered. But it was unfortunate that the attitude persisted and persists. The church is entirely christocentric.[139] He faulted christocentric theology on three points:

1. It created a doctrine of Divine activity in which Christ occupies an exclusive position.
2. It has created a situation in which the Church preached that Christ is the solution to every problem in human life, in spite of the evidence to the contrary.
3. It introduced the concept of "salvation in Christ" whose exclusive nature consigns the majority of humanity to Hell.[140]

Christocentric theology needed to be changed, according to Parkes, because it "has not only led the Church into deplorable beliefs and activities, but has failed, of itself, to meet the whole of human need."[141] If theology remains christocentric, it would also mean that Jews would remain outside the boundaries of God's

---

[139] *Prelude to Dialogue*, op. cit., p. 208.
[140] Ibid., p. 208.
[141] Ibid., p. 210.

people, and Judaism would continue to be perceived as having no truth left in it. Conversion would be the only way Jews could once again share in God's truth. Parkes argued that a move back to theocentric theology would help avoid the problems christocentric theology presented to Jewish–Christian relations, and that it would also insure that the doctrine of the Trinity would be more faithfully represented in theology. As Parkes saw it, christocentric theology tended to reduce the significance of the first and third persons of the Trinity. In his opinion, this prevented the Church from forming an active concept of a personal and immediate God. As we have seen, Parkes was quite critical of theologians like Barth, whose christocentric theology makes God into a Wholly Other who has no contact with human history on a daily basis. He argued that christocentric theology made Christian theology too narrow in its concept of God, and thus the Church is unable to see the activities of God as revealed in religions other than Christianity. What Parkes proposes is a new Christian theology that is theocentric in nature, but that does not destroy Christian self-identity or exclude Judaism as a valid source of divine revelation. In general terms, I think we could say that Parkes is attempting here to apply some of his Modernist theology to the whole question of Jewish–Christian relations.

His ideas for this theology is based on his application of the Christian doctrine of the Trinity to explain the meaning of God's revelations and his own anthropology. We have already discussed the change in terminology Parkes made in speaking about the Trinity. The term "person" is changed to "channel" because Parkes believed that his helped to avoid the metaphysical problems the term "person" introduces. He also believed that the term "channel" helped to clarify the way God acts in the World.

In defining his anthropology, Parkes wrote that the individual experiences life in three ways: (1) as a social being, (2) as a person, and (3) as a seeker of truth. It is his contention that these three experiences of the individual are absolutely necessary to the whole person, but that none of the three are subject to the others, or is the lesser of the three experiences. As in the Christian Trinity, there is one individual with three distinct modes of activity. Parkes then shifts from speaking about anthropology to speaking about theology. "So, I believe," he wrote, "it is with the three expressions of the experience of man in Judaism, Christianity, and Humanism. They are related to each other as are the three circles of the Trinity."[142]

Parkes believed that his move from christocentric to theocentric theology enabled him to broaden the dimensions of the Christian interpretation of God's revelatory activity, and enabled Christianity to accommodate other revelations besides Calvary. Unlike christocentric theology, Parkes' theocentric theology accepted a doctrine of progressive revelation that clearly bore the marks of Modernist theology. Parkes argued that there were different revelations of God, and once a revelation occurs it is not to be superseded by a later one. "The stages of God's revelation once achieved are never lost," he wrote.[143] With this thesis, Parkes simply argued that Sinai, Calvary, and the Renaissance were all revelations of God that occurred in their proper time in history, and from which certain aspects of God and His power can still be ascertained and tapped. In reference to his own theological and historical work, Parkes wrote that he was "forced into the apparently absurd proposition that both Christianity and Judaism are needed by man."[144]

In relating this theory of revelation back to his anthropology, Parkes understood the role of the three revelations of God as corresponding to the three expressions of the human experience. Sinai is the first revelation, and the channel through which flows the power of God as it relates to man as social being. Parkes argued that the central message of Sinai is that "God is active as Ruler in the ordering of people in society, and it is with that activity that Judaism was constantly preoccupied."[145] Unlike traditional Christian interpretations of Sinai that have made it only a forerunner or an incomplete form of Christianity, Parkes argued that Sinai represents a source of divine power flowing into history that reveals God to man the social being, and that this power is still channeled through Sinai today, through Judaism.

---

[142] Ibid., p. 216.
[143] *Good God*, op. cit., p. 92.
[144] James Parkes, *A Reappraisal of the Christian Attitudes to Judaism*, pp. 20–21.
[145] *God at Work*, op. cit., p. 94.

Parkes wrote that "the center of Judaism is a natural community. Its whole emphasis is on man as social being, related to other men through righteousness and justice. It insists on human responsibility, on definable and achievable objectives."[146] And, continuing his attack upon the antisemitic tradition of Christianity, Parkes wrote that "the only right attitude is one which recognizes the equality of the synagogue as the vehicle of a divine purpose of fulfillment, the recipient of a still valid divine revelation."[147]

Some Jewish critics of Parkes have felt that the image of Judaism in Parkes' system is incomplete and misleading. Parkes does not deny that Judaism is concerned about other experiences of life as well, but he is convinced that at its center is man as a social being.

> It would be absurd to pretend that Judaism is unaware that man is person, and that the relationship of persons is through love, or that man is a seeker, and that what he seeks is truth. But, Judaism has not developed these possibilities with the same intensity and the emphasis on the way of life of a community does not lend itself naturally to that development.[148]

In addition, with Parkes' interpretation, the Law in Judaism takes on a meaning different from the usual negative connotations it has in the minds of most Christians because it is through the Law that the power of God is incorporated into the teachings of the people themselves.

According to his scheme, Christianity serves as the channel through which God reveals Himself in terms of man as person. Parkes accepted the Christian doctrine of the Incarnation as providing the explanation of the concept of God-in-human-life. It was through the life of Jesus of Nazareth that this power flowed into human history, power concerned with man as person. Parkes argues "that the Christian, recognizing Jesus' divinity as well as his humanity, believes that Jesus saw far more than death in the crucifixion is as true as that the Jews see more in the Torah than a

---

[146] *Prelude to Dialogue*, op. cit., p. 217.
[147] *Judaism and Christianity*, op. cit., p. 174.
[148] *Prelude to Dialogue*, op. cit., p. 217.

law of commandments and ordinances."[149] The revelation at Sinai is not completed with the advent of Christianity. Christianity is but another revelation of God that has no superiority over any other revelation before or after Calvary. As with Sinai, Parkes does not imply that man as person is the only concern of Christianity. Rather, he argued that while Christianity is aware of man as a social being and a seeker, "it has constantly tried to subordinate this to the personal aspects of life."[150] Whereas Judaism has emphasized the fulfillment of God's will in human history, Christianity has emphasized the future life of the individual.[151] Both religions are concerned with these problems, but their emphasis is different. They also have had different views about messianic expectations. Parkes believed that Judaism was being faithful to its own beliefs by not recognizing in Jesus as the promised Messiah since the Christian Messiah fulfills so little of the Jewish expectations. According to Parkes, "as long as Christianity remains a living religion it will rest on the bold statement that God himself, of His own free will entered into human life and history," and thus its emphasis will remain on man as a person.[152]

A good illustration of the contrast between the two religions that Parkes is trying to make can be found in the different mystics they have produced. I can no more imagine a Hasidic rebbe living in a monastery than I can imagine a Trappist monk singing and dancing at a Purim celebration. The Hasid needs the community around him to find God. The monk needs solitude and quiet for his personal search for God. One emphasizes the social being in relation to God, while the other emphasizes the person in relation to God.

In addition, Parkes thinks that the concept of the "chosen people" is also a useful concept by which to understand the differences between Judaism and Christianity. This concept has, of course, been used by Christians to present a derogatory picture of Jews, and to claim that Christians, not the Jews, were the

---

[149] *The Foundations of Judaism and Christianity*, op. cit., p. 164.

[150] *Prelude to Dialogue*, op. cit., p. 217.

[151] James Parkes, *The Concept of the Chosen People in Judaism and Christianity*, p. 12.

[152] *God and Human Progress*, op. cit., p. 20.

"chosen people." Parkes believed that the concept operated in both religions, albiet in different ways. This idea of a chosen people was very important in the development of his thought:

> It was, therefore, of fundamental importance to the development of my theology that I gradually came to see that the main distinction between Judaism and Christianity was that the one was the Divine imperative to an *elect nation*, and the other a similar imperative to the *elect from every nation*. The natural community was the subject of Judaism, and all descriptions of Judaism as *a church* were completely false. On the other hand, Christianity was, from its very beginning, a body *called out*—which, after all is what ecclesia means— from the natural community of which each person happens to be a member.[153]

Parkes saw the differences between the two religions expressed clearly in their understanding of the nature of their call, but he also argued that their callings were of equal value.

To complete his trinitarian model, Parkes argued that the Age of Truth, the Renaissance, marked the revelation of God as it concerned man as seeker of truth. "In the revelation of the Indwelling Spirit, God released the power to understand and to control the world he had devised, including man himself."[154] Humanism has been the channel through which this power has been sent, and the search for truth remains its one objective. Parkes saw this third revelation as caring less for the other two experiences of man, and said that "it tends to be the most intolerant, perhaps because it is the youngest of these revelations."[155] His opinions about the Renaissance show the influence of his Modernist training. Rather than seeing it as an enemy of religion, Parkes saw the Renaissance as being an essential part of God's revelation and plan for His world. It is a bit unusual, but it is not out of character, given Parkes' theological position on other

---

[153] *Prelude to Dialogue*, op. cit., p. 193. See also *The Concept of the Chosen People*, p. 32.
[154] *God at Work*, op. cit., p. 149.
[155] *Prelude to Dialogue*, op. cit., p. 218.

questions. It is with this revelation that Parkes' unique revelation trinity is complete.

On this theology of equality Parkes hoped to establish a new Jewish–Christian relationship. This new relationship would be based on the premise that Judaism is a valid revelation of God, whose importance is equal to that of Christianity. There is no question of Judaism being a dead religion, or of Jews being cursed by God for being a deicidal people. Parkes also rejects the idea that salvation could be found only in Jesus Christ. "There must be no suggestion that one nature or activity of God is more or less important than another. All are equally divine, and in contact with any we are in contact with God."[156] Parkes is not suggesting that both religions are the same or that the hope of the future is the denial of the particular nature of either Judaism or Christianity. What Parkes is saying is that God has revealed Himself differently at different times through different "channels," and that each channel, while important in the overall divine plan, is also able to stand alone as a particular source of divine power. One channel does not succeed another in the order of their appearance. What this theology of equality is trying to do is to make Christians more aware of their particular place in God's creation without feeling the need to deny God's activity elsewhere. There is certainly no motive on Parkes' part to convert Jews to Christianity; indeed, his theology of equality makes conversion unnecessary and undesirable. Judaism is part of God's overall plan for creation, and as such, it is necessary for it to survive intact and to continue to be a channel of God's power. They do not need to become Christians.

> In this time and generation, not only do I not desire to see the conversion of all Jews to present forms of Christianity, but I do not seek the union of the two religions. That may happen in the future. But it can only happen when I can bring all that I value of the Christian tradition to the common pool and the Jew can equally openly bring all that he values of the Jewish tradition. And that day is certainly not yet, and in our present circumstance a religion made out of patches and compromises

---

[156] *God at Work*, op. cit., p. 63.

and superficial synthesis would be a monster lacking the very qualities which give each tradition its permanent value to humanity.[157]

Parkes did not want Judaism or Christianity to give up the necessary exercise of determining its own identity or belief system, but he did suggest that Christianity do this with an awareness of the dynamic and fluid relationship God has with his creation. His historical work made it necessary for Parkes to urge Christianity to recognize the contributions Judaism has made both as a religion and as a people, and also to recognize in Christian teachings. "It is to proclaim," he wrote, "the legitimacy, indeed the necessity, of Jewish survival that I have so long paid so much attention to the theological aspect of Jewish–Christian relationship; and have insisted on the theological equality of the revelation of Sinai and the Incarnation."[158] In adding up the factors involved in creating a new Christian attitude toward Jews and the creation of a new theology, Parkes came to the conclusion that a recognition of the equal validity of the two religions *via* his theology of equality will provide the means by which Christianity can make a positive step forward in truly eliminating antisemitism from its theology.

In examining Parkes' work, one finds that he has provided Christian theology and the Church itself with many of the historical and theological correctives needed in order that the quest to create a theology free of antisemitism might succeed. Malcolm Diamond is correct when he writes that "as we survey the work of James Parkes it will soon be obvious that his understanding of Christian dogma and his singular view of the relation between Judaism and Christianity are not likely to be shared by many Christians. Yet, because of his penetrating insights into Judaism and his thoroughly documented and trenchantly expressed views on Christian responsibility for antisemitism, his work presents a challenge which no Christian can ignore."[159] Since Parkes was a

---

[157] *Judaism and Christianity*, op. cit., p. 12.
[158] *Jewry and Jesus of Nazareth*, p. 19.
[159] Diamond, "Honesty in the Christian–Jewish Interchange," *The Journal of Bible and Religion*, vol. 33, no. 2 (April 1965).

pioneer in the field of Jewish–Christian relations, much of his work is seminal, particularly the theological writings. He was one of the first Christians to deal with this problem of Christian antisemitism and its consequences, and his work has influenced many of the theologians now grappling with this problem. His work on the history of Christian antisemitism still remains the major contribution of a Christian in this field, and his theology of equality helped to point the way for other Christians to follow.

There have been critics of Parkes' position in both the Jewish and the Christian community. Rabbi Levi Olan has argued that Parkes still falls into the traditional Christian trap of making Judaism appear to nothing more than an incomplete form of Christianity. He believed that the stress that Parkes placed on the communal aspect of Judaism made it look like Judaism was deficient in answering man's personal needs. Olan argued that this was unacceptable to Jews since they find in Judaism the total answer for man. Olan is aware of the qualifications that Parkes has put on his views of the different emphasis in Judaism and Christianity, but Olan does not find them adequate.[160]

The Canadian Protestant scholar Alan Davies, while appreciating the work that Parkes has done, finds it to be problematic on a number of points. Like Olan, he also thinks that Parkes' distinctions between Judaism and Christianity are forced, and that the ideas Parkes has about the Trinity, revelation, and anthropology are really a celebration of human progress. Davies finds Parkes to be somewhat guilty of making Christianity into a romantic religion in much the same way Leo Baeck had done. Given Parkes' Modernist background, however, this criticism may reflect a disagreement between Davies and Parkes on more fundamental theological issues. Davies is clearly in error when he claims that Parkes "slavishly follows" Franz Rosenzweig in creating a neat, logical pattern of functional equality between the two religions, for Parkes stated that he did not accept the Rosenzweig solution:

> There was the view popularized by Rosenzweig that Judaism was the Divinely intended religion for the Jews, and Christi-

---

[160] Rabbi Levi Olan, "Christian Jewish Dialogue: A Dissenting Opinion," *Religion in Life*, vol. 41, no. 2 (summer 1972), pp. 168–69.

anity for the Gentiles. . . . I came to the conclusion that there were two fundamental points which had to be accepted for any solution. The first was that Jews and Gentiles formed a single humanity with the same needs. The solution of Rosen-zweig would therefore have worked had the two religions been identical in character. Since they were not, there was either something which was missed, or each possessed some-thing which was erroneous or superfluous. If the former, then each ultimately needed the other; of the latter, then they could combine by each dropping what was particular to themselves. The latter seemed to me an impossible solution. I was prepared to assert of both religions that they contained human imperfections and errors; that both could still grow and develop. but I was quite certain that neither could surrender what made it different from the other, and showed as its essential identity and quality. I was definitely not going to give up my belief in the Divinity of Christ or in the doctrine of Atonement. I was equally sure that Jewry would not surrender its doctrine of Torah and of the covenant relation-ship of God and Israel. . . . What prevented me from leaving the matter there, and compelled me to go on to my present position, was my life-long concern with the world of the natural community, the world of politics, and international relations, and with the disillusion with the typical Christian attitude thereto. And it was in these fields that I discovered the strength of Judaism.[161]

It should also be pointed out that Parkes does not see Judaism in the "ahistorical" role given it by Rosenzweig.

The Catholic theologian, John Pawlikowski, has a deep appreci-ation for Parkes, and he has written a valuable critique of Parkes. He faults Parkes, though, for not giving enough attention to philosophical questions related to his position, and says that "his model and vision need expansion and refinement. But in his writings we have witnessed a terribly important break-

---

[161] *Prelude to Dialogue*, op. cit., p. 198.

through."[162] Pawlikowski characterized Parkes' methodology as follows:

> If we were to describe the movement in Parkes' method, it would be from personal experience to history (corporate experience) to theology to meaning. And if we were to describe Parkes' methodological orientation from the philosophical-theological viewpoint especially, we could characterize it as Buberian, progressivistic, historical, transcendental, neo-orthodox and holistic.[163]

Father Pawlikowski believes that Parkes is basically sound in his historical work, and he greatly appreciates Parkes' work on the Pharisees and their influence on the teachings of Jesus. He believes that modern scholarship supports what Parkes was saying in the 1930s about this issue. He thinks, however, that Parkes' philosophical–theological position suffers from not being more clearly defined. But this did not mean that Parkes should not be read more widely by Christians. In closing his critique of Parkes he gives the following evaluation of Parkes' works:

> In my view Parkes was saying as far back in the thirties what Paul Tillich proposed in his final public lecture, "The Significance of the History of Religions for the Systematic Theologian": "He (Adolph Harnack) once said that Christianity in its history embraces all elements of the history of religions. This was a partially true insight, but he did not follow it through. He did not see that if this is so, then there must be a much more positive relationship between the whole history of religions and the history of the Christian Church." Tillich was a better philosopher than Parkes, Parkes more of an historian. Yet both saw that they could no longer speak of the Church without seeing its relationship to the other great religions and ideological movements in a world in which Christians are becoming more and more of a minority. Both saw by implication that inter-Christian ecumenism is only an

---

[162] John Pawlikowski, "The Church and Judaism: The Thought of James Parkes," *Journal of Ecumenical Studies* (fall 1969).
[163] Ibid., p. 6.

important, minor concern which is basically an internal dispute compared to the possible significance and importance of the encounter of Christianity with other world religions and the cultures they have created. And Parkes went beyond Tillich in trying to work out a detailed model for at least one phase of this encounter. Thus, though Harnack, Baur, Dallinger and Mahler may get more of the headlines, James Parkes has given a more radical and more valid answer to the problem of the church and history with which all of these thinkers have struggled.[164]

A. Roy Eckardt is a Protestant theologian-ethicist who acknowledges his indebtedness to both Parkes and Reinhold Niebuhr. It was Eckardt who called Parkes "an Anglican of the Anglicans." Eckardt thinks that Parkes' historical work has presented a challenge to the Christian community that it can ignore only at its peril. He also appreciates the fact that Parkes does not try to gloss over the differences between Judaism and Christianity in the name of tolerance. He says that Parkes accepted

> the trend away from the calculated blurring of the differences that was prevelant during an earlier day. To be sure, a Judaism that was prepared to reduce the events of Sinai to an interesting piece of folklore and a Christianity that was prepared to relegate Jesus' claim to divinity to a Hellenistic mystery relic could easily join hands. But the price had to be the denial of the essential truths embodied in each religion.[165]

Eckardt is favorable to Parkes' idea of Christianity and Judaism being religious traditions in tension with each other. But he also thinks that Parkes does not explain his position clearly enough. Eckardt points out that Parkes always refers to the tension as between Sinai and Calvary, but what of the resurrection? Parkes doesn't have much to say about it, even though it is a major point

---

[164] Ibid., p. 21.
[165] A. Roy Eckardt, *Elder and Younger Brother*, op. cit., pp. 82–89.

of contention between Jews and Christians.[166] For Eckardt, this is a problem in Parkes.

Also, Eckardt thinks that Parkes does not deal adequately with the tension between Christianity's belief in a redeemed world and the Jewish belief in the unredeemability of the world. He thinks that these two tensions color the way in which both communities live out their faith on many levels, and complicate their relationship to each other. Parkes' rather rational, well-ordered attempt to balance the two religious traditions strikes Eckardt as a little too artificial.

One place where Eckardt and Parkes did agree is in their view that history needs to inform our theology. Both thinkers believed that Christian thought can no longer ignore those portions of its theology that are based upon bad history or inaccurate historical information. Eckardt has recently presented a full-blown theology based on this idea in his book *For Righteousness' Sake*. On Parkes, Eckardt wrote: "As a scholar and a man he combines historical empiricism, traditional Christian dogma, moral responsibility, toleration in the best sense, and, last but in no way least, religious individualism. In all this, we are blessed by an Anglican of the Anglicans."[167]

In his survey of Christian thought since the Holocaust, Michael McGarry provides a fine summary of Parkes' ideas. McGarry places Parkes in what he calls the "two-covenant" theology espoused by other Christian thinkers like Peter Chirico, Eva Fleischner and J. Coert Rylaarsdam. Others like A. Roy Eckardt and Rosemary Ruether share this position to some degree. McGarry points out that Parkes' use of the Trinity is unique

---

[166] Parkes does make a statement about the resurrection in an article published in *The Times* on March 28, 1970. He doesn't think that one can prove it happened, but he isn't bothered by that fact. Such demands for the actual bones or grave strike him as Victorian materialism. Rather one should admit it was an unique event, and then ask why it happened. One needs to ask about Jesus' task which had to be fulfilled rather than asking for an empty tomb. "Of course, it is unprovable, but why not? Have we explored all the powers of the spirit over matter?" Eckardt's point is a good one. Since much of Christian triumphalism stems from the belief that the resurrection proves the Christian claims for Jesus, Parkes needed to give it more attention than he did.

[167] Eckardt, op. cit., p. 89.

among these thinkers, and that he is singular in suggesting that the most contested doctrine between two communities can actually help interpret their relationship. Like Davies, McGarry sees his overall position as closely related to Franz Rosenzweig's. While I think it is useful to discuss Parkes in this manner, we must realize that Parkes does not limit revelation to Christianity and Judaism. He had a much more universalist idea of revelation, with God acting in different ways with different peoples to reveal the divine will. I think Parkes is probably closer to Ernst Troeltsch than to Rosenzweig.[168]

It is not clear to me that Parkes may not be more at home in the one-covenant school, even though his views on the tensions between Judaism and Christianity appear to support a two-covenant idea. Parkes does not argue that Christianity is merely Judaism for Gentiles. But he does seem to think that all the world religions have some rootedness in God and the divine plan. If he can be characterized as a single-covenant theologian, it is on a much more universalist basis than one would think by just reading his works on Jewish–Christian relations.

I would again argue that Parkes was ahead of his time here as well in seeing religious pluralism as a key issue for Christians in the modern age. If nothing else, he surely believed that God's ability to redeem far exceeded our ability to comprehend that redemption. The idea that one revelatory experience took priority over all others was rejected by Parkes. Still, he understood that the particularness of any one experience for those in that particular community could well have universal significance for all. He says, for example, that "I hold the Atonement wrought on Calvary to be of equal significance, whether they accept it or not, to all men."[169] Thus the fact that a Christian could experience the power of God through the living Christ does provide a glimpse at God's saving power, but it is always a glimpse and never the whole picture. Any absolutist claim on behalf of the Christian experience can only be made paradoxically on the grounds that it is an absolute experience for me, but it cannot be used to negate other

---

[168] Michael McGarry, *Christology After Auschwitz*, pp. 61–99. This is an excellent survey of Christian thought concerning Jewish–Christian relations.
[169] *The Conflict in the Church and Synagogue*, op. cit., p. 200ff.

experiences of the divine in human life. This is why I think Parkes always felt it possible to claim to be an orthodox Christian, even while he was challenging traditional orthodox claims for the finality of Christianity. It is a difficult position to maintain, but one which seems to be attracting more Christians.

It can safely be assumed that Parkes' ideas did not receive universal acceptance in the Christian community. For many conservative/fundamentalist Christians, Parkes simply was giving away too much of the Christian tradition. His tracing the roots of antisemitism back to Christian teachings and the New Testament itself was simply unacceptable for many. They would certainly reject his position that salvation is not an exclusive commodity, and they were decidedly opposed to his rejection of the whole mission/conversion enterprise of the Church toward the Jews. Perhaps, the most consistent opponent to Parkes was Jacob Jocz. Jocz was a solid theologian of the Barthian school who had converted from Judaism. He and Parkes had an ongoing argument over the mission question, much of which appeared as articles in the Church of England newspaper.

Jocz took Parkes very seriously, and he did not hesitate to praise Parkes for his battle against antisemitism. He paid Parkes the extreme compliment that his theology is so pervasive and influential within the Churches of Great Britain and America that it needs to be continually dealt with by those who hold opposing ideas. It is interesting to note that those who tend to side with Parkes have always felt his work did not get anywhere the kind of attention Jocz credits it with having. Nonetheless, Jocz's critique of Parkes is interesting because it is a good example of how someone holding to the traditional ideas of Christianity's relationship to Judaism reacted to Parkes.

Jocz took immediate issue with Parkes' critique of christocentric theology. "For the Church to reduce her high christology," Jocz wrote, "in order to accommodate the synagogue would spell dissolution. She stands and falls with the confession that Jesus is Lord."[170] Unlike many critics of Parkes, Jocz acknowledges the history of Christian antisemitism, but he feels that this is the very reason that Christians should bring the "Good News" of the

---

[170]   Jacob Jocz, *Christians and Jews: Encounter and Missions*, p. 33.

Gospels to the Jews. Jocz argued that Parkes' understanding of Christianity as a missionary religion, as one not to save lost sheep but to serve the world and its Creator, is entirely Jewish in its outlook. Nowhere in Parkes' works did Jocz see the saving message of redemption in Christ. While Jocz was appreciative of Parkes' concern for Jewish life and values, he seriously questioned whether Parkes could make good his claim to being an "orthodox" Christian. Jocz attributed this problem directly to Parkes' attempt to produce a theocentric Christian theology.

Jocz was also troubled by Parkes' idea that Judaism and Christianity live in creative tension. What was one to make of Parkes' notion of revelation in Christ? Jocz was clearly opposed to any Modernist theological thinking, and he challenged Parkes on the revelation question:

> Revelation for Dr. Parkes is not tied to the Bible: Judaism, Christianity, and Humanism all have a share of it, each standing for a particular emphasis—righteousness, love, truth. These three virtues are not incompatible but neither are they interchangeable. It is for this reason that mission is out of place. The tension arising from the encounter of these three positions must not be resolved but maintained in the form of dialogue.[171]

Jocz placed Parkes in the two-covenant school of thought, and questioned why Parkes was not more bothered by the Pauline vision in Ephesians about Jesus Christ breaking down the barriers between Gentile and Jew. He rejected Parkes' view of the necessary tension between the two faiths on the grounds that Parkes never explained what purpose this "creative tension" serves. Jocz also argued that Parkes never really explained clearly enough what reconciliation wrought by Christ is all about. For Jocz, there was little left to Christianity after Parkes was through with it.

---

[171] Jacob Jocz, *The Jewish People and Jesus Christ After Auschwitz: A Study in the Controversy between the Church and the Synagogue*, p. 86. Jocz does not think that the Holocaust demands a radical rethinking of the Christian faith. This book is a very good discussion of current thinking on Jewish–Christian relations from a decidedly evangelical/conservative, Barthian point of view. Jocz is in opposition to Parkes on almost every issue raised in this book.

Jocz was very critical of Parkes and Reinhold Niebuhr because of their opposition to missions to the Jews. He appreciated both men for their concern that the mission activity is just another form of Christian superiority, but he thought that they reached the wrong conclusion when they rejected missions to the Jews. Missions must continue, but it must be done with a sense of humility.[172] What Jocz meant by that is not very clear. But, of all of Parkes' critics, Jocz was the one who offered the most cogent alternative to Parkes' new ideas. It is not clear to me, however, that Jocz was ever able to free his theology from a decidedly anti-Jewish bias despite his best intentions.

Given these critical appraisals, Parkes still remains one of the essential figures in the Christian quest for a theology without antisemitism. In many ways, his work must be seen as seminal in nature, though it is hardly a complete, systematic theology. Yet it does provide a glimmer of hope that it is possible to develop a Christian theology that can free itself of the need to denigrate Judaism and perpetuate the evil of antisemitism. It is, as it were, a kind of signpost that points the concerned Christian in the proper direction. It is no accident that so many of the people involved in the modern dialogue between Christians and Jews point to Parkes as one of the major influences in their thinking. Even if they do not follow Parkes entirely in their thinking, he is still seen as the one who opened their eyes to the problem. Parkes helped to enlist many in the Church into the battle against antisemitism, what he called "a battle for decency and fellowship in communal life."[173]

The Holocaust was a turning point for many Christians in the battle against antisemitism. Parkes' greatness stems from his uncanny ability to identify the demonic depths of Christian antisemitism many years before the events of the Holocaust were to unfold. He was one of the first Christian thinkers to take the Church to task for its responsibility in creating and perpetuating antisemitism. He was equally one of the first to deal with the theological implications of his discovery. It is easy to forget just how lonely a prophetic voice James Parkes actually was, now that

---

[172] Jocz, *Christians and Jews*, op. cit., p. 12.
[173] *Judaism and Christianity*, op. cit., p. 179.

so much of what he was concerned with has become the concern of a growing number of Christians.

A. Roy Eckardt has asked the question: "Does the affirmation that the task of the Christian Church is to bring the world into the Covenant through Jesus the Jew contribute in and through itself to the perpetuation of antisemitism? In the measure that the answer is yes, the Christian gospel can no longer be preached."[174] More than any person in modern times, James Parkes attempted to show that it was possible to preach the Christian message without having to include in that message anything remotely related to antisemitism. In order for his ideas to succeed, Christians will have to make some major changes in their thinking, but for those willing to apply a "hermeneutic of suspicion" to the Christian tradition concerning Jews and Judaism, James Parkes is an important guide. For with the writings of James Parkes, one can get a good start on the quest for a Christian theology free of antisemitism.

---

[174] A. Roy Eckardt, *Your People, My People*, op. cit., p. 249.

6

Christian Apology for Israel

Perhaps on no other issue are Christians quite as perplexed by the Jewish experience as by the State of Israel and its meaning to Jews. There is simply no parallel in the Christian experience that couples land and people, religion and politics, piety and society in quite the same way. Throughout the Jewish tradition, the land of Zion, Israel, has been an integral part of the Jewish consciousness as reflected in the unbroken covenant between God and His people Israel. The geopolitical dimension of Jewish theological self-understanding has always been a stumbling block to Christianity, and today, the debate in Christian circles over the State of Israel reflects the continuation of Christian difficulties with a Jewish state.[1] Except for a small but vocal group of Christians, official Christian attitudes, e.g. World Council of Churches, National Council of Churches, Vatican, etc., reflect either indifference to the Jewish state or outright hostility. While Christian opponents of Israel deny that their opposition to the Jewish state is motivated by antisemitism, their inability to deal with the success of the Jewish state often reflects a long-standing tradition in Christianity that stated that Jews should always remain in a subjugated state of existence. The refusal of the Vatican officially to recognize Israel as a state can be seen as an example of such a Christian viewpoint. The refusal of Christians to appreciate the centrality of the land in the Jewish experience reveals, I think, the determination on the part of Christians to continue to define

---

[1] Uriel Tal, "Jewish Self-Understanding and the Land and State of Israel," *Union Seminary Quarterly Review*, vol. 26, no. 4 (summer 1971), p. 352.

Judaism solely in Christian categories, rather than coming to terms with Judaism itself.

Within Christian circles, James Parkes has been a most articulate apologist for Israel. Parkes wrote extensively on many of the issues related to Israel, and his work represents the most sustained effort yet made by a non-Jew to defend the creation of the Jewish state. He has written on the political problems associated with Israel's statehood, dealing at length with the British Mandate, Zionism, and Arab reactions.[2] However, Parkes devoted most of his attention to an examination of Jewish claims to the land of Palestine, and his work can properly be seen as an attempt to justify those claims on the basis of theological, historical and moral grounds. He gave proper attention to Arab claims, but on the whole, Parkes was concerned with showing that the creation of a Jewish state in Palestine was both proper and correct. While sympathetic to Zionism, he was often times critical of Zionist historiography and propaganda. Parkes believed that the Zionist aspiration was but one part of Israel's claim to statehood, and he believed that Israel's strongest case is to be made on other grounds. Parkes was also aware that many non-Jews believe that Jews suddenly appeared to take Arab land in 1948 to create their own state. If this were indeed the case, it is doubtful that Parkes would be a supporter of Israel. At the root of Parkes' work was his desire to show how Jewish claims to the land are based on a long religious and historical connection to the land, which spans nearly 2,500 years. It is here, not in twentieth-century politics, that Parkes believed Israel could make its strongest claim to the land. In this chapter, we shall examine the way in which Parkes constructs his case for Israel, with particular attention being given to Parkes' own historical methodology.

There are two unique features in Parkes' work that need mention at the onset. Being both an historian and a theologian, Parkes draws on theology as well as history for material on which to build his argument. The religious dimensions of the Jewish claims to the land are just as essential in his view as are the historical factors. This does not mean that he holds to the belief

---

[2] There are three books by Parkes one should consult on these problems: *The Emergence of the Jewish Problem*; *Whose Land?*; *A History of the Jewish People*.

that God gave the Jews the land and no one else can have it. Parkes is not a biblical fundamentalist. But he took very seriously the role that the land has played in the development of Jewish self-identity, and he viewed this role as crucial to any interpretations of the Jewish point of view concerning the land. He realized that this is often where non-Jews become confused about the Jewish position, since neither Islam nor Christianity have such a relationship with a particular land. Thus Parkes went to great lengths to explain the religious dimensions of the Jewish claim. Purists in either history or theology may be troubled by this aspect of Parkes' work, but he firmly believed that the interplay between theology and history is an important factor in understanding not only Jewish claims, but human history as well.

The other unique feature is the emphasis Parkes put on the history of Palestine itself. Unlike many histories of Israel that begin with the Zionist movement in nineteenth-century Europe, Parkes began his attempt to understand the Jewish claim to the land in Palestine itself. As we shall see, Parkes viewed Zionism as being a part of Jewish identity centuries before Hertzl created the World Zionist Organization. We need now, however, to turn to Parkes' work itself.

Although Parkes was writing about the Zionist question in 1939, his sustained study of the question of a Jewish state began in 1946. In that year, Parkes traveled to Palestine to see for himself what the situation was. He saw immediately how incompatible the Jewish and Arab claims were, and he perceived the inevitable failure of the British Mandate. What impressed him most was the ignorance on the part of all concerned of even the most basic historical facts concerning the land and its people. On his return to England, he undertook the task of writing a history of Palestine and the relationship that the three different religious traditions and different peoples had with the land. He gave the following explanation for undertaking this task:

> In 1946 my wife and I spent three months in Palestine, and I asked so many historical questions, to which I could not get a satisfactory answer from anyone, that I came home and spent the next couple of years in writing the history of Palestine from 135 to 1948. For this task I had three assets. I was

personally involved in the issue. I was concerned equally with
Jews, Christians, and Moslems, and I had no *parti pris*.
Advocacy of the Zionist programme had at that time not been
part of my concern. Secondly I was as much a theologian as a
historian, and again was concerned with the whole theological background Jewish, Christian, and Islamic. Thirdly as a
historian I was concerned with the whole of Jewish history, so
that any discoveries I made about Palestinian Jewish history,
found an inevitable background in my knowledge of Jewish
history outside Palestine at the time with which I was
concerned.[3]

The result of Parkes' efforts during this two-year period was the
book *Whose Land: A History of the Peoples of Palestine.* The book
dealt with the changing history of Palestine over a two-thousand-
year period, and examined the links that Christianity, Islam, and
Judaism all had to it. Parkes' research led him to the conclusion
that the Jewish claims to the land were the most unique among
the three claims. As he pointed out, Islam appeared in Palestine
around 636. As far as Moslems were concerned, the land of
Palestine was not a Holy Land; rather their interest was in
Jerusalem as a Holy City. It was said that from Jerusalem the
prophet Muhammad had been transported up to heaven, where
his vocation was recognized by his prophetic predecessors. In
Islamic tradition, Jerusalem is the third holy city. For Christians,
Palestine was a Holy Land because it was where Jesus had lived
and conducted his ministry. It never became a center of the
Christian religion nor did Christians believe that living on the
land was a religous obligation. Christians concerned themselves
mainly with the security of holy places and access for pilgrimages.
It is only when one turns to Judaism that one finds the land itself
viewed as being of ultimate value and importance.

Within Judaism, the land is an integral part of the covenant
between God and His people, the Jews. It is the "Promised Land,"
and Parkes points out that this is very distinct from the Christian
concept of Palestine as the Holy Land.

---

[3] "Notes on the Long Haul to Peace in the Middle East," p. 2.

For Jews the Land is a Holy Land in the sense of being a Promised Land, and the word indicates an intensity of re-lationship going beyond that of either of the other two religions. As it is for Christians, the Land is unique; but the nature of its unique appeal goes further, and has throughout the centuries involved the idea of settlement and return, and an all-pervading religious centrality possessed by no other land.[4]

In Parkes' view, this is the key for understanding the basis of the Jewish claim to the land. The land is not merely a piece of real estate, but a unique factor in Jewish life and identity. Parkes believed that the full implications of the land in Jewish history are reflected in the very nature of the Jewish religion.

Throughout his work, Parkes defined Judaism as a religion that is communally oriented. "The center of Judaism," he wrote, "is the natural community. Its whole emphasis is on man as a social being, related to other men through righteousness and justice. It insists on human responsibility, on definable and achievable objectives."[5] The covenant between God and Israel is one in which emphasis is placed on the way men should live their lives in a community. Compared to Christianity or Islam, Judaism is little concerned with questions of the afterlife; rather the emphasis falls on life in the world, in the community. While Judaism does not ignore individual responsibility, it nevertheless understands itself and its mission as that of a chosen people. The covenant that called Israel forth as a people also included in it the promise of a land in which Israel could be a nation and a people. Parkes pointed out that from biblical times onwards this land has always been believed by Jews to be Palestine.

The history of a community cannot be divorced from its geographical and historical setting and it is the historical fact that this setting was Palestine during the whole formative period in Judaism which gives to the soil of Palestine its unique place in Jewish thought and life, a place which

---

[4] *Whose Land?*, p. 135.
[5] *Prelude to Dialogue*, p. 217. See also my article on Parkes' theology in *Christian Attitudes on Jews and Judaism*, no. 52 (February 1977).

remains unique even among those Jews who have followed the secularist tendencies of the age in their attitude to religious tradition and revelation. . . . For the Jew the intimate geographical link is, however, not concerned only with the past. The "promises" concern the future also.[6]

In Parkes' view, the relationship of the people to the land is ongoing and not limited to a time in the past. The land itself has been crucial in helping Judaism define itself and its mission. Because Islam and Christianity have no such similar relationship to a land nor a concept of peoplehood like that of Judaism, this aspect of Judaism is often very troublesome to non-Jews. Parkes argued, however, that one needs to clearly understand the relationship of the land and the people of Israel, if one is to correctly understand the Jewish claim to the land.

Parkes' view of the interplay between history and theology is evident in this discussion of the land and its intimate connection with the life of the Jewish people. Obviously there are historical realities that contribute to this relationship, but these realities have often been expressed religiously within the Jewish tradition. Judaism concerned itself with all aspects of the life of the people, not just the religious aspect, and the land was seen as providing a physical dimension to Judaism. Parkes' understanding of the role the land plays is found in the following passage:

> The intimate connection of Judaism with the whole life of a people, with its domestic, commercial, social, and public relations as much as with its religion and its relations with its God, has historically involved an emphasis on roots in physical existence and geographical actuality such as is found in neither of the other two religions. *The Koran* is not the history of the Arab people; New Testament contains the history of no country; it passes freely from the landscape of the Gospels to the hellenistic and Roman landscape of later books; and in both it records the story of a group of individuals with a larger environment. But the whole religious significance of the Jewish Bible—the "Old Testament"—ties it to the history of a single people and the geographical actuality of

---

[6] Ibid., p. 111.

a single land. The long religious development which it re-
cords, its law-givers and prophets, all emerge out of, and
merge into, the day by day life of an actual people with its
political fortunes and social environment. Its laws and customs are based on the Land and the climate of the Land; its
agricultural festivals follow its seasons; its historical festivals
are linked to events in its history—the joyful rededication of
the Temple at the feast of Hanukkah, the mourning for its
destruction on the month of Av, and above all the commemo-
ration of the original divine gift of the Land in the feast of
Passover. The opening words of the Passover ritual conclude
with the phrase: now we are here, but next year may we be in
the land of Israel; now we are slaves, but next year may we be
free men. And the final blessing is followed by the single
sentence "next year in Jerusalem."[7]

In this passage, Parkes gives his account of the role the land plays
in developing both the theological and historical consciousness of
Judaism. While the "Promised Land" is rooted in the divine
covenant between God and Israel, it also provides the backdrop
for even the most mundane activities of the Jews. In Parkes'
interpretation, removing the land as a factor in Jewish history
and identity would leave one bewildered as to the meaning of
Judaism and its tradition. The concept of peoplehood, so central to
Judaism, would have no meaning if not linked somehow to the
land. It is out of this very intimate connection between the land
and all that is considered Jewish that Parkes discovered the roots
of the Jewish claim to the land. One can also get from this passage
a clear view of why Parkes refused to keep theology and history in
separate compartments. They both provide clues as to the meaning of the land in Jewish thought, and as such, they are both
drawn upon freely.

Parkes has written that "It was only in the course of this study
(1946) that the uniqueness of the Jewish relationship and its
amazing quality became clear. I did not acquire the idea ready
made from any previous writer."[8] It is important that we realize

---

[7] *Whose Land?*, op. cit., p. 137.
[8] "Notes on the Long Haul to Peace in the Middle East," op. cit., p. 3.

how impressed Parkes was by the intimate relationship the land has with all aspects of Jewish life. This impression colors all his future work, and moves him in a direction contrary to most Zionist historians. Parkes wished to argue that Zionism itself is unintelligible without a complete understanding of how the land is intimately linked to Jewish identity and survival, and he is adamant in insisting that Israel's claims do not rest on the political and legal decisions made in the nineteenth and twentieth centuries. As far as he is concerned, the Balfour Declaration and the League of Nations Mandate of 1923 merely recognized the connection of the Jewish people to the land and their right to a homeland. He believed that if the Arab reaction to this decision— "Palestine is an Arab country that Great Britain had no right to give to the Jews"—is countered by the Jewish reaction—"Jews have claimed nothing that has not been legally granted to them"—the Arabs have the stronger case.

> If these two statements really represented the whole of the facts, the Arab refusal to recognize the whole transaction would be morally justified. Political legality is not in itself an unchanging moral authority, and in any case, a legal document could not make moral anything if it were fundamentally immoral.[9]

Parkes is not saying that the decision to establish a Jewish homeland was wrong, but he is expressing his own concern that Zionist arguments in Israel's defense often miss the point. His own research had led him to conclude that: (1) it misses every essential quality of the country in its long recorded history to say simply that Palestine is an Arab country; and (2) the Jewish case does not rest on the legality of two twentieth-century documents, but on a unique and unbroken historical relationship.[10] Thus Parkes went to great lengths to prove Jewish links to the land, and also to correct what he perceived to be errors in Zionist historiography. His purpose in explaining the role the land played in developing Jewish theological self-understanding, was to make clear why and how Jews came to have such links with the land.

---

[9] *Arabs and Jews in the Middle East: A Tragedy of Errors*, p. 6.
[10] Ibid., p. 6.

For it is these links that form the fundamental basis of the Jewish claims to the land.

Parkes faults Jewish historiography for three errors that he believed weaken the case for Israel. In his view, Zionist apologies usually commit these particular errors, and he believed it necessary that these errors be recognized and corrected if one was to present Israel's strongest case. Parkes was sensitive to the need of answering Israel's critics (who claim that Jews took land that was not theirs to take), and his criticism of Jewish historiography reflected this aspect of his work. It is important, therefore, to consider Parkes' criticism of Jewish historiography on Israel.

Parkes believed that his discovery of the unique quality of the relationship between the land and the people would not have been such a surprise had Jewish historians been writing about it. However, its very uniqueness was the reason no one felt the need to explain it. It was such an essential part of Jewish life and identity that Jewish historians simply took it for granted. Therefore, no one felt the need to question and analyze precisely what that relationship meant and entailed. While this is understandable to Parkes, he believed that the neglect of this issue became problematic when Arab nationalism began to challenge the Zionists.

> It was only when the Jewish primary interest was challenged by Arab nationalism and its supporters that the *quality* of the Jewish relationship (to the land) became a matter of supreme significance; and by that time, the argument from legality, so strong in Jewish minds because of Jewish history, had assumed unchallengeable authority in Zionist and Israeli publicity.[11]

Parkes believed this to be a serious error, and one that had led Zionist apologists to construct their positions without access to the strongest factors in Israel's favor. Thus Parkes urged Zionist historiography to go back and reconsider some of its basic presuppositions concerning the essential elements needed to present the

---

[11] "The Palestinian Jews: Did Someone Forget?" *The New Middle East* no. 13 (October 1969, p. 49.

strongest case possible for Israel. In Parkes' view, the history of nineteenth- and twentieth-century Zionism or a history of British Mandate policies and decisions are insufficient when answering the charges made by Israel's critics.

A second criticism is more academic in nature, and it raises questions about the whole enterprise called Jewish history. In Parkes' view, the reason the Jewish relationship to the land was ignored by most Jewish historians can be traced back to the authority of Heinrich Graetz and his work in the field of Jewish history. Parkes argued that Eastern European Jewry, Jewish mysticism, and oriental Jewry were viewed through the "nationalist" eyes of Graetz and his disciples, and thus, they were not given the attention they deserved. Parkes pointed out that

> up to the present the whole tradition of Jewish historiography has been to present the Jew of Europe and later of America, as their heir to an earlier Jew of the Middle East . . . Because of the long stagnation of the area, the Jewish historian decided to forget that substantial Jewish communities went on living there, except when there was a European Jewish interruption such as the population of 16th century Safed.[12]

In his view, such historiography gives an unbalanced and incomplete picture of the Jewish experience, and it neglects Israel's strongest claims. "A true picture of Jewish history," wrote Parkes, "must balance the essential contributions of both West and East and expound why the Western appeared of exclusive significance during the formative years of the modern age."[13] Parkes wanted to argue that although Zionism manifested itself in the late nineteenth century as a purely European affair, usually in nineteenth-century secularist and political forms, its roots lay deep in the qualities and hopes of Judaism itself. If one was not aware of these roots, Parkes did not believe that Zionism could be correctly understood or interpreted. In much of his

---

[12] *Prelude to Dialogue*, op. cit., p. 126.
[13] Ibid., p. 127.

writing, Parkes appears to be attempting to correct these mistakes in Jewish historiography on Israel.

The third criticism Parkes has of Jewish historiography concerns its neglect of Palestinian Jewry. Parkes believed that an essential clue to Jewish history is found in the Palestinian Jewish experience. Yet conditions at the turn of the century had caused that community to experience a serious decline, and thus it is not surprising that the early Zionists overlooked its importance. Parkes argued, however, that at very crucial times in Jewish history, it was the Palestinian community which provided the necessary energy and life force needed to keep Judaism alive. In addition, Palestinian Jews were responsible for keeping a physical link to the land, and the continual presence of this Jewish community marks the most important argument in favor of Jewish claims to the land. Parkes also believed that the Jewish presence in Israel was of vital importance to the Jews living in the Diaspora. For Parkes, any examination and explanation of Jewish claims to the land must take serious account of the history of the Jewish community in Palestine. He believed Jewish historiography has failed to do this adequately, and thus ignored a very important, perhaps the most important, argument in Israel's favor. As we shall see, Parkes devoted a good deal of attention to this problem.

Although these criticisms of Parkes may be subject to debate within Zionist historical circles, they are essential to Parkes' own position. The fact that he did not begin writing on Israel from within the Zionist fold may explain how he comes to his particular position. Parkes was not writing to justify Zionism as Zionism, but rather, he attempted to justify the existence of the state of Israel to those outside the Jewish experience. He believed that this effort required him to speak of issues beyond the Zionist movement. He is trying to establish a position that will move beyond political debates, and establish the rights of Jews to the land in such a way that political ideology will not be a factor. As a theologian, he was also sensitive to the religious dimensions of Israel's case that have generally been played down by Zionist writers, many of whom were in sharp opposition to the religious orthodoxy of their day. Parkes was perhaps more sensitive to the Arab position, particularly in terms of understanding the inevitable clash between Arab and Jewish nationalist sentiment; thus he was very aware that Israel's case needed to rest on more than Jewish nationalist needs and interest, however important they may be.

We need to mention also Parkes' interpretation of Jewish history and the role played by Israel. In his opinion, Jewish history has been based on a tension between universalism and particularism. In religious terms, this has been expressed as the experience of Exile and Return. The land plays an important role in providing the framework within which one important key to Jewish history and survival is to be found. For Parkes, one can only understand Jewish history by reference to the relationship between Israel and the Diaspora, which he believed to be characterized by particularism and universalism.

Parkes argued that the exilic experience was an important factor in Jewish history. Yet that experience has always been understood and made bearable by reference to the land of Zion and the hoped for restoration. Psalm 137 is the classical expression of this experience. Parkes wrote, "A diaspora community shows itself, on the one hand, conscious of its 'exile' and its need to 'return' to the homeland. but, on the other hand, it regards itself as autonomous, it creates its own religious forms; and it accepts influences from its non-Jewish environment."[14] Israel, on the other hand, keeps the Diaspora community aware of its Jewish identity, and prevents it from total assimilation into the non-Jewish world. He spoke of this mutual relationship between Israel and the Diaspora as follows:

> What then is the basis of a true relationship? It is the traditional one unchanged, save by temporary necessity. The diaspora community feeds into the heart of Jewry in Israel the experience, spiritual, cultural, social, and material which it garners in its life with the Gentile world. Israel feeds back into each diaspora community the same experience digested and transiented by the values inherent in the Jewish way of life.[15]

---

[14] *Israel and the Diaspora*, p. 12.
[15] James Parkes, *End of An Exile*, p. 171.

Parkes believed that this constant exchange between Israel and the Diaspora is essential for Jewish survival, and the key to understanding Jewish history.

Two ideas are at work here. First, Parkes was trying to establish the centrality of the land of Israel in the whole of Jewish history. Second, he was attacking the idea that since there is now a Jewish state all Jews should move there. "Nothing could be falser," he wrote, "than the conception, which has found too frequent expression in recent years, that the appearance of Israel has made the survival of the diaspora unnecessary."[16] In his view, neither assimilationists nor extreme Jewish nationalists have a proper view of Jewish history and its meaning. He argued that Jewish survival is concerned with both a moral and a geographical identity, and it would be disastrous to Jewish survival to choose one or the other.[17] Both are essential since neither one alone represents the whole Jewish experience.

> In the permanent relationship between Israel and the diaspora there is a spiritual as well as a material thread. for the reinterpretation of Judaism can only be achieved by drawing on the total experience of the Jewish people, and the Israel of today represents a fraction of that experience as will indeed the Israel of the future.

In Parkes' view, Jewish history is a combination of non-cosmopolitan universalism and non-exclusive particularism. It is Israel that prevents the universalism from degenerating into cosmopolitanism; it is the Diaspora that saves Israel from becoming arrogant, or parochial in her particularism.[18] Without Israel, the Diaspora would collapse into an ethical monotheism or universalist position devoid of Jewish identity. Without the Diaspora, Israel would become another Levantine state that would lack spirit and energy.[19] Parkes believed that this held true throughout Jewish history, and it remains true today. While the danger in the past has been in forgetting Israel (a reference made in his

---

[16] Ibid., p. 178.
[17] *Israel and the Diaspora*, op. cit., p. 38.
[18] *End of an Exile*, op. cit., p. 176.
[19] Ibid., p. 164.

criticism of Jewish historiography), today the danger was in letting Israel overshadow the importance of the Diaspora. It was in the Diaspora that Jews began to shed their separatism and develop universal ideas and intellectual activities. But it is in Israel where these pursuits were constantly filtered through the Jewish experience. In Parkes' view, "The main reason for Jewish survival lies in those Jewish qualities which Jews recognized to be obligatory to all men, but found to be better taught and practiced within the Jewish fold than outside."[20] In his opinion, this is only possible if there is a constant flow of ideas and activities between Israel and the Diaspora.

Parkes appreciated the need for a place where Jews can be Jews, and such a place is the state of Israel. The centrality of the land and its Jewish community in Jewish history is unmistakable in Parkes' thought. It is one half of the determinative factors in Jewish history. But his view of Jewish history is one that appreciates the influence the Diaspora has had on Jewish experience, and the counterbalance it provides to Jewish parochialism. From this view of Jewish history, Parkes believed that one could establish the Jewish claim to the land, given the land's overwhelming importance in Jewish life. But it also cautions against extreme nationalism, which he believes would reduce the function and importance of Israel in Jewish life.

Whether one can view Jewish history as being a struggle between universalism and particularism is a matter of debate. Jewish historians do not usually talk in these terms, and Arthur Hertzberg has pointed out that these categories could well reflect Parkes' Christian background. Christians are usually troubled by the tension in Judaism between universalism and particularism, and Hertzberg suggests that Parkes may be reflecting this concern in approaching Jewish history in this matter.[21] However, one should not dismiss Parkes on this point, for his argument is cogent. I would suggest that Parkes' view of Jewish history reflects his sensitivity to both non-Jewish hostility to Israel and

---

[20] *Israel and the Diaspora*, op. cit., p. 37. See also *Israel and the Arab World*, pp. 12–15.
[21] This view was pointed out to me by Professor Hertzberg in a seminar on Zionism, in the spring of 1978 at Columbia University.

the situation of Jews in the Diaspora. By presenting this view of Jewish history, Parkes attempted to explain why all Jews need not move to Israel, while maintaining the importance of having a Jewish state. The use of categories not usually employed by Jewish historians may reflect Parkes' recognition of his role as an apologist for Israel to non-Jews, and thus he uses categories familiar to his audience in making his case. On the whole, I think Parkes' historiography offers much useful information and direction on this point.

Parkes acknowledged that the case for Israel is often difficult to appreciate because it is so complex and involved. Israel's critics can simply say that the Jews took Arab land that was not theirs to take. Obviously, Parkes did not believe this to be the case, but he did believe that Jewish claims need to be carefully presented if they are to counter the claims of Israel's critics:

> The Jewish case is not so easy to appreciate. For it rests on a long history little known even to many Jews and not easy to assess in terms of a political decision. But without some knowledge of that past association, no fair judgment can be made; and, however dimly appreciated, it was acceptance of that past connection which moved many Englishmen, Lord Balfour among them, to make a unique decision.[22]

Parkes, therefore, was to concern himself with presenting Israel's claims to the land by stressing the unique historical relationship the Jews have had with the land. In this way, he hoped to establish the idea that this long historical connection is the core of Jewish claims to the land. To do this, Parkes describes what he calls the "Five Roots of Israel."

In discussing these five roots, Parkes drew freely from Jewish religious tradition and Jewish history. The Jewish claims are based on certain religious ideas, as well as on historical factors in Jewish history, both ancient and modern. It is essential, in Parkes' opinion, that one realize that the Jewish claims are based on a number of different factors, each of which is significant in and of itself, but also dependent on the other factors for creating the whole case for Israel. Parkes believed that a purely religious

---

[22]   *End of an Exile*, op. cit., p. 3.

explanation of Israel or a purely secular explanation fails to adequately account for Israel's claims. He summed up the five roots as follows:

> The tree of Israel springs from five roots deeply embedded in the experience of the Jewish people. The first and deepest is Judaism as the religion of a community. The second is the Messianic hope, intimately connected ever since the destruction of the Jewish state with the expectations of a return to the Promised Land. The third is Jewish history, and the long experience of dispersion and insecurity. The fourth is the continuity of Jewish life in Palestine. The fifth is the unique relationship between the Jewry of Palestine and the whole of Jewish people.[23]

From these five roots, Parkes constructed his position concerning Israel's right to exist as a nation among nations in the Middle East.

We have already mentioned Parkes' definition of Judaism as a religion of the community, and the consequences of such a definition regarding the land of Zion. Parkes was aware that this is often a most difficult concept for Christians to understand about Judaism. To the outsider, Judaism presents the paradox of claiming to be a universal religion, while being bound up at the same time with the Jewish nation. Parkes did not believe Judaism could be understood simply as an ethical monotheism or a national religion. Rather, Judaism is a religion that expresses its religious concerns communally, while it does not basically concern itself with the individual.[24] "The nature of Judaism," wrote Parkes,

> is such that, in all his wanderings, each individual Jew was conscious that he was a member of a single people—he would not have understood had he been asked whether that people constituted a religious or national community—and that the fulfillment of his own destiny was inextricably bound up with the safety and restoration of his people.[25]

---

[23] Ibid., p. 3.
[24] Ibid., p. 5.
[25] Ibid., p. 5.

Parkes believed that his is such a fundamental part of Judaism that even secular Zionists must admit the influence it had on their own thinking. Despite the debate between religious and secular Zionists concerning the nature of Zionism, Parkes maintained that "the deepest root from which the state of Israel has sprung is the Jewish religion."[26]

Parkes argued for the position that at Sinai Israel was chosen to be a particular people with a particular relationship to the land. Throughout their history, Jews have maintained a concept of peoplehood and an attachment to a particular geographical entity which is unique among the religions of the world. Non-Jews frequently misunderstand the Jewish concept of "chosenness" as implying special privileges. The prophets and rabbis, however, viewed being God's chosen people as a responsibility given to the Jewish people. It is always to the people or nation of Israel that this responsibility was given, along with God's promise to the land. The themes of Exile and Return in Jewish tradition were bound up in this covenant. Exile being seen as punishment for Israel's refusal to keep the covenant; Restoration of the land as a sign of God's faithfulness to His people. Even non-religious Zionists, many of whom rejected outright the religious orthodoxy of their day, often explained their mission in similar terms. Secular Zionists also spoke of Jews as being "chosen" for a special role in history, but "chosen" for reasons more in tune with the political needs of the time. Israel would be the great socialistic state, or democratic state, etc.[27] Again, the secularist call was to a people and to corporate responsibility. Thus Parkes believed that secular Zionists expressed a feeling inherent in Judaism, and he argued that, in spite of their rejection of religious orthodoxy, they are really the heirs of a deep-seated feeling for the whole people implanted by religious orthodoxy.[28]

There have been movements in Judaism that have tried to make Judaism into a purely ethical monotheism, and that often spiritualized the concept of the people and the land. For years,

---

[26] Ibid., p. 5.
[27] See Arthur Hertzberg's introduction to his book *The Zionist Idea*, pp. 15–101, for a historical survey of Zionist positions.
[28] *End of an Exile*, op. cit., p. 8.

liberal or Reform Judaism opposed the Zionist movement *per se*. Opposition also came from the ultra-orthodox who believed that only the Messiah should restore Israel. On the whole, however, Parkes' understanding of Judaism and the religious roots of Israel's claims to the land seem to be solidly established in Jewish tradition. In Parkes' view, it was the religious tradition of the Jews that accounts for the intimate link between the people and the land, and he believed that the influence of this religious tradition was felt by both religious and secular Zionists. Thus, for Parkes, the religion of the Jews was where Israel's deepest root is to be found.

The messianic hopes that run through Jewish tradition was the second root of Israel in Parkes' view. Messianic hope is common to both Jews and Christians, but Jewish hopes differ greatly from Christian hopes. This difference is often a source of great misunderstanding between the two religions. Unlike Christians, Jews have never understood the Messiah as simply a redeemer of souls. Rather, the hoped-for Messiah would restore Israel to all its glory. With the coming of the Messiah, Jerusalem would be rebuilt and the Promised Land would be restored to the Jews. The Jewish messianic hopes have a historical dimension that is lacking for the most part in Christian messianic hopes. The messianic hopes are intimately connected with the community of Israel as a whole, and thus, with the land of Israel itself. As Parkes understood it, "the Messiah's prime function was the gathering in of the dispersion, and the restoration of the Jewish people to the land of their fathers, the land they believed theirs by divine promise."[29] Secular Zionists would discount this, but in many ways, secular Zionism had its own messianic consciousness about itself. Many secularists spoke of the gathering in of the dispersion and restoring the land in a way very reminiscent of religious messianic hopes. Despite the early debate between the "practical" and "political" Zionists over where to establish a homeland, the messianic image that many Zionists had of themselves is closely related to traditional messianic thought. Parkes saw this as more evidence of the influence Judiasm as a religion had on the Zionist enterprise.

---

[29] Ibid., p. 11.

Parkes believed that an understanding of this root of Israel is often difficult for non-Jews to grasp, particularly Christians. The role played by the Messiah in the restoration of Israel is contrary to Christian beliefs about the Messiah. Yet the messianic hopes concerning the restoration of Israel are an essential part of Jewish tradition, and they help to illustrate just how deeply rooted the Jewish experience is in the land of their forebearers. At a very deep level, the Jewish soul is directly linked to the land, even to the point of viewing the Messiah's primary function to be the restoration of the people to the land. These messianic hopes helped to keep alive the hope of eventual return to the land by the Jews even during the most awful of times in the Diaspora. Parkes believed that the Jewish claims cannot be fully understood without grasping the significance of the link between the land and Jewish messianic visions.

Parkes considered the historic situation that Jews found themselves in while living in Christian and Moslem societies as being the third root of Israel. He wrote that

> the third root of Israel was based on long experience of inequality and insecurity under the rule of both Christianity and Islam, and on the shattering disillusion which followed the high hopes of complete emancipation in the liberal democracies in Europe.[30]

This situation produced an urgent need for a homeland for the Jews where they would not be a subjugated racial or religious minority. Parkes believed there was a correlation between this situation of the Jews and the fact that messianic hopes were kept alive over centuries of alien rule. The restoration to the land was always viewed as a solution to the problems. The ultimate failure of the European emancipation and the rise of nationalist feelings in nineteenth-century Europe provided the catalyst for Zionism to become a fully developed political movement. Parkes believed, however, that only an appreciation of Zionism's roots in Jewish tradition and history can account for either its development or its goals. The historical situation alone cannot account for Zionism.

---

[30] Ibid., p. 18.

Parkes also observed that the Jewish experience in the Diaspora contributed to the feeling among Zionists that the legal aspect of their claims provided them with their strongest case. Jews were often at the mercy of Christian and Moslem authorities, and this gave rise to an interest in the Jewish communities in establishing their legal rights. This was done in order to try to provide some security for Jews in an alien environment. Parkes believed that this dependence on legal documents in the Jewish experience heavily influenced Zionists in their desire to establish Jewish claims to the land by means of legal documents. As we mentioned, Parkes argued that Jewish claims are founded on stronger grounds, and he believed appeals to legality did more harm than good. While he saw this aspect of Zionist apology as being understandable in light of Jewish history, he strongly urged Zionists to reconsider their position on this issue since he did not believe that it produced the results desired.

By considering the historic experience of Jews in Christian and Moslem countries as a factor in Jewish claims, Parkes moved toward a historiography that considered unconscious and collective memories important factors in history. Thus he moved away from a position that would consider Zionism as simply another example of nineteenth-century nationalism. Parkes was looking for the rationale behind Zionism, and he was asking why they chose to go to Palestine. As it happened, the late nineteenth century provided the necessary framework in which a political expression for the Zionist impulse could manifest; but, for Parkes, it was a serious error to view Zionism as simply a Jewish version of Western nationalism. That Zionism became politically active in the nineteenth century is more an accident of timing rather than necessity. What is more essential in Parkes' thinking is how Zionism manifested impulses long in existence within Judaism, and how the historical situation of Jews contributed to its manifestation at a particular time.

The first three roots in Parkes' scheme established the importance the land had in Jewish tradition and self-identity. The fourth and fifth roots, however, attempted to establish the actual physical links that Jews have had with Palestine. Parkes realized that just being an integral part of Jewish tradition was not sufficient reason to support Jewish claims to the land. He attempted in his summary of the fourth and fifth roots to describe the historical link of Jews to the land and its meaning in Jewish history.

Parkes believed that the continuity of Jewish life in Israel constitutes the strongest argument on behalf of Jewish claims and the fourth root of Israel. The actual number of Jewish inhabitants is meaningless to Parkes because the population was often subject to radical changes due to outside pressures.

> If the number of Jewish inhabitants has constantly varied, it has been because of circumstances outside Jewish control, and not because Jews had themselves lost interest in living in their "promised land." On the whole it may be said that it was always as large as was possible in view of conditions existing at any one time.[31]

Parkes traced the historical condition of the Jews in Palestine, describing their constantly changing historical situation, while stressing the importance of their presence for all Jews. In his opinion, the Jewish population of Palestine was always considered to be the ambassador of the Jewish people; they were the physical reminders of the long-awaited return to the land of Zion. Throughout its history, this Jewish community was the recipient of aid and support from Jews all over the world, allowing it to survive even during the worst of times.

Parkes considered this to be a crucial root of Jewish claims to the land. The charges against Israel as being a creation of Western imperialism or that Jews took land from Arabs are challenged by the fact that there has been a Jewish presence in the land for centuries. Parkes also pointed out that this root is not religious in nature and cannot be dismissed out of hand by atheists or secular critics.[32] Jews had struggled over the centuries to preserve their presence in Palestine, and Parkes believed that this is an important factor in the rise of political Zionism. Jews had been immigrating in varying numbers to Israel for centuries. The Zionists were a new type of immigrant, but certainly not unique.

---

[31] Ibid., p. 19.
[32] *Whose Land?*, op. cit., p. 138.

"They were the successors and reinforcement," wrote Parkes, "to a Jewish community which through all vicissitudes had remained a part of the land of Israel."[33] Parkes argued that unless this is clearly understood there will be confusion about Jewish claims to the land. The idea that Jews suddenly reappeared in Israel in 1948 to take land away from Arabs is not true. Jews had never left the land. That Zionist immigrants increased the Jewish population is no more nefarious than the fact that the Arab population also grew by immigration during this time. What is essential is the fact that Jews had been struggling for many centuries to keep alive their community through the land.

We cannot stress enough the importance of this root of Israel in Parkes' thought. Parkes believed that Zionist history often neglects this aspect of Jewish history; yet it provides an important counter to claims that Jews had no right to take Arab land, and that Jews only came to Palestine because of the Holocaust. The centrality of the land in Jewish religious thought is given physical evidence by the determined effort of Jews to maintain their presence in the land, often at great personal risk. Parkes believed that Zionist propaganda has often been its own worst enemy by not giving enough attention to this aspect of Jewish history.

> But a real tragedy is that the Zionists were their own worst propagandists. They ignored not merely their strongest argument but their real case. They were not bridging a gap of 2000 years. They were augmenting a Jewish population which had never ceased to exist in the country, and which survived largely because every successive Muslim ruler recognized that it had a right to be there. The Zionists ignored this vital relationship, probably because they were in opposition to the religious conservatism of eastern European Judaism, and simply saw the existing Jews of Palestine as exponents of a religious fanaticism they disliked. But from the point of view of Arab reaction, the real justification of the Zionist presence is that the Jewish population of Palestine has always been as

---

[33] *End of an Exile*, op. cit., p. 23.

large as could find the humblest means of existence in the Land of Israel.[34]

Throughout his writings, Parkes was very critical of Jewish arguments that seem to imply that after two thousand years Jews suddenly reappeared in the land of Zion. He continually rebuked the Israeli propaganda that perpetuates this idea. Therefore, this fourth root of Israel—the continuity of Jewish life in Israel—is fundamental to Parkes' position.

The fifth root of Israel is closely related to the fourth root, and it also relates to Parkes' criticism of Jewish historiography. Parkes believed that the history of Palestinian Jewry has been neglected by Jewish historians, and thus its central role in Jewish history has been obscured. Parkes considered this lapse a grave error. In his view, Palestinian Jewry has played a fundamental role in shaping Jewish history, and he believed that recognition of this fact strengthens the arguments supporting the significance of the Jewish presence in the land. Parkes argued that at four crucial points in Jewish history it was Palestinian Jewry that provided Jewry with direction and leadership.

> The Jewish people never gave up their corporate existence in Palestine. They were constantly reduced in numbers, but they were always there in the maximum that could find any means of support—including increasingly the charity of more fortunate Jewish communities. There would be neither Jewish people nor Judaism, without the *scholars of Jabne*, who evolved a Judaism which needed no geographical center, no sanhedrin, no political or religious hierarchy; the Masoretes of Tiberias who produced a text of the Old Testament, and recalled Jewish scholars to its significance, at a moment when the center of Jewish life was moving from Islam to Christendom, and so provided one vital link between the two religions (for Islam had no interest in the Old Testament text, though it is Holy Scripture for Christians); the mystics of Safed who created an inner world of light and joy opened to the Jewish

---

[34] *Arabs and Jews in the Middle East*, op. cit., p. 21.

communities of Eastern Europe during centuries of other-wise intolerable denigration and derelictions; and the *foun-ders of Zionism* who alone offered a physical and psychologi-cal redemption to the survivors of the Holocaust.[35]

On these grounds, Parkes argued for the centrality of Palestinian Jewry in Jewish history.

If one accepts this view of Parkes, there can be no question of Palestinian Jewry's role in Jewish history, and it is not an insignificant role. On matters of religious tradition, politics, and survival, Parkes places Palestinian Jewry at the center of Jewish life. It is out of the Jewish community in Palestine that the synagogue developed, as well as a religious tradition capable of sustaining its adherents in alien societies. "The Rabbis of Gali-lee," wrote Parkes, "laid the foundation which allowed the Jewish people not only to survive, but to retain their creative power."[36] One also finds the creation of the Talmud and the beginings of biblical studies rooted in this community. Christians, as well as Jews, came to benefit from this activity. In Parkes' historical framework, Palestine was the source from which new energy flowed into a decaying European Jewry in medieval times. The mystics of Safed, Joseph Caro and his *Shulcan Aruch*, and Isaac Luria's teachings all contributed to a revival of Jewish learning and mysticism. The influence of Safed on the developing Hasidic movement in Eastern Europe is unmistakable, and Parkes be-lieved this was essential in helping Jews of Eastern Europe survive times of persecution and suffering. Finally, Parkes saw the Zionist settlers providing an answer to the breakdown of the emancipation and assimilation of Jews in Europe. As we men-tioned previously, Parkes believed that Zionism as a political movement represented a basic impulse in the Jewish conscious-ness that existed long before Hertzl's World Organization.[37] Parkes saw the various positions taken by Zionists, as well as the support of Zionism by various Christian groups, as indicating that

---

[35] James Parkes, *Israelis and other Palestinians in the Perspective of History*, pp. 7–8.
[36] *End of an Exile*, op. cit., p. 27.
[37] Ibid., p. 31.

Zionism entailed much more than Jewish nationalism. Nonetheless, Parkes did see Palestine again being the central focus of Jewish history during a time of crisis. Parkes believed that had the British fully appreciated Nazi intentions in Europe, Palestine could have been a haven for many more Jews than it was. As it was, the state of Israel became a symbol of redemption for Jews who survived the Holocaust. Thus, Parkes had no patience with those who would argue that Jews suddenly returned to Palestine after two thousand years. Jews had always lived there, and they had made substantial contributions to Jewish life.

These are the five roots of Israel on which Parkes builds his case for Israel. We again see an interplay between theology and history, and Parkes firmly maintained that one cannot be separate from the other. It will be noted that little mention of antisemitism has been made by Parkes as a contributing factor to Israel's creation. The third root of Israel, dealing with the historical situation of Jews in Christian Europe, of course addresses this problem, but Parkes believed that European antisemitism should not be seen as an essential factor of Israel's case. The Arabs would be rightly indignant over being told that they had to pay the price for Europe's evil. Parkes believed that Israel's case rests more soundly on events and ideas central to Judaism and the Jewish people themselves and not on problems imposed on Jews from outside. Antisemitism was undoubtedly a motivation for Hertzl and other nineteenth-century Zionists, but Parkes stressed those factors that made Palestine the logical choice for a Jewish homeland rather than the political conditions that led to the development of Zionism as a political movement. This is an important feature of Parkes' position, and it seems, I think, from his sensitivity to the charge often leveled at Israel by non-Jewish circles that Jews took land that was not theirs. In his five roots of Israel, Parkes attempted to demonstrate the legitimacy of Jewish claims to the land on religious and historical grounds.

A clue to why Parkes approached this problem in this particular way can be found, I think, in an essay written in 1963 entitled *Continuity of Jewish Life in the Middle East*. Parkes mentions an article by Dr. Charles Malik, a prominent Lebanese Christian of high standing in the World Council of Churches, that appeared in *Foreign Affairs* in 1952. Malik took a critical stand against Israel, and Parkes believed he voiced opinions commonly found in non-Jewish circles. Malik claimed that Israel does not fit anywhere into the Middle East picture since the West is represented by Christianity and the East by Islam, making Lebanon, not Israel, the logical crossroads of the two. In Malik's view, Israel is grounded in neither one. Parkes disagrees, saying that both Christianity and Islam are grounded in Israel. However, Parkes saw an even greater problem at stake:

> Dr. Malik in succeeding pages recognized that Israel had become a *fait accompli* in the political situation, but still refused to accept her permanence. He argued that you can force yourself upon unwilling neighbours, but you cannot stay there permanently. And that also is, I believe, a fairly widespread opinion among non-Jews who are interested in one way or another in the area. . . . Moreover if Israel established herself in a completely alien territory simply by force of arms then one would have to agree that Dr. Malik was right. Such a situation is ultimately untenable. Not only do comparative forces change their balance, but it is impossible to maintain, generation after generation, the same *elan* which once sufficed to secure a victory against enormous odds and to maintain a foothold on alien soil[38]

In Parkes' view, Malik raised two points. First, the transformation of Palestine into a "national home" was an alien decision. Hence, Parkes' fear of using the Balfour Declaration as a central argument. Second, the idea that Israel provided economic advantages to Arabs. As it developed, economic conditions were not high in Arab priorities, and thus they had little impact on Arab sentiments about Israel. Parkes believed that both these positions have crumbled, and that we need to go back to the true foundations of Israel. "For in fact," wrote Parkes, "Israel today is a Middle Eastern country both in history and population."[39] In his view, the only issue left to debate is that of the boundaries of the Middle Eastern countries concerned, and Parkes believed this to be no different than problems found between any neighboring

---

[38] James Parkes, *The Continuity of Jewish Life in the Middle East*, p. 4.
[39] Ibid., p. 5.

states. Parkes then went on to outline the history of the Jews in Palestine, but he also referred to the fact that in population Israel today is also a Middle Eastern nation. This he attributed to the influx of Jews forced out of Arab nations after 1948. Parkes also argued that Israel's dependence on help from the West is paralleled by Egypt's need for help, thus making it foolish to see Israel as the sole Western nation in the Middle East or a product of imperialism.

I think this is an important part of Parkes' work and it deserves our attention. He was well aware of the arguments Israel's critics, particularly Christian critics, set forth, and he always had them in mind while making his case for Israel. As such, he moved his arguments away from traditional Zionist appeals to the Balfour Declaration and improvement of the Arab economic tradition because he did not believe they answered the critics. Instead, he attempted to illustrate that there can be no denying Jewish rights to the land based on their historical and religious ties, which go back centuries, even before Arabs populated the land. Thus, while Parkes disagreed with classical Zionist propaganda, he did so because he realized that it failed to counter the charges of Israel's critics adequately. In his view, Israel has a sound case, but the Zionists usually fail to make it.

In this regard, Parkes' work can clearly been seen as an apology for Israel aimed directly at her critics, particularly those in Christian circles. This is no way implies that his work was dishonest or slanted. All we wish to do is to show what motivated Parkes to take up Israel's cause, and what questions he had in mind when examining the material. Parkes' scholarship was always sound, but in reading his work, it makes a great deal of sense to bear in mind that for many years he was a lone voice speaking on behalf of Israel to a very hostile community. Thus his work is less an apology for Zionism than it is a defense of Jewish claims in general. Parkes realized this often left him in a no-man's land, pleasing neither pro-Zionists nor anti-Zionists, but he believed that the facts led to no other position.[40]

We have so far considered that part of Parkes' work that concentrates primarily on the historic and religious roots of

---

[40] *The Emergence of the Jewish Problem*, preface.

Israel's claims to the land. We need to mention briefly some of his thoughts on the political questions involved.[41]

Parkes believed that the changes in the political situation that have occurred since the time of the Balfour Declaration makes for great confusion concerning the establishment of the state. The use of Palestinian nationalism introduced a factor not present when the initial decisions were made. In Parkes' view, the unique Jewish situation allowed normal political concerns to be overridden, but therefore placed upon the Zionists the task of explaining the situation to the Arabs. Instead, the Zionists reiterated the legal arguments, which did little to help the situation. On the whole, however, Parkes believed the decision for a Jewish homeland in Palestine did the Arabs little harm, except for the harm they imposed on themselves by refusing to cooperate in any way with the decision. In Parkes' view, peace could come if the Arabs willed it.[42]

Parkes believed that the Arabs do themselves great harm by insisting that Arab unity is a reality, when in essence, the only things Arabs have in common is their hostility to Israel, which Parkes believed to be detrimental to Arabs and their countries. The issue that is usually used to generate the most hostility to Israel is the Palestinian refugee problem—a problem most frequently used by Christian critics of Israel to support their opposition to Israel. In Parkes' view, blame for this problem cannot be placed on one side or the other, and he believed that the refugees have been used by Arab states for their own propaganda.

> From any humanitarian standpoint the non-absorption of approximately a million human victims of the conflict, more than a dozen years after the termination of warfare, is a deeply distressing event. But in relation to the fundamentals the Arab refugee problem is a red herring; and these human beings are being used as a kind of scapegoat to emphasize the more fundamental problem and the world's responsibility to it.[43]

---

[41] For the details of Parkes position, see his *The Emergence of the Jewish Problem* and *Whose Land?*
[42] *End of an Exile*, op. cit., pp. 36–48.
[43] *Israel and the Arab World*, op. cit., p. 3.

Parkes pointed out that there was no single reason the Arabs fled, and notes that those who stayed have prospered. He also noted that the status of refugee is incorrect.

> Finally it is significant that the accepted basis on which the League of Nations and its successor the United Nations have dealt successfully with the problems caused by the presence of many millions of refugees since the First World War, the Palestinian Arab refugees would not be accepted under the international definition of refugees at all. Other victims of the cruelty of man to man have been refused official international help although they were in need similar to that of the displaced Palestinian Arabs. But they have been referred to the governments of the countries where they were living, and to voluntary organizations such as the Red Cross or the Save the Children Fund, willing to help them.[44]

Unlike other refugees, the Palestinians settled in countries similar in ethnic group, religion, and culture, and they are represented by Arab states in world forums. But as Parkes pointed out, "the problem rests insoluble because the Arab states are determined that it shall be so because they see the Palestinians and parade them as evidence of a basic injustice done to the Arab people as a whole.[45] Parkes also believed that given the number of Jewish refugees from Arab lands that Israel has absorbed, it is foolish to expect Israel to bear the total burden of the Palestinian problem. Parkes saw something of as fair exchange between the two.

I have mentioned this issue because it continues to be a source of antagonism toward Israel in Christian circles. Parkes attempted to show that Israel did not create the problem alone, and that the problem has been perpetuated by the Arabs. Parkes was not unsympathetic to the Palestinian plight, but he opposed the idea that Israel alone should be responsible for its solution. He urged Israel to recognize the needs of the Palestinian and realize that the time had come to help the Palestinians create their own

---

[44] Ibid., p. 6.
[45] Ibid., p. 7.

homeland.[46] However, he did not see how this situation can come about as long as the Arab states use the Palestinians for propaganda purposes and continue to instil hatred for Jews in their hearts. He pointed out that the center of anti-Jewish propaganda today is found in the Arab offices in various countries, and that much of the material has been imported from Nazi Europe, making the so-called anti-Zionist material indistinguishable from antisemitism.[47] Perpetuation of this kind of hate within Arabs can only strengthen Israel's resolve not to deal with her enemies. In Parkes' view, the Arabs must take the necessary steps to normalize their relations with Israel if peace is to come.

Throughout his writings, Parkes wrote about Israel in the context of the overall history of the land. Yes, Jews have claims to the land that are unique, but Jews need to recognize that this land is shared by others as well. Parkes was most concerned for Israel because its claim had been seriously and continuously challenged, but that does not mean he ignored the claims of Arabs, Moslem and Christian. If there is to be peace in the future, Parkes believed that both Arabs and Israelis need to admit that they share the land and strive to find ways to make this coexistence tolerable and just to both sides.

> For each of the three actors in the drama of the Land the future cannot be easy. For the Palestine Arab the task is to find his own identity and to develop the whole organic expression of the identity in ways more creative than terrorism. For the Arab states it is not easy to stand back and allow the Palestinian Arab to choose for himself, while it is so much easier to provide him with weapons and vicious propaganda to spur him on to redeem vicariously the honor of the Arab people after their humiliating defeat. For Israel it is a long task of adjustment in which she is bound to be involved once she is not insatiably seeking more land, but recognizes that she is one part of an ancient common history within a small territory.[48]

---

[46] *End of an Exile*, op. cit., p. 42.
[47] *Israel and the Arab World*, op. cit., p. 3. See also Alice and A. Roy Eckardt, *Encounter with Israel—Challenge to Conscience*, pp. 219–21.
[48] *Whose Land?*, op. cit., pp. 321–22.

Whatever the future may be, James Parkes was convinced that Israel had a right to be part of it. We have tried to show how Parkes argued for the right of Israel to exist as a nation among nations. He has done a great service by trying to explain why the Jewish claims have as much validity as other claims to the land, and by so doing, he raised issues that are fundamental to the Middle East situation. His work challenges those who would question the right of a Jewish state to exist, and he ably illustrated that the only questions that should be asked today about Israel concern how Israel and her neighbors can learn to live together. As a Christian, Parkes is representative of a small but important circle of Christians who support Israel and challenge the hostility often found in high Christian circles. With his reasoned and calm presentation of Israel's case, Parkes made it impossible for Christians to remain hostile to Israel without running the risk of refusing to admit the truth. As an outsider, Parkes also raised issues for Jewish and Zionist historians that they might have otherwise overlooked.

It needs to be said that Parkes was not uncritical of Israeli policy after 1968. He thought it was a mistake for Israel to hold on to the West Bank and Gaza. He foresaw the problems that Israel faces today, occupying territory in which so many Palestinians live. He believed that some kind of political arrangement had to be made with the Palestinians that would allow them to have a state of their own, although he does not spell out the precise formula for such a position. Here his friendship with both Martin Buber and Judah Magnes may have had an influence. He urged a solution that would achieve peaceful coexistence between Israelis and Arabs. While he is adamant in arguing that Israel cannot be blamed for the entire Palestinian problem, and he expressed concern about the increased use of antisemitic propaganda in Arab views of Israel, he still believed that it was possible for a political solution to be found.

Parkes believed that Israelis needed to ask themselves hard questions about whether their security was based merely on geography or if there was not just as much value in gaining security from changing the attitude of the other side. Palestinians likewise need to give up their political fantasies and deal realistically with Israel's existence.

There is undoubted room for a prosperous Israel and a prosperous Palestinian state in the area involved. There is always the danger that intransigence on the one side creates intransigence on the other. Once there are real negotiations for a real peace, I am convinved that there would be few in Israel who would not thankfully agree that the "security" of frontiers depends not on geography but on the attitude of those on the other side.[49]

For Parkes, peace could come to the Middle East only if both sides came to recognize the fact that two peoples have authentic roots in the land. An Israel with a Christian and Arab minority is not "Nazi racialism" but merely a "Jewish" state that contains minorities, a situation not unlike most other countries that contain minorities. The Arabs also need to cease their hysterical hatred of Israel. Clearly, Parkes would be unhappy with some present Israeli policy, but he would also be unhappy with the refusal of the Arab world to come to terms with Israel. Parkes would probably fall in with the "Peace Now" movement in Israel, but he would be distressed over the fact that there is no similar movement in the Arab world. Like Magnes and Buber before him, Parkes' vision of an Israel living peacefully side by side with a Palestinian state remains a dream thwarted by political passions and dogmatism. Still, his belief that the solution to this problem requires both sides to deal honestly with the historical facts of the attachment to the land of both Jews and Palestinians, makes his work in this area an important source for any future negotiations.

---

[49] *Israeli and Other Palestinians in the Perspective of History*, op. cit., p. 14.

7

Epilogue

James Parkes was one of those rare thinkers whose works contribute something new to our thinking on a particular problem. He is acknowledged by those familiar with his works as being a pioneer in the field of Jewish–Christian relations, and the wide range of materials Parkes produced on the many aspects of this problem remains unsurpassed. Many of his books remain classics in the field, particularly *The Conflict of the Church and Synagogue, Judaism and Christianity,* and *Whose Land?*. In this dissertation, I have tried to show the richness of Parkes' thought and its significance for the modern Jewish–Christian dialogue. While I began this study with a good deal of interest in the thought of James Parkes, my appreciation of his work has grown considerably as the study progressed. I discovered many things about Parkes that I did not know before I began my research, and this new knowledge only confirmed my initial regard for the man and his work.

As one who has been continually instructed by the fresh insights of Dr. Parkes, I remain amazed by the relative obscurity of his writings. Here is a thinker whose ideas constitute a serious challenge and yet open new possibilities to the Christian faith, particularly as it relates to Judaism and the Jewish people, who, nevertheless, has received little attention from the Christian community. I cannot but think that part of the reason for this stems from an indifference to Jews in Christian circles. Parkes' passionate concern for the Jewish people seems terribly irrelevant to many Christians. Another reason may well be the refusal of the Christian community to deal seriously with the long antisemitic tradition of the Christian Church so ably revealed in

310

the writings of Dr. Parkes. For Christians unwilling to acknowledge and confront Christian antisemitism, Parkes provides little interest. Yet antisemitism remains a Christian problem, and there is a growing interest on the part of Christians to come to grips with the problem. The awareness that the Holocaust and the creation of the state of Israel are events as important for Christians as they are for Jews is motivating some Christians to re-examine their traditional attitudes toward Jews and Judaism. As this re-examination takes place in the Christian community, there will be, as there already has been, a call for change in the way Christians view Jews and their religion. The Christian community will need theologians and historians to help them think through the problems and to reassess what it means to be a Christian. James Parkes has gone further than most thinkers to date in giving the Church the historical facts and the theological direction needed to make this reassessment. It is for this reason that I believe Parkes should be considered one of the most important Christian thinkers of this century, and certainly deserving of far more attention than he has received.

To give such praise to Parkes is not to imply that there are no problems in using him as a model for the modern Jewish–Christian dialogue. I do not think it is incorrect to say that Parkes' work as a historian is essential for anyone dealing with the problem of Jewish–Christian relations. Any new Christian understanding of Judaism and the Jewish people must take into account the long and dreadful history of Christian antisemitism. It must also become aware of postbiblical Judaism, and thus understand something about the Judaism of today. Parkes' works go a long way to correct historical misconceptions and misunderstandings in the Christian mind. His work on the question of the state of Israel is also quite important. From the historical point of view, then, Parkes is essential reading.

The theological alternatives offered by Parkes may prove unsatisfactory for a number of reasons. A major part of this study has been devoted to showing the roots of Parkes' thinking in the Modernist movement that was so influential during his days at Oxford and the time immediately following. That Modernism has lost much of its influence today, and it often leaves Parkes looking like a romantic visionary rather than a hard-thinking theologian.

Modernism was becoming outdated even before World War II, and the war undercut many Modernist positions. Particularly problematic was its view of evil. The Modernist view seemed unable to deal realistically with the horrors of war. Modernist ideas about moral progress seemed to be shattered by the events of 1930–45. News of the Holocaust introduced the problem of evil in a way never before imagined. The neo-orthodox view of sin and man's moral depravity seemed much more closer to the truth than the Modernist view of the goodness of man. While Parkes was certainly aware of the problem of evil, I think his Modernist roots make his stand on the problem quite unconvincing to many today.

The Modernist idea of progress may also be problematic to some. While it is certainly true that there has been considerable material progress in the last fify years, it is not clear that there has been similar progress in morality and politics. The optimism that pervades Modernist theology about the nature of man and his accomplishments sounds rather hollow after the atrocities of the twentieth century. Modernism put a good deal of faith in reason, education and science, and it appears to have been betrayed by all three. A critic of Parkes like Alan Davies may be correct in thinking that Parkes' celebration of progress limits his ability to influence people in the world today. At best, the Modernist position seems a bit naive; at worst, it seems outdated and useless.

Some of Parkes' key concepts in his theology of equality have decidedly Modernist overtones to them. His anthropological interpretation of the Trinity, for instance, is a good example of the way Modernist ideas influenced Parkes. It is also an example of an idea that strikes non-Modernist and post-Modernist theologians as being artificial and forced. Linked to that Trinitarian interpretation is the celebration of the Renaissance and Humanism as a key part of God's revelatory plan. This is rather unique to Parkes, and clearly of Modernist tone. Yet in this century of atrocities such a celebration is premature. It is true that Modernism felt very much at home with the humanist position, so much so that its opponents could hardly distinguish between the two. Part of the problem Parkes' position may present to many Christians is that it is not Christian enough, and that it has given away too much of essential Christianity to really be useful.

What is important to realize is that this criticism of Parkes stems from his Modernist background and not from his position on Judaism. His views on Jewish–Christian relations are, as we have tried to show, a logical outgrowth of his Modernist perspective. Yet the insights he gained can be seen as fully valid from other theological positions. This is a very significant point. Parkes does not create an artificial scheme in order to say favorable things about Judaism. He simply applied his Modernist viewpoint to the problem and developed his position accordingly. One does not have to accept that Modernist position to understand what Parkes was about here. He has shown that it is possible to create a Christian theology that takes the Jewish experience seriously and sympathetically. He was able to do this without impairing his Christian faith, although it was a faith interpreted from a Modernist stance.

It should also not be inferred that because Parkes is a Modernist his ideas are suspect or worthless. Quite the contrary is the case. While the Modernist position has come under attack, it is by no means dead. A good many Modernist ideas have been generally accepted by mainline Protestantism and Catholicism, and they offer valuable insights for dealing with the modern world. Modernist views on the interpretation of the Bible are accepted by a good number of Christians, and are very helpful in reassessing traditional Christian views about Judaism. Modernist appreciation of historical facts as a necessary component of theological thinking is also very commendable to today's Christians. The emphasis given to the world creation and human endeavor is an important counter to the view that reduces all human effort to sinfulness and meaningless activity. Viewing Christianity as part of God's larger plan for creation opens the way for an appreciation of other faiths. Coupled with this is the idea of progressive revelation. The work that Parkes did provides an example of how a Christian can reexamine traditional views with the attitude that change is possible without forfeiting his faith. So, while his Modernist views may prove problematic to many, that by no means negates the work that he did. He is thus able to provide a role model for Christians involved in creating a new Christian attitude toward Jews and Judaism, even if one does not accept everything that Parkes said.

Parkes' "theology of equality" may strike many as an artificial construction, designed more to fit his ideas than to fit the facts. I think the use of the word "equality" poses a problem simply because it introduces an idea not commonly found in theological thinking, particularly as it concerns Christianity's relationship to Judaism. For Parkes "equal" here means different rather than same. It means that one religion does not offer a way to God or an understanding of God that is superior to any other religion. "God's hand" is present in both religions, according to Parkes. It would be quite erroneous to interpret this as meaning that he sees no difference between the two. In fact, he said quite the opposite. Parkes' unique ability to interpret both Christianity and Judaism judiciously and sympathetically made him well aware of the differences between the two. He knew perfectly well that Jews would never accept or understand the "hellenized" Christian concept of the Trinity, any more than Christians would appreciate the significance of the kosher laws. Parkes did not say that Judaism and Christianity contained the same beliefs with different interpretations. He is clear in maintaining that there are real differences that made them equal in importance because each was needed by God to introduce into creation important ideas and aspects about the divine nature of God and His relationship to His creation. For Parkes, a theology of equality seemed to be the only way in which it was possible to express how essential both Judaism and Christianity were to God's ultimate plan for creation.

Parkes may well have been a man ahead of his time. While the traditional idea of Christianity's superiority over Judaism is still rather prevalent in Christian thinking, those Christians who can no longer hold such a position must struggle to find a way in which to interpret Christianity in such a way that the validity of Judaism remains intact. In this regard, Parkes is perhaps the only Christian thinker who has attempted to provide a complete theological system that aims to do just that. Whatever weakness may remain in Parkes' system cannot undercut the value of his work in this regard.

Nor should the serious thinker disregard the importance of his work on the question of Zionism and the state of Israel. While he was clearly sympathetic toward the Zionist cause, his writings on the issue are not marked by any undue prejudice. He has provided quite valuable historical and theological insights into the complex issue of the Middle East, and one can still profit from reading Parkes' material. Nor can Parkes be written off as another in the long and odd line of British Christian Zionists. For him, the case for the establishment of the state of Israel rested in no way on Christian eschatology. He dealt with Jewish issues on their own terms, and he did not impose a Christian superstructure on them. Recent events have shown the Christian community to be less than supportive of Israel, except for a small group of Christians who see the survival of Israel as a crucial issue for Christianity. Parkes provides an important counterforce to the anti-Israel, pro-PLO churchmen who are dominant in so many mainline Protestant churches in America and elsewhere. The fact that Parkes came out of a traditional Christian Church, the Anglican Church, makes his voice all the more important.

Toward the end of his life, Parkes devoted a good deal of attention to the question of how the Christian liturgy contributes to the perpetuation of antisemitism in the Churches. For example, the reading of Scripture on Good Friday repeats the deicide charge year after year. Although there has been some effort to educate the clergy on this point, it still is the case that most Holy Week services portray the Jewish people in a negative light. The problem of the New Testament view of Judaism was also of great concern to Parkes. All the work of scholars to correct the negative image of Judaism and Jews in the New Testament is for naught if there is no attempt to instruct local congregations about the problem. Parkes wrote

> that there is nothing equivalent to this in the relations to Christianity to any other religion, and I do not believe that Christendom can for long continue to ignore the fact that here lies the ultimate reason why six million Jews died in the Holocaust, and why Israel is left so wrongly and pathetically isolated in its struggle for survival.[1]

Parkes believed that if the Church continued to teach that the Jews were a deicidal race who are to be eternally punished by God

---

[1] *Judaism and the Jewish People in their World Setting at the End of 1973.* Postscript added in July 1971, p. 18.

for their sins, there was little hope in fostering sympathy and support in Christian circles for the Jewish state. The changes that Parkes thought necessary in traditional Christian teachings would go a long way to removing some of these problems. The inability of so many Christians to deal with the reality of the Jewish state on its own terms reflects just how difficult it is to change the old way of thinking. Like Parkes, I ascribe to the thesis that Christian antisemitism was largely responsible for the Holocaust that befell European Jewry. I also agree that the hostility shown Israel in many Christian quarters is but a continuation of traditional Christian anti-Jewish behavior. Unless some changes are forthcoming, the Church may once again find itself overtly or covertly responsible for a second Holocaust—the destruction of the state of Israel. For such a fate to befall the Church twice within a century would constitute, in my mind, a deathblow to Christian survival.

James Parkes was a unique thinker and individual. His personal life is itself worth a study. But it is his thought that has left a lasting legacy. The issues that he dealt with in his lifetime are issues we have still to resolve today. Parkes was perceptive enough to see the evil inherent in the long tradition of Christian antisemitism before the Holocaust took place, and Christians living in the post-Holocaust era are under a moral imperative to re-examine those parts of the tradition that contribute to antisemitism and to do away with them. After remaining silent while Jews were slaughtered in Nazi Europe, Christians of today are morally obligated to speak out on behalf of Jewish life whenever it is threatened. This is true whether the threat comes from Soviet Russia or Arab extremism. While it is true that much of Parkes' work is seminal in nature, it also marks one of the very few efforts of a Christian to deal honestly with the historical and theological roots of the Jewish people, and one of the few efforts to offer an alternative to traditional Christian ways of thinking about Judaism and the Jewish experience. This makes James Parkes an important figure in contemporary Christian thought and worthy of close attention.

I hope that this study will introduce Parkes to a broader audience, and encourage some to study him in greater detail. The quest for a Christian theology freed of antisemitic overtones will be a hard and long battle. As more Christians join in this struggle, I believe that they will find, as I have, that James Parkes has provided the concerned Christian with a fine start on that quest. If this study has done nothing else, I hope it has conveyed the importance of James Parkes to the modern Christian and to the future of the Christian Church.

Bibliography of the Works of James Parkes

This bibliography lists all the known published and unpublished works of James Parkes, including the works written under his *nom de plume*, John Hadham. Most helpful in preparing this bibliography was *A Bibliography of the Printed Works of James Parkes with Selected Quotations*, by Sidney Sugarman and Diana Bailey, and edited, with additions and amendments, by David A. Pennie (Southampton: The University of Southampton, 1977).

The bibliography is divided into eight sections: I. Books; II. Journal Articles; III. Pamphlets; IV. Introductions and Forewords; V. Lectures and Interviews; VI. Newspaper Articles; VII. Unpublished Works; and VIII. Selected Book Reviews. Sections I through VIII are listed chronologically and separate entries are made for each new edition, translation, and revision.

I. Books

The Jew and His Neighbour: A Study of the Causes of Antisemitism. London: Student Christian Movement Press, for International Student Service, 1930.

The Jew and His Neighbour: A Study in the Causes of Antisemitism. New York: R. R. Smith, 1931.

Evrei sredi naradov: obzor' prichin' antisemitizma. Paris: YMCA Press, 1932.

International Conferences: A Handbook for Conference Organisers and Discussion Leaders. Geneva: International Student Service, in collaboration with *The Inquiry*, New York, 1933.

The Conflict of the Church and the Synagogue: A Study in the Origins of Antisemitism. London: The Soncino Press, 1934.

Jesus, Paul and the Jews, with a foreword by Herbert M. J. Loewe. London: Student Christian Movement Press, 1936.

The Jew and His Neighbour: A Study of the Causes of Antisemitism. 2nd revised edition. London: Student Christian Movement Press, 1938.

The Jew in the Medieval Community: A Study of His Political and Economic Situation. London: The Soncino Press, 1938.

The Jewish Problem in the Modern World. London: Thornton Butterworth, 1939.

God in a World at War, by John Hadham. Harmondsworth: Penguin Books, 1940.

Good God: Sketches of His Character and Activities, by John Hadham. Harmondsworth: Penguin Books, 1940.

Between God and Man, by John Hadham: London: Longman, Green, 1942.

God and Human Progress, by John Hadham. Harmondsworth: Penguin Books, 1944.

An Enemy of the People: Antisemitism. Harmondsworth: Penguin Books, 1945.

The Emergence of the Jewish Problem, 1878–1939. London: Oxford University Press, 1946.

An Enemy of the People: Antisemitism. New York: Penguin Books, 1946.

The Jewish Problem in the Modern World. Revised edition. New York: Oxford University Press, 1946.

Antisemitismus: ein Feind des Volkes. Nürnberg: Nest-Verlag, 1948.

Judaism and Christianity. London: Victor Gollancz, 1948.

Judaism and Christianity. Chicago: The University of Chicago Press, 1948.

Die Judenfrage als Weltproblem. Durisburgh: H. E. Visser, 1948.

A History of Palestine from 135 A.D. to Modern Times. London: Victor Gollancz, 1949.

A History of Palestine from 135 A.D. to Modern Times. New York: Oxford University Press, 1949.

The Story of Jerusalem. London: The Cresset Press, 1949.

The Story of Jerusalem. 2nd revised edition. London: The Cresset Press, 1950.

God at Work in Science, Politics and Human Life. London: Putnam, 1952.

God at Work in Science, Politics and Human Life. New York: Philosophical Library, 1952.

Il problema ebraico nel mondo moderno. Firenze: la Nuova Italia, 1953.

End of an Exile: Israel, the Jews and the Gentile World. London: Vallentine, Mitchell, 1954.

End of an Exile: Israel, the Jews and the Gentile World. New York: Library Publishers, 1954.

The Foundations of Judaism and Christianity. London: Vallentine, Mitchell, 1960.

The Foundations of Judaism and Christianity. Chicago: Quadrangle Books, 1960.

Common Sense about Religion, by John Hadham. London: Victor Gollancz, 1961.

Common Sense about Religion, by John Hadham. New York: Macmillan, 1961.

The Conflict of the Church and the Synagogue: A Study in the Origins of Antisemitism. Cleveland: The World Publishing Company; Philadelphia: The Jewish Publication Society of America, 1961.

A History of the Jewish People. London: Weidenfeld and Nicolson, 1962.

Antisemitism: A Concise World History. London: Vallentine, Mitchell, 1963.

A History of the Jewish People. Chicago: Quadrangle Books, 1963.

Antisemitism. Chicago: Quadrangle Books, 1964.

Antisemitismus. Munich: Rütten & Loening Verlag, 1964.

Fin d'exil: Israel, les Juifs et le monde de la gentilite. Paris: editions SIPEP, 1964.

Five Roots of Israel. London: Vallentine, Mitchell, 1964.

Geschiedenis van het Joodse volk. The Hague: Kruseman, 1964.

A History of the Jewish People. Revised edition. Harmondsworth: Penguin Books, 1964.

A History of the Jewish People. Revised edition. Baltimore: Penguin Books, 1964.

Antisemitismo. Buenos Aires: Editorial Paidos, 1965.

Good God: Sketches of His Character and Activities, by John Hadham. Revised edition. Cincinnati: Forward Movement Publications, 1965.

Historia del pueblo judio. Buenos Aires: Editorial Paidos, 1965.

Good God, by John Hadham. Revised edition. London: SCM Press, 1966.

The Conflict of the Church and the Synagogue: A Study in the Origins of Antisemitism. New York: Atheneum, 1960.

Prelude to Dialogue: Jewish–Christian Relationships, with a foreword by A. J. Heschel. London: Vallentine, Mitchell, 1969.

Prelude to Dialogue: Jewish–Christian Relationships, with a foreword by A. J. Heschel. New York: Schocken Books, 1969.

Voyage of Discoveries, by John Hadham. London: Victor Gollancz, 1969.

The Emergence of the Jewish Problem, 1878–1939. Westport, Conn.: Greenwood Press, 1970.

Whose Land? A History of the Peoples of Palestine. Harmondsworth: Penguin Books, 1970.

Whose Land? A History of the Peoples of Palestine. New York: Taplinger Publishing Co., 1971.

The Conflict of the Church and the Synagogue: A Study in the Origins of Antisemitism. New York: Hermon Press, 1974.

The Jew in the Medieval Community: A Study of His Political and Economic Situation. 2nd edition, with a new introduction; foreword by Morton C. Fierman. New York: Hermon Press, 1976.

II. Journal Articles

"Demobilization: The Situation Made Clear." *Punch* (February 26, 1919)

"The Jews." *The Student Movement*. London: Student Christian Movement. (July 1930): 1.

"God and My Furniture" and "Revelation and a Duster." (N.p., 1931).

"Der jüdische Student." In: *Die Juden im Gemeinschaftsleben der Volker: Bericht uber die zweite Tagung des Weltstudentenwerks zum Studium der judischen Frage in den Hochschulen, Nyon, 13–18 (April 1931).* Genf: Weltstudentenwerk (i.e., International Student Service), (1931): 10–18.

"God and My Furniture." *The Student Movement*. London: Student Christian Movement. (March 1931).

"Revelation and a Duster." *The Student Movement*. London: Student Christian Movement. (May 1931).

"The Jewish Problem in Eastern Europe." *The Student World*. Geneva: World Student Christian Federation. (1931): 391–401.

"Peace." *The Student Movement*. The Student Christian Movement. (1932).

"The Nature of Anti-Semitism." *The Church Overseas: an Anglican Review of Missionary Thought and Work*. London, issued for the Missionary Council of the Church Assembly by the Press and Publications Board, Church House, Westminster. Vol. 6, no. 24 (October 1933): 302–10.

"Judaism—Jews—Antisemites: Thoughts of a Non-Jew." *Jewish Review*. London: The Soncino Press. No. 8 (March–June 1934): 26–34.

"Quelques reflexions sur la Conference Juive Mondiale." *Israelitisches Wochenblatt fur die Schweiz/Journal Israelite Suisse*. Zurich. Jahrgang 34, Nr. 37 (September 1934).

"Can Christianity be detached from the Old Testament? I." *The East and West Review: An Anglican Missionary Quarterly Magazine*. London: Society for Promoting Christian Knowledge and Press and Publications Board of the Church Assembly. Vol. I, no. 4 (October 1935): 352–57.

"Post-war Anti-Semitism, in the Light of the Letter of Resignation of Mr. James G. McDonald." *The Jewish Academy*. London: Inter-University Jewish Federation. Vol. 2, no. 1 (March 1936): 6–9.

"The Church and Usury." *The Fig Tree: a Douglas Social Credit Quarterly Review*. London: Social Credit Secretariat Ltd. No. 1 (June 1936): 18–24.

"Rome, Pagan and Christian." In: *Judaism and Christianity*. Vol. 2: The Contact of Pharisaism with Other Cultures: Essays . . . (by various authors), edited by H. Loewe. London: The Sheldon Press. (1937): 113–44.

"The Jewish Money-Lender and the Charters of the English Jewry in Their Historical Setting." *The Jewish Historical Society of England Miscellanies*. London. Part 3 (1937): 34–41. Bibliographical note: 40–41.

"A Challenge to Christians: The Attitude of the Jews to Christianity." *The Torch*. Vol. 15, no. 11 (November 1937).

"The Foundations of Antisemitism." Toronto: The Committee on Jewish–Gentile Relationships. (1938).

"How Russian Jews Came to the West." Toronto: The Committee on Jewish–Gentile Relationships (1938).

"The Jew as Usurer." Toronto: The Committee on Jewish–Gentile Relationships. (1938).

"Judaism and Christianity." Toronto: The Committee on Jewish–Gentile Relationships. (1938).

"Anti-Semitism from Caesar to Luther." *Query*. Book no. 2: The Jews (1938): 12–13.

"The eternal significance of religion." *The Liberal Jewish Monthly*. London: Jewish Religious Union. Vol. 9, no. 1 (April 1938): 2–5.

"The Jews in New Testament Teaching." *Religion in Education*. London: Student Christian Movement. Vol. 5, no. 4 (October 1938): 220–23.

"Christian Influence on the Status of the Jews in Europe." *Historia Judaica*. New York. Vol. 1, no. 1 (November 1938): 31–38.

"Judaism and Christianity." In: *Problems in Modern Education* (addresses given at the Conference of Young Public School Masters, Harrow in January 1938). Edited by E. D. Laborde. Cambridge: Cambridge University Press. (1939): 49–59.

"The History of the Jews." *The Listener*. London: British Broadcasting Corporation. (April 27, May 25, June 8, 1939).

"Anti-Semitism." *The Religious Book Club Bulletin*. London: SCM Press. No. 10 (May 1939): 1–4.

"Ways Forward." *Hasholom*. Durban: Durban Jewish Club. Vol. 17, no. 1 (September 1939): 12, 36.

"The Fate of the Jews." *The Christian News-Letter*. London: J. H. Oldham, for the Council on the Christian Faith and the Common Life. No. 6 (December 6, 1939: supplement): 5–8.

"These Jews." *St. Martin's Review*. London: Longmans, Green. No. 601 (March 1941): 93–95.

"The God We Believe in," by John Hadham. *St. Martin's Review*. London: Longmans, Green. Nos. 602–07. (April–September 1941).

University Sermon delivered in Great St. Mary's Church. *The Cambridge Review*. Cambridge: W. Heffer & Sons. (May 2, 1941): 385–88.

"The Jewish Question Today." *The Christian News-Letter*. London: J. H. Oldham, for the Council on the Christian Faith and the Common Life. No. 102 (October 8, 1941: supplement): 3–6.

"These Jews." *The Bulletin of the Society of Jews and Christians*. London. Vol. 2, no. 3 (November 1941): 3–4.

"Jews, Christians . . . and God." London: Youth Council on Jewish Christian Relations. (1942).

"God and the Church," by John Hadham. *St. Martin's Review*. London. Nos. 616–21 (June–November 1942).

"Jews in the Post-War World." *The Jewish Bulletin*. London: Jewish Issues, in collaboration with the Office of the Chief Rabbi of the British Empire. No. 11 (July 1942): 1–2.

"Jews in Britain: Origin and Growth of Anglo-Jewry." London: The Council of Christians and Jews. (1943).

"The Parson in the Pew," by John Hadham. *The Listener*. London: British Broadcasting Corporation. (February 11, 1943): 178.

"New Calls of a New Age," by John Hadham. *The Listener*. London: British Broadcasting Corporation. (April 8, 1943): 422.

"God and the Church," by John Hadham (2nd series). *St. Martin's Review*. London. Nos. 631–32 (September–October 1943).

"Judaism, Christianity and Antisemitism." *The Left News*. London: Victor Gollancz. No. 88 (October 1943): 2616–22.

"The Jewish Problem." *The Modern Churchman*. Oxford: Basil Blackwell. Vol. 33, nos. 7, 8 and 9 (October–December 1943): 226–36.

"Amdat ha-Yehudim be-Angliyah." *Metsudah* (Fortress). London: Ararat Publishing Co. (December 1943): 64–75.

"The Jewish Problem." Oxford: (no publisher, printed by Holywell Press, Oxford). (1944).

"Judaism, Christianity and Antisemitism: Reply to Sidney Dark . . . and to Max Binderman." *The Left News*. London: Victor Gollancz. No. 91 (January 1944): 2724–25.

"Liberal Theology and Churchmanship." *The Modern Churchman*. Oxford: Basil Blackwell. Vol. 34, no. 1 (June 1944): 23–30.

"Communion in the Messiah." *The East and West Review: An Anglican Missionary Quarterly*. London: Society for Promoting Christian Knowledge and Press and Publications Board of the Church Assembly. Vol. 10, no. 3 (July 1944): 88–90.

"The Future of the Jews." *The London Quarterly of World Affairs*. Oxford: Basil Blackwell, for the London Institute of World Affairs. (July 1944): 13–17.

"A Christian Looks at the Christian Mission to the Jews." *Theology*. London: Society for Promoting Christian Knowledge. Vol. 47, no. 292 (October 1944): 218–24.

"It Can't Happen Here," by John Hadham. *St. Martin's Review*. London. No. 644. (October 1944): 117–118.

"A Problem for the Gentiles." London: Peace News. (1945).

"The Real Jewish Problem." London: Peace News. (1945).

"A Programme for the Nations and the Jews." *Gentile and Jew: A Symposium on the Future of the Jewish People*, compiled and edited by Chaim Newman. London: Alliance Press. (1945): 209–17.

"A Possible Way Out." In: *Palestine Controversy: A Symposium;* papers prepared for the Fabian Colonial Bureau, with an introduction by H. N. Brailsford. London: Fabian Publications and Victor Gollancz. (1945): 11–18.

"The Jewish World since 1939." *International Affairs*. London: The Royal Institute of International Affairs. Vol. 21, no. 1 (January 1945): 87–99.

"Target for 1945." *St. Martin's Review*. London. No. 648 (February 1945): 17–19.

"Ha-Mission ha-Notsri le-Yisra'el-be'einei Notsri." *Metsudah* (Fortress). London: Ararat Publishing Co. (June 1945): 104–09.

"The Jewish Conception of the Chosen People." *Chayenu: Organ of Jewish Religious Labour*. London: Brit Chalutzim Datiim and the Torah Va'Avodah Organisation. Vol. 8, no. 7/8 (July–August 1945): 3–4; Vol. 8, no. 9 (September 1945): 4–6.

"The Jewish Case through Gentile Eyes." *The Jewish Forum*. London, distributed by APC (Anglo-Palestinian Club) Book Club. (November 1945): 52–60.

"The Zionist Movement." *Christians and Jews: An Occasional Review*. London: The Council of Christians and Jews. (April 1946): 25–28.

"Palestine in the Spring of 1946." *The New Judæa*. London: The Press Printers, for the Central Office of the Zionist Organisation. Vol. 22, no. 9 (June 1946): 162–63.

"The Issue in Palestine." *The Christian News-Letter*. London: J. H. Oldham, for the Christian Frontier Council. No. 266. (August 7, 1946: supplement): 7–12.

"Judaism and Palestine." *Chayenu: Organ of Jewish Religious Labour*. London: Brit Chalutzim Datiim and the Torah Va'Avodah Organisation. Vol. 10, no. 10 (October 1946): 7–8.

"Judaism and Zionism: A Christian View." *Some Religious Aspects of Zionism: A Symposium* (by various authors). London: Palestine House. (1947): 7–12.

"Arab-Jewish Unity." *Chayenu: Organ of Jewish Religious Labour*. London: Brit Chalutzim Datiim and the Torah Va'Avodah Organisation. Vol. 11, no. 6 (June 1947): 3–4.

"A Christian Speaks." *Free Synagogue Weekly Bulletin*. New York. (September 16, 1947): 5.

"Hanukkah: A Famous Christian Clergyman Compares the Jewish with the Christian Seasonal Feast." *The Jewish Outlook*. London: The Jewish Fellowship. Vol. 2, no. 5 (November/December 1947): 5.

"Anti-Semitism." *Common Wealth Review*. London. Vol. 4, no. 6 (December 1947): 6–7.

"A Living Faith." London: The Modern Churchmen's Union. (1948).

"An Interpretation of Judaism." *The Gates of Zion*. London: The Central Synagogue Council of the Zionist Federation. Vol. 2, no. 3 (April 1948): 17–19.

324 *Christianity without Antisemitism*

"The Jews as a World-wide Community." *The Listener.* London: British Broadcasting Corporation. (August 12, 1948): 229–30.

"The Future of Jewish Defence." *The Gates of Zion.* London: The Central Synagogue Council of the Zionist Federation. Vol. 3, nos. 2–3 (April 1949): 25–29.

"The Emergence of Israel." *The Christian News-Letter.* London: The Christian Frontier Trust. No. 338 (May 25, 1949): supplement: 167–76.

"Jewry, Judaism, Israel." *Congregational Quarterly.* London: Independent Press. Vol. 27, no 3 (July 1949): 218–26.

"The Religious Future of Jerusalem." *The Hibbert Journal.* London: Allen & Unwin. Vol. 47, no. 4 (July 1949): 328–34.

"The Religious Future of Jerusalem." *Public Opinion.* London. (July 29, 1949): 77.

"The Permanence of Sinai as God's Revelation of Man in Society." *St. Martin's Review.* London. Nos. 701–04. (August–November 1949).

"Politics and Pacifism," by John Hadham (in collaboration with James Parkes). *St. Martin's Review.* London. Nos. 708–10. (March–May 1950).

"Religion in Britain since 1900," by G. Stephens Spinks in collaboration with E. L. Allen and James Parkes. London: Andrew Dakers. (1952).

"Church and Synagogue in the Middle Ages." *The Jewish Historical Society of England Transactions.* London. Sessions 1945–1951. Vol. 16 (1952): 25–33.

"The Religious Situation in Jewry." *The Modern Churchman.* Oxford: Basil Blackwell. Vol. 42, no. 2 (June 1952): 83–90.

"Life is with People: The Story of the Little-town Jews of Eastern Europe." *Common Ground.* London: The Council of Christians and Jews. Vol. 6, no. 5 (August–October 1952): 16–21.

"The Story of Three David Salomons at Broomhill." Southborough, Kent: David Salomons House (1953).

"The History of the Jewish Community in Gentile Society." *The Jewish Historical Society of England Transactions.* London. Sessions 1951–52. Vol. 17 (153): 11–22.

"The Problems of Jewish Orthodoxy Today." *The Gates of Zion.* London: The Central Synagogue Council of the Zionist Federation. Vol. 7, no. 2 (January 1953): 4–8.

"Israel and Jerusalem." *Zionist Newsletter.* Jerusalem: Information Department of the Jewish Agency and the World Zionist Organisation. Vol. 5, no. 18 (July 14, 1953): 10–14.

"Israel and the Diaspora: A Christian Point of View." *Zionist Newsletter.* Jerusalem: Information Department of the Jewish Agency and the World Zionist Organisation. Vol. 5, no. 19 (July 28, 1953): 7–10.

"Religion and Responsibility." *Common Ground.* London: The Council of Christians and Jews. Vol. 7, no. 4 (July–August 1953): 16–18.

"Progressive Judaism." *The Modern Churchman.* Oxford: Basil Blackwell. Vol. 43, no. 3 (September 1953): 207–17.

"Israel and the Diaspora." *Judaism: A Quarterly Journal of Jewish Life and Thought.* New York: American Jewish Congress. Vol. 2, no. 4 (October 1953): 291–306.

"Judaism and Christianity in the Purpose of God." *The University of Chicago Round Table.* Chicago. No. 813 (November 8, 1953): 11–19.

"Law and Custom in Ancient Israel: How the Old Testament System Grew Up." *The Church of England Newspaper.* London. (December 11, 1953).

"The Faith and Laws of the Rabbis: Who Were the Pharisees and Sadducees?" *The Church of England Newspaper.* London. (December 18, 1953): 7.

"The German Treatment of the Jews." In: *Survey of International Affairs 1939–1946.* (vol. 4): *Hitler's Europe,* edited by Arnold Toynbee and Veronica M. Toynbee. London: Oxford University Press, issued under the auspices of the Royal Institute of International Affairs. (1954): 153–64.

"The History of the Anglo-Jewish Community." In: *A Minority in Britain: Social Studies of the Anglo-Jewish Community,* by James Parkes and others; edited by Maurice Freedman. London: Vallentine, Mitchell. (1955): 3–51.

"The Separation of Church and Synagogue." *The Liberal Jewish Monthly.* London: The Union of Liberal and Progressive Synagogues. Vol. 27, no. 1 (January 1955): 2–5.

"The Chosen People." *The Georgia Review.* Athens, Georgia: University of Georgia Press. Vol. 9, no. 1 (Spring 1955): 45–55.

"Relations between Synagogue and Church since the Rise of Christianity." *The Liberal Jewish Monthly.* London: The Union of Liberal and Progressive Synagogues. Vol. 26, no. 7 (July 1955): 112–16; Vol. 26, no. 8 (October 1955): 131–35.

"Perspective on the Arab Refugees." *Reconciliation: A Monthly Review of the Things of Peace.* London: The Fellowship of Reconciliation. Vol. 33, no. 4 (April 1956): 65–66.

"The British Mandate," *Land Reborn: The Holy Land and the Contemporary Near East.* New York: The American Christian Palestine Committee. Vol. 7, no. 2 (May–June 1956): 3–13.

"A Great Clergyman's Objections." *Jewish Newsletter.* New York: William Zukerman. Vol. 12, no. 16 (July 20, 1956): 3–4.

"The Present State of Jewish–Christian Relations." *Conservative Judaism.* New York: The Rabbinical Assembly. Vol. 10, no. 2 (Winter 1956): 11–12.

"Jewish Contributions to Civilization." *Jewish Heritage.* Washington, D.C.: B'nail B'rith Department of Adult Jewish Education. Vol. 1, no. 1 (Fall–Winter 1957): 23–24, 55.

"The Bogery of Double Loyalty." *Jewish Newsletter.* New York: William Zukerman. Vol. 15, no. 14 (July 13, 1959): 4.

"Christendom and the Synagogue." *Frontier.* London. Vol. 2, no. 4 (Winter 1959): 271–77.

"Early Christian Hebraists." *Studies in Bibliography and Booklore.* Cincinnati: The Library of Hebrew Union College – Jewish Institute of Religion. Vol. 4, no. 2 (December 1959): 51–58; Vol. 6, no. 1 (Spring 1962): 11–28.

"Continuing the Dialogue: James Parkes to Bernard Bamberger." *Central Conference American Rabbis Journal.* New York. No. 28 (January 1960): 11–17.

"New Approaches to Anti-Semitism." *Jewish Newsletter.* New York: William Zukerman. Vol. 16, no. 11 (May 30, 1960): 3.

"The Parkes Library." *Studies in Bibliography and Booklore.* Cincinnati: The Library of Hebrew Union College – Jewish Institute of Religion. Vol. 4, no. 3 (June 1960): 123–32.

"Charles Singer 1876–1960." *Common Ground.* London: The Council of Christians and Jews. Vol. 14, no. 3 (Autum 1960): 17–18.

"The Jewish Background of the Incarnation." *The Modern Churchman*. Ludlow: The Modern Churchmen's Union. New series, Vol. 4, no. 1 (October 1960): 33–44.

"Jewish–Christian Relations in England." In: *Three Centuries of Anglo-Jewish History: A Volume of Essays*; edited by V. D. Lipman. Cambridge: W. Heffer, for The Jewish Historical Society of England. (1961): 149–68.

"Religion and Peoplehood in the History of the Diaspora." In: *World Congress of Jewish Studies*, 3rd, 1961. Synposes of Lectures, Section: Plenary and Special Sessions, Third World Congress of Jewish Studies, at the Hebrew University, Jerusalem, July 25–August 1st, 1961. Jerusalem: The Hebrew University. (1961): X–X/2.

"L'Enseignement chretien concernant les juifs: une enquete." *Evidences: Revue Publiee sour l'Egide de l'American Jewish Committee*. Paris. No. 88 (Mars–Avril 1961): 8–11.

"Christians and Antisemitism." *Cajex: Magazine of the Association of Jewish Ex-Servicemen & Women*. Cardiff. Vol. 11, no. 2 (June 1961): 92–93.

"The World of the Rabbis." *The Liberal Jewish Monthly*. London: The Union of Liberal and Progressive Synagogues. Vol. 32, no. 7 (July 1961): 132–35; Vol. 32, no. 8 (September 1961): 153–55.

"God and the Jews." *The Twentieth Century*. London. Vol. 170. (Autumn 1961): 51–57.

"A Reappraisal of the Christian Attitude to Judaism." *The Journal of Bible and Religion*. Garden City, New York: The National Association of Biblical Instructors. Vol. 29, no. 4 (October 1961): 299–307.

"Toynbee and the Uniqueness of Jewry." *The Jewish Journal of Sociology*. London: William Heinemann, on behalf of the World Jewish Congress. Vol. 4, no. 1 (June 1962): 3–13.

"The Bar Mitzvah of Israel." In: *The Mission of Israel*, edited by Jacob Baal-Teshuva. New York: Robert Speller & Sons. (1963): 165–68.

"Unique Power of the Cross," by John Hadham. *The Leader: Britain's Christian Voice in Industry*. Manchester: M. Z. Brooke. (January 1963): 2.

"The Co-operation of Theists and A-theists for World Peace." *Views*. London. No. 2 (Summer 1963): 43–47.

"The Meaning of Torah." *Common Ground*. London: The Council of Christians and Jews. Vol. 17, no. 2 (Summer 1963): 11–16.

"It's the Individual Who Counts . . . Just What is God After?," by John Hadham. *The Leader: Britain's Christian Voice in Industry*. Bala, North Wales: A. J. Chapple (Bala Press) Ltd. (September 1963): 2.

"Jules Isaac." *Common Ground*. London: The Council of Christians and Jews. Vol. 17, no. 4 (Winter 1963): 19–20.

"Jews and Christians in the Constantinian Empire." In: *Studies in Church History: Papers Read at the First Winter and Summer Meetings of the Ecclesiastical History Society*, edited by C. W. Dugmore and Charles Duggan. Vol. 1. London: Nelson. (1964): 69–79.

"Lewis Way and His Times." *The Jewish Historical Society of England Transactions*. London. Sessions 1959–61. Vol. 20 (1964): 189–201.

"Hanging on to the Good Things in Life," by John Hadham. *The Leader: Britain's Christian Voice in Industry*. Bala, North Wales: A. J. Chapple (Bala Press) Ltd. (January 1964): 2.

"God's Great Canvas," by John Hadham. *The Leader: Britain's Christian Voice in Industry.* Bala, North Wales: A. J. Chapple (Bala Press) Ltd. (February 1964): 2.

"The Bible, the World and the Trinity." *The Journal of Bible and Religion.* Philadelphia: American Academy of Religion. Vol. 33, no. 1 (January 1965): 5–16.

"The Parkes Library." *Common Ground.* London: The Council of Christians and Jews. Vol. 19, no. 3 (Autumn 1965): 21–24.

"The Parkes Library." *Jewish Affairs.* Johannesburgh: The South African Jewish Board of Deputies. Vol. 20, no. 11 (November 1965): 24–26.

"Facing the World Today: The Dilemma of Creed and Mitsvoth in Judaism and Christianity." *The Synagogue Review.* London: The Reform Synagogues of Great Britian. Vol. 4, no. 4 (December 1965): 77–79.

"Unexpected Israel." London: The Anglo-Israel Association. (1966).

"Jewish–Non-Jewish relations and Southampton University." *Christian News from Israel.* Jerusalem: Government of Israel, Ministry of Religious Affairs. Vol. 17, nos. 2–3 (September 1966): 38–40.

"In The Fulness of Time." *For Health and Healing: The Magazine of the Guild of Health.* London. (September–October 1966): 132–34, 144–48; (November–December 1966): 162–63, 174–76.

"Israel, the Dispersion, and the World Outside." *The Listener.* London: British Broadcasting Corporation. (October 27, 1966): 600–01.

"Arabs and Jews in the Middle East: A Tragedy of Errors." London: Victor Gollancz. (1967).

"The Millennial Interplay of Judaism and Jewry." *The Jewish Journal of Sociology.* London: William Heinemann, on behalf of the World Jewish Congress. Vol. 9, no. 1 (June 1967): 72–91.

"The End of the Way." *Encounter Today: Judaism and Christianity in Contemporary World.* Paris. Vol. 2, no. 3 (Summer 1967): 90–93.

"The Covenant Relationship." *Common Ground.* London: The Council of Christians and Jews. Vol. 21, no. 3 (Autumn 1967): 5–8.

"The German Treatment of the Jews." In: *Survey of International Affairs 1939–1946.* Vol. 4: *Hitler's Europe,* edited by Arnold Toynbee and Veronica M. Toynbee. New York: Johnson Reprint Corporation. (1968): 153–64.

"Now is Christ Risen." *For Health and Healing: the Magazine of the Guild of Health.* London. (March–April 1968): 35–38.

"Jews, Christians and the World of Tomorrow." Southampton: The Parkes Library. (1969).

"Lecture on the Long Haul to Peace in the Middle East." London: The Anglo-Israel Association. (1969).

"Note on the Long Haul to Peace in the Middle East." (N.p.). (1969).

"Dialogue—with Whom?" *Common Ground.* London: The Council of Christians and Jews. Vol. 23, no. 1 (Spring 1969): 17–20.

"The Palestinian Jews: Did Someone Forget?" *The New Middle East.* London. No. 13 (October 1969): 29–33.

"The Palestinian Jews: Did Someone Forget?" New York: The American Jewish Committee. (1970).

"Contribution." In: *The Sunflower*; with a symposium; editor, Simon Wiesenthal. London: W. H. Allen. (1970).

"Aftermath of War: Middle East, June 1967 – February 1970." In: *History of the 20th Century: Our World Today.* Vol. 7, chapter 102: "Israel and the Arabs:

The New Eastern Question." London: Purnell, for BPC Publishing. (1970): 165–68.

"Let My People Go! 1280 B.C." In: *Milestones of History*. Vol. 1: *Ancient Empires*; editor, S. G. F. Brandon. London: Weidenfeld and Nicolson. (1970): 51–55.

"Who Wants the Nobel Peace Prize? How to get it." *The New Middle East*. London. No. 21 (June 1970): 39–40.

"Parkes on Pawlikowski on Parkes." *Journal of Ecumenical Studies*. Philadelphia. Vol. 7, no. 4 (Fall 1970): 790–94.

"A Blockbuster or Not Even a Whimper: The Conference of Modern Churchmen Planned for 1970." *The Modern Churchman*. Ludlow: The Modern Churchmen's Union. New series. Vol. 14, no. 1 (October 1970): 113–17.

"The Holy Land of Christianity." In: *Christianity in Israel*, edited by A. Roy Eckardt. New York: American Academic Association for Peace in the Middle East. (1971): 10–25.

"Brodetsky, Selig (1888–1954)." In: *The Dictionary of Natural Biography, 1951–1960*, edited by E. T. Williams and Helem M. Palmer. London: Oxford University Press. (1971): 143–44.

"Holy Places," by J. W. Parkes, R. Posner and S. P. Colbi. In: *Encyclopaedia Judaica*, Vol. 8. Jerusalem: Keter Publishing House. (1971): Columns 920–40.

"Protestants: Up to World War II." In: *Encylopaedia Judaica*, Vol. 13. Jerusalem: Keter Publishing House. (1971): Columns 1247–1350.

"Tradition and the Challenge." *Israel Today*. London. (December 1971): 12–13.

"Christian Antisemitism." London: The Jewish Information Service. (1972).

"Israel in the Middle-East Complex." London: The Anglo-Israel Association. (1972).

"A Contemporary Theology of Survival." *Inward Light*. Washington D.C., sponsored by the Friends Conference on Religion and Psychology. Vol. 35, no. 82 (Fall 1972): 26–33.

"The Jews." In: *Dictionary of World History:* general editor, G. M. D. Howat; advisory editor, A. J. P. Taylor. London: Nelson. (1973): 770–71.

"The Faiths and the Faithful: The Paradox of Jerusalem." *New Middle East*. London. No. 54 (March 1973): 20–22.

"Israelis and other Palestinians in the Perspective of History." *Britain and Israel*. London. Commentary no. 25 (August 1973): 1–4.

"Tomorrow and All Our Yesterdays." *Common Ground*. London: The Council of Christians and Jews. Vol. 27, no. 3 (Autumn 1973): 25–29.

"Bridging a Chasm." *The Tablet*. London. (December 8, 1973): 1171–72.

"The Palestinian Reality." *The Tablet*. London (January 12, 1974): 29–30.

"William Wynn Simpson." *Common Ground*. London: The Council of Christians and Jews. Vol. 28, no. 3 (Augumn 1974): 5–10.

"The Lord's Prayer." *The Churches Fellowship for Psychical and Spiritual Studies Quarterly Review*. (London?). No. 83 (Spring 1975): 12–13.

"A Theology for the Coming of Age." *The Modern Churchman*. Ludlow: The Modern Churchmen's Union. New series. Vol. 18, no. 4 (Summer 1975): 151–55.

"Jewish Mysticism." *The Churches Fellowship for Psychical and Spiritual Studies Quarterly Review*. (London?). No. 87 (Spring 1976): 9–13.

"Christianity, Jewish History and Antisemitism." Southampton: The Parkes Library. (1976).

III. Pamphlets

The Jewish Student. Geneva: International Student Service, 1933.

Palestine. Oxford: Clarendon Press, 1940.

The Jewish Question. Oxford: Clarendon Press, 1941.

Palestine Yesterday and To-morrow. London: British Association for the Jewish National Home in Palestine, 1945.

Judaism, Christianity and Islam in the History of Palestine. London: Palestine House, 1948.

The Concept of a Chosen People in Judaism and Christianity. New York: The Union of American Hebrew Congregations, 1954.

The Parkes Library: A Centre for the Study of Relations between the Jewish and Non-Jewish Worlds. Barley: The Parkes Library, 1956.

Some English Books Interpreting Jews to Christians. London: The Jewish Book Council, 1959.

Jewish–Christian Relations in England. London: The Jewish Historical Society of England, 1960.

A Reappraisal of the Christian Attitude to Judaism. Barley: The Parkes Library, 1960.

The Parkes Library: A Centre for Research into the Nature and Causes of Antisemitism and the Relationship between the Jewish and Non-Jewish Worlds. Barley: The Parkes Library, 1961.

The World of the Rabbis. Barley: The Parkes Library, 1961.

The Theology of Toleration. London: The Liberal Jewish Synagogue, 1961.

Toynbee and the Uniqueness of Jewry. Barley: The Parkes Library, 1962.

The Parkes Library: Relations between Jews and Non-Jews. London: The Wiener Library Bulletin, 1962.

The Continuity of Jewish Life in the Middle East, with a comment by Sir William Fitzgerald. London: The Anglo-Israel Association, 1963.

Jews in the Christian Tradition. Barley: The Parkes Library; London; The Council of Christians and Jews, 1963.

The Bible, the World and the Trinity. Barley: The Parkes Library, 1964.

Jewry and Jesus of Nazareth, by Maurice Eisendrath and James Parkes. Barley: The Parkes Library, 1964.

The Parkes Library: Its Formation and Transfer to the University of Southampton. Southampton: The Parkes Library, 1965.

The Interplay of Judaism and Jewish History. Southampton: The Parkes Library; London: The Council of Christians and Jews, 1967.

Israel and the Arab World. New York: Anti-Defamation League of B'nai B'rith, 1967.

The Concept of a Chosen People in Judaism and Christianity. (Revised edition). New York: The Union of American Hebrew Congregations, 1969.

Tradition and the Challenge of the Times and Judaism and Politics. Southampton: The Parkes Library; London: The Friends of Bar-Ilan University, 1971.

Israeli and other Palestinians in the Perspective of History. Southampton: The Parkes Library, 1973.

Judaism and the Jewish People in Their World Setting at the End of 1973. Toronto: The Canadian Council of Christians and Jews, 1974.

IV. Introductions and Forewords

Dinter, Arthur. *The Completion of the Protestant Reformation*; with a foreword by James Parkes. London: Friends of Europe, 1937, pp. 4–5.

Emden, Paul H. *Jews of Britain: A Series of Biographies*; with a foreword by James Parkes. London: Sampson Low, Marston, 1943, pp. vii–ix.

Rabinowitz, L. *Soldiers from Judaea: Palestinian Jewish Units in the Middle East, 1941–1943*; with an introduction by James Parkes. London: Victor Gollancz, 1944, pp. 7–9.

Rosenberg, Stuart E. *Bridge to Brotherhood: Judaism's Dialogue with Christianity*; with a foreword by James Parkes. London: Abelard-Schuman, 1961, pp. v–viii.

Strizower, Schifra. *Exotic Jewish Communities*; with a foreword by James Parkes. London: Thomas Yoseloff, 1962, p. 7.

Cosgrove, I. K. *To Visit the Sick*; with a foreword by James Parkes. Barley: The Parkes Library, 1963, pp. 5–6.

Rosenfeld, Elsbeth. *The Four Lives of Elsbeth Rosenfeld*, as told by her to the BBC; with a foreword by James Parkes. London: Victor Gollancz, 1964, pp. 9–12.

Oesterreicher, John M. *Jerusalem the Free*; with an introduction by James Parkes. London: The Anglo-Israel Association, 1973, p. 3.

V. Lectures and Interviews

Israel and the Diaspora. London: The Jewish Historical Society of England, 1952. (The Arthur Davis Memorial Lecture, 1952).

The Meaning of Torah. London: London Diocesan Council for Christian–Jewish Understanding, 1963. (Considered as Parkes Library pamphlets, 11).

The New Face of Israel. Leeds: Leeds University Press, 1964. (Selig Brodetsky Memorial Lecture, 6th, 1964).

Regligious Experience and the Perils of its Interpretation. Southampton: The University of Southampton, 1972. (Montefiore Memorial Lecture, 9th, 1972).

Directions: (transcript of an interview with James Parkes). New York: ABC News International, 1974. Duplicated typescript; transcript of a televised interview between James Parkes and George Watson, recorded in Southampton on July 17, 1974 for ABC News International, New York, and broadcast in their *Directions* religious series later in 1974.

VI. Newspaper Articles

"The Oxford League of Nations." *Isis*, November 2, 1921.

"J. W. Parkes (Elizabeth College and Hertford College) Founder of Oxford International Assembly." Men of the Year. *Isis*, May 24, 1922.

"Jewish Reconstruction: A Non-Jew's View of Jewish Problems." *The Jewish Chronicle.* London. (February 6–20, 1942).

"Jews Must Fight as Jews: A Challenge to Every Jew." *The Jewish Chronicle.* London. (October 30, 1943): 1, 5.

"In My View . . ." *The Jewish Chronicle.* London. (November 26, 1948): 13.

"100 Years of the Jewish Chronicle." *The Jewish Chronicle.* London. (March 31, 1950): 15, 20.

"Jewish–Christian Relations." *The Jewish Chronicle, Special Supplement: Tercentenary of the Resettlement of the Jews in the British Isles, 1656–1956.* London. (January 27, 1956): 25.

"Missions to the Jews: A Theological Dispute." *The Jewish Chronicle.* London. (November 27, 1959): 11.

"Do We Need Missions to the Jews? No, says Dr. J. W. Parkes." *The Church of England Newspaper,* November 5, 1954, p. 9.

"Our Relations with Judaism are Unique." *The Church of England Newspaper,* April 29th, 1955, p. 11.

"Are Missions to the Jews Justified? . . . No—If Judaism and Christianity are not Alternative Schemes of Salvation." *The Church of England Newspaper,* April 24, 1959, p. 11.

"An Anglo-Jewish Bicentenary." *The Observer.* London. (April 3, 1960): 16.

"A Philosopher of Zionism: (Ahad Ha-Am)." *The Jewish Chronicle.* London. (March 10, 1961): 21.

"The Mentality of the Persecutor and Persecuted." *The Scotsman.* Edinburgh. (May 24, 1961): 9.

"Eichmann: Persecutors & Persecuted." *The Birmingham Post.* Birmingham. (May 26, 1961): 6.

"The Attitude to Early Christianity." *The Jewish Chronicle.* London. (August 4, 1961): 17.

"After the Eichmann Verdict." *The Observer.* London. (December 17, 1961): 8.

"Silhouette: Albert Polack." *The Jewish Chronicle.* London. (March 30, 1962): 15.

"Teaching Morality Today." *The Observer,* January 3, 1963, p. 10.

"Christians and Jews: Like and unlike." *The Observer.* London (December 22, 1963): 6.

"Christians and Jews: Like and Unlike." *The Globe and Mail.* Toronto. (December 25, 1963): 7.

"Behind the Split: The Fear of Change." *The Sunday Times.* London. (April 26, 1964): 4.

"Middle East Reality." *The Jewish Chronicle.* London. (July 24, 1964): 9.

"Grudging Prudence." *The Jewish Chronicle.* London. (November 12, 1965): 7.

"Jews and Christians Face the Same Crisis." *The Observer.* London. (April 9, 1967): 11.

"The Brighter Side of Advent." *The Times,* November 29, 1969, p. 8.

"Why Try to Prove the Resurrection?" *The Times,* March 28, 1970, p. 10.

"Three Channels for God's Giving." *The Times,* June 27, 1970, p. 10.

"The Holy Places." *The Jewish Chronicle.* London. (July 3, 1970): 7.

"Crossroads of Faith.". *The Jewish Chronicle.* London. (July 10, 1970): 7.

"Israel and the Christian World." *The Jewish Chronicle,* February 12, 1971, p. 9.

"Crossroads of Faith." *The Jewish Chronicle,* May 28, 1971, p. 13.

"The Willow in the Lulav—Christianity and Judaism." *Ends and Odds: Study Papers from the Anglican Archbishopric in Jerusalem,* September 4, 1971, No. 4, pp. 1–3.

"If only! . . . buy why not?: Miracle at Bar-Ilan." *The Jewish Chronicle,* November 12, 1971, pp. 34–35.

"Defending Spiritual Wealth of 1662 Communion Service." *The Times*, January 20, 1973, p. 16.

"Israel in the Middle East Complex." *Jewish Echo*. Glasgow. Vol. 46, no. 18 (4 May 1973: supplement: "Israel: The First Quarter Century): iii–v.

VII. Unpublished Works (Dates listed where known)

"Politics and the Doctrine of the Trinity." 1929.

"Introduction to Politics and the Doctrine of the Trinity." 1929.

"Politics and the Person of Christ." 1929.

"The Community in the Purpose of God." 1929.

"The Teaching of the Old Testament in Mission Schools." July 1935.

"Jewish Christian Relations." 1935.

"Antisemitism in the East End." November 1936.

"The Legacy of Jewish Life and Thought: A Broadcast for Schools between Dr. James Parkes and Mr. E. N. Wall." December 1939.

"Christianity and Judaism—Conversion or Co-operation?, memorandum no. 2. Comments on the letter of John Campbell of May 9, 1942." May 1942.

"Christianity and Judaism—Conversion or Co-operation?, memorandum no. 3." September 1942.

"Note on 'ex aequo' discussion between Jews and Christians." February 1944.

"The Council of Christians and Jews and the Christian Missions to the Jews. Confidential." March 1944.

"Faith and Institutions." June 1944.

"Faith and the Future." Lecture for a Conference of American Chaplains. November 1944.

"Comment on: *A Message for Israel*." Second Draft of Assembly Commission II on "God's Design and Man's Witness," Study 47/E/230 (B). April 1948.

"The Church and the Jewish People in Light of Biblical Teachings." Memorandum for Conference on "The Church and the Jewish People," March 24–30, 1949. Ecumenical Institute, Chateau de Bossey. November 1948.

"God and His Creation." April 1950.

"The Interpretation of the Law in Judaism." November 1953.

"A New Approach to the Doctrine of the Trinity." 1951.

"The Law in the Old Testament." November 1953.

"The Jew as Presented in Roman Catholic Education." 1961.

"Notes on the Possible Treatment of Jewish Questions at the Proposed Vatican Council." Confidential for the World Jewish Congress. March 1963.

"Judaism and the Reformed Churches." November 1964.

"An Economic Trinitarianism." January 1974.

"The Jew in the Medieval Community: Introduction to the Edition of 1976 (unrevised)." October 1975.

"Judaism and Christianity: Their Tasks and Their Relations in the Present Phase of the Evolving World." October 1978.

VIII. Selected Book Reviews

Williams, A. Luklyn. *Adversus Judaeos. Jewish Chronicle*, February 21, 1936.

Trachenburg, Joshua. *The Devil and the Jews. Occasional Review*, June 1944.

Sartre, Jean-Paul. *Antisemite and Jew. The New Republic*, December 1948.

Jocz, Jakob. *The Jewish People and Jesus Christ. Jewish Chronicle*, November 1949.

Hedenquist, Goto. *The Church and the Jewish People. Church of England Newspaper*, May 1954.

Sandmel, Samuel. *A Jewish Understanding of the New Testament. Jewish Social Studies*, 1956.

Herberg, Will. *Protestant–Catholic–Jew. Jewish Chronicle*, January 1956.

Winter, Paul. *On the Trail of Jesus. The Jewish Journal of Sociology*, September 1961.

Simon, Leon. *Adad Am-am. The Jewish Chronicle*, February 1961.

Hilberg, Raul. *The Destruction of the European Jews. The Observer*, November 1961.

Selected General Bibliography

Arendt, Hannah. *The Origins of Totalitarianism.* Part one: "Antisemitism." New York: Harcourt, Brace & World, Inc., 1951, 1968.

Ballie, John. *The Idea of Revelation in Recent Thought.* New York and London: Columbia University Press, 1964.

Bea, Augustine. *The Church and the Jewish People.* New York: Harper and Row, 1966.

Beck, Norman. *Mature Christianity.* Selinsgrove, Pa.: Susquehanna Press, 1985.

Bishop, Clair Huchet. *How Catholics Look at Jews: Inquiries into Italian and French Teaching Materials.* New York: Paulist Press, 1974.

Bratton, Fred Galdstone. *The Crime of Christendom: The Theological Sources of Christian Anti-Semitism.* Boston: Beacon Press, 1969.

Coakley, Sarah. *Christ Without Absolutes: A Study in the Christology of Ernst Troeltsch.* Oxford: Claredon Press, 1988.

Davies, Alan T. *Anti-Semitism and the Christian Mind: The Crisis of Conscience after Auschwitz.* New York: Herder and Herder, 1969.

Davis, Alan T. editor, *Antisemitism and the Foundations of Christianity.* Introduction by James Parkes. New York, Ramsey and Toronto: Paulist Press, 1979.

Davies, W. D. *Jewish and Pauline Studies.* Philadelphia: Fortress Press, 1984.

Diamond Malcolm. "Honesty in the Christian–Jewish Interchange," *The Journal of Bible and Religion,* vol. XXXIII, no. 2, April 1965.

Eckardt, A. Roy. *Christianity and the Children of Israel.* New York: King's Crown Press, 1948.

Eckardt, A. Roy. *Elder and Younger Brothers: The Encounter of Jews and Christians.* New York: Charles Scribner's Sons, 1967.

Eckardt, A. Roy with Alice Eckardt. *Encounter with Israel: Challenge to Conscience.* New York: Associated Press, 1970.

Eckardt, A. Roy. *Your People, My People.* New York: Quadrangle Books, 1974.

Eckardt, A. Roy with Alice Eckardt. *Long Night's Journey into Day: Life and Faith after the Holocaust.*, revised edition New York: Holocaust Library, 1987.

Eckardt, A. Roy. *For Righteousness' Sake.* Bloomington, Indiana: Indiana University Press, 1987.

Everett, Robert A. "Christian Theology after the Holocaust, Parts 1 & 2," *Christian Attitudes on Jews and Judaism* (London). October and December 1976.

Everett, Robert A. "The Theology of James Parkes," *Christian Attitudes on Jews and Judaism* (London). February 1977.

Everett, Robert A. "A Christian Apology for Israel," *Christian–Jewish Relations* (London), vol. 15, no. 4 (1982).

Everett, Robert A. "A Reply to Hyam Maccoby" in *The Origins of the Holocaust: Christian Antisemitism*. R. Braham, editor. Columbia University Press, distributors, 1986.

Everett, Robert A. "Dealing Honestly with Jews and Judaism: A Study in the Thought of James Parkes," *Journal of Ecumenical Studies,* Winter 1986.

Everett, Robert A. "James Parkes: A Model for Christians in the Time after the Holocaust" in *Remembering for the Future.* Yehuda Bauer, editor. Oxford: Pergamon Press, 1989.

Everett, Robert A. "James William Parkes" in *The Encyclopedia of the Holocaust,* Israel Gutman, editor. New York: Macmillan, 1990.

Fierman, Morton. "Dr. James Parkes—An Affectionate Statement on his Eightieth Birthday" in *C.C.A.R. Journal,* Winter 1977.

Flannery, Edward. *The Anguish of the Jews.* New York: Macmillan, 1965.

Fleischner, Eva. *Judaism in German Theology since 1945.* Metuchen, N. J.: Scarecrow Press, 1975.

Fleischner, Eva. *Auschwitz: Beginning of a New Era? Reflections on the Holocaust.* New York: KTAV, 1977.

Fussell, Paul. *The Great War and Modern Memory.* London: Oxford University Press, 1977.

Gager, John. *The Origins of Antisemitism: Attitudes toward Judaism in Pagan and Christian Antiquity.* New York and Oxford: Oxford University Press, 1983.

Gaston, Lloyd. *Paul and the Torah.* Vancouver: University of British Columbia Press, 1983.

Grayzel, Solomon. *The Church and the Jews in the XIIth Century.* New York: Herman Press, 1966.

Gutteridge, Richard. *Open Thy Mouth for the Dumb: The German Evangelical Church and the Jews 1879–1950.* Oxford: Basil Blackwell, 1976.

Hay, Malcolm. *Thy Brother's Blood: Christian Roots of Antisemitism.* New York: Hart Publishing Co., 1975.

Heer, Friedrich. *God's First Love.* London: Weybright and Tally, 1967.

Hertzberg, Arthur. *The French Enlightenment and the Jews.* New York: Schocken, 1964.

Hertzberg, Arthur. *The Zionist Idea.* New York: Atheneum, 1970.

Isaac, Jules. *The Teaching of Contempt.* New York: Holt, Rinehart and Winston, 1964.

Jocz, Jacob. *Christians and Jews: Encounter and Missions.* London: SPCK, 1966.

Jocz, Jacob. *The Jewish People and Jesus Christ after Auschwitz.* Grand Rapids Mich.: Baker Books, 1981.

Johnson, Humphrey J. T. *Anglicanism in Transition.* London & New York: Longmans, Green & Co., 1938.

Katz, Jacob. *From Prejudice to Destruction: Antisemitism, 1700–1933*. Cambridge, Mass: Harvard University Press, 1980.

Kaylor, R. David. *Paul's covenant Community: Jews and Gentiles in Romans*. Atlanta: John Knox Press, 1988.

Klein, Charlotte. *Anti-Judaism in Christian Theology*. Philadelphia: Fortress Press, 1975.

Knitter, Paul. *No Other Name? A Critical Survey of Christian Attitudes toward the World Religions*. Maryknoll, N.Y.: Orbis Books, 1985.

Kulka, Otto Dov and Mendes-Flohr, Paul, eds. *Judaism and Christianity under the Impact of National Socialism*. Jerusalem: The Historical Society of Israel and the Zalman Shazar Center for Jewish History, 1987.

Lewis, Rose. "James Parkes" in *Midstream*, 1982.

Littell, Franklin. *The Crucifixion of the Jews: The Failure of Christians to Understand the Jewish Experience*. New York: Harper and Row, 1975.

Littell, Franklin and Hubert Locke, eds., *The German Church Struggle and the Holocaust*. Detroit: Wayne State Press, 1974.

Lloyd, Roger. *The Church of England in the Twentieth Century, Vol. II*. London: Longman, Green & Co., 1950.

Major, H. D. A. *English Modernism: Its Origins, Methods and Aims*. Cambridge, Mass: Harvard University Press, 1927.

McGarry, Michael. *Christology After Auschwitz*. New York: Paulist Press, 1977.

Niebuhr, Reinhold. *The Godly and the Ungodly: Essays on the Religious and Secular Dimensions of Modern Life*. London: Faber and Faber Limited, 1958.

Niebuhr, Reinhold. *Essays in Applied Christianity: The Church and the New World*, D. B. Robinson, ed. New York: Meridian Books, 1959.

Olan, Levi. "Christian–Jewish Dialogue: A Dissenting Opinion" in *Religion in Life* (Vol. ILI, no. 2) (Summer 1972).

Olson, Bernard. *Faith and Prejudice*. New Haven: Yale University Press, 1963.

Osten-Sacken, Peter von der. *Christian–Jewish Dialogue: Theological Foundations*. Philadelphia: Fortress Press, 1986.

Pannenberg, Wolfhart. *Jesus—God and Man*, 2nd edition. Philadelphia: Westminster Press, 1968.

Pawlikowski, John. *Christ in the Light of the Jewish–Christian Dialogue*. New York: Paulist Press, 1982.

Pawlikowski, John. "The Church and Judaism: The Thought of James Parkes" in *Journal of Ecumenical Studies*, Fall 1969.

Peck, Abraham, ed., *Jews and Christians after the Holocaust*. Philadelphia: Fortress Press, 1982.

Pinson, Koppel, ed., *Essays in Antisemitism*. New York: Conference on Jewish Relations, 1946.

Poliakov, Leon. *The History of Antisemitism, Vol. I*. New York: Schocken Books, 1974.

Poliakov, Leon. *The History of Antisemitism, Volumes II & III*. New York: Vanguard Press, 1975.

Ramsey, Arthur Michael. *An Era of Anglican Theology*. New York: Charles Scribner's Sons, 1960.

Rashdall, Hastings. *Ideas and Ideals*. Oxford: Basil Blackwell, 1928.

Richardson, Herbert. *Toward an American Theology.* New York: Harper and Row, 1967.

Richardson, Peter with David Granskou. *Anti-Judaism in Early Christianity,* Vol. I: *Paul and the Gospels;* Vol. II: *Separation and Polemic.* Waterloo, Ontario: Wilfrid Laurier University Press, 1986.

Rosenzweig, Franz. *The Star of Redemption.* New York: Holt, Rinehart, and Winston (University of Notre Dame Press edition), 1985.

Ruether, Rosemary. *Faith and Fratricide: The Theological Roots of Antisemitism,* introduction by Gregory Baum. New York: Seabury Press, 1974.

Sanders, E. P. *Paul and Palestinian Judaism.* Philadelphia: Fortress Press, 1977.

Sanders. E. P. *Paul, the Law and the Jewish People.* Philadelphia: Fortress Press, 1983.

Sanders, E. P. *Jesus and Judaism.* Philadelphia: Fortress Press, 1985.

Simon, Marcel. *Verus Israel: A Study in the Relationship between Christians and Jews in the Roman Empire (AD 135–425).* Oxford: Oxford University Press, 1986.

Simon, Ulrich. *A Theology of Auschwitz.* London: Victor Gollancz, 1967.

Schoeps, Hans Joachim. *The Jewish–Christian Argument: A History of Theologies in Conflict.* New York: Holt, Rinehart and Winston, 1963.

Tal, Uriel. *Christians and Jews in Germany.* Ithaca and London: Cornell University Press, 1975.

Tal, Uriel. *Religious and Anti-Religious Roots of Modern Antisemitism.* Leo Baeck Memorial Lecture. No. 14. New York 1971.

Tal, Uriel. "Jewish Self-Understanding and the Land and State of Israel" in *Union Seminary Quarterly Review,* Vol. XXVI, no. 4 (Summer 1971).

Temple, William. *Nature, Man and God.* London: Macmillan, 1960.

Thoma, Clemens. *A Christian Theology of Judaism.* New York and Ramsey: Paulist Press, 1980.

Troeltsch, Ernst. *Christian Thought: Its History and Application.* London: The University of London Press, 1923.

Tuchman, Barbara. *The Guns of August.* New York: Dell Publishing Co., 1962.

Tuchman, Barbara. *The Proud Tower.* New York: Macmillan, 1966.

Van Buren, Paul. *A Theology of the Jewish–Christian Reality, Part I: Discerning the Way.* New York: Seabury Press, 1980.

Van Buren, Paul. *A Christian Theology of the People of Israel, Part II: A Theology of the Jewish–Christian Reality.* New York: Seabury Press, 1983.

Van Buren, Paul. *Christ in Context, Part III: A Theology of the Jewish–Christian Reality.* San Francisco: Harper and Row, 1988.

Vidler, Alec R. *Witness to the Light: F. D. Maurice's Message for Today.* New York: Charles Scribner's Sons, 1948.

Vermes, Geza. *Jesus the Jew: A Historian's Reading of the Gospels.* London: Fontana/Collins. 1976.

Wasserstein, Bernard. *Britain and the Jews of Europe 1939–1945.* New York: Oxford University Press, 1979.

Wiesenthal, Simon. *The Sunflower.* New York: Schocken Books, 1977.

Wilken, Robert, L. *Judaism and the Early Christian Mind: A Study of Cyril of Alexandria's Exegesis and Theology.* New Haen and London: Yale University Press, 1971.

Wilken, Robert L. *John Chrysostum and the Jews.* Berkeley: University of California Press, 1983.

Williamson, Clark. *Has God Rejected His People? Anti-Judaism in the Christian Church.* Nashville: Abingdon Press, 1982.

Wood, James E., ed., *Jewish–Christian Relations in Today's World.* Waco, Texas: Baylor University Press, 1971.

Index

342   *Index*